MATHEMATICAL FOUNDATIONS OF LIFE INSURANCE

Lewis C. Workman, BS, FSA, MAAA
Actuarial Vice President
Central Life Assurance Company

FLMI Insurance Education Program
Life Management Institute LOMA
Atlanta, Georgia

LOMA (Life Office Management Association, Inc.) is an international association founded in 1924. Through education, training, research, and information sharing, LOMA is dedicated to promoting management excellence in leading life and health insurance companies and other financial institutions.

The **FLMI Insurance Education Program** consists of two levels—Level I, "Fundamentals of Life and Health Insurance," and Level II, "Functional Aspects of Life and Health Insurance." Level I is designed to help students achieve a working knowledge of the life and health insurance business. Level II is designed to further the student's career development by providing a more detailed understanding of life and health insurance and related business and management subjects. Upon the completion of Level I, the student is awarded a certificate. Upon the completion of both levels, the student is designated a Fellow of the Life Management Institute (FLMI) and is awarded a diploma.

ISBN 0-915322-52-8

Library of Congress Catalog Card Number: 82-80669

Printed in the United States of America

Dedicated to Sally Ann

Helper, supporter, proofreader,
and wife extraordinaire

PREFACE

The primary aim of this book is to enable students of the Life Office Management Association's (LOMA) Life Management Institute to understand the fundamental mathematical principles that underlie much of the work in a life insurance company. Such an understanding should give students more insight into their jobs and a better awareness of how all the jobs in an insurance company fit together. The book is also suitable for a college course in life insurance mathematics. There, it would appeal particularly to insurance or business students who do not have extensive mathematical background.

This book replaces the text *Fundamental Mathematics of Life Insurance* by Lewis C. Workman and the late Floyd S. Harper, previously used in the FLMI Insurance Education Program. Much of the material presented in that textbook has been updated for this book, and many of the explanations have been expanded. In addition, chapters have been added specifically to explain (1) the role of mathematics in the various departments of a life insurance company and (2) the mathematical principles used in group insurance and health insurance. At the end of each chapter, a "Chapter Summary" and "Learning Objectives" are presented. The "Chapter Summary" lists the important points from the chapter, while the "Learning Objectives" provide a checklist of what the student should have learned from the chapter. Answers are given for all exercises, along with explanations or hints for working each one.

The approach is to lead students through the material a step at a time, beginning with the most elementary concepts. In this way, even the beginning student should have little difficulty understanding the explanations. Straightforward illustrations are given throughout the book, and the steps in the calculations are shown and explained. The use of actuarial symbols, which could become complicated and confusing, has been kept to a minimum. Extensive use is made of the *line diagram*, which should help students considerably in visualizing the elements of each problem. The manner of presentation will enable the student to proceed through the content without classroom instruction.

Chapter 1 explains the importance of mathematical principles to many areas of life insurance and briefly describes the role of an actuary. Chapter 2 is for students who need a reacquaintance with certain areas of arithmetic which will be used later (over and above elementary addition, subtraction, multiplication, and division). These areas are: fractions, decimals, common multipliers, equations, and exponents. Chapters 3 through 6 cover the subject of compound interest. Chapter 7 describes the subject of probability and its use with mortality tables. Chapters 8 through 14 present the mathematics of individual annuity and insurance contracts, wherein compound interest is combined with probability. Chapter 15 describes group life insurance, emphasizing the mathematical principles involved, and Chapter 16 presents the highlights of the subject of health insurance, again, emphasizing mathematical principles.

The author is indebted to a number of people who spent many hours reviewing and checking the drafts of this book and helping with the mechanical preparation. These include, particularly, Theresa Wells and Sandra Schwartz of the Central Life Assurance Company staff, Margaret Walsh, FLMI, Kenneth Huggins, and Iris Hartley, FLMI, of LOMA's Life Management Institute, and Raymond Maneval, Educational Consultant to LOMA. A special debt of gratitude is also due to the members of LOMA's Curriculum Review Committee for their invaluable suggestions:

Chairman: Kenneth A. LaSorella, FLMI, FSA
Assistant Actuary
Sun Life Assurance Company of Canada

Donald F. Behan, FSA, MAAA, EA, PhD
Director
Deloitte Haskins & Sells

Warren A. Carter, ASA
Second Vice President
Teachers Insurance and Annuity Association

E. Jennifer Randall, FLMI
Manager, Product Development and Actuarial Programming
Confederation Life Insurance Company

Robert P. Robinson, FSA
Assistant Vice President and Associate Actuary
Kansas City Life Insurance Company

James E. Drennan, FSA, MAAA
Second Vice President and Associate Group Actuary
Philadelphia Life Insurance Company

Des Moines, Iowa   Lewis C. Workman
May 1982

CONTENTS

vii

1

The Mathematical Basis of Life Insurance

This first chapter is designed to familiarize the student with the importance of the mathematical foundations that underlie the operations of a life insurance company. It describes some of the day-to-day work which is based on these mathematical principles and tries to show that every job in a life insurance company relates in some way to these principles.

Most of the mathematical bases and calculations used in life insurance are developed by persons called *actuaries*, and the bulk of this chapter will acquaint the student with the work of life insurance actuaries and the operations of the *actuarial department*. While this type of work has sometimes been characterized as excessively difficult, it is the aim of this book to present the material in an easily understandable and practical manner.

1.1 INTRODUCTION

The premiums which are paid for a life insurance policy are not determined by guess work. Similarly, the promises and the guarantees which an insurance company makes to its policyowners are not pulled out of thin air or based on mere hopes about the future. On the contrary, the buyers of life insurance can have a great deal of assurance that the premiums they pay are fair and meaningful and that the company's promises will be met. Such assurance is possible because of the sound and proven mathematical basis on which modern-day life insurance rests.

In the early days of life insurance, policyowners could not be so assured. For example, in some life insurance arrangements, benefits were provided by assessing each insured person a share of every death claim payment whenever a death occurred. Other life insurance practices were also conducted on unscientific bases, such as charging older and younger insured persons the same premium rates. Such arrangements generally ended in complete failure, because companies were unable to pay legitimate claims.

The mathematical basis for life insurance rests on two chief foundation stones: *compound interest* and *probability*. This book will explain each of these subjects separately and then show how actuarial practice combines the two areas to guarantee that the life insurance business operates on a sound and scientific basis.

The aim of this book is not to turn the reader into an actuary, but to give nonactuaries a useful insight into the mathematics and theories underlying the operations of life insurance. By learning these basics, any person employed by a life insurance company will come to a better understanding of his or her own job and how it interacts with other jobs in the company.

The student will learn about many aspects of the actuarial process in a life company: how to determine and use the time value of money, how to use probabilities of living and dying, how premiums are calculated, how the company's operations are affected by these calculations, and how the actuary's calculations are affected by various governmental requirements. In particular, the student should learn how the parts of the insurance process are interrelated and depend on one another and how all areas of the company's operations relate to the mathematical foundations which form the basis of insurance.

1.2 WHAT IS AN ACTUARY?

In Ancient Rome, an *actuarius* was the recorder at the proceedings of the Senate. In Medieval England, this name referred to the recorder of court decisions. About 200 years ago the name was shortened to *actuary* and used to describe an administrative officer of an insurance company.

Today an actuary is a person who deals with contingencies, that is, with events which may or may not happen. Among the contingent events that affect people (and their pocketbooks) most dramatically are birth, death, marriage, retirement, sickness, accidents, and unemployment. In dealing with such events, the actuary must know how to determine the *probabilities* of such events occurring and how to use those probabilities to make important calculations and forecasts.

Unlike in the professions of law and medicine, there are no governmental examinations to be passed or licenses to be issued before a person can call himself or herself an actuary or practice actuarial work. However, several actuarial organizations exist in North America, and membership in one or more of such organizations is widely recognized as evidence that a person is competent to give actuarial advice and perform actuarial work. A professional designation is awarded by these organizations to those members who have demonstrated sufficient knowledge and ability. This generally requires the passing of rigorous examinations.

While actuaries are employed by many different governmental and business organizations, this book is concerned primarily with the work of the life insurance actuary. Therefore, it is appropriate to describe in more detail the primary responsibilities of such a person in a life insurance company. In general, it is the duty of insurance actuaries to see that the operations of the company are conducted on a sound mathematical basis. Although much of their work is of a technical, mathematical nature, the overall duties of actuaries are broad and widely diversified.

PRINCIPAL RESPONSIBILITIES. The life insurance actuary's principal responsibilities are as follows:

1. *Designing products.* This requires making decisions on the particular terms and conditions of policies to be sold. The actuary must draw up insurance policies that will be popular, reasonable in cost, practical to administer, and competitive with those of other companies. In this product-design role, the actuary must work very closely with the sales and legal departments of the company. In Chapter 14, we will deal with some of the mathematical methods used to compare the competitive positions of two different insurance policies.

2. *Drafting policies.* Actuaries play a significant role in the actual drafting of the policy documents themselves. They must furnish the figures for the various tables which appear in the policies, such as the tables of *settlement options* (described in Chapter 8) and *nonforfeiture values* (described in Chapter 13). Here again, the actuary works closely with the sales, legal, and other departments.

3. *Calculating the premiums that should be charged in order to offer insurance benefits.* Chapter 10 explains many of the principles involved in these calculations.

4. *Reviewing the premium rates periodically to make sure they continue to be appropriate as conditions change.* This requires frequent studies of the company's own experience with death and disability among its policyowners, with its investment results, and with its expenses.

5. *Calculating the amounts to be set aside into funds or as policy reserves to guarantee the payment of policy benefits in the future.* The actuary must make certain that such amounts comply with the strict legal requirements regarding policy reserves in all the jurisdictions in which the company does business. These policy reserves normally constitute the primary liabilities on a life insurance company's balance sheet. Chapters 11 and 12 will explain *reserves.*

6. *Assisting the accounting staff in preparing the company's regular financial statements.* The annual statement of a life insurance company is required to bear the signature of an actuary.

7. *Engaging in corporate planning and operations research.* The expression "operations research" generally refers to using mathematical techniques to explore the effects which certain assumed events or courses of action would have on the company's operations. This might include evaluating a proposed company merger or developing new plans for agency financing or opening new markets.

It should be pointed out that most of the above responsibilities apply just as much to those working in the *group insurance* actuarial staff as to those in the *individual insurance* side of the company. (Chapter 15 discusses the mathematical bases of group insurance.)

COMPUTERS. The majority of the computations in today's life insurance offices is actually done by electronic data processing machines or computers. A considerable portion of this work is based on actuarial principles. The computer is one of the actuary's most valuable tools. It makes it possible to produce a huge number of calculations in a very short time and solve very complex problems. Actuaries must become virtual experts on the computer. They must be able to develop new applications for the computer, and they must advise persons working in the computer department on the uses and applications of these principles in the preparation of computer software programs, that is, instructions to the computer.

1.3 THE ACTUARIAL DEPARTMENT OF A LIFE INSURANCE COMPANY

The actuarial department of a large or medium-sized life insurance company is typically organized into sections, each one of which is responsible for certain aspects of the over-all actuarial function. Generally, the company's chief actuary oversees the entire department, with each section headed by an actuary who either holds a professional designation gained from an actuarial organization or is actively pursuing such a professional designation.

Day-to-Day Transactions. One section typically is involved in performing calculations of a day-to-day nature. These have to do with regular transactions requiring calculations, such as the amount payable for a particular death claim or the amount which a particular policyowner can borrow and the amount of interest thereon or the amount of nonforfeiture value due if premium payments are stopped. In companies where much of this type of calculating is done by computers, actuaries play important roles in setting up the correct computer application to handle such calculations.

Nonrecurring Transactions. Another section usually deals with less routine work, that is, with projects which are unique and nonrecurring. These require a broad knowledge of the company's insurance policies and premiums. Examples might include the calculation of illustrative figures used in sales material or the calculation of dividends to be paid to the owner of a very unusual type of policy issued many years previously.

Policy Changes. A third major area of actuarial responsibilities is dealing with policy changes in conjunction with the company's policyowner service function. When the owner of a policy which is already in force wishes to alter that policy in some way, such as changing the number of years it is scheduled to remain in force in the future, certain calculations must be made to determine the amounts of money which should change hands and the entries to be made on the company's records.

Statistics. Yet another section typically is concerned with regularly gathering and compiling statistics about the company's operations. Some of these statistics are necessary in producing the company's annual financial statement. Others are required by the company's management for its own use.

Research Activities. Finally, a section of actuaries is generally detached from the day-to-day routine operations of the company and engaged in a variety of research activities. Examples include making periodic studies of the company's experienced death rates, calculating the premiums and values to be used with new types of insurance policies, and conducting various operational research projects.

Of course, not all actuaries in an insurance company work in the actuarial department itself. For example, some may work in the data processing department, preparing instructions for the computer to perform some of the calculations mentioned above.

1.4 THE APPROACH OF THIS BOOK

This book will concentrate on basic principles and will teach basic calculation methods, although in practice, actuaries have developed and use more sophisticated methods (such as derived tables and computers). The student will learn the theories and principles which underlie the sophisticated methods but will do the calculations by hand as an aid in the learning process.

This text assumes that the student is familiar with the four fundamental arithmetical operations: addition, subtraction, multiplication, and division. Certain additional aspects of arithmetic and algebra will be reviewed in Chapter 2. This review should make it evident that many aspects of the actuarial process can be understood even by persons who do not work in the actuarial field.

For some students, the review in Chapter 2 may be unnecessary; for many, it will serve as an adequate review; for others, it may reveal deficiencies and indicate a need for additional help.

CHAPTER SUMMARY

- The sound mathematical principles underlying life insurance calculations provide assurance to policyowners that the amount they pay as premiums is justified and the insurance company will meet its promises.

- Compound interest and probability are the chief foundation stones that underlie the mathematical basis of life insurance.

- An actuary deals with contingent events, calculating their probabilites and making forecasts.

- Actuaries who work for life insurance companies generally have the following principal responsibilities:
  a) deciding on the benefits to include in policies (product design);
  b) drafting the actual documents for policies;
  c) calculating the premiums to be charged for policies;
  d) studying the company's own experience with death claims, investment results, and expenses;

e) calculating policy reserves to meet legal requirements and to assure adequate funds for the future;

f) preparing the company's financial statements with the accounting staff; and

g) engaging in corporate planning and operations research.

- Electronic computers have become invaluable in actuarial work. Therefore, when consulting with the computer department, an actuary must be familiar with the potentials and limitations of computers in order to determine their best use as actuarial aids.

- Typically, the different sections of the actuarial department in a life insurance company are assigned the tasks of:

  a) day-to-day calculations involving regular transactions;

  b) nonrecurring calculations, such as sales illustrations, as required;

  c) calculating policy changes;

  d) gathering statistics; and

  e) research assignments, such as making studies and producing new kinds of policies.

- The departments in a life insurance company are interdependent, and the actuarial department is vital to almost every area of operation. A study of basic actuarial principles should give every insurance company employee a better understanding of his or her own job.

- Performing basic calculations by hand will help a student considerably in learning these basic principles.

2

Fundamentals of
Mathematics

The purpose of this chapter is to review certain basic concepts of mathematics (such as fractions, decimals, factoring, equations, and exponents) which will be used throughout this textbook to explain and calculate life insurance mathematics. Some students will find the material presented in this chapter quite familiar. Others, however, who are less sure of their mathematical background, will probably find that the chapter is a necessary preparation for the material ahead. For students who study this chapter thoroughly and still feel the need for further review, a list of study aids is given at the end of this chapter.

Remember, a thorough grasp of the concepts presented in this chapter is essential for understanding the mathematics in the remainder of the book.

2.1 ARITHMETICAL CALCULATIONS

Letters of the alphabet are often used instead of numbers when arithmetical calculations are written. Using letters indicates that the exact number is unknown or that what is being written is general in nature. When letters are used, one letter stands for an entire number, not one letter for each digit of the number.

When two or more numbers are multiplied together and letters are being substituted for numbers, it is customary to write the two letters beside each other. For example,

ab means a times b, or $a \times b$

$4c$ means 4 times c, or $4 \times c$

ORDER OF OPERATIONS. When a series of arithmetical calculations involves more than one of the four fundamental operations, multiplication and division are performed before addition and subtraction. For example, to calculate

$2 + 3 \times 5 - 1$

the multiplication of 3×5 is performed first:

$$2 + 15 - 1$$

Then the addition of 2 and subtraction of 1 (either operation first) are performed, to give

$$16$$

As a second example, to calculate

$$10 - 12 \div 4$$

first divide 12 by 4, then subtract the result, 3, from 10:

$$10 - 3$$

giving the answer of

$$7$$

FACTORS. The factors of a number are those smaller whole numbers which, when multiplied together, equal that number. For example,

$$60 = 5 \times 12$$

$$60 = 6 \times 10$$

$$60 = 4 \times 15$$

$$60 = 3 \times 10 \times 2$$

The numbers 5 and 12 are factors of 60. The numbers 6 and 10 are also factors of 60, as are 4 and 15, etc.

When letters are used instead of numbers, the expression

$$C = DE$$

is a way of making a general statement of the fact that D and E are factors of C. The examples given above, such as $60 = 5 \times 12$, are specific instances of this general statement.

QUANTITIES. A *quantity* is all the numbers and letters which are included inside a pair of parentheses or brackets. For example, in the following expression

$$5 + 4(A - 5) + 2B$$

$(A - 5)$ is a quantity. In performing arithmetical calculations, each quantity is treated as if it were one number.

Any number or letter written beside a quantity is to be multiplied by that quantity, such as 4 in the expression above. When a quantity is being multiplied by a number or letter, that quantity may instead be written showing each number inside the parentheses multiplied by that number or letter. For example, the above expression, $5 + 4(A - 5) + 2B$, may be written instead showing the A and the -5 each multiplied by the 4, as follows:

$$5 + (4A - 20) + 2B$$

This does not change the value of the expression.

As a second example, the expression

$$-6(a - 2)$$

may be written showing the *a* and the −2 each multiplied by the −6:

$$-6 \times a = -6a$$

and $$-6 \times (-2) = + 12$$

Notice that multiplying two negative numbers results in a positive answer. So the expression may be written as:

$$-6a + 12$$

2.2 FRACTIONS

When an item is divided into four equal parts, each part is known as one fourth of the item and is represented by the symbol

$$\frac{1}{4}$$

The number below the line indicates division into "fourths." This number is known as the *denominator* and tells how many parts there are altogether. The number above the line is known as the *numerator*. It tells how many of the parts are being considered. The entire symbol is known as a *fraction*.

Fractions are, in fact, a way of indicating division. For example, $\frac{1}{4}$ indicates the division of 1 by 4; $\frac{3}{4}$ indicates the division of 3 by 4.

When the numerator and denominator are equal to each other, the fraction has the value of 1. This is because any number divided by itself equals 1. For example,

$$\frac{6}{6} = 1,$$

or $$\frac{bc}{bc} = 1$$

The value of a fraction is not changed if the numerator and denominator are both multiplied or both divided by the same amount. For example, if both the numerator and denominator of the fraction $\frac{3}{4}$ are multiplied by 2, the fraction becomes

$$\frac{3 \times 2}{4 \times 2} = \frac{6}{8}$$

The value of the fraction is not changed, that is,

$$\frac{3}{4} = \frac{6}{8}$$

As another example, if both the numerator and denominator of the fraction

$\frac{10}{15}$ are divided by 5, and the fraction becomes

$$\frac{10 \div 5}{15 \div 5} = \frac{2}{3}$$

The value of the fraction is not changed, that is,

$$\frac{10}{15} = \frac{2}{3}$$

REDUCING FRACTIONS. It is generally considered good practice to *reduce* all fractions to their lowest terms, that is, to divide the numerator and denominator by as large a number as possible (the same number) so that the remaining numerator and denominator are as small as possible (with the value of the fraction being unchanged). This is exactly what is done above when the fraction $\frac{10}{15}$ is reduced to $\frac{2}{3}$. The value is not changed but the numbers are smaller.

To Illustrate—Reduce the fraction $\frac{6}{18}$ to its lowest terms.

Solution—Both the numerator and the denominator can be divided evenly by 2, and the fraction becomes

$$\frac{6 \div 2}{18 \div 2} = \frac{3}{9}$$

The fraction is now expressed in lower terms, but it can be reduced still more. Both the numerator and the denominator of the fraction $\frac{3}{9}$ can be divided evenly by 3, and the fraction becomes

$$\frac{3 \div 3}{9 \div 3} = \frac{1}{3}$$

The value is unchanged throughout, that is,

$$\frac{6}{18} = \frac{3}{9} = \frac{1}{3}$$

The original fraction, $\frac{6}{18}$, could have been reduced to $\frac{1}{3}$ without an intermediate step, by dividing both the numerator and the denominator by 6:

$$\frac{6 \div 6}{18 \div 6} = \frac{1}{3}$$

To Illustrate Again—Reduce the fraction $\frac{2A(2B + C)}{4(2B + C)}$ to its lowest terms.

Solution—The items included inside the parentheses represent a quantity, which is treated as if it were one number. The numerator is

$$2 \times A \times (2B + C)$$

that is, three items multiplied together. The denominator is

$$4 \times (2B + C)$$

that is, two items multiplied together. Since the quantity $(2B + C)$ appears in both the numerator and the denominator as a multiplier, then the first step in reducing is to *divide* both the numerator and the denominator by this quantity:

$$\frac{2A(2B + C) \div (2B + C)}{4(2B + C) \div (2B + C)} = \frac{2A}{4}$$

The fraction may be reduced further by dividing both the numerator and the denominator by 2:

$$\frac{2A \div 2}{4 \div 2} = \frac{A}{2}$$

CANCELLATION METHOD. The cancellation method is a helpful shortcut for reducing numbers which appear as multipliers in both the numerator and denominator of a fraction. In this method, division is indicated by simply drawing lines through the common multipliers. For example, the fraction shown above

$$\frac{2A(2B + C)}{4(2B + C)}$$

can be reduced as follows:

$$\frac{2A\,\cancel{(2B + C)}}{4\,\cancel{(2B + C)}} = \frac{2A}{4}$$

Then, after dividing the numerator and denominator by 2, the fraction can be shown as

$$\frac{\cancel{2}A}{\cancel{4}_2} = \frac{A}{2}$$

ADDITION AND SUBTRACTION OF FRACTIONS. Before two or more fractions can be added or subtracted, they must have a *common denominator.* Each of the fractions to be added or subtracted can be altered in form (but not in value) by multiplying both the numerator and denominator by some number that will result in all the fractions having the same denominator. For example, the fractions

$$\frac{2}{3} \text{ and } \frac{1}{6}$$

may be expressed with a common denominator, 6, by multiplying both the numerator and the denominator of the first fraction by 2, as follows:

$$\frac{2 \times 2}{3 \times 2} = \frac{4}{6}$$

The first fraction $\frac{2}{3}$, may thus be expressed as

$$\frac{4}{6}$$

It now has the same denominator as the second fraction, $\frac{1}{6}$; that is, the two have a common denominator.

As another example, the fractions

$$\frac{2}{3} \text{ and } \frac{1}{4}$$

may be altered in form so that they have a common denominator, 12, by multiplying both the numerator and the denominator of the first fraction by 4, and by multiplying both the numerator and the denominator of the second fraction by 3:

$$\frac{2 \times 4}{3 \times 4} = \frac{8}{12}$$

$$\frac{1 \times 3}{4 \times 3} = \frac{3}{12}$$

A common denominator can always be found by multiplying together the denominators of the fractions to be added or subtracted, such as 3×4 in the above example. Very often, a smaller common denominator can be used, however, such as 6 in the first example.

When fractions are added or subtracted, the answer is a fraction which has a numerator equal to the numerators of the individual fractions added or subtracted and a denominator equal to the common denominator.

For example,

$$\frac{9}{12} - \frac{6}{12} + \frac{2}{12} = \frac{9 - 6 + 2}{12}$$

$$= \frac{5}{12}$$

To Illustrate—Add the following fractions:

$$\frac{1}{6} + \frac{B}{2A}$$

Solution—A common denominator can be used which is found by multiplying the two denominators together. However, in this case a smaller common denominator can be used, and is determined as follows:

Multiply the numerator and denominator of the first fraction by A; multiply the numerator and denominator of the second fracation by 3 to get the common denominator:

$$\frac{1}{6} + \frac{B}{2A} = \frac{1 \times A}{6 \times A} + \frac{B \times 3}{2A \times 3}$$

Perform each of the multiplications (fractions then have a common denominator):

$$= \frac{A}{6A} + \frac{3B}{6A}$$

Add numerators of individual fractions; place over common denominator:

$$= \frac{A + 3B}{6A}$$

MULTIPLICATION OF FRACTIONS. When fractions are multiplied, the answer is a fraction which has a numerator equal to the numerators of all of the individual fractions multiplied together and a denominator equal to the denominators of all the individual fractions multiplied together.

To Illustrate—Calculate $\frac{8}{3} \times \frac{3}{4}$ and express the answer in its lowest terms.

Solution—

Multiply the numerators; multiply the denominators:

$$\frac{8}{3} \times \frac{3}{4} = \frac{8 \times 3}{3 \times 4} = \frac{24}{12}$$

Reduce the fraction by dividing both the numerator and denominator by the same number:

$$= \frac{24 \div 12}{12 \div 12}$$

$$= \frac{2}{1} = 2$$

The cancellation method could shorten the above work, by drawing lines through the 3 that appears as a multiplier in both the numerator and denominator:

$$\frac{8 \times \cancel{3}}{\cancel{3} \times 4} = \frac{8}{4}$$

Then, simplifying this fraction by dividing numerator and denominator by 4 can be shown as

$$\frac{\cancel{8}^2}{\cancel{4}} = 2$$

DIVISION OF FRACTIONS. When one fraction is divided by another, the numerator and denominator of the second fraction are inverted (switched) and the answer is then found by multiplying the two fractions together.

To Illustrate—Calculate $\frac{5}{6} \div \frac{8}{3}$ and express the answer in its lowest terms.

Solution—

Invert the second fraction and multiply:

$$\frac{5}{6} \div \frac{8}{3} = \frac{5}{6} \times \frac{3}{8}$$

Multiply the numerators; multiply the denominators:

$$= \frac{5 \times 3}{6 \times 8}$$

$$= \frac{15}{48}$$

Reduce the fraction by dividing both the numerator and denominator by the same number:

$$= \frac{15 \div 3}{48 \div 3}$$

$$= \frac{5}{16}$$

To Illustrate Again—Calculate $\frac{5}{8} \div 7$.

Solution—The number 7 may be written as $\frac{7}{1}$.

Invert the second fraction and multiply:

$$\frac{5}{8} \div \frac{7}{1} = \frac{5}{8} \times \frac{1}{7}$$

Multiply the numerators; multiply the denominators:

$$= \frac{5 \times 1}{8 \times 7}$$

$$= \frac{5}{56}$$

EXERCISES, SET 1

1. What does XY mean, that is, two numbers written beside each other?

2. Find the value of $20 - 18 \div 3 + 6$.

3. How would the expression $3(3 + A - B)$ be written without parentheses?

4. How is $14B \div 9$ written in fraction form?

5. Before any number of fractions can be added or subtracted, what must first be done?

6. What is the smallest common denominator that can be used for adding $\frac{2}{3} + \frac{3}{4}$?

7. $\dfrac{1}{2} + \dfrac{4}{5} = ?$

8. $\dfrac{5}{6} - \dfrac{3}{4} = ?$

9. $\dfrac{7}{8} + \dfrac{1}{2} + \dfrac{3}{4} = ?$

10. $\dfrac{3}{4} \times \dfrac{A}{(B + 6)} = ?$

11. $\dfrac{1}{3} \div \dfrac{1}{4} = ?$

12. $\dfrac{22}{7} \div 11 = ?$

13. $\dfrac{2}{5} \times \dfrac{15}{16} = ?$

(Choose the correct answer.)

14. The expression (27 + 3 × 4 − 2) equals

    (1) 33   (3) 60

    (2) 37   (4) 118

2.3 DECIMALS

Decimals occur with great frequency in insurance work because (1) the monetary systems in the United States and Canada are decimal systems and (2) decimals are usually easier to handle than fractions in making calculations.

A *decimal point* is a dot or period. Its appearance between two digits of a number means that all the digits to the right of the decimal point actually constitute a fraction. For example, the number

    28.217

is actually the number 28 plus a fraction.

The fraction which is indicated by the digits to the right of the decimal point has a numerator equal to the number formed by those digits, and a denominator equal to 1 followed by as many zeros as there are digits in the numerator. For example, the number

    28.217

could be written as

$$28 + \frac{217}{1,000}$$

The digits to the right of the decimal point, namely 217, constitute the numerator. There are three such digits; hence the denominator is 1 followed by three zeros (1,000).

Any number without a decimal point (that is, a *whole number*) is assumed to have a decimal point at the end.

The value of a decimal number is not affected by adding any number of zeros to the right of the decimal number because, if the decimal were expressed in fraction form, adding zeros would similarly increase both the numerator and denominator, leaving the value of the fraction unchanged. For example, .01 is the same as the fraction $\frac{1}{100}$. If two zeros are added, the decimal number becomes .0100 which is the same as the fraction $\frac{100}{10,000}$. But this second fraction is equal to the first one, which can be seen by dividing both the numerator and denominator by 100.

When writing a fraction in decimal form, zeros may be placed *between* the decimal point and the digits which follow in order to achieve the total number of places needed to express the denominator. For example, it may be desired to express the fraction

$$\frac{23}{1,000,000}$$

in decimal form. Since there are six zeros in the denominator, there must be six digits following the decimal point. However, 23 has only two digits. The decimal form, then, would be

.000023

with the four zeros inserted to position the decimal point correctly.

ADDITION AND SUBTRACTION OF DECIMALS. Before adding or subtracting decimals, all the numbers should be given the same number of digits (*decimal places*) following the decimal point. This is done by adding the necessary number of zeros to the right of the numbers. After making sure the decimal point of each number lies directly below the decimal point of the number above, the numbers are then added or subtracted in the usual manner.

To Illustrate—Add the numbers 10.07, .047, 1,800, and 176.4.

Solution—10.07 has two decimal places; .047 has three decimal places; 1,800 has no decimal places; and 176.4 has one decimal place. The greatest number of decimal places is three, so zeros are added where necessary to produce three decimal places in each number.

$$
\begin{aligned}
10.07 &= 10.070 \\
.047 &= .047 \\
1,800 &= 1,800.000 \\
176.4 &= \underline{176.400} \\
&\quad 1,986.517 \text{ Total}
\end{aligned}
$$

The decimal point is placed in the answer so that there are three decimal places to the right.

MULTIPLICATION OF DECIMALS. *To multiply two or more decimals, first multiply the numbers in the usual manner. Place the decimal point in the answer so that the number of decimal places is equal to the total of the number of decimal places in the numbers being multiplied.*

To Illustrate—Multiply 14.231 by 1.04.

Solution—First multiply the numbers in the usual manner (ignoring the decimal points):

$$14231 \times 104 = 1480024$$

Because 14.231 has three decimal places and 1.04 has two decimal places, a decimal point must then be placed so that the answer will have five decimal places:

$$14.231 \times 1.04 = 14.80024$$

When decimals are being multiplied by 10 or 100 or 1,000, etc., the answer is easily found by shifting the decimal point to the right by as many places as there are zeros in the multiplier.

To Illustrate—Calculate 12.4717×100.

Solution—The multiplier, 100, has two zeros. Hence the answer is found by shifting the decimal point in 12.4717 two places to the right:

$$12.4717 \times 100 = 1247.17$$

DIVISION OF DECIMALS. *To divide two decimals, first divide the numbers in the usual manner. Place the decimal point in the answer so that the number of decimal places is equal to the number of decimal places in the number that is being divided into minus the number of decimal places in the number that it is being divided by.*

To Illustrate—Calculate $8.586 \div .3$.

Solution—First divide the numbers in the usual manner (ignoring the decimal points):

$$8586 \div 3 = 2862$$

Because 8.586 has three decimal places and .3 has one decimal place, a decimal point must be placed so that the answer will have two decimal places:

$$8.586 \div .3 = 28.62$$

It is often useful to add zeros at the end of the number being divided into so that the answer can be expressed with more decimal places.

To Illustrate—Calculate $.3 \div 8.586$, and show four decimal places in the answer.

Solution—If the division were performed in the usual way (ignoring the decimal points), the answer would be zero plus a remainder

$$3 \div 8586 = 0 \text{ (plus remainder)}$$

because the number that is being divided into (.3) is smaller than the number it is being divided by (8.586). In this example, the number .3 may be written as

.3000000

This number contains seven decimal places. Now divide in the usual manner:

$$3000000 \div 8586 = 349 \text{ (plus a small remainder)}$$

According to the rule for division of decimals, the answer will have four decimal places, because .3000000 has seven decimal places and 8.586 has three decimal places:

$$.3 \div 8.586 = .0349$$

The number of zeros to be added is related to the number of decimal places desired in the answer. Usually the number of decimal places is specified in the problem.

When a number is divided by 10 or 100 or 1,000, etc., the answer is easily found by shifting the decimal point to the *left* by as many places as there are zeros in the number it is being divided by.

To Illustrate—Calculate 487.72 ÷ 100.

Solution—The number that 487.72 is being divided by (100) has two zeros. The answer is found by shifting the decimal point in 487.72 two places to the left:

$$487.72 \div 100 = 4.8772$$

CHANGING FROM FRACTIONS TO DECIMALS. Because fractions indicate that the numerator is divided by the denominator, fractions can be changed to decimals by actually performing this division. For example, the fraction $\frac{1}{8}$ can be changed into decimal form by dividing 1 by 8. The 1 can be expressed as

$$1.000$$

The division, according to the rule given above, would be 1.000 ÷ 8 with three decimal places in the answer:

$$1.000 \div 8 = .125$$

Thus

$$\frac{1}{8} = .125$$

Every fraction has its decimal equivalent. The following decimal equivalents of certain fractions are useful to know because they occur quite commonly:

$\frac{1}{2} = .5$	$\frac{1}{8} = .125$	$\frac{1}{5} = .2$
$\frac{1}{4} = .25$	$\frac{3}{8} = .375$	$\frac{2}{5} = .4$
$\frac{3}{4} = .75$	$\frac{5}{8} = .625$	$\frac{3}{5} = .6$
	$\frac{7}{8} = .875$	$\frac{4}{5} = .8$

Some fractions produce a decimal equivalent which can never be expressed exactly: for example, the fraction $\frac{1}{3}$. When 1 is divided by 3, the result will be .33333. . . , with no end to the 3's, regardless of how many decimal places are used in the answer.

ROUNDING OFF DECIMALS. Decimals may express either exact or approximate values. The values are approximate if the decimal has been *rounded off*. The decimal .002, meaning $\frac{2}{1,000}$, is exact. The decimal .125, which is the equivalent of $\frac{1}{8}$, is also exact. However, if the decimal .08333. . . , which is the equivalent of $\frac{1}{12}$, is rounded off to four decimal places and written .0833, then it is approximate.

Consider the decimal .2168528, which is correct to seven decimal places. If six decimal places only are needed, it would not be correct just to drop the digit 8 in the seventh decimal place, and write the number as .216852. It would be more accurate to write .216853, because the latter is a closer approximation to the true value, .2168528. Similarly, if the given decimal were to be retained to only five decimal places, the correct result would be .21685.

Hint: When a particular number of decimal places are needed in an answer, the accuracy of the answer is increased by calculating to one decimal place more than is needed, then rounding off.

The rule for rounding off is: If a decimal is to be rounded off to a fewer number of places, drop the digits to be eliminated; then, if the first digit dropped is 5 or more (that is, 5, 6, 7, 8, 9), add 1 to the last remaining digit of the number; if the first digit dropped is less than 5 (that is, 0, 1, 2, 3, 4), make no adjustment in the remaining number.

For example, if the decimal .42649 is to be rounded off to four decimal places, the last digit, 9, is dropped. Since the digit dropped is 5 or more, 1 is added to the last remaining digit:

.4265

If this same decimal, .42649, is to be rounded off to three decimal places, the last two digits, 49, are dropped. Since the first digit dropped, 4, is less than 5, the remaining number needs no adjustment:

.426

To Illustrate—Round off each of these decimals to four places; to three places; and to two places: .24382, .52696, .84285, .77655, and .42852.

Solution—

Decimal	Four Places	Three Places	Two Places
.24382	.2438	.244	.24
.52696	.5270	.527	.53
.84285	.8429	.843	.84
.77655	.7766	.777	.78
.42852	.4285	.429	.43

It is important to note that a decimal which has been rounded off to three decimal places, such as .429, may have originally been as small as .4285000, or as large as .4294999.... Whenever calculations are performed using decimals which have been rounded off, the fact that they are not exact should be kept in mind.

For example, when adding 10.7 and 4.852, two zeros are added to 10.7 so that both numbers will have the same number of decimal places:

$$10.700$$
$$+ \ \ 4.852$$
$$15.552$$

However, to judge whether all of the decimal places in the answer are exact, it is necessary to know whether 10.7 is exact or rounded off. If 10.7 has been rounded off, then the answer, 15.552, is an inexact or approximate answer.

It is also important to observe that rounding in successive steps may result in a different answer (not so accurate) from rounding in one step. For example, if .42649 is to be rounded off to three decimal places, the answers would be as follows:

> *One step*:   .426
> *Two steps*: .4265, .427

2.4 COMMON MULTIPLIER

Consider the problem of finding the total wages to be paid to a person who works on three consecutive days for 7.6 hours, 9.2 hours, and 8.4 hours, respectively, at an hourly wage of $4.25. The total wages may be represented by

$$\underbrace{7.6 \times \$4.25}_{\text{1st day}} + \underbrace{9.2 \times \$4.25}_{\text{2nd day}} + \underbrace{8.4 \times \$4.25}_{\text{3rd day}}$$
$$= \$32.30 + \$39.10 + 35.70$$
$$= \$107.10$$

(Notice adherence to the rule that, in a series of arithmetical calculations, multiplications and divisions are performed before additions and subtractions.)

It is simpler to write the expression

$$7.6 \times \$4.25 + 9.2 \times \$4.25 + 8.4 \times \$4.25$$

in the following manner:

$$\$4.25(7.6 + 9.2 + 8.4)$$

The items inside the parentheses constitute a quantity. They are all treated the same, that is, multiplied by $4.25. The quantity itself is treated as a single number; in this case the quantity is, $(7.6 + 9.2 + 8.4) = 25.2$, the total number of hours worked. Therefore, the total wages are

$$\$4.25 \times 25.2 = \$107.10$$

Removing the factor $4.25 from each of the three original terms and writing it as a common multiplier has reduced the number of multiplications from three to one. The number of additions has been left unchanged.

This operation of removing the common multiplier is called *factoring out a common multiplier*.

To Illustrate—Calculate $573 \times 291 + 846 \times 291 - 755 \times 291$.

Solution—Factor out the common multiplier 291 to give the expression $291(573 + 846 - 755)$.

Add and subtract within the parentheses:

$$291(573 + 846 - 755) = 291 \times 664$$

Multiply:

$$= 193,224$$

To Illustrate Again—Calculate $\dfrac{475}{1.03} - \dfrac{325}{1.03} + \dfrac{250}{1.03}$.

Solution—This expression may be written as

$$475\left(\frac{1}{1.03}\right) - 325\left(\frac{1}{1.03}\right) + 250\left(\frac{1}{1.03}\right)$$

showing that $\left(\dfrac{1}{1.03}\right)$ is a common multiplier.

Factor out the common multiplier:

$$475\left(\frac{1}{1.03}\right) - 325\left(\frac{1}{1.03}\right) + 250\left(\frac{1}{1.03}\right) = \frac{1}{1.03}(475 - 325 + 250)$$

Add and subtract within parentheses:

$$= \frac{1}{1.03}(400)$$

Multiply:

$$= \frac{400}{1.03}$$

Divide the numerator by the denominator; round to two decimal places:

$$= 388.35$$

It should be noted that when factoring out a common multiplier, it is most efficient to factor out the *greatest common multiplier*, thereby deriving the simplest expression. For example, in the expression, $36 + 40 - 28$, 2 and 4 are both common multipliers. If only 2 is factored out, $2(18 + 20 - 14)$, the expression has still not been reduced to the simplest state that factoring can take it, $4(9 + 10 - 7)$.

To Illustrate—Factor out the greatest common multiplier from the expression $4ab - 2ac + 8abc$.

Solution—Each of the numbers has 2 and a as common multipliers. Therefore, factoring out the greatest common multiplier, $2a$, shows

$$4ab - 2ac + 8abc = 2a(2b - c + 4bc)$$

EXERCISES, SET 2

1. Express the fraction $\frac{2}{100,000}$ in decimal form.

2. Add the following: 12, 4.62, .007, 14.88.

3. How many decimal places would appear in the answer to this multiplication:

    $18.773 \times .005$

4. Calculate $47.0001 \times .04$.

5. Calculate the decimal equivalent of the fraction $\frac{3}{7}$, showing four decimal places in the answer.

6. Calculate each of the following:

    a) 33.43×10 d) $746 \div 10$
    b) $.0674 \times 100$ e) $13.8147 \div 100$
    c) 10.7×100 f) $42.77 \div 1,000$

7. Round off this number to three decimal places, then round off the original number to two places:

    13.17452

8. Factor out the common multiplier from each of the following expressions, then calculate each answer:

    a) $14 \times 12 + 8 \times 12 + 3 \times 12$
    b) $\$1,000(1.05) + \$250(1.05) + \$750(1.05)$
    c) $\dfrac{\$100}{1.08} + \dfrac{\$250}{1.08} + \dfrac{\$50}{1.08}$

9. Factor out the greatest common multiplier from each of the following:

    a) $4A + AX$
    b) $5B - 15BC + 20C$

10. The expression $4.31 \times 1,000$ is equal to

    (1) .00431   (3) 431
    (2) .431   (4) 4,310

2.5 ESTIMATING THE ANSWER

In order to avoid any gross error, estimate the magnitude and nature of an answer in advance. In addition, consider the reasonableness of an answer. This is especially important when multiplying or dividing decimals.

For example, suppose it is necessary to multiply 23.64 by 41.73. It can be estimated that the answer should be a little larger than 20×40, or 800. When the two numbers are multiplied together, the resulting digits are 9864972. The estimate indicates the answer must be 986.4972, not 98.64972 nor 9864.972.

As a second example, suppose a person terminates a life insurance policy and receives the policy's value of $476.10 for each $1,000 of insurance. If this policy provides $12,000 of insurance (or 12 thousands), the amount to be received by the policyowner will be approximately $500 \times 10 = \$5,000$. The $476.10 is in the neighborhood of $500, and the 12 thousands of insurance is in the neighborhood of 10. (The actual amount, of couse, is $476.10 \times 12 = \$5,713.20$.)

A similar procedure is applicable in estimating for division. For example, suppose it is necessary to calculate 15,475.1 ÷ 288. It can be estimated that the answer should be in the neighborhood of 15,000 divided by 300. Both 15,000 and 300 can be divided by 100 by shifting the decimal point in each number two places to the left, giving 150 divided by 3. Thus, the answer should be in the neighborhood of 50. After the actual calculation, when the digits 537 (plus a small remainder) are the first three digits of the answer, the decimal point must be placed to show 53.7, which is in the neighborhood of 50.

Always remember: It pays to estimate the answer in advance to assure that the answer, when obtained, is reasonable.

EXERCISES, SET 3

The multiplications and divisions in the following examples have been performed without placing decimal points in the answers. Determine, by estimating, the correct positions of the decimal points.

1. $251.722 \times 3.11 = 78286$
2. $41.4771 \times .533 = 221073$
3. $2.6774 \times 1.062 = 28434$
4. $36,874 \times .01187 = 43769$
5. $2,000 \div 96.88 = 20644$
6. $.036 \div 114.87 = 313$

2.6 EQUATIONS

A mathematical statement that two things are equal to each other is known as an *equation*. For example, the following expression used first in Section 2.2 is an equation:

$$\frac{2A \div 2}{4 \div 2} = \frac{A}{2}$$

Equations are useful in solving a variety of problems. For example, the selling price of an item is made up of its cost to the seller and the profit. If the selling price is represented by S, the cost to the seller by C, and the profit by P, their relationship may be expressed in symbols as the equation

$$C + P = S$$

that is, cost plus profit equals selling price.

The profit from selling an article is equal to the difference between the selling price and the cost to the seller. Using the same symbols as above, this relationship, which is also an equation, is represented by

$$P = S - C$$

that is, profit equals selling price minus cost.

This simple illustration suggests that an equation can be changed from one useful form to another. The question naturally arises as to the kinds of changes which can properly be made on an equation without destroying the equality which exists between the amount on the right-hand side of the equal sign, and the amount on the left-hand side of the equal sign. The following rules apply:

- The same amount can be added to both sides of an equation without destroying the equality.
- The same amount can be subtracted from both sides of an equation without destroying the equality.
- Both sides of an equation can be multiplied by the same amount without destroying the equality.
- Both sides of an equation can be divided by the same amount without destroying the equality.
- The two sides of an equation can be interchanged (as a whole) without destroying the equality.

These five principles may be summarized in the single statement: *If both sides of an equation are increased, reduced, multiplied, or divided by the same amount, or if the sides are interchanged, the equality between the two sides of the equation is preserved.*

To Illustrate—If $S - C = P$, find the values of S. (This is known as *solving for S.*)

Solution—As a working procedure in solving equations, first inspect the equation to decide what operations must be performed on the equation (that is, addition, subtraction, multiplication, or division) so that the item being sought will stand alone on one side of the equation, and the answer on the other. Add C to both sides of the equation:

$$S - C + C = P + C$$

Now, on the left-hand side of the equation, the $-C$ offsets the $+C$ and the equation becomes

$$S = P + C$$

To Illustrate Again—If $P + C = S$, solve for P.

Solution—Subtract C from both sides of the equation:

$$P + C - C = S - C$$

Again, on the left-hand side of the equation, the $+C$ offsets the $-C$, and the equation becomes

$$P = S - C$$

Shortcut: When moving an amount from one side of the equal sign to the other, changing the sign of the amount (plus to minus, minus to plus) will provide the same result as adding or subtracting the same amount on both sides of the equation.

To Illustrate Again—If the hourly wage rate, R, is equal to total income, T, divided by the number of hours worked, H, express this fact in equation form and solve the equation for T.

Solution—

Given relationship:

$$\text{Hourly Rate} = \frac{\text{Total Income}}{\text{Hours Worked}}$$

Express the equation in symbols:

$$R = \frac{T}{H}$$

Multiply both sides by H:

$$HR = H\left(\frac{T}{H}\right)$$

Express the right-hand side in an equivalent form:

$$HR = \frac{HT}{H}$$

Reduce the fraction $\dfrac{HT}{H}$:

$$HR = T$$

To Illustrate Again—Given the equation $HR = T$, solve for H.

Solution—

Given equation:

$$HR = T$$

Dividing both sides R:

$$\frac{HR}{R} = \frac{T}{R}$$

Reducing the fraction $\dfrac{HR}{R}$:

$$H = \frac{T}{R}$$

Note that the result in each illustration can be verified by common-sense reasoning. In every problem, the answer should be examined to test its reasonableness.

To Illustrate Again—If $\left(\dfrac{4R}{5} + 3\right) = R$, find R.

Solution—Note that R appears on both sides of the equation. To solve for

R, it is necessary to make it stand alone on one side only. Also note that R is part of a fraction on the left-hand side, so that the fraction must be operated on to express it in nonfractional form.

Given equation:

$$\left(\frac{4R}{5} + 3\right) = R$$

Multiply both sides by 5:

$$5\left(\frac{4R}{5} + 3\right) = 5R$$

Multiply each item in parentheses by 5:

$$\frac{20R}{5} + 15 = 5R$$

Reduce the fraction $\frac{20R}{5}$:

$$4R + 15 = 5R$$

Subtract $4R$ from each side:

$$4R - 4R + 15 = 5R - 4R$$

$$15 = R$$

This answer can be checked if, in the original equation, R is replaced by its value, 15. The equation, $\left(\frac{4R}{5} + 3\right) = R$, then becomes

$$\frac{4 \times 15}{5} + 3 = 15$$

The calculation on the left-hand side may be performed by multiplying 4×15 (which equals 60), then dividing by 5 (which gives 12), and then adding 3 (which gives 15). This proves that the value $R = 15$ is correct and that the equation was properly solved.

To Illustrate Again—Solve the following equation for B:

$$K + 4 = \frac{3K}{B}$$

Solution—

Given equation:

$$K + 4 = \frac{3K}{B}$$

Multiply both sides by B:

$$B(K + 4) = \frac{3K}{B} \times B$$

Simplify the right side by cancellation:

$$B(K + 4) = \frac{3K}{\cancel{B}} \times \frac{\cancel{B}}{1}$$

$$B(K + 4) = 3K$$

Divide both sides by $(K + 4)$:

$$\frac{B(K + 4)}{(K + 4)} = \frac{3K}{(K + 4)}$$

Reduce the fraction on the left side:

$$\frac{B\cancel{(K + 4)}}{\cancel{(K + 4)}} = \frac{3K}{K + 4}$$

$$B = \frac{3K}{K + 4}$$

A desirable series of steps to use in solving equations would be as follows:

1. Eliminate fractions by multiplying both sides of the equation by a number which will eliminate the denominators:

$$\frac{4C}{B} = \frac{2(C + 6)}{B}$$

$$\frac{B}{1} \times \frac{4C}{B} = \frac{2(C + 6)}{B} \times \frac{B}{1}$$

$$\frac{\cancel{B}}{1} \times \frac{4C}{\cancel{B}} = \frac{2(C + 6)}{\cancel{B}} \times \frac{\cancel{B}}{1}$$

$$4C = 2(C + 6)$$

2. Eliminate parentheses (quantities) by multiplying each item inside parentheses by the multiplier:

$$4C = 2(C + 6)$$

$$4C = 2C + 12$$

3. Get all the items involving the letter being solved for onto one side of the equation and everything else onto the other side:

$$4C = 2C + 12$$

$$4C - 2C = 2C - 2C + 12$$

$$2C = 12$$

4. Combine all items possible, then divide both sides by the appropriate number to make the letter solved for stand alone on one side:

$$2C = 12$$
$$2C \div 2 = 12 \div 2$$
$$C = 6$$

2.7 EXPONENTS

Multiplying two 10's together (10×10) may be written as

$$10^2$$

Multiplying three 10's together ($10 \times 10 \times 10$) may be written as

$$10^3$$

Multiplying four 10's together ($10 \times 10 \times 10 \times 10$) may be written as

$$10^4$$

The small number appearing above and to the right of the 10 is called an *exponent* or sometimes a *power*. It tells how many 10's are multiplied together. The number being multiplied, 10, is called the *base*.

In more general terms (using letters):

$$A^n$$

means A multiplied by itself n times ($A \times A \times A \times A \ldots$), whatever number n represents. The base is A; the exponent is n.

Some other illustrations of exponents are:

$7 \times 7 = 7^2$—read as "seven to the second power" or "seven squared"

$2 \times 2 \times 2 \times 2 \times 2 \times 2 \times 2 = 2^7$—two to the seventh power

$(1.03)(1.03)(1.03) = 1.03^3$—1.03 to the third power or 1.03 cubed

$(1 + i)(1 + i)(1 + i)(1 + i) = (1 + i)^4$—$(1 + i)$ to the fourth power

$\left(\dfrac{1}{1 + i}\right)\left(\dfrac{1}{1 + i}\right)\left(\dfrac{1}{1 + i}\right) = \left(\dfrac{1}{1 + i}\right)^3$—$\left(\dfrac{1}{1 + i}\right)$ to the third power

Note that everything inside the parentheses is kept together.

Let us see what happens when we *multiply* two numbers which have the same base. For example:

$$B^3 \text{ multiplied by } B^2$$

The first number can be expressed as $B \times B \times B$, and the second number as $B \times B$. If the two are multiplied, the answer is $B \times B \times B \times B \times B$. Notice that multiplying three B's by two B's is the same as multiplying five B's.

There is, in fact, a convenient rule to use when multiplying or dividing numbers which have the same base: *If two or more numbers having the same base are multiplied together, the answer will be this base with an exponent equal to the total of the individual exponents. If two numbers having the same base are divided, the answer will be this base with an exponent equal to the difference between the two exponents.*

To Illustrate—Multiply 1.02^4 and 1.02^7.

Solution—The two numbers to be multiplied together have the same base, namely 1.02; therefore, the answer will have this base. The exponent in the answer is found by adding the two exponents, 4 and 7:

Add the exponents:

$$1.02^4 \times 1.02^7 = 1.02^{(4+7)}$$

$$= 1.02^{11}$$

To Illustrate Again—Multiply $(R + 3)^B(R + 3)^J(R + 3)^M$. Note that this means $(R + 3)^B$ *times* $(R + 3)^J$ *times* $(R + 3)^M$.

Solution—The base, in each case, is in the form of a quantity which must be kept intact, namely $(R + 3)$. The answer will have the base $(R + 3)$; its exponent will be equal to the total of the three exponents:

$$(R + 3)^B \times (R + 3)^J \times (R + 3)^M = (R + 3)^{B+J+M}$$

To Illustrate Again—Divide M^9 by M^3.

Solution—To divide it is necessary to subtract the exponents; hence, the exponent in the answer is the difference between 9 and 3:

Subtract the exponents:

$$M^9 \div M^3 = M^{(9-3)}$$

$$= M^6$$

To Illustrate Again—Find the value of $\dfrac{(1 + i)^5}{(1 + i)^4}$.

Solution—Remember that a fraction indicates the division of two numbers:

Subtract the exponents:

$$\frac{(1 + i)^5}{(1 + i)^4} = (1 + i)^{(5-4)}$$

$$= (1 + i)^1$$

A number with the exponent 1 is that number itself:

$$= (1 + i)$$

The use of exponents is essential in the study of compound interest. Therefore, it will be an important part of almost every subject presented in this book.

2.8 COMMON MULTIPLIERS IN EQUATIONS

The process of factoring out common multipliers (described in Section 2.4) is often useful in working with equations.

To Illustrate—Solve the following equation for X:

$$AX + BCX = D$$

Solution—

$$AX + BCX = D$$

Factor out the common multiplier X:

$$X(A + BC) = D$$

Divide both sides by $(A + BC)$:

$$\frac{X(A + BC)}{(A + BC)} = \frac{D}{(A + BC)}$$

$$X = \frac{D}{(A + BC)}$$

When factoring out a common multiplier, it is important to remember that any number by itself can be expressed as that number multiplied by one. For example, in the equation

$$S = 10 + 10(1.03) + 10(1.03)^2 + 10(1.03)^3$$

each of the numbers on the right-hand side has the number 10 as a factor, since the 10, which stands by itself, can be expressed as 10×1. After factoring out the common multiplier, 10, this equation appears as follows:

$$S = 10[1 + 1.03 + 1.03^2 + 1.03^3]$$

Note that the first number inside the bracket is a 1.

The common factor may be a letter, such as the letter R in the equation

$$T = R + R(1.03) + R(1.03)^2 + R(1.03)^3$$

The R which stands by itself can be expressed as $R \times 1$. Therefore, after factoring out the common multiplier, the equation appears as

$$T = R[1 + 1.03 + 1.03^2 + 1.03^3]$$

In some equations, as noted in Section 2.4, there may be more than one multiplier which can be factored out. For example, in the equation

$$U = P(1 + i) + P(1 + i)^2 + P(1 + i)^3$$

the three items on the right-hand side can be expressed as

$$P \times (1 + i) \times 1$$

$$P \times (1 + i) \times (1 + i)$$

and $P \times (1 + i) \times (1 + i)^2$, respectively.

Thus, two common multipliers, P and $(1 + i)$, appear in every item. [Also note that the rule for multiplying and dividing with exponents has been used, since $(1 + i)(1 + i)^2$ has been used as being equivalent to $(1 + i)^3$.] After factoring out the two common multipliers, the equation appears as follows:

$$U = P(1 + i)[1 + (1 + i) + (1 + i)^2]$$

In some equations, the common multiplier may be a fraction, as in the second illustration in Section 2.4. Another example of a fractional common multiplier would be the equation

$$V = \frac{Q(1 + i)}{(a + b)^2} + \frac{Q(1 + i)^2}{(a + b)^3} + \frac{Q(1 + i)^3}{(a + b)^4}$$

The three items on the right-hand side can be expressed as

$$\frac{Q(1 + i)}{(a + b)^2} \times 1$$

$$\frac{Q(1 + i)}{(a + b)^2} \times \frac{(1 + i)}{(a + b)}$$

and $\quad \dfrac{Q(1 + i)}{(a + b)^2} \times \dfrac{(1 + i)^2}{(a + b)^2}$

Thus, the greatest common multiplier

$$\frac{Q(1 + i)}{(a + b)^2}$$

appears in every item. After factoring out the common multiplier, the equation appears as follows:

$$V = \frac{Q(1 + i)}{(a + b)^2}\left[1 + \frac{(1 + i)}{(a + b)} + \frac{(1 + i)^2}{(a + b)^2}\right]$$

EXERCISES, SET 4

In Exercises 1 through 12, determine the value of the unknown quantity (the letter):

1. $G - 3 = 10$

2. $2D = D + 3$

3. $4A + 1 = 17$

4. $17 - C = 3C + 1$

5. $\dfrac{K}{5} = 3$

6. $3B - 1 = \dfrac{B}{2}$

7. $2(L - 2) = 3$

8. $3(E + 1) = 2(E + 6)$

9. $3(2R - 1) = 9$

10. $\dfrac{2}{R} + 1 = 17$

11. $\dfrac{L - 2}{3} = 2(L - 1)$

12. $\dfrac{K}{7} = \dfrac{4K}{2} - 1$

13. Solve the following equation for N:

$$R + \frac{N}{3} = 4(R - N)$$

In Exercises 14 through 18, write each expression as the base 10 with a single exponent:

14. $10^3 \times 10^4$

17. $10^8 \div 10^5$

15. $10^2 \times 10^7 \times 10^2$

18. $10^{10} \div 10^9$

16. $10^2 \times 10^3 \times 10^5 \times 10^6$

In Exercises 19 through 23, write each expression as the appropriate base with a single exponent:

19. $B^7 \times B^8 \times B^3$

20. $(1.08)^4(1.08)^8$

21. $v^{18} \div v^{10}$

22. $\left(\dfrac{1}{1+i}\right)^8 \times \left(\dfrac{1}{1+i}\right)^2 \times \left(\dfrac{1}{1+i}\right)$

23. $\left(\dfrac{a}{4}\right)^3 \div \left(\dfrac{a}{4}\right)$

In Exercises 24 through 26, factor out all the common multipliers:

24. $A^2 + A$

25. $5(1.075) + 15(1.075)^2 + 25(1.075)^3$

26. $\dfrac{50}{1.06} + \dfrac{150}{(1.06)^2} + \dfrac{50}{(1.06)^3} + \dfrac{200}{(1.06)^4}$

27. The expression, $\dfrac{(b+c)^{10}(b+c)^6}{(b+c)^4}$, has the same value as

    (1) $(b+c)^4$ (3) $(b+c)^{12}$

    (2) $(b+c)^8$ (4) $(b+c)^{20}$

CHAPTER SUMMARY

- Substituting letters for numbers indicates that the exact number is unknown or that a *general statement*, which is true for more than one number, is being shown.

- Numbers written beside each other indicate multiplication.

    $4JC = 4 \times J \times C$

- Order of performing arithmetic: multiplication and division first, addition and subtraction last.

- Quantities (within parentheses or brackets) are treated as one number.

- If a number is multiplied by a quantity, the result is that number multiplied separately by each item within the parentheses.

$$Y(4 + B) = 4Y + YB$$

- Fractions indicate division (numerator divided by denominator).

$$\frac{2}{A} = 2 \div A$$

- Multiplying or dividing both numerator and denominator by the same number will not change the value of the fraction.

$$\frac{1}{3} = \frac{1}{3} \times \frac{2}{2}$$

- Any number divided by itself equals one.

$$\frac{B + 6}{B + 6} = 1$$

- Any number divided by one equals that same number.

$$\frac{R}{1} = R$$

- To add or subtract fractions, express them all with a common denominator, then add or subtract numerators.

$$\frac{1}{2} + \frac{1}{3} + \frac{1}{6} = \frac{3}{6} + \frac{2}{6} + \frac{1}{6}$$

- To multiply fractions: multiply numerators by numerators, multiply denominators by denominators.

$$\frac{M}{N} \times \frac{P}{Q} = \frac{MP}{NQ}$$

- To divide one fraction by another, invert the second fraction and multiply.

$$\frac{D}{E} \div \frac{F}{G} = \frac{D}{E} \times \frac{G}{F}$$

- In a decimal number, the numbers to the right of the decimal point indicate the numerator of a fraction. The denominator of the fraction is 1 followed by as many zeros as there are digits in the numerator.

$$4.732 = 4\,\frac{732}{1,000}$$

- To multiply or divide decimals by 10, 100, 1,000, etc., move the decimal point right or left as many places as there are zeros.

$$114.8 \div 100 = 1.148$$

$$114.8 \times 100 = 11480.0$$

- To round off a decimal number, drop digits not wanted, then add 1 to the final digit if the first digit dropped is 5 or larger.

  81.7266 = 81.73 when rounded to two decimal places.

- It is advisable to estimate the general size of an answer in advance.
- An equation is a mathematical statement that two things are equal to each other.
- The same amount can be added to (or subtracted from) both sides of an equation without affecting the validity.
- The same amount can be multiplied by (or divided into) both sides of an equation without affecting the validity.
- "Solving an equation" means rearranging the equation until the *unknown* (letter of the alphabet) stands alone on one side, thus showing its value.
- In an expression such as A^n, A is the *base* and n is the *exponent*.
- The exponent tells how many times the base is to be multiplied by itself.

  $10^3 = 10 \times 10 \times 10$

- When multiplying numbers with the same base, simply add the exponents; when dividing, subtract the exponents.

  $(1 + i)^3 \times (1 + i)^4 = (1 + i)^7$

  $v^8 \div v^2 = v^6$

LEARNING OBJECTIVES

After reading this chapter, the student should know

- How letters of the alphabet are used to substitute for numbers.
- Which operations to perform first when a series of numbers must be added, subtracted, multiplied, and divided.
- What is meant by writing numbers inside parentheses or brackets.
- How a quantity multiplied by a number can be rewritten.
- The meaning of a fraction.
- How to change the numbers in a fraction without changing the value of the fraction.
- How to add, subtract, multiply, and divide fractions.
- How to convert a decimal into a fraction and vice versa.
- How to multiply and divide decimals.
- How to factor out a common multiplier.
- How to add, subtract, multiply, or divide on both sides of an equation without changing the fact that it is still a true equation.
- The meaning of "solving an equation."
- How to solve an equation.
- How to cancel out numbers which appear as multipliers in both a numerator and a denominator.

- The meaning of *exponent* and *base*.

- How to handle exponents when multiplying or dividing numbers which have the same base.

- How to factor out the common multiplier when exponents are involved.

Suggested Study Aids

Any one of the books listed below will provide the student a more extended review of the basic mathematics covered briefly in Chapter 2 of this textbook. Most of them should be available in local libraries, book stores, or schools.

Bernstein, Allen L., and Wills, David W. *Trouble Shooting Mathematics Skills*. New York: Holt, Rinehart & Winston, 1979.

Clark, Gerlena Reed; Lawton, Marjorie Sherman; Molina, Angela L.; and Wantuck, Laurence R. *Holt General Mathematics*. New York: Holt, Rinehart & Winston, 1982.

Denholm, Richard A.; Underhill, Robert G.; and Dolciani, Mary P. *Part 1, Elementary Algebra*. new ed. Boston: Houghton Mifflin Co., 1977.

Dressler, Isidore. *Review Text in Preliminary Math*. New York: AMSCO School Publications, Inc., 1962.

Jacobs, Russell F. *Basic Skills in Mathematics*. New York: Harcourt Brace Jovanovich, Inc., 1975.

Keedy, Mervin L., and Bittinger, Marvin L. *Review of Basic Mathematics for Part 6*. Reading, MA: Addison-Wesley Publishing Company, Inc., 1980.

Learning to Compute. 2 vol. 4th ed. New York: Harcourt Brace Jovanovich, Inc., 1981.

Meserve, Bruce E., and Sobel, Max A. *Contemporary Mathematics*. 2nd ed. Englewood Cliffs, NJ: Prentice Hall, Inc., 1977.

Saxon, John H., Jr. *Algebra I, An Incremental Development*. Norman, OK: Grassdale Publishers, Inc., 1981.

Introduction to Accumulated Values

After paying current benefits and expenses, the investment department of a life insurance company must invest the company's excess income, that is, money which will be needed to pay future obligations. *Compound interest* is the basic principle used in calculating the income of investments. This chapter and the following three will discuss this principle.

In this chapter, the nature of simple and compound interest will be explained and the calculation of interest will be shown. The concept of *accumulated value* (that is, the total amount of money originally invested plus the interest) will also be explained, and the student will learn how to figure accumulated values using both simple and compound interest.

Three important problem-solving tools (to be used throughout the book) will be introduced in this chapter: *equations* (or *formulas*), *line diagrams*, and *tables*.

- *Equations* provide a convenient way of using numbers and symbols to represent the relationships between mathematical ideas. The most important equations in this book will be highlighted when they first appear and will also be listed in the back of the book.
- A *line diagram*, much like a sentence diagram in grammar, acts like a map to all the essential elements of a problem. It helps the student understand the reasoning behind a problem.
- The *tables* are lists of figures already calculated for use in standard mathematical problems involving interest rates (and, in later chapters, *mortality rates*). All the student needs to do in certain cases is turn to the appropriate table, choose the appropriate figure, and insert it in an equation to help find a solution.

3.1 SIMPLE ACCUMULATED VALUE

Money paid for the use of money is known as *interest*. Banks, for example, pay depositors interest on money in savings accounts because banks generally invest the depositors' money for their own profit. A person who borrows money pays interest to the person or institution (bank, insurance company, etc.) who made the loan because the borrower has the use of the money during the period of the loan. Life insurance companies also pay interest on amounts such as money held for a beneficiary or policyowner dividends left with the company.

Interest is calculated by multiplying the amount of money originally invested or borrowed by a number called the *interest rate* or *rate of interest*. Whenever an interest rate is referred to without specifying a period of time, it is assumed to be the rate for calculating one year's interest. Interest rates are generally stated as being a certain percent (%), which means hundredths. For example, 3% means $\frac{3}{100}$, or .03. The money originally invested plus the total interest earned on that investment is known as the *accumulated value*.

To Illustrate—Find the accumulated value of $100 at the end of one year, if interest is earned at the rate of 3% per year.

Solution—The rate of interest, 3%, means that at the end of one year .03 times the sum invested will be due as interest. Consequently, the amount of interest earned is

$$.03(\$100) = \$3$$

and the accumulated value of $100 at the end of one year (the total of the original $100 investment plus the amount of interest earned) is

$$\$100 + \$3 = \$103$$

Sometimes interest rates are used which involve fractions, such as $2\frac{1}{2}\%$. In decimal form, this interest rate is expressed as .025. As another example, $5\frac{3}{4}\%$ is expressed as .0575. In general, the decimal form is easier to use in computing interest.

To Illustrate Again—If money is assumed to accumulate at the annual rate of .025 or $2\frac{1}{2}\%$, find the accumulated value of $750 at the end of one year.

Solution—The amount of interest earned on $750 at the end of one year at $2\frac{1}{2}\%$ is

$$\$750(.025) = \$18.75$$

The accumulated value of $750 at the end of one year ($750 plus the amount of interest earned) is

$$\$750 + 18.75 = \$768.75$$

These problems involve the same operation: adding the dollar amount of interest earned to the amount of money invested to obtain the accumulated value. If the letter A is used to represent the amount of money invested, the letter I to represent the amount of interest, and the letter S to represent the accumulated value, all such problems are represented by the equation:

$$S = A + I$$

If the interest rate per year is i, the amount of interest earned in one year is equal to the amount of money invested multiplied by the interest rate, that is,

$$I = Ai$$

Since this equation says I is equal to Ai, we can substitute Ai for I in the first equation above:

First equation above:

$$S = A + I$$

Substitute Ai for I:

$$S = A + Ai$$

Factor out common multiplier A:

$$S = A(1 + i)$$

This last equation states an important principle: *To accumulate an amount of money for one year at a specified rate of interest, multiply the amount of money by the quantity (1 plus the rate of interest), which is called the accumulation factor.* Using this method, the solution of the last illustration above may be written:

Basic equation for accumulating:

$$S = A(1 + i)$$

Substitute $750 for A, .025 for i:

$$= \$750(1 + .025)$$

Add 1 plus .025 inside the parentheses:

$$= \$750(1.025)$$

Multiply:

$$= \$768.75$$

The answer is the same as above.

LINE DIAGRAMS. As previously mentioned, a *line diagram* is a device which is helpful in clarifying many problems involving the transfer of money from one party to another. A line diagram makes it possible to see at a glance the essential elements of any problem, such as the amounts of money and the dates on which they are paid or invested, the rate of interest, and the number of years involved. It also shows another essential element, *the evaluation date*, which means the date used to determine the unknown or sought-after amount of money in the problem.

The following line diagram for the last illustration shows all of the essential information in the problem:

The amount of money *A* at the beginning of the year is $750. The rate of interest *i* is placed under the line with the horizontal brace ⌣ indicating the period for which this rate applies (one year in this diagram). The value of *S*, indicated by a question mark, is to be determined as of the evaluation date. This date is indicated by the asterisk*.

Thus far, examples have been confined to what is called *simple interest*, that is, interest payable only on the amount of money originally borrowed or invested.

3.2 ACCUMULATED VALUE AT COMPOUND INTEREST

The accumulated value of $100 at the end of one year at 3% interest is $100 multiplied by the *accumulation factor* (1 + .03), that is, $100(1.03). Now, suppose that the accumulated value of $100 at the end of *two* years is desired.

To obtain the accumulated value of $100 for two years, it is important to realize that the amount of money at the beginning of the second year is the same as the accumulated value at the end of the first year. Consider the following line diagram. This illustrates that $100 accumulated for one year at 3% interest equals $100(1.03). When this amount is accumulated for one more year, the accumulated value as of the evaluation date (the end of two years) is represented by *S*.

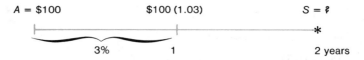

The amount of money at the end of the first year, or the beginning of the second year, is $100(1.03). This amount, accumulated for one more year at 3% is $100(1.03)(1.03). Therefore, we may write

$$S = \$100(1.03)(1.03)$$
$$= \$100(1.03)^2$$

This is the accumulated value of $100 based on the concept of *compound interest*, in which interest is payable on both the original amount and the accumulated interest.

Similarly, $100(1.03)^3$ is the accumulated value of $100 at the end of three years; $100(1.03)^4$ is the accumulated value of $100 at the end of four years; and, using the letter n to represent any number of years, $100(1.03)^n$ is the accumulated value of $100 at the end of n years at 3% interest per year.

More generally, if A dollars are invested at interest rate i per year, the accumulated values at the end of two, three, and four years, respectively, are

$$A(1 + i)^2$$
$$A(1 + i)^3$$
and $$A(1 + i)^4$$

It follows, therefore, that the accumulated value at the end of any number of years, n, is

$$S = A(1 + i)^n$$

To Illustrate—What is the accumulated value of $1,000 at the end of two years, if it earns interest at the rate of 6% per year?

Solution—The line diagram appears as follows:

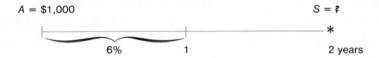

$A = \$1,000$ $S = ?$

6%   1   2 years

Using the equation just given:

Basic equation for accumulating:

$$S = A(1 + i)^n$$

Substitute $1,000 for A, .06 for i, and 2 for n:

$$= \$1,000(1 + .06)^2$$

$$= \$1,000(1.06)(1.06)$$

Multiply the first two numbers:

$$= \$1,060(1.06)$$

Multiply again; round to the nearest cent:

$$= \$1,123.60$$

During the second year, interest is earned on the interest which was earned during the first year. The fact that this interest is earned on interest gives rise to the term *compound interest*. In this text, the term interest will always mean compound interest unless otherwise stated.

To Illustrate Again—If a person leaves $500 on deposit with an insurance company at 5% interest per year, how much will this investment amount to at the end of four years?

Solution—The line diagram appears as follows:

If $500 accumulated at 5% for four years equals S, then using the equation for accumulating:

Basic equation for accumulating:

$$S = A(1 + i)^n$$

Substitute $500 for A, .05 for i, and 4 for n:

$$= \$500(1.05)^4$$

To avoid recalculating values which are used frequently (such as the value of 1.05^4), tables of these values have been prepared. Such tables are generally based on a payment of $1 (or on a series of payments of $1 each). The values shown in the tables may then be multiplied directly by the amount of the particular payment involved. For example, instead of obtaining the value of 1.05^4 by multiplying the four factors—(1.05)(1.05)(1.05)(1.05)—its value may be found in column (1) of Table I (for 5%) in the back of this book. Table I includes values of $(1 + i)^n$ (the "Accumulated Value of 1") at various interest rates for 1 to 25 periods, inclusive. Each page of Table I shows values at a different interest rate.

If $i = .05$ (or 5%) and $n = 4$, column (1) of Table I (5%) shows the value of $(1 + i)^n$ to be 1.215506. Therefore, the problem above can be solved as follows:

Basic equation for accumulating:

$$S = A(1 + i)^n$$

Substitute $500 for A, .05 for i, and 4 for n:

$$= \$500(1.05)^4$$

Substitute 1.215506 for 1.05^4:

$$= \$500(1.215506)$$

Multiply; round to nearest cent:

$$= \$607.75$$

To Illustrate Again—To what sum will $500 accumulate in 20 years at 4% interest per year?

Solution—The line diagram appears as follows:

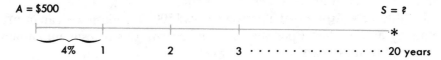

Basic equation for accumulating:

$$S = A(1 + i)^n$$

Substitute $500 for A, .04 for i, and 20 for n:

$$= \$500(1.04)^{20}$$

Substitute the value for 1.04^{20} from Table I (4%):

$$= \$500(2.191123)$$

Multiply; round to nearest cent:

$$= \$1,095.56$$

Two Notes. Table I shows the values to six decimal places, that is, they have been rounded off to six decimal places. This is generally sufficient for most practical calculations. In the offices of insurance companies, actuaries and others often work with tables that show ten or more decimal places. On the other hand, for less exacting calculations, the values in the table can be rounded off to fewer places.

Sometimes the interest rate may change during the time that the money is invested. In this case, the multiplier of $(1 + i)^n$ will use the first interest rate and first number of years, and a *second* multiplier of $(1 + i)^n$ will use the second interest rate and second number of years. For example, if $100 is loaned at 6% for three years and 8% for another four years, the amount owed at the end of the entire seven years is

$$\$100(1.06)^3(1.08)^4$$

3.3 CONSTRUCTION OF INTEREST ACCUMULATION TABLES

When a table is not available, it may be necessary to calculate certain values of $(1 + i)^n$. Interest accumulation tables can be constructed by starting with the value of $(1 + i)$ and multiplying each successive value by $(1 + i)$ to obtain the next value.

To Illustrate—Construct a table of values of $(1 + i)^n$ for 2%, that is, 1.02^n, for the values of n from $n = 1$ through $n = 5$, correct to six decimal places.

Solution—Remember, to construct a table correct to six decimal places, it is generally necessary to carry all calculations to at least seven decimal places and then round off each value to six decimal places. Remembering, also, the rule that exponents are added when multiplying numbers with the same base, the calculation is as follows:

$$1.02^1 = 1.0200000$$
$$1.02^2 = (1.02)(1.02) = 1.0404000$$
$$1.02^3 = (1.02)^2(1.02) = (1.0404000)(1.02) = 1.0612080$$
$$1.02^4 = (1.02)^3(1.02) = (1.0612080)(1.02) = 1.0824321$$
$$1.02^5 = (1.02)^4(1.02) = (1.0824321)(1.02) = 1.1040807$$

and the table is

n	1.02^n
1	1.020000
2	1.040400
3	1.061208
4	1.082432
5	1.104081

These values agree with the values in column (1) of Table I at 2% interest.

If a value from an interest accumulation table is known, the succeeding value can be determined by multiplying the known value by $(1 + i)$.

To Illustrate—Given $1.04^4 = 1.170$, find the value of 1.04^5.

Solution—Applying the above rule, the value of 1.04^5, which is the value succeeding 1.04^4 in a 4% table, can be found by multiplying:

Multiply known value by $(1 + i)$:

$$(1.04)^5 = (1.04)^4(1.04)$$

Substitute 1.170 for 1.04^4 as given above:

$$= 1.170(1.04)$$

Multiply; round to three decimal places:

$$= 1.217$$

If a value from an interest accumulation table is known, the preceding value can be determined by dividing the known value by $(1 + i)$.

To Illustrate—Given $1.04^5 = 1.217$, find the value of 1.04^4.

Solution—Applying the above rule, the value of 1.04^4, which is the value preceding 1.04^5, may be found by dividing:

Divide known value by $(1 + i)$:

$$1.04^4 = 1.04^5 \div 1.04$$

Substitute 1.217 for 1.04^5 as given above:

$$= 1.217 \div 1.04$$

Divide; round to three decmal places:

$$= 1.170$$

In dealing with problems like these, it is important to consider in advance whether the number sought will be larger or smaller than the given number. For example, when 1.04^4 is given and 1.04^5 is asked for, the answer would be expected to be larger than the given number, so that multiplication is indicated instead of division.

It should also be noted that these two illustrations make use of the rules given in Section 2.7 regarding the use of exponents for multiplying or dividing numbers having the same base.

To Illustrate—Find the value of 1.035^7, assuming that tables of values of the accumulation factor at $3\frac{1}{2}\%$, that is, 1.035^n, are not available.

Solution—

Multiply to obtain 1.035^2:

$$1.035^2 = (1.035)(1.035)$$

$$= 1.071225$$

Multiply to obtain 1.035^4:

$$1.035^4 = (1.035)^2(1.035)^2$$

$$= (1.071225)(1.071225)$$

$$= 1.147523$$

Multiply the values necessary for finding 1.035^7:

$$1.035^7 = (1.035)^4(1.035)^2(1.035)$$

$$= (1.147523)(1.071225)(1.035)$$

$$= 1.272279$$

EXERCISES, SET 5

1. Verify the answers in the last column without reference to any table:

Amount Invested (A)	Interest Rate per Year (i)	Years (n)	Accumulated Value (S)
$ 100.00	.06	1	$ 106.00
200.00	.05	1	210.00
86.47	.14	1	98.58
1,000.00	.125	1	1,125.00
750.00	.08	2	874.80
300.00	.06	3	357.30

2. Verify the answers in the last column, making use of accumulation factors from Table I:

Amount Invested (A)	Interest Rate per Year (i)	Years (n)	Accumulated Value (S)
$ 100.00	.10	6	$ 177.16
1,250.00	.025	10	1,600.11
500.00	.02	8	585.83
312.63	.04	17	608.97
898.04	.06	25	3,854.27
1,000.00	.05	12	1,795.86

3. A corporation borrows $15,000 from an insurance company, giving in return a note promising to pay in a single payment at the end of ten years the $15,000 with interest at 10% compounded annually. What will be the amount of the payment?

4. A person receives $500 from a friend's will and decides to invest the full $500 in a savings and loan association at 5% interest compounded annually. To what amount will the person be entitled at the end of four years?

5. In Table I, the value shown for 1.06^{25} is 4.291871. Calculate the value of 1.06^{26}.

6. The actuarial department needs to make a calculation using the value of 1.04^{35}. If they have Table I available, what value would they use?

7. If the value of $1 accumulated at an annual interest rate of 8% for 20 years is equal to $(1.08)^{20}$, then the value $1 accumulated at the same interest rate for 19 years is equal to

(1) $(1.08) \div (1.08)^{20}$ (3) $(1.08)^{20}(1.08)$

(2) $(1.08)^{20} - (1.08)$ (4) $(1.08)^{20} \div (1.08)$

3.4 ACCUMULATING MONEY FOR PERIODS OF TIME OF LESS THAN ONE YEAR

When interest is compounded once a year and it is necessary to find the interest earned by a sum of money for a period of *less* than one year, it is customary to calculate the interest in proportion to the time. For example, the interest for half a year is equal to half of the interest for a whole year, and the interest for two thirds of a year is equal to two thirds of the interest for a whole year.

To Illustrate—Find the interest on, and the accumulated value of, $250 for nine months at 8% interest per year.

Solution—The interest for nine months is $\frac{9}{12}$ or $\frac{3}{4}$ of the interest for a whole year. The amount of interest earned for a whole year is

$$.08(\$250) = \$20$$

Therefore, the amount of interest earned for $\frac{3}{4}$ of a year is

$$\frac{3}{4}(\$20.00) = \$15.00$$

The accumulated value at the end of nine months is the original sum plus interest:

Basic equation:

$$S = A + I$$

Substitute $250 for A, $15.00 for I:

$$= \$250 + \$15.00$$

Add:

$$= \$265.00$$

If the period of time is expressed in terms of days instead of months, it is often assumed, to simplify calculations, that the number of days in one year is 360. When this assumption of 360 days is made, it is also customary to assume that each of the 12 months contains 30 days. To find the exact number of days between dates, count either the first or final date but not both.

To Illustrate—Find the interest on, and accumulated value of, $500 for 60 days at 5% interest per year.

Solution—If one year is assumed to be 360 days, the interest for 60 days is $\frac{60}{360}$ or $\frac{1}{6}$ of the interest for a whole year. The amount of interest earned for a whole year is

$$.05(\$500) = \$25$$

Therefore, the amount of interest earned for $\frac{1}{6}$ of a year is

$$\frac{1}{6}(\$25) = \$4.17$$

The accumulated value at the end of 60 days is the original sum plus interest:

Basic equation:

$$S = A + I$$

Substitute $500 for A, $4.17 for I:

$$= \$500 + \$4.17$$

Add:

$$= \$504.17$$

3.5 NOMINAL AND EFFECTIVE INTEREST RATES

NOMINAL INTEREST RATES. It is customary to quote interest rates on a yearly basis. In this text the rate of interest quoted always means an *annual* interest rate unless otherwise stated. When interest is calculated each year on both the amount invested and the interest from preceding years, the interest is being compounded annually.

However, interest is often compounded more frequently than once a year—for example, semiannually or quarterly. In such a case, an *annual* interest rate may be quoted which is equal to twice the semiannual rate or four times the quarterly rate. Such a quoted figure is referred to as a *nominal interest rate.* If the nominal interest rate is divided by the number of compounding periods per year, the result is the interest rate per compounding period. For example, a nominal 6% compounded semiannually means that interest at the rate of 3% is added to the amount invested each half-year. An investment of $100 at such a rate would earn $100(.03) = $3 interest during the first half-year. The accumulated sum would then be $100 + $3 = $103. During the second half-year, the interest earned would be $103(.03) = $3.09; and so on.

Up to this point, the i and n in the equation

$$S = A(1 + i)^n$$

have been interpreted as the interest rate per year and the number of years, respectively, during which A accumulates to S. Such a restriction is unnecessary, however; all that is necessary is that i and n refer to the same period of time. For example, if i is the interest rate per half-year, then n must be measured in half-years. Similarly, if i is the interest rate per quarter, then n must be measured in quarters, and if i is quoted as the interest rate per month, then n must be measured in months.

To Illustrate—Find the accumulated value of $250 at the end of two years at a nominal 8%, compounded quarterly.

Solution—Since there are four quarters in one year, the interest rate is one fourth of 8%, or 2% each quarter. The line diagram appears as follows:

Since the interest rate is a rate per quarter, the time, two years, must be measured in quarters. Since there are four quarters in one year, then there are $4 \times 2 = 8$ quarters in two years. The problem therefore deals with eight periods, that is, the interest will be compounded eight times during the two years.

Basic equation for accumulating:

$$S = A(1 + i)^n$$

Substitute $250 for A, .02 for i, 8 for n:

$$= \$250(1.02)^8$$

Substitute the value for 1.02^8 from Table I (2% for 8 periods):

$$= \$250(1.171659)$$

Multiply; round to nearest cent:

$$= \$292.91$$

To Illustrate Again—Find the accumulated value of $2,000 at the end of five and a half years if the interest rate is 4% compounded annually during the first two years and a nominal 5% compounded semiannually during the last three and a half years.

Solution—The line diagram appears as follows:

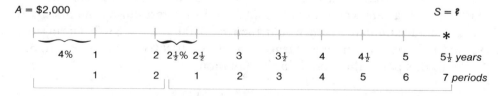

The accumulated value must be found in two steps, since only one rate of interest is used at a time in applying the accumulation formula $S = A(1 + i)^n$. The first step is to find the accumulated value at the end of the period (two years) during which interest is earned at the rate of 4%:

Basic equation for accumulating:

$$S(\text{end of 2 years}) = A(1 + i)^n$$

Substitute $2,000 for A, .04 for i, 2 for n:

$$= \$2,000(1.04)^2$$

The second step is to accumulate this value to the end of the entire period, that is, for the three and a half years during which the interest rate is a nominal 5% compounded semiannually. This means that $2\frac{1}{2}\%$ interest will be compounded for seven periods. The beginning value, A, in this case will be the same as the ending value, S, found at the end of two years:

Basic equation for accumulating:

$$S(\text{end of entire period}) = A(1 + i)^n$$

Substitute $2,000(1.04)^2 for A, .025 for i, 7 for n:

$$= \underbrace{\$2,000(1.04)^2}_{A}(1.025)^7$$

Substitute values from Table I for 1.04^2 and 1.025^7:

$$= \$2,000(1.081600)(1.188686)$$

Multiply; round to nearest cent:

$$= \$2,571.37$$

UNKNOWN RATE OF INTEREST. Sometimes it is desired to learn what rate of interest has been earned when the beginning value, A, and the accumulated value, S, are known. A procedure for finding the *approximate* rate of interest is as follows:

Basic equation for accumulating:

$$S = A(1 + i)^n$$

Divide both sides by A:

$$\frac{S}{A} = (1 + i)^n$$

At this point, tables of $(1 + i)^n$ (such as Table I) can be consulted to find which interest rate will give a value of $(1 + i)^n$ nearest to the actual value of $\frac{S}{A}$.

To Illustrate—An investment of $500 made ten years ago, with interest being compounded annually, has grown in value to $750. What interest rate per year was earned during that time?

Solution—The line diagram appears as follows:

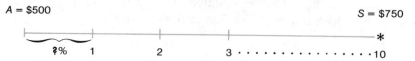

Equation derived above:

$$\frac{S}{A} = (1 + i)^n$$

Substitute $750 for S, $500 for A, and 10 for n:

$$\frac{\$750}{\$500} = (1 + i)^{10}$$

Divide $750 by $500:

$$1.5 = (1 + i)^{10}$$

From Table I, the values of $(1 + i)^{10}$, for various values of i, are as follows:

i	$(1 + i)^{10}$
2%	1.218994
$2\frac{1}{2}$%	1.280084
3%	1.343916
4%	1.480244
5%	1.628895
6%	1.790848
10%	2.593742

The rate of interest being sought is the one which will yield a value of 1.5 for $(1 + i)^{10}$. An examination of the values of $(1 + i)^{10}$ above shows that 4% yields a value of 1.480244 (which is smaller than the 1.5), and 5% yields a value of 1.628895 (which is larger than the 1.5). Therefore, the exact interest rate being sought must lie between 4% and 5%.

Greater accuracy in determining the exact rate earned could be achieved by using tables with more intervening interest rates or by using some methods of higher mathematics.

EFFECTIVE INTEREST RATES. When interest is compounded more frequently than once a year, an annual interest rate can be found which will produce the same accumulated values as the given nominal rate. This annual interest rate is called the *effective interest rate* and is actually the true interest rate earned.

For example, in the second paragraph of this section it was pointed out that $100 earning a nominal 6% compounded semiannually would earn $3 interest the first half-year, and the resultant $103 would earn $3.09 the second half-year. Therefore, the $100 would grow to $106.09 at the end of one year. If, instead, the interest rate were 6.09% compounded annually, the accumulated value at the end of one year would be

Basic equation for accumulating:

$$S = A(1 + i)$$

Substitute $100 for A, .0609 for i:

$$= \$100(1 + .0609)$$

Add inside the parentheses:

$$= \$100(1.0609)$$

Multiply:

$$= \$106.09$$

This is the same accumulated value as was produced by a nominal 6% compounded semiannually. Therefore, 6.09% may be said to be the effective interest rate which corresponds to a nominal 6% compounded semiannually.

Whenever two interest rates produce the same accumulated value in the same period of time, they are said to be *equivalent rates*. Therefore, in the example above, a nominal 6% compounded semiannually is equivalent to 6.09% compounded annually. The two rates were shown to be equivalent since they produced the same accumulated value at the end of one year; furthermore, if this is true, the two rates will necessarily produce the same accumulated value at the end of any number of years.

It is common to see advertisements by banks and other savings institutions in which two interest rates are quoted for the same type of savings account: one is the nominal rate and the other is the effective rate. Using the example given above, one might see an advertisement (or a sign posted in the bank) something like this:

> CURRENTLY PAYING ON SAVINGS ACCOUNTS
> 6% Compounded Semiannually
> 6.09% Effective Annual Yield

The *effective* rate corresponding to any given *nominal* rate may be calculated by the equation

$$\text{Effective Rate (decimal)} = (1 + i)^n - 1$$

where n is the number of periods per year, and i is the interest rate per period. This answer will be expressed in decimal form. It must be multiplied by 100 if it is to be expressed in percentage form:

$$\text{Effective Rate (\%)} = [(1 + i)^n - 1]100$$

To Illustrate—Find the effective interest rate which is equivalent to a nominal 10% compounded quarterly.

Solution—In using the above equation, it must be recognized that there are four periods in a year (because interest is compounded quarterly), and the interest rate per quarter is $2\frac{1}{2}\%$ (because $10\% \div 4 = 2\frac{1}{2}\%$).

Equation given above:

$$\text{Effective Rate (decimal)} = (1 + i)^n - 1$$

Substitute .025 for i, 4 for n:

$$= 1.025^4 - 1$$

Substitute the value for 1.025^4 from Table I:

$$= 1.103813 - 1$$

Subtract:

$$= .103813$$

This is the effective rate expressed in decimal form. If this answer is desired in percentage form, it must be multiplied by 100:

$$.103813 \times 100 = 10.3813\%$$

To Illustrate Again—A bank advertises that it is now paying interest on special one-year investments as follows:

> 8.96% Compounded Semiannually
> 9.16% Effective Annual Yield

Prove that the two interest rates are equivalent to each other.

Solution—There are two periods in a year (because interest is being compounded semiannually), and the interest rate per half-year is 4.48% (because $8.96\% \div 2 = 4.48\%$). In decimal form, this is $i = .0448$.

Basic equation:

$$\text{Effective Rate (decimal)} = (1 + i)^n - 1$$

Substitute .0448 for i, 2 for n:

$$= 1.0448^2 - 1$$

Substitute 1.091607 for 1.0448^2 (because $1.0448 \times 1.0448 = 1.091607$):

$$= 1.091607 - 1$$
$$= .091607$$

To express the answer in the desired percentage form, it must be multiplied by 100:

$$.091607 \times 100 = 9.1607\%$$

Since this is equal to 9.16% when rounded to two decimal places, the two interest rates shown in the advertisement are equivalent.

In a life insurance company, interest is being paid and received with various frequencies, and it is often necessary to compute the effective rate paid or earned. For example, the company's investment department must choose among many possible places to invest the company's funds, and the interest to be received is usually paid on monthly, quarterly, or semiannual bases. As another example, the company pays interest on money which is left on deposit with the company under policy settlement options. Such payments may generally be made with any frequency desired. The actuarial department must make certain that such payments are equivalent, regardless of the frequency chosen. Often the policyowner services department must explain the options available to the payee and explain why the various options and frequencies of payment are equivalent to each other.

To Illustrate—An insurance company's investment department has a choice between two investment opportunities. The first will pay the company a nominal 8% compounded quarterly. The second will pay a nominal 8.06% compounded semiannually. Which of the two investments would pay a higher effective annual interest rate?

Solution—In the case of the first investment, it should be recognized that there are four periods in a year (because interest is compounded quarterly), and the interest rate per quarter is 2% (because 8% ÷ 4 = 2%).

Basic equation:

Effective Rate (decimal) $= (1 + i)^n - 1$

Substitute .02 for i, 4 for n:

$$= 1.02^4 - 1$$

Substitute the value for 1.02^4 from Table I:

$$= 1.082432 - 1$$
$$= .082432$$

In percentage form, the first investment yields

$$.082432 \times 100 = 8.2432\%$$

The second investment opportunity is compounded semiannually, so there are two periods in a year. The interest rate per half-year is 4.03% (that is, half of 8.06%).

Basic equation:

Effective Rate (decimal) $= (1 + i)^n - 1$

Substitute .0403 for i, 2 for n:

$$= 1.0403^2 - 1$$

Multiply 1.0403×1.0403:

$$= 1.08222409 - 1$$
$$= .08222409$$

In percentage form, the second investment yields

$$.08222409 \times 100 = 8.222409\%$$

Therefore, the effective rate earned on the first investment would be better than the effective rate earned on the second.

FREQUENT COMPOUNDING. Nominal interest rates compounded semiannually, quarterly, and monthly are very common in many businesses. As the frequency of compounding increases, the corresponding effective rate increases because more interest is earned on interest. The following tabulation shows this specifically for a nominal interest rate of 6% compounded semiannually, quarterly, monthly, weekly, and daily:

6% Nominal Rate	Effective Rate
Compounded semiannually	6.090%
Compounded quarterly	6.136%
Compounded monthly	6.168%
Compounded weekly	6.180%
Compounded daily	6.183%

It is interesting to note that if the compoundings were to take place at increasingly shorter intervals of time, such as every hour, minute, second, etc., the corresponding effective interest rate in the above table would ultimately approach 6.184% (rounded off to three decimal places). This is said to be the effective rate when the money is compounded continuously.

It becomes increasingly impractical to compound money more and more frequently. However, this frequent calculation can be avoided by computing the accumulation at the equivalent effective interest rate. This is what is actually done by banks and savings and loan associations which advertise that money deposited with them is compounded daily or continuously.

EXERCISES, SET 6

1. Using the assumption of 360 days in one year, calculate the amount of interest which a borrower would owe at the end of 180 days on a $100 loan, if the interest rate were 6%.

2. Using the assumption of 360 days in a year and 30 days in a month, calculate the accumulated value on November 25 of $1,000 which an insurance company invested at 8% interest on March 4.

3. Calculate the accumulated amount at the end of four years of $100 which earns interest at a nominal 5% compounded semiannually.

4. If $1,000 earns interest at 6% compounded annually from March 15, 1983, to March 15, 1990, and the accumulated amount is then withdrawn and invested elsewhere at a nominal 8% compounded quarterly, what will be the accumulated value on June 15, 1992?

5. If a loan is made at a nominal interest rate of 10%, which one would be most likely to seek a very frequent compounding: the borrower or the lender?

6. What effective interest rate is equivalent to a nominal 10% compounded semiannually?

7. What effective interest rate is equivalent to a nominal 4% compounded quarterly?

8. Approximately what annual rate of interest has been paid by an insurance company on $1,000 deposited with the company if the accumulated value at the end of 20 years is $2,191.12?

9. Approximately what nominal rate of interest, compounded semiannually, has been earned on $2,000 if the accumulated value at the end of five years is $2,600?

10. On October 1, 1979, Karen Jolly deposited $1,300 in a savings account paying 6% interest compounded semiannually. On October 1, 1980, the bank announced that, beginning on that date, it would pay interest at 6% compounded quarterly. Ms. Jolly made no further deposits and no withdrawals. The amount in her account on April 1, 1982, was

(1) $1,300(1.03)^2(1.015)^6$ (3) $1,300(1.03)^4(1.015)^3$
(2) $1,300(1.015)^{10}$ (4) $1,300[(1.03)^2 + (1.015)^6]$

CHAPTER SUMMARY

- The amount of interest for a certain period of time is found by multiplying the amount of money invested by the interest rate for that same period of time. For this calculation, the interest rate must be expressed in decimal form.

- Unless specified otherwise, any interest rate quoted is an *annual* rate.

- The original amount invested plus the interest earned is called the *accumulated value*.

- If further interest is earned on the accumulated value, it is called *compound interest*.

- The accumulated value (S) of an amount of money invested (A) at an interest rate (i) per period for a number of periods (n) is calculated as:

$$S = A(1 + i)^n$$

- Tables of the values of $(1 + i)^n$ are published for various values of i and n.

- The next value in such a table can be found by multiplying the given value by $(1 + i)$. The previous value in such a table can be found by dividing the given value by $(1 + i)$.

- When an annual rate of interest is given, the amount of interest for less than one year is proportional to the time. For example, interest for one sixth of a year is one sixth of an entire year's interest.

- A yearly interest rate which is compounded more often than once a year is called a *nominal interest rate*. For example, 12% compounded monthly means 1% per month, and 12% is a nominal interest rate.

- When calculating accumulated value using the equation $S = A(1 + i)^n$ and when the interest rate given is a nominal rate, then i refers to the rate per period, and n refers to the number of periods.

- A yearly interest rate which produces the same accumulated value at the end of one year as a given nominal rate is said to be the *equivalent effective interest rate*.

- The effective interest rate which is equivalent to a given nominal rate can be found by this equation:

Effective Rate $= (1 + i)^n - 1$

where i is the rate per period and n is the number of periods in a year. Multiply this answer by 100 to get a percent rather than a decimal.

LEARNING OBJECTIVES

After reading this chapter, the student should know

- What is meant by accumulated value.
- How to draw line diagrams.
- How accumulated value at compound interest is calculated.
- How to use tables of $(1 + i)^n$.
- How to find a value of $(1 + i)^n$ if the preceding or succeeding value is known.
- How to calculate interest for periods of time less than a year.
- What is meant by nominal, effective, and equivalent interest rates.
- How to calculate accumulated values when a nominal rate is given.
- How to calculate effective interest rates.

4

More on Accumulated Values

In the last chapter, the student was shown the meaning of accumulated value and how to calculate the accumulated value of an amount of money which is loaned or invested. In this chapter, those same concepts will be carried further and applied to a "series" of payments rather than to a single amount of money. As will be seen, there are many instances in life insurance in which a series of payments is encountered—most importantly, the premiums paid for a life insurance policy.

Once the idea of a series of payments is established, the student will be introduced to the various kinds of series of payments. For example, some series may require that payments be made at the beginning of a certain period of time, while other may require that payments be made at the end of each period.

Finally, the student will be shown how to calculate how big each payment in a series needs to be in order to produce a definite amount of accumulated value.

The simplest series of payments is one in which each payment is of the same amount, and payments are made with constant frequency (for example, $100 paid on the first day of every month). This book generally confines itself to such simple cases and deals only with payments that are made with the same frequency as the interest compoundings.

Although the use of symbols in this book has been kept to a minimum, the student will be introduced in this chapter to certain symbols which are commonly accepted and used throughout the financial world. They are short ways of writing complex concepts, such as the accumulated value of a given number of payments at a given rate of interest. The student should find that the symbols used in this chapter and throughout the book simplify otherwise complicated mathematical expressions.

4.1 KINDS OF ANNUITIES

Any series of payments made or received at regular intervals of time is known as an *annuity*. Some examples found in everyday life are payments on mortgages, salaries, pensions, rents, regular periodic deposits in savings accounts, social security checks, payments for installment purchases, and life insurance premiums.

Every instance of an annuity represents payments going out from the viewpoint of the payor and payments coming in from the viewpoint of the receiver. The accumulated values explained in this chapter are applicable from either viewpoint.

In general, annuities fall into two broad classifications:

1. *Annuities certain*—which involve a fixed number of payments. An example would be the payment for a television set by regular monthly installments for two years. Another example would be the payments which an insurance company receives every month for 20 years to repay a mortgage loan which the company had made. Life insurance companies do not sell annuities certain, but they do use the concept in their calculations.
2. *Contingent annuities*—in which the continuation of payments depends on the occurrence or nonoccurrence of some event. An example would be the premiums for a life insurance policy which stop when the insured dies. In that case, the continued payment of the premiums is contingent on the life of the insured. Another example would be the payments made by an insurance company to a person who is disabled, each payment being made only if that person is still alive and still disabled.

Attention will be limited in this and the next two chapters to annuities certain. Chapter 8 will be devoted to a study of contingent annuities. Within the broad classification of annuities certain, there are two other classifications, depending on the time when each payment is made:

1. *Annuities immediate*—in which the payments are made at the *end* of each interval of time. An example would be salaries which are paid in arrears, that is, after the work period has ended.
2. *Annuities due*—in which the payments are made at the *beginning* of each interval of time. An example would be rents which are paid in advance, that is, before the start of the tenancy period.

In this text, the word *annuity* by itself refers to an annuity in which payments are made at the end of each interval of time, that is, an annuity immediate.

4.2 THE ACCUMULATED VALUE OF AN ANNUITY IMMEDIATE

The accumulated value, at the time of the last payment, of a series of payments of 1 each,* made at the end of each period for n periods, at interest rate i per period, is represented by the symbol

$$s_{\overline{n}|i}$$

The symbol is read as: "s angle n at rate i." The n and the i are written slightly lower than the s and are called subscripts. This means that they are

---

* Throughout this book, the phrase "of 1" or "of 1 each" means one unit of money of any kind.

part of the whole symbol, not something which is being multiplied by *s*.

For example, consider a series of five payments of $1 each, made at the end of each year, accumulating at an interest rate of 4% per year. The line diagram appears as follows:

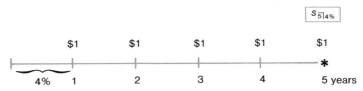

Since the number of payments is five and the interest rate is 4%, the accumulated value of the annuity at the end of five years is represented by the symbol

$$s_{\overline{5}|4\%}$$

This symbol is read as: "*s* angle 5 at 4%." The number under the angle is the number of payments. The number beside the angle is the rate of interest.

If each payment had been $10, then the accumulated value of the above annuity would have been $10 multiplied by the above value, that is,

$$\$10 s_{\overline{5}|4\%}$$

The line diagram, then would appear as follows:

The accumulated value of this annuity at the end of the five years can be calculated as follows: Ten dollars is deposited at the end of the first year. This deposit will grow to $10(1.04) at the end of the second year, at which time the second deposit of $10 will increase the balance to

$$\$10(1.04) + \$10 = \$20.40$$

In one more year, this amount will have grown to $20.40(1.04), and will be increased by a third deposit of $10, giving

$$\$20.40(1.04) + \$10 = \$31.22$$

In the fourth year, this amount will have grown to $31.22(1.04), and will be increased by a fourth deposit of $10, giving

$$\$31.22(1.04) + \$10 = \$42.47$$

Similarly, at the end of the fifth year, the amount will have accumulated to

$$\$42.47(1.04) + \$10 = \$54.17$$

A SECOND METHOD. The same accumulated value can be calculated by a second method, namely, by accumulating each deposit of $10 to the evaluation date and then finding the total of these five accumulations. The following line diagram illustrates this second method.

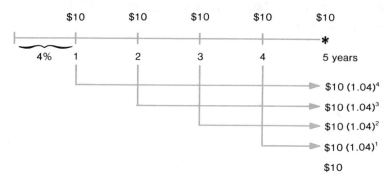

The first $10 deposit, made at the end of the first year, accumulates for four years; the second $10 deposit accumulates for three years; the third $10 deposit accumulates for two years; and the fourth $10 deposit accumulates for one year, all at 4% interest. The fifth $10 deposit, made on the evaluation date, earns no interest. Using the equation for accumulating, $S = A(1 + i)^n$, separately for each deposit, the total accumulated value is

$$\$10s_{\overline{5}|4\%} = \$10(1.04)^4 + \$10(1.04)^3 + \$10(1.04)^2 + \$10(1.04)^1 + \$10$$

The final $10 is not multiplied by any accumulation factor, since that deposit is made on the evaluation date. In the above expression, the common multiplier, $10, can be factored out (noting that the final $10 can be expressed as $10 × 1):

$$\$10s_{\overline{5}|4\%} = \$10[1.04^4 + 1.04^3 + 1.04^2 + 1.04^1 + 1]$$

Each expression inside the brackets can be looked up in column (1) of Table I (4%) and a substitution made:

$$\$10s_{\overline{5}|4\%} = \$10[1.169859 + 1.124864 + 1.081600 + 1.040000 + 1]$$

$$= \$10(5.416323)$$

$$= \$54.16$$

This answer is one cent different from that obtained above by the first method. This small difference is the result of rounding off at various stages of the calculations.

To use general terms: if the accumulated value at the end of n periods of a series of payments of 1, made at the end of each period for n periods, at interest rate i, is desired, the first term of the series will be $(1 + i)^{n-1}$, because there will be only $(n - 1)$ periods for the first payment to accumulate. The succeeding terms will be $(1 + i)$ with exponents diminishing by one each period, as follows:

$$s_{\overline{n}|i} = (1 + i)^{n-1} + (1 + i)^{n-2} + \cdots + (1 + i)^2 + (1 + i)^1 + 1$$

(The group of dots in the right-hand side of the equation indicates that a number of items are left out but that the series continues in the same manner as the previous items.)

Note that 1.04^1 in the example above could have been written simply as 1.04; also that $(1 + i)^1$ could have been written simply as $(1 + i)$. This text will usually omit the exponent 1.

TABLES OF VALUES. Values of $s_{\overline{n}|i}$ for periods of 1 to 25, inclusive, are given in column (3)—"Accumulated Value of 1 per Period"—of Table I at the various interest rates.

To Illustrate—Calculate the accumulated value of the annuity of $10 per year for five years at 4%, which was discussed above, by using values of $s_{\overline{n}|i}$ from Table I (4%).

Solution—

$$\text{Accumulated Value} = \$10 s_{\overline{5}|4\%}$$

Substitute the value of $s_{\overline{5}|4\%}$ from Table I:

$$= \$10(5.416323)$$

Multiply; round to nearest cent:

$$= \$54.16$$

The answer is the same as was derived above. Using values of $s_{\overline{n}|i}$ from Table I saves a great deal of calculation, especially as the number of periods increases.

4.3 CONSTRUCTION AND USE OF TABLES OF $s_{\overline{n}|i}$

The basic equation given above,

$$s_{\overline{n}|i} = (1 + i)^{n-1} + (1 + i)^{n-2} + \cdots + (1 + i)^2 + (1 + i) + 1$$

indicates a way to construct a table of accumulated values of an annuity of 1 per year ($s_{\overline{n}|i}$). The right-hand side of the equation represents the addition of terms, each of which can be found in a table of values of $(1 + i)^n$, such as Table I, column (1).

As an example, consider the 5% page of values shown in Table I. The first value, $s_{\overline{1}|5\%}$, will be equal to 1.000000, because in an annuity of just one payment, the payment will be made on the evaluation date and, hence, earns no interest. This is always true, regardless of the interest rate:

$$s_{\overline{1}|i} = 1$$

Each succeeding value in the $s_{\overline{n}|i}$ column may be found by adding, successively, the value from the $(1 + i)^n$ column, that is:

$$s_{\overline{2}|5\%} = s_{\overline{1}|5\%} + (1.05)^1$$

$$s_{\overline{3}|5\%} = s_{\overline{2}|5\%} + (1.05)^2$$

$$s_{\overline{4}|5\%} = s_{\overline{3}|5\%} + (1.05)^3$$

etc.

To derive the value of $s_{\overline{2}|5\%}$, substitute the actual values for $s_{\overline{1}|5\%}$ and $(1.05)^1$ shown in the table, then add.

$$s_{\overline{1}|5\%} = 1.000000$$

$$(1.05)^1 = 1.050000$$

$$1.000000 + 1.050000 = 2.050000$$

This answer agrees with the value shown in the table. To derive the value of $s_{\overline{3}|5\%}$, we would add $s_{\overline{2}|5\%} + (1.05)^2$, which is $2.050000 + 1.102500 = 3.152500$. This also agrees with the value shown in the table.

It is important to remember that the two values to be added are taken from the same line in the table, that is, the same number of periods are used for $s_{\overline{n}|i}$ and $(1 + i)^n$. The result is the value for $s_{\overline{n+1}|i}$, that is, for the next larger number of periods.

If an entire table of values of $s_{\overline{n}|i}$ is being calculated by this method of adding successive values of $(1 + i)^n$, great care should be exercised to see that no errors are made, for all succeeding values will be in error after the first error is made.

VALUES GREATER THAN SHOWN IN TABLE. It is sometimes necessary to find the value of $s_{\overline{n}|i}$ when the number of payments, n, is greater than the number shown in an available table. For example, Table I in this book shows such values for any number of periods up to and including 25. The equation for calculating such a value when n is larger than 25 is

$$s_{\overline{n}|i} = s_{\overline{25}|i} + s_{\overline{n-25}|i} (1 + i)^{25}$$

A line diagram of a specific example showing accumulation of payments for 30 years helps to visualize this relationship:

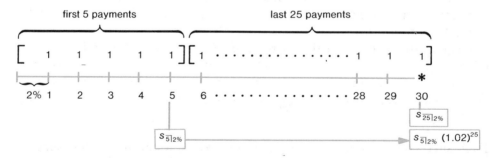

The accumulated value of the last 25 payments of 1 is $s_{\overline{25}|2\%}$. The accumulated value of the first five payments, accumulated to the date when the fifth payment is due, is $s_{\overline{5}|2\%}$. This latter value, accumulated to the true evaluation date, is

$$s_{\overline{5}|2\%}(1.02)^{25}$$

Therefore, the accumulated value of the 30 payments is

$$s_{\overline{30}|2\%} = s_{\overline{25}|2\%} + s_{\overline{5}|2\%}(1.02)^{25}$$

To Illustrate—Assume that a person in a company's actuarial department is working with a particular annuity certain which has 35 payments. How can this person calculate the value of $s_{\overline{35}|4\%}$, using only Table I?

Solution—Using the above equation:

Basic equation:

$$s_{\overline{n}|i} = s_{\overline{25}|i} + s_{\overline{n-25}|i}(1 + i)^{25}$$

Substitute 35 for n, .04 for i:

$$s_{\overline{35}|4\%} = s_{\overline{25}|4\%} + s_{\overline{10}|4\%}(1.04)^{25}$$

Substitute the values from Table I for $s_{\overline{25}|4\%}$, $s_{\overline{10}|4\%}$, and 1.04^{25}:

$$= 41.645908 + 12.006107(2.665836)$$

Multiply the last two numbers; round to six decimal places:

$$= 41.645908 + 32.006312$$

Add:

$$= 73.652220$$

TWO RATES OF INTEREST. Sometimes it is necessary to find the accumulated value of an annuity over a period of time during which the interest rate changes. The same technique can be used as was shown above when the number of periods exceeds that shown in the table, namely, to consider the series in two parts.

To Illustrate—An insurance company is investing $900 at the end of each year in a certain fund which credits 5% for the first three years and 6% thereafter. At the end of five years, what asset can the insurance company expect to show on its books for the money it invested in this fund?

Solution—The answer requires that we calculate the accumulated value of this five-year annuity, which has two interest rates (sometimes referred to as *dual interest rates*). The funds accumulate at 5% for the first three years and at 6% for the final two years. The line diagram appears as follows:

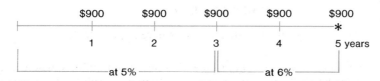

The accumulated value of the first three payments, evaluated at the time of the third payment, is

$$\$900\,s_{\overline{3}|5\%}$$

At this point (the beginning of the fourth year), the interest rate changes to 6%. Therefore, in order to find the accumulated value of these three payments at the end of the entire five-year period, the above value must be multiplied by $(1.06)^2$, that is, using the new interest rate for these last two years:

$$\$900\,s_{\overline{3}|5\%}(1.06)^2$$

A line diagram showing just the first three payments should help to make this clear:

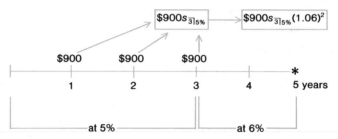

Finally, the last two payments in the series must also be accumulated to the evaluation date, and this calculation will use only the 6% rate:

$$\$900\,s_{\overline{2}|6\%}$$

A line diagram showing just the final two payments should help make this clear:

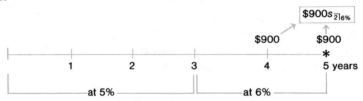

The total accumulated value of the entire series of five payments will be the two parts added together:

$$\$900\,s_{\overline{3}|5\%}(1.06)^2\ +\ \$900\,s_{\overline{2}|6\%}$$

Substituting values from Table I, this becomes:

$$\$900(3.152500)(1.123600) + \$900(2.060000) = \$5{,}041.93$$

EXERCISES, SET 7

(Draw line diagrams for all exercises where appropriate)

1. Write the symbol that means "the accumulated value of an annuity where each payment is 1, there being 30 such payments, and they accumulate at the rate of 11% each payment period."

2. Calculate the value of $s_{\overline{3}|5\%}$ by accumulating the value year by year of the payments to date, as was done in the first method in Section 4.2.

3. Calculate the value of $s_{\overline{3}|5\%}$ by accumulating each payment individually to the evaluation date and totaling them, as was done in the second method in Section 4.2.

4. Calculate the value of $\$625s_{\overline{12}|\ 2\frac{1}{4}\%}$.

5. If a person deposits $250 at the end of each year into a savings account earning 6% interest per year, how much will the account have to its credit at the end of four years?

6. If a bank is receiving deposits of $100 at the end of every three months from one of its depositors, how much will the bank owe the depositor at the end of five years if it allows interest at a nominal 8% compounded quarterly?

7. Every year a policyowner receives a dividend of $50 from a life insurance policy and leaves it on deposit with the insurance company. Interest is credited at 7%. If the first deposit is paid on June 1, 1983, then $\$50s_{\overline{5}|7\%}$ represents the value of these deposits on what date?

8. Calculate the value of $s_{\overline{50}|3\%}$. Calculate to four decimal places.

9. A loan of $500 is to be repaid at the end of five years with interest at 10%. In order to repay this loan, the borrower deposits $100 at the end of each year for five years in a savings account which earns interest at the rate of 5%. At the end of five years, what additional amount will be needed to pay the obligation?

4.4 THE ACCUMULATED VALUE OF AN ANNUITY DUE

In Section 4.1, an *annuity due* was described as a series of payments made or received at the beginning of each regular interval of time. Many such annuities are encountered in everyday living situations (such as rent payments, which generally must be made at the beginning of each rental period). Such annuities are also important and frequently encountered in the operations of a life insurance company, as will be seen throughout the remainder of this book.

Since payments in an annuity due are made at the beginning of each period, this means that the accumulated value is calculated as of one time period after the last payment.

The accumulated value, at the end of the period of the last payment, of a series of payments made at the beginning of each period for n periods, at interest rate i per period, is represented by the symbol

$$\ddot{s}_{\overline{n}|i}$$

The two dots over the s indicate that payments are made at the beginning of each period.

For example, consider a series of four payments of $1 each, made at the beginning of each year, accumulating at an interest rate of 3% per year. The line diagram appears as follows:

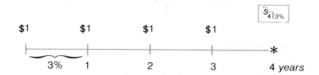

Since the number of payments is four, and the interest rate is 3%, the accumulated value (at the end of the four years, one year after the time of the last payment) is

$$\ddot{s}_{\overline{4}|3\%}$$

If each payment had been $50, then the accumulated value of the above annuity due would have been $50 multiplied by the above value:

$$\$50\ddot{s}_{\overline{4}|3\%}$$

The value can be calculated by accumulating each deposit of $50 to the evaluation date and then finding the total of these four accumulations. The following line diagram illustrates this procedure:

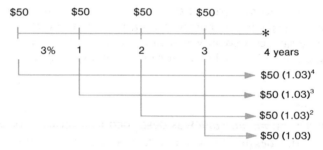

The first $50 deposit, made at the beginning of the first year, accumulates for four years; the second $50 deposit accumulates for three years; the third $50 deposit accumulates for two years; and the last $50 deposit accumulates for one year. Using the equation for accumulating, $S = A(1 + i)^n$, separately for each deposit, the total accumulated value is

$$\$50\ddot{s}_{\overline{4}|3\%} = \$50(1.03)^4 + \$50(1.03)^3 + \$50(1.03)^2 + \$50(1.03)$$

The common multiplier, $50, can be factored out, as follows:

$$\$50\ddot{s}_{\overline{4}|3\%} = \$50[1.03^4 + 1.03^3 + 1.03^2 + 1.03]$$

Each expression inside the brackets can be looked up in Table I (3%) and the values substituted:

$$\$50\ddot{s}_{\overline{4}|3\%} = \$50[1.125509 + 1.092727 + 1.060900 + 1.030000]$$

$$= \$50(4.309136)$$

$$= \$215.46$$

To use general terms: if the accumulated value at the end of n periods of a series of payments of 1, made at the beginning of each period for n periods, at an interest rate of i per period, is desired, the first term of the series will be $(1 + i)^n$. The succeeding terms will be $(1 + i)$ with exponents diminishing by one each period, as follows:

$$\ddot{s}_{\overline{n}|i} = (1 + i)^n + (1 + i)^{n-1} + \cdots + (1 + i)^2 + (1 + i)$$

Assuming that a table of values of $(1 + i)^n$ is available, this equation can be used to construct a table of accumulated values of an annuity due $(\ddot{s}_{\overline{n}|i})$. The procedure would be similar to that described in Section 4.3 for the construction of tables of $s_{\overline{n}|i}$.

RELATIONSHIPS BETWEEN $\ddot{s}_{\overline{n}|i}$ *AND* $s_{\overline{n}|i}$. Tables of $\ddot{s}_{\overline{n}|i}$ are not shown in this text and are not frequently found in practice. This is because there are two different relationships by which any desired value of $\ddot{s}_{\overline{n}|i}$ can be readily calculated by using a table of $s_{\overline{n}|i}$ (the accumulated value of an annuity immediate). This must be done quite often in the every-day work in various departments of a life insurance company, and the particular situation at hand will determine which one of these two relationships will be the easier to use.

The first such relationship is that *the accumulated value of an annuity due is equal to the accumulated value of the corresponding annuity immediate, for the same number of periods, multiplied by* $(1 + i)$.

This relationship between an annuity due and an annuity immediate can be expressed by the general equation:

$$\ddot{s}_{\overline{n}|i} = (1 + i)s_{\overline{n}|i}$$

This relationship may be demonstrated by use of the first equation given in this section, namely,

$$\ddot{s}_{\overline{n}|i} = (1 + i)^n + (1 + i)^{n-1} + \cdots + (1 + i)^2 + (1 + i)$$

Using as an example a six-payment annuity due, this equation would be

$$\ddot{s}_{\overline{6}|4\%} = 1.04^6 + 1.04^5 + 1.04^4 + 1.04^3 + 1.04^2 + 1.04$$

Factoring out the common multiplier 1.04

$$\ddot{s}_{\overline{6}|4\%} = 1.04[1.04^5 + 1.04^4 + 1.04^3 + 1.04^2 + 1.04 + 1]$$

The expression inside the brackets is exactly the same as the expression for $s_{\overline{6}|4\%}$, using the equation given in Section 4.2. Therefore, substituting $s_{\overline{6}|4\%}$

for the expression inside the brackets, the relationship becomes

$$\ddot{s}_{\overline{6}|4\%} = (1.04)s_{\overline{6}|4\%}$$

To Illustrate—Find the accumulated value at the end of four years of an annuity due of $50 per year at an interest rate of 3%.

Solution—The line diagram appears as follows:

This is the same annuity due which was calculated above. The accumulated value was given as $50\ddot{s}_{\overline{4}|3\%}$. Now this value can be calculated more readily by using the relationship:

$$\ddot{s}_{\overline{n}|i} = (1 + i)s_{\overline{n}|i}$$

as follows:

Basic equation:

$$\$50\ddot{s}_{\overline{n}|i} = \$50(1 + i)s_{\overline{n}|i}$$

Substitute 4 for n, .03 for i:

$$\$50\ddot{s}_{\overline{4}|3\%} = \$50(1.03)s_{\overline{4}|3\%}$$

Substitute the value from Table I for $s_{\overline{4}|3\%}$:

$$= \$50(1.03)(4.183627)$$

Multiply; round to six decimal places:

$$= \$50(4.309136)$$

Multiply; round to nearest cent:

$$= \$215.46$$

This answer agrees with that previously calculated.

A second relationship is that *the accumulated value of an annuity due is equal to the accumulated value of the corresponding annuity immediate for one more period, minus the amount of one payment.*

This relationship can be expressed in general terms by the equation:

$$\ddot{s}_{\overline{n}|i} = s_{\overline{n+1}|i} - 1$$

This relationship may be demonstrated by the equation:

$$\ddot{s}_{\overline{n}|i} = (1 + i)^n + (1 + i)^{n-1} + \cdots + (1 + i)^2 + (1 + i)$$

Using as an example a six-payment annuity due, this equation would be

$$\ddot{s}_{\overline{6}|4\%} = 1.04^6 + 1.04^5 + 1.04^4 + 1.04^3 + 1.04^2 + 1.04$$

Adding 1 to both sides

$$\ddot{s}_{\overline{6}|4\%} + 1 = 1.04^6 + 1.04^5 + 1.04^4 + 1.04^3 + 1.04^2 + 1.04 + 1$$

The right-hand side is exactly the expression for $s_{\overline{7}|4\%}$, with the exponent of the first term one less than the number of payments. Therefore, substituting $s_{\overline{7}|4\%}$ for the right-hand side, the above equation becomes

$$\ddot{s}_{\overline{6}|4\%} + 1 = s_{\overline{7}|4\%}$$

Subtracting 1 from both sides

$$\ddot{s}_{\overline{6}|4\%} = s_{\overline{7}|4\%} - 1$$

To Illustrate—Find the accumulated value at the end of four years of an annuity due of $50 at interest rate 3% (the same annuity due as in the last illustration), this time using $\ddot{s}_{\overline{n}|i} = s_{\overline{n+1}|i} - 1$.

Solution—

Basic equation:

$$\$50\ddot{s}_{\overline{n}|i} = \$50(s_{\overline{n+1}|i} - 1)$$

Substitute 4 for n, 3% for i:

$$\$50\ddot{s}_{\overline{4}|3\%} = \$50(s_{\overline{5}|3\%} - 1)$$

Substitute the value from Table I for $s_{\overline{5}|3\%}$:

$$= \$50(5.309136 - 1)$$

Subtract inside the parentheses:

$$= \$50(4.309136)$$

Multiply; round to nearest cent:

$$= \$215.46$$

This answer agrees with that calculated above.

WHICH EQUATION TO USE? Both of the two basic equations give the same result. In deciding which one to use, the student must be governed by the information given in a particular problem. For example, in order to use the equation $\ddot{s}_{\overline{n}|i} = (1 + i)s_{\overline{n}|i}$, it is necessary to know the interest rate. In order to use the equation $\ddot{s}_{\overline{n}|i} = s_{\overline{n+1}|i} - 1$, the value of $s_{\overline{n+1}|i}$ must be known. Where both items of information are known, it is generally easier to subtract

1 from the known value than to multiply by $(1 + i)$. This is very often the case in real-life situations, since the actuarial or investment department generally has published tables of values of $s_{\overline{n}|i}$ at various interest rates (such as in Table I in this text). Values of $\ddot{s}_{\overline{n}|i}$ are often needed, and must therefore be derived using one of the two basic equations.

To Illustrate Again—Calculate the accumulated value at the end of ten years of a series of deposits of $20 each made at the beginning of each half-year. Interest is credited at a nominal 5% compounded semiannually.

Solution—Since deposits are made each half-year for ten years, there are 20 deposits in all. The rate of interest is $2\frac{1}{2}\%$ (half of 5%) compounded every half-year. The line diagram appears as follows:

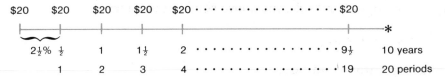

This series of deposits constitutes an annuity due, since deposits are made at the beginning of each period and the evaluation date comes one time period after the last payment. Hence, the accumulated value is $20\ddot{s}_{\overline{20}|2\frac{1}{2}\%}$.

Basic equation:

$$\$20\ddot{s}_{\overline{n}|i} = \$20(s_{\overline{n+1}|i} - 1)$$

Substitute 20 for n, $2\frac{1}{2}\%$ for i:

$$\$20\ddot{s}_{\overline{20}|2\frac{1}{2}\%} = \$20(s_{\overline{21}|2\frac{1}{2}\%} - 1)$$

Substitute the value from Table I for $s_{\overline{21}|2\frac{1}{2}\%}$:

$$= \$20(27.183274 - 1)$$

Subtract inside the parentheses:

$$= \$20(26.183274)$$

Multiply; round to nearest cent:

$$= \$523.67$$

WHICH TYPE OF ANNUITY? In order to determine whether a series of payments represents an annuity immediate or an annuity due, it is sometimes necessary to note where the final payment falls due in relation to the evaluation date. It should be remembered that in an *annuity immediate*, the accumulated value is calculated as of the same date as the final payment. In an *annuity due*, the accumulated value is found as of a date one period after the date of the final payment.

To Illustrate—A person deposits $100 in a savings account every July 1, from July 1, 1980 to July 1, 1984, inclusive. If interest is added to the account at 5%, how much will be in the account on July 1, 1984?

Solution—The problem does not specify whether the payments are made at the beginning or the end of each period. When no reference to the evaluation date is made, the line diagram appears as follows:

```
          $100    $100    $100    $100    $100
  ---+------+-------+-------+-------+-------+-------+---
  ··· 7/1/79  7/1/80  7/1/81  7/1/82  7/1/83  7/1/84  7/1/85 ···
```

It is impossible to tell by looking at this diagram whether this series of payments represents an annuity immediate or an annuity due. However, when an evaluation date (July 1, 1984) is added, the line diagram appears as follows:

```
          $100    $100    $100    $100    $100
                                          *
  ---+------+-------+-------+-------+-------+-------+---
  ··· 7/1/79  7/1/80  7/1/81  7/1/82  7/1/83  7/1/84  7/1/85 ···
```

Since the final payment falls upon the evaluation date, this represents an annuity immediate; that is, payments are made at the end of each period.

$$\text{Accumulated Value} = \$100 s_{\overline{5}|5\%}$$

Substitute the value of $s_{\overline{5}|5\%}$ from Table I:

$$= \$100(5.525631)$$

Multiply; round to nearest cent:

$$= \$552.56$$

4.5 SINKING FUND PAYMENTS

A regular periodic payment into a fund, made for the purpose of accumulating a certain amount on a certain date, is known as a *sinking fund payment*. The fund which is being accumulated is known as a *sinking fund*. An example would be a situation where parents deposit regular, periodic payments into a savings account in order to accumulate $10,000 for their child's college expenses by the time the child becomes 18 years old.

Up to this point, the amount of the regular periodic or sinking fund payment has been known and the accumulated value of the fund had to be calculated. Now, the converse problem will be considered: The accumulated value of the payments is known, but the amount of each payment must be calculated.

Suppose that sinking fund payments are being made for n years, and are being credited with interest at the rate of i per year. If each sinking fund payment is made at the end of the year, then these payments constitute an annuity immediate. The equation for the accumulated value at the time of the last payment is

$$\left(\begin{array}{c} \text{Sinking Fund} \\ \text{Payment} \end{array}\right) s_{\overline{n}|i} = \text{Accumulated Value}$$

The line diagram is as follows:

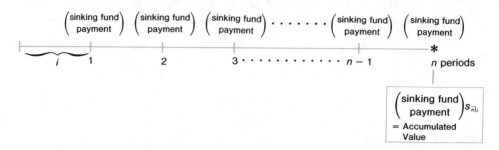

Since it is the sinking fund payment which is wanted, both sides of the equation can be divided by $s_{\overline{n}|i}$, to give an equation for the sinking fund payment:

$$\left(\begin{matrix}\text{Sinking Fund}\\ \text{Payment}\end{matrix}\right) = \frac{\text{Accumulated Value}}{s_{\overline{n}|i}}$$

This equation states that the known accumulated value is divided by $s_{\overline{n}|i}$ to arrive at the desired sinking fund payment.

To Illustrate—How large a sinking fund payment must be made at the end of each year for four years to yield an accumulated value of $600 at the end of four years? Assume an interest rate of 6%.

Solution—The line diagram appears as follows:

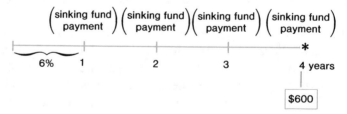

Basic equation:

$$\left(\begin{matrix}\text{Sinking Fund}\\ \text{Payment}\end{matrix}\right) = \frac{\text{Accumulated Value}}{s_{\overline{n}|i}}$$

Substitute $600 for accumulated value, 4 for n, 6% for i:

$$= \frac{\$600}{s_{\overline{4}|6\%}}$$

Substitute the value of $s_{\overline{4}|6\%}$ from Table I:

$$= \frac{\$600}{4.374616}$$

Divide; round to nearest cent:

$$= \$137.15$$

It can be shown that the annual sinking fund payment of $137.15 in the above illustration will actually accumulate to the desired $600 in four years. The following schedule shows the progress of the sinking fund year by year:

(1) Year	(2) Total in Fund Beginning of Year (Col. 6 of Previous Year)	(3) Interest Earned during Year (Col 2 × .06)	(4) Deposit End of Year	(5) Growth in Fund for One Year (Col. 3 + Col. 4)	(6) Total in Fund End of Year (Col. 2 + Col. 5)
1	$ 0	$ 0	$137.15	$137.15	$137.15
2	137.15	8.23	137.15	145.38	282.53
3	282.53	16.95	137.15	154.10	436.63
4	436.63	26.20	137.15	163.35	599.98

The shortage of 2 cents is the result of rounding off all figures to the nearest cent.

PAYMENTS AT THE BEGINNING OF EACH PERIOD. Sinking fund payments may be made at the beginning of each period instead of at the end. In this case, the payments constitute an annuity due. The equation for the accumulated value of sinking fund payments made at the beginning of each year for n years at interest rate i per year is

$$\left(\begin{array}{c}\text{Sinking Fund}\\\text{Payment}\end{array}\right)\ddot{s}_{\overline{n}|i} = \text{Accumulated Value}$$

An expression for the sinking fund payment can be derived as before by dividing both sides of the equation by $\ddot{s}_{\overline{n}|i}$, giving

$$\left(\begin{array}{c}\text{Sinking Fund}\\\text{Payment}\end{array}\right) = \frac{\text{Accumulated Value}}{\ddot{s}_{\overline{n}|i}}$$

If the value of $\ddot{s}_{\overline{n}|i}$ is not tabulated, it must first be calculated by using one of these two equations:

$$\ddot{s}_{\overline{n}|i} = (1 + i)s_{\overline{n}|i}$$

or

$$\ddot{s}_{\overline{n}|i} = s_{\overline{n+1}|i} - 1$$

To Illustrate—How large a sinking fund payment must be made at the beginning of each year for four years to yield an accumulated value of $600 at the end of that time? Assume the interest rate being credited to the fund is 6%.

Solution—This is comparable to the last illustration, except that the payments now constitute an annuity due. The line diagram appears as follows:

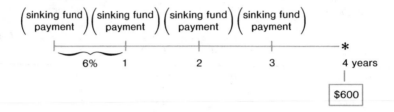

Using the equation for finding sinking fund payments which are made at the beginning of each period:

Basic equation:

$$\left(\begin{array}{c}\text{Sinking Fund}\\\text{Payment}\end{array}\right) = \frac{\text{Accumulated Value}}{\ddot{s}_{\overline{n}|i}}$$

Substitute $s_{\overline{n+1}|i} - 1$ for $\ddot{s}_{\overline{n}|i}$, since values of $\ddot{s}_{\overline{n}|i}$ are not tabulated:

$$= \frac{\text{Accumulated Value}}{s_{\overline{n+1}|i} - 1}$$

Substitute $600 for accumulated value, 4 for n, 6% for i:

$$= \frac{\$600}{s_{\overline{5}|6\%} - 1}$$

Substitute the value of $s_{\overline{5}|6\%}$ from Table I:

$$= \frac{\$600}{5.637093 - 1}$$

Subtract in the denominator:

$$= \frac{\$600}{4.637093}$$

Divide; round to nearest cent:

$$= \$129.39$$

The following schedule shows that this annual sinking fund payment of $129.39 will actually accumulate to the desired $600 in four years:

(1) Year	(2) Fund at Beginning of Year (Col. 6 of Previous Year)	(3) Deposit Beginning of Year	(4) Total in Fund Beginning of Year (Col. 2 + Col. 3)	(5) Interest Earned during Year (Col. 4 × .06)	(6) Total in Fund End of Year (Col. 4 + Col. 5)
1	$ 0	$129.39	$129.39	$ 7.76	$137.15
2	137.15	129.39	266.54	15.99	282.53
3	282.53	129.39	411.92	24.72	436.64
4	436.64	129.39	566.03	33.96	599.99

The difference of one cent is, as before, the result of rounding off all figures to the nearest cent.

COMPARING THE TWO KINDS OF SINKING FUND PAYMENTS. In comparing the last two illustrations, it will be observed that the deposit of $129.39, needed at the beginning of each year, is smaller than the corresponding deposit of $137.15, needed at the end of each year. This is logical because the deposit made at the beginning of each year has one more year in which to earn interest. In fact, this is the exact relationship between the two payments:

$$\$129.39(1.06) = \$137.15$$

As another example, if it is known that $100 deposited at the *beginning* of each period will accumulate to a desired amount on a certain date, then it is true that the same amount can be accumulated on the same date by making payments at the *end* of each period of $100(1 + i)$.

The reverse relationship should also be noted. If it is known that a given payment deposited at the *end* of each period will accumulate to a desired amount on a certain date, the same amount can be accumulated on the same date by making payments at the *beginning* of each period which are equal to the payment at the end of the year divided by $(1 + i)$.

EXERCISES, SET 8

(Draw line diagrams for all exercises where appropriate)

1. Calculate the value of $\ddot{s}_{\overline{12}|2\frac{1}{2}\%}$ by using both of the usual equations. Compare the two answers as a check.

2. Calculate the value of $\ddot{s}_{\overline{3}|5\%}$ by accumulating the value year by year of the payments to date. Check the answer by accumulating each payment individually to the evaluation date and totaling them.

3. In a life insurance company, the investment department needs to know the value

of $100 \ \ddot{s}_{\overline{10}|5\%}$. Calculate the value, assuming the only tables available are the Table I figures in this book.

4. If a person deposits $400 at the beginning of each year into a savings account earning 6% interest per year, how much will the account have to its credit at the end of six years?

5. On the day of their child's birth, the parents deposit $75 into a bank paying interest at the rate of a nominal 5% compounded semiannually. If they make a similar deposit at the beginning of each half-year thereafter, what is the total amount credited to the account on the child's tenth birthday? Assume they make no deposit on that day.

6. If $25 is deposited at the beginning of each year at 5% interest, what is the accumulated value at the end of five years, including a deposit then being made for the sixth year?

7. By what amount will the accumulated value of an annuity due of $300 for five years at $2\frac{1}{2}\%$ interest exceed the accumulated value of an annuity immediate of the same amount, duration, and rate of interest?

8. What amount must be deposited at the end of each year for seven years at 10% interest to yield an accumulated value of $750 at the end of the seventh year?

9. In order to accumulate a sinking fund having $10,000 at the end of five years, at a nominal 8% compounded quarterly, what payment must be made into the fund at the beginning of each quarter?

10. It is known that $24 deposited at the beginning of each month, earning a nominal 6% compounded monthly, will accumulate to $1,682.85 at the end of five years. What monthly deposit made at the end of each month will yield this same $1,682.85 in five years?

11. If $200 is deposited in a savings account every year, with the first deposit on June 1, 1981, and the final payment on June 1, 1991, how much will be in the account on June 1, 1992, if interest is credited at 5%?

12. The expression $\ddot{s}_{\overline{3}|7\%}$ is equal to

(1) $(1.07)^3 + (1.07)^2 + (1.07)$ (3) $s_{\overline{2}|7\%} + 1$

(2) $(1.07)^2 + (1.07) + 1$ (4) $s_{\overline{3}|7\%}(1.07) - 1$

CHAPTER SUMMARY

- A series of regular payments is called an *annuity*.
- If the number of payments is fixed (not dependent on some possible event), it is called an *annuity certain*.
- In an annuity immediate, or simply an annuity, payments are made at the *end* of each period. The accumulated value is evaluated as of the same date as the final payment.
- In an annuity due, payments are made at the *beginning* of each period. The accumulated value is evaluated as of the date one period after the final payment.

- The symbol meaning the accumulated value of an annuity of n payments of 1 each at an interest rate of i per period is $s_{\overline{n}|i}$.

- The accumulated value of such an annuity may be found by calculating the accumulated value of each payment separately:

$$s_{\overline{n}|i} = (1+i)^{n-1} + (1+i)^{n-2} + \cdots + (1+i)^2 + (1+i)^1 + 1$$

- A value of $s_{\overline{n}|i}$ may be found where the number of payments is greater than shown in the table. The technique involves splitting the series into segments, each of which contains the maximum number of payments shown in the table (or fewer), and evaluating each segment as of the evaluation date. For example, if the table shows a maximum of 25 payments and the number of payments being solved for is 30, the equation used would be

$$s_{\overline{30}|i} = s_{\overline{25}|i} + s_{\overline{5}|i}\,(1+i)^{25}$$

- The symbol meaning the accumulated value of an annuity due of n payments of 1 each at an interest rate of i per period is $\ddot{s}_{\overline{n}|i}$.

- The accumulated value of such an annuity may be found by calculating the accumulated value of each payment separately:

$$\ddot{s}_{\overline{n}|i} = (1+i)^n + (1+i)^{n-1} + \cdots + (1+i)^2 + (1+i)$$

- If a table is available showing the accumulated value of an annuity immediate $(s_{\overline{n}|i})$, the accumulated value of an annuity due can be found by either of these equations:

$$\ddot{s}_{\overline{n}|i} = (1+i)s_{\overline{n}|i}$$

or

$$\ddot{s}_{\overline{n}|i} = s_{\overline{n+1}|i} - 1$$

- Regular payments made to accumulate a desired amount are called *sinking fund payments*.

- If such payments are made at the *end* of each period, then each such payment equals

$$\frac{\text{Accumulated Value}}{s_{\overline{n}|i}}$$

- If, on the other hand, such payments are made at the *beginning* of each period, then each such payment can be found by substituting $\ddot{s}_{\overline{n}|i}$ for $s_{\overline{n}|i}$ in the above expression.

- If the sinking fund payments made at the *beginning* of each period are known, then sinking fund payments made at the *end* of each period which accumulate to the same final value can be found by multiplying the known payment amount by $(1+i)$. The reverse is also true. If payments made at the *end* of each period are known, then payments made at the *beginning* of each period which accumulate to the same final value can be found by dividing the known payments by $(1+i)$.

LEARNING OBJECTIVES

After reading this chapter, the student should know

- What is meant by the word annuity.
- How to calculate the accumulated value of an annuity by accumulating each individual payment separately.
- What is meant by the symbol $s_{\overline{n}|i}$.
- The general equation defining $s_{\overline{n}|i}$.
- How to use tables of $s_{\overline{n}|i}$.
- What is meant by annuity immediate and annuity due.
- Where the final payment falls in relation to the evaluation date for each of the two kinds of annuities.
- What is meant by the symbol $\ddot{s}_{\overline{n}|i}$.
- The differences between the general equations defining $\ddot{s}_{\overline{n}|i}$ and $s_{\overline{n}|i}$.
- How to use the two equations relating $\ddot{s}_{\overline{n}|i}$ to $s_{\overline{n}|i}$.
- How to use the evaluation date to determine whether an annuity is an annuity immediate or an annuity due.
- What is meant by sinking fund payments.
- How to calculate sinking fund payments.

Introduction to Present Values

In Chapters 3 and 4, the student was introduced to the concept of accumulated value, that is, a total amount of money invested plus interest. In Chapters 5 and 6, the student will be introduced to the concept of *present value*, that is, the amount of money which must be invested at the beginning of a transaction in order to grow to a specified amount at a later date. An example of how present value may be used can be seen in the following example: If $1,412.86 is the balance now in a savings account, how much was deposited three years earlier to produce this balance? The original deposit is the present value of the $1,412.86.

Finding present values, sometimes called *discounting*, is of special importance to life insurance companies because they are always concerned with the present value of premiums, benefits, investments, and policy loans that will be paid or received in the future. For example, calculating present value is necessary to guarantee that, when a loan is made, the present value of the amount to be repaid will equal the amount originally borrowed. Present value is also used to find the amount of money which should be invested originally in order to provide a desired amount of money at a later date.

This chapter will show the basic methods used to determine present value for a single payment and a series of payments, both annuities immediate and annuities due.

5.1 BASIC CONCEPT

In Chapter 3, it was demonstrated that the accumulated value, S, of a given amount of money, A, at the end of n periods, at interest rate i per period, can be calculated by using the accumulation equation

$$S = A(1 + i)^n$$

This same equation gives us the basis for solving the converse and equally important problem of determining A, the amount of money that must be deposited or invested for n periods at an interest rate of i per period in order to accumulate to the given amount, S.

As S is called the accumulated value of A, now A is called the *present value* of S. It is also sometimes referred to as the *discounted value*. For example, in the equation

$$\$103 = \$100(1.03)$$

$103 is the accumulated value of $100 for one year at 3%. Conversely, $100 is the present value (or discounted value) at 3% of $103 due at the end of one year.

Finding the present value of an amount of money is finding its equivalent value at an earlier date. For example, the present value of $100 due in five years at 3% is that amount of money which will accumulate at 3% interest to $100 in five years.

5.2 PRESENT VALUES

In finding a present value, the original amount to be invested, A, is sought. The accumulation equation can be solved for A, as follows:

Basic equation for accumulating:

$$S = A(1 + i)^n$$

Divide both sides by $(1 + i)^n$:

$$\frac{S}{(1 + i)^n} = A\left[\frac{(1 + i)^n}{(1 + i)^n}\right]$$

Drop $\frac{(1 + i)^n}{(1 + i)^n}$ because it equals 1:

$$\frac{S}{(1 + i)^n} = A$$

This equation, $\dfrac{S}{(1 + i)^n} = A$, specifies that the known accumulated value, S, is divided by $(1 + i)^n$ to arrive at the desired present value, A. Since values of $(1 + i)^n$ are shown in Table I, this procedure can be followed.

A simpler procedure is possible, however. The equation, $A = \dfrac{S}{(1 + i)^n}$, may also be written as

$$A = S\left[\frac{1}{(1 + i)^n}\right]$$

This indicates that the known accumulated value, S, is multiplied by the fraction $\dfrac{1}{(1 + i)^n}$ to arrive at the desired present value, A. For convenience the fraction $\dfrac{1}{1+i}$ is often expressed as v. Accordingly, the fraction $\dfrac{1}{(1+i)^n}$ is written as v^n. The equation for finding present values (that is, discounting) thus becomes

$$A = Sv^n$$

Therefore, v^n is the factor by which an amount of money, S, should be multiplied in order to determine its value n periods earlier, at interest rate i per period. It is important to remember that multiplying by v^n is the same as dividing by $(1+i)^n$. Values of the factor, v^n, are given for various interest rates in column (2) (present value of 1) of Table I for periods of 1 to 25, inclusive.

Note that the interest rate being used, i, does not appear directly in the factor for discounting, v^n, as it does in the factor for accumulating, $(1+i)^n$. Therefore, while an equation for accumulating might be written as

$$S = \$100(1.03)^{10}$$

an equation for discounting should be written as

$$A = \$134.39(v^{10} \text{ at } 3\%)$$

To Illustrate—How much money must be deposited in a bank paying 6% interest per year on deposits so that \$100 will be available at the end of one year?

Solution—The line diagram for this illustration appears as follows with A as the unknown:

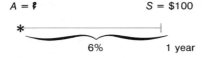

Use the basic equation for discounting:

$$A = Sv^n$$

Substitute \$100 for S, 1 for n; note interest rate is 6%:

$$= \$100(v^1 \text{ at } 6\%)$$

Substitute value of v^1 at 6% from Table I:

$$= \$100(.943396)$$

Multiply; round to nearest cent:

$$= \$94.34$$

This amount, \$94.34, is called the present value (or discounted value) of \$100 due in one year at 6%.

Note that the expression v^1 in the above solution could also have been written simply as v.

To Illustrate Again—How much money must be deposited in a bank paying 6% interest per year on deposits so that $100 will be available at the end of ten years?

Solution—The line diagram for this illustration appears as follows:

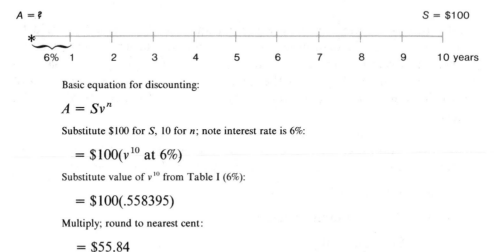

Basic equation for discounting:

$$A = Sv^n$$

Substitute $100 for S, 10 for n; note interest rate is 6%:

$$= \$100(v^{10} \text{ at } 6\%)$$

Substitute value of v^{10} from Table I (6%):

$$= \$100(.558395)$$

Multiply; round to nearest cent:

$$= \$55.84$$

This amount, $55.84, is called the present value or discounted value of $100 due in ten years at 6%.

COMPARING DIFFERENT PRESENT VALUES. The preceding examples illustrate that (at a given interest rate) *when the number of periods is increased, the present value is decreased.* This is true because in a longer period of time more interest is earned; hence, a smaller amount of money is required at the beginning to accumulate to a specified amount.

Similarly, *when the interest rate is increased, the present value is decreased.* This is true because a higher interest rate will produce more interest over a given period; hence, a smaller amount of money is required at the beginning to accumulate to a specified amount.

To Illustrate—Parents wish to invest an amount of money for their child, age ten, which will provide a $5,000 educational fund when the child reaches age 18. What amount should they invest if the fund earns a nominal 10% compounded semiannually? What amount should they invest if the fund earns a nominal 12% compounded semiannually?

Solution—Since the child is now age ten, and the fund is needed when the child is age 18, the total time is eight years. However, because interest is compounded every half-year, there are 16 periods. The interest rate of a nominal 10% compounded semiannually means 5% every half-year; the interest rate of a nominal 12% compounded semiannually means 6% every half-year. The line diagram appears as follows:

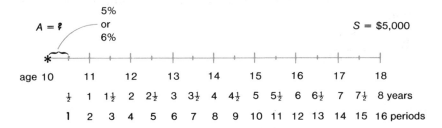

For a nominal 10% compounded semiannually:

Basic equation for discounting:

$$A = Sv^n$$

Substitute $5,000 for S, 16 for n; note interest rate is 5%:

$$= \$5,000(v^{16} \text{ at } 5\%)$$

Substitute value of v^{16} from Table I (5%):

$$= \$5,000(.458112)$$

Multiply; round to nearest cent:

$$= \$2,290.56$$

For a nominal 12% compounded semiannually:

Basic equation for discounting:

$$A = Sv^n$$

Substitute $5,000 for S, 16 for n; note interest rate is 6%:

$$= \$5,000(v^{16} \text{ at } 6\%)$$

Substitute value of v^{16} from Table I (6%):

$$= \$5,000(.393646)$$

Multiply; round to nearest cent:

$$= \$1,968.23$$

The answers show that the higher interest rate produces the lower present value.

5.3 CONSTRUCTION OF TABLES OF PRESENT VALUES

Present value tables at any desired interest rate may be constructed by starting with the value of v, which is found by dividing 1 by $(1 + i)$, and multiplying each successive value by v to progress down the table.

To Illustrate—Construct a table of values of v^n at 2%, for values of n from $n = 1$ to $n = 3$, inclusive, correct to six decimal places.

Solution—To construct a table correct to six decimal places, it is generally necessary to carry all calculations to at least seven decimal places and then round off each value to six decimal places. The calculation is as follows, remembering the rule that exponents are added when multiplying numbers with the same base:

$$v^1 \text{ at } 2\% = \frac{1}{(1.02)}$$

$$= .9803922$$

$$v^2 \text{ at } 2\% = v(v)$$

$$= (.9803922)(.9803922)$$

$$= .9611689$$

$$v^3 \text{ at } 2\% = v^2(v)$$

$$= (.9611689)(.9803922)$$

$$= .9423225$$

and the table is

n	v^n
1	.980392
2	.961169
3	.942323

These values check with the values in Table I at 2% interest, except for the last one. Table I shows the value of v^3 at 2% to be .942322. The reason for this difference in the sixth decimal place lies in the number of decimal places used in the calculation. It is not unusual in this type of calculation for two independent computations of the same problem to arrive at answers which differ in the last decimal place.

VALUES GREATER THAN SHOWN IN TABLE. It may be necessary to find the value of v^n at i when the number of payments, n, is greater than the number shown in an available table. For example, when n is larger than 25 (highest n shown in Table I), the equation for calculating such a value is

$$v^n \text{ at } i = v^{25} \text{ at } i \times v^{n-25} \text{ at } i$$

To Illustrate—Calculate the value of v^{35} at 5%.

Solution—

$$v^{35} \text{ at } 5\% = v^{25} \text{ at } 5\% \times v^{10} \text{ at } 5\%$$

Substitute the values from Table I for v^{25} and v^{10} at 5%:

$$= .295303 \times .613913$$

Multiply; round to six decimal places:

$$= .181290$$

EXERCISES, SET 9

1. Without using values from any table, verify the present values listed in the last column of the following schedule:

S	Interest Rate per Period (i)	Periods (n)	Present Value (A)
$ 800.00	.07	1	$ 747.66
1,200.00	.03	1	1,165.05
7,500.00	.04	1	7,211.54
427.50	.02	2	410.90
963.84	.05	2	874.23
1,250.00	.12	2	996.49

2. Using present value factors from Table I, verify the discounted values listed in the last column of the following schedule:

S	Interest Rate per Period (i)	Periods (n)	Discounted Value (A)
$1,500.00	.03	5	$1,293.91
5,000.00	.025	9	4,003.64
125.00	.04	15	69.41
750.00	.06	20	233.85
1,465.96	.10	6	827.50
943.83	.05	18	392.18

3. Which one of the following does not represent the present value of $100 due five years later?

a) $\dfrac{\$100}{(1 + i)^5}$ b) $\$100v^5$ c) $\$100(1 + i)^5$ d) $\$100\left[\dfrac{1}{(1 + i)^5}\right]$

4. How much money must be deposited now in an account paying 6% interest per year in order to provide $1,500 at the end of one year?

5. How much money must be deposited now in an account paying 6% interest per year in order to provide $1,500 at the end of ten years?

6. Calculate the present value of $1,000 due in five years, if the interest rate is a nominal 10% compounded quarterly.

7. To assist in financing the future college education of a newborn child, what amount of money should a parent immediately deposit in a savings account earning 6% interest annually so that $20,000 will be available when the child is age 18?

8. How much money would the parent in Exercise 7 have to deposit immediately so that the child would have available $5,000 each year for the 4 consecutive years starting when the child is age 18? (Hint: Find the present value as if there were four separate payments, then add.)

9. Using Table I, calculate the value of v^{30} at 3%.

10. At an interest rate of 12% per year compounded quarterly, the present value of $5,000 due in four years is shown by the expression

(1) $\$5,000s_{\overline{16}|3\%}$ (3) $\$5,000v^{16}$ at 3%

(2) $\$5,000(1.03)^{16}$ (4) $\$5,000v^{4}$ at 3%

5.4 THE PRESENT VALUE OF AN ANNUITY IMMEDIATE

At this point we are ready to begin studying the methods of finding the present value of a *series* of payments (that is, an annuity). A common example of such a problem is that of a debt repaid by periodic payments. The amount of the debt, plus interest, must be paid exactly by the series of payments. This is the same as saying that the present value of the payments must be equal to the original debt.

A savings account from which periodic withdrawals will be made provides another example involving present value of a series of payments. The original amount in the account, plus the interest that will be earned, must be exactly sufficient to provide for the series of withdrawals. This is the same as saying that the present value of the future withdrawals must equal the amount originally in the account.

In a life insurance company, calculating the present value of annuities is an everyday requirement. For one example, the investment department must see that the present value of repayments it is to receive on its investments will be equal to the amount originally invested. Both the actuarial department and the policyowners service department make frequent calculations involving the company's *settlement options* (to be explained fully in Chapter 8), wherein the present value of a series of amounts the company pays out must equal the company's original obligation.

SYMBOL FOR PRESENT VALUE OF ANNUITY. The present value at the beginning of the first period of a series of payments of 1 each made at the end of each period for n periods at interest rate i per period is represented by the symbol

$$a_{\overline{n}|i}$$

The symbol is read as: "a angle n at rate i." The number under the angle is the number of payments. The number beside the angle is the rate of interest.

For example, consider a series of four withdrawals of $1 each made at the end of each year from a savings account earning 5% interest per year. The line diagram appears as follows:

Since the number of payments is four, and the interest rate is 5%, the present value (at the beginning of the four years) of these payments is

$$a_{\overline{4}|5\%}$$

This symbol is read as: "a angle 4 at 5%."

If each withdrawal had been $20, then the present value of the above annuity would have been $20 multiplied by the above value, that is

$$\$20a_{\overline{4}|5\%}$$

The line diagram, then, would appear as follows:

CALCULATING PRESENT VALUE. The present value can be calculated by discounting (that is, finding the present value of) each withdrawal of $20 separately, and then finding the total of these four present values. The following diagram illustrates this procedure:

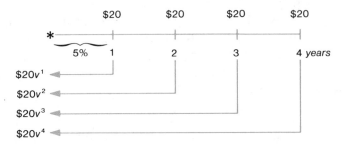

The first $20 withdrawal, made at the end of the first year is discounted for one year; the second $20 withdrawal is discounted for two years; the third $20 withdrawal is discounted for three years; and the fourth $20 withdrawal is discounted for four years, all at 5% interest. Using the equation for finding present values, $A = Sv^n$, separately for each withdrawal, the total value is

$$\$20a_{\overline{4}|5\%} = \$20v^1 + \$20v^2 + \$20v^3 + \$20v^4, \text{ all } v\text{'s at } 5\%$$

In the above expression, the common multiplier, $20, can be factored out:

$$\$20a_{\overline{4}|5\%} = \$20(v^1 + v^2 + v^3 + v^4), \text{ all } v\text{'s at } 5\%$$

A value for each expression inside the parentheses can be found in Table I

(5%), column (2), and substituted in the equation

$$\$20a_{\overline{4}|5\%} = \$20(.952381 + .907029 + .863838 + .822702)$$

$$= \$20(3.545950)$$

$$= \$70.92$$

Note that the expression v^1 in the above example could also have been written simply as v.

To use general terms: If the present value at the beginning of n periods of a series of payments of 1 made at the end of each period for n periods is desired, the first term of the series will be v. The succeeding terms will have exponents increasing by one each period. The exponent of the final term will be n. The equation is

$$a_{\overline{n}|i} = v + v^2 + \cdots + v^{n-1} + v^n$$

TABLES OF $a_{\overline{n}|i}$. Values of $a_{\overline{n}|i}$ for periods of 1 to 25, inclusive, at various interest rates are given in column (4) (Present Value of 1 per Period) of Table I. An inspection of these values shows that $a_{\overline{n}|i}$ is always *less than* the value of n. For example, $a_{\overline{1}|i}$ is less than 1, $a_{\overline{2}|i}$ is less than 2, etc. This occurs because each of the payments is being evaluated at a date earlier than its due date. Hence, the total of the present values is less than the total of the payments themselves. For instance, in the previous example, the four $20 payments totaled $80 while their present value was only $70.92.

In contrast, an inspection of the values in a table of accumulated values $s_{\overline{n}|i}$, column (3), shows values which are *greater than* the value of n (except for $s_{\overline{1}|i}$, which always equals 1). This occurs because each of the payments is being accumulated to a date later than its due date (except for the last payment). Hence, the total of the accumulated values is greater than the total of the payments themselves.

To Illustrate—Calculate the present value of the annuity of $20 per year for four years (the four withdrawals discussed above) by using values of $a_{\overline{n}|i}$ at 5% from Table I.

Solution—

Present Value $= \$20a_{\overline{4}|5\%}$

Substitute the value of $a_{\overline{4}|5\%}$ from Table I:

$$= \$20(3.545950)$$

Multiply; round to nearest cent:

$$= \$70.92$$

The answer is the same as was derived above without the use of a table of values of $a_{\overline{n}|i}$. Using values of $a_{\overline{n}|i}$ from Table I saves a great deal of calculation, especially as the number of periods increases.

It can be demonstrated that the present value in the above illustration will actually provide the desired four withdrawals. The following schedule shows the condition of the savings account year by year:

(1)	(2)	(3)	(4)	(5)	(6)
		Interest	Total		Balance
	Amount	Earned	in Account		in Account
	in Account	During Year	End of Year		End of Year
	Beginning	(Col. 2 ×	(Col. 2 +	Payment	(Col. 4 −
Year	of Year	.05)	Col. 3)	End of Year	Col. 5)
1	$70.92	$3.55	$74.47	$20.00	$54.47
2	54.47	2.72	57.19	20.00	37.19
3	37.19	1.86	39.05	20.00	19.05
4	19.05	.95	20.00	20.00	0

To Illustrate Again—If a person is paying off a debt to a bank by payments of $75 at the end of each quarter for five years, calculate the amount of the debt. Assume that interest is charged on the debt at a nominal 8% compounded quarterly.

Solution—The debt is equal to the present value of the periodic payments. Since payments are made quaterly (four times per year) for five years, there are 20 payments altogether. The rate of interest is equal to 2% (one fourth of 8%) compounded every quarter. The line diagram appears as follows:

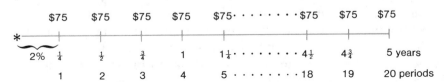

This series of payments constitutes an annuity of 20 payments, with interest at 2% per period. Hence:

$$\text{Present Value} = \$75 a_{\overline{20}|2\%}$$

Substitute the value of $a_{\overline{20}|2\%}$ from Table I:

$$= \$75(16.351433)$$

Multiply; round to nearest cent:

$$= \$1,226.36$$

Therefore, the amount of the debt was originally $1,226.36.

5.5 CONSTRUCTION AND USE OF TABLES OF $a_{\overline{n}|i}$

The basic equation given above, namely,

$$a_{\overline{n}|i} = v + v^2 + \cdots v^{n-1} + v^n$$

indicates a way to construct a table of present values of an annuity of 1 per year ($a_{\overline{n}|i}$). The right-hand side of the equation represents the addition of terms, each of which can be found in a table of values of v^n, such as Table I, column (2).

As an example, refer to the 5% page of values shown in Table I. The first value, $a_{\overline{1}|5\%}$, will be equal to v^1 (that is, .952381), because in an annuity of just one payment, the payment will be made one period after the evaluation date. Hence, it is discounted for one period to find its present value.

Each succeeding value in the $a_{\overline{n}|i}$ column may be found by adding, successively, the value from the v^n column, that is:

$$a_{\overline{2}|5\%} = a_{\overline{1}|5\%} + v^2$$

$$a_{\overline{3}|5\%} = a_{\overline{2}|5\%} + v^3$$

$$a_{\overline{4}|5\%} = a_{\overline{3}|5\%} + v^4$$

etc.

Substituting the actual values shown in the table, to derive the value of $a_{\overline{2}|5\%}$, we would add $a_{\overline{1}|5\%}$, $+ v^2$, which is .952381 + .907029 = 1.859410. This answer agrees with the value shown in the table. To derive the value of $a_{\overline{3}|5\%}$, add $a_{\overline{2}|5\%}$, $+ v^3$, which is 1.859410 + .863838 = 2.723248. This also agrees with the value shown in the table.

It is important to remember that the value of v^n to be added to the previous annuity value is taken from the *next* line in the table from the line where the previous annuity value appears. (This is in contrast to the procedure shown in Section 4.3 for constructing tables of the *accumulated* value of an annuity, $s_{\overline{n}|i}$, where the two values to be added are taken from the *same* line.) That is, the values of $a_{\overline{n}|i}$ and v^{n+1} are added to produce the value of $a_{\overline{n+1}|i}$.

$$a_{\overline{n+1}|i} = a_{\overline{n}|i} + v^{n+1}$$

To Illustrate—Given $a_{\overline{10}|5\%} = 7.721735$, calculate the value of $a_{\overline{11}|5\%}$, assuming that tables of v^n are available.

Solution—Using the above equation:

Basic equation:

$$a_{\overline{n+1}|i} = a_{\overline{n}|i} + v^{n+1}$$

Substitute 10 for n, 5% for i:

$$a_{\overline{11}|5\%} = a_{\overline{10}|5\%} + v^{11} \text{ at } 5\%$$

Substitute the given value of $a_{\overline{10}|5\%}$ and value of v^{11} at 5% from Table I:

$$= 7.721735 + .584679$$

Add:

$$= 8.306414$$

To repeat the caution given in Chapter 4: Great care should be exercised to see that no errors are made when using this method of constructing a table. All succeeding values will be in error after the first error is made. Also, it would be desirable to use values of v^n with more decimal places than the number to be shown in the answer, $a_{\overline{n}|i}$.

VALUES GREATER THAN SHOWN IN TABLE. It is sometimes necessary to find the value of $a_{\overline{n}|i}$ when the number of payments is greater than the number of periods shown in an available table. Table I, for example, shows such values for any number of periods up to and including 25. The equation for calculating such a value when n is larger than 25 is

$$a_{\overline{n}|i} = a_{\overline{25}|i} + a_{\overline{n-25}|i}\,v^{25}$$

A line diagram of a specific example showing the present value of payments of $1 for 30 years helps visualize this relationship:

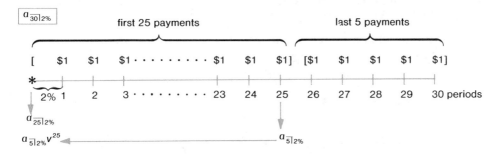

The present value of the first 25 payments of 1 is $a_{\overline{25}|2\%}$. The present value of the last five payments, discounted to the beginning of the last five-year period, is $a_{\overline{5}|2\%}$. This latter value, discounted to the true evaluation date, is

$$a_{\overline{5}|2\%}\,v^{25}$$

Therefore, the present value of the 30 payments is

$$a_{\overline{30}|2\%} = a_{\overline{25}|2\%} + a_{\overline{5}|2\%}\,v^{25}$$

To Illustrate—Calculate the value of $a_{\overline{35}|4\%}$, using Table I.

Solution—

Basic equation:

$$a_{\overline{n}|i} = a_{\overline{25}|i} + a_{\overline{n-25}|i} v^{25}$$

Substitute 35 for n, 4% for i:

$$a_{\overline{35}|4\%} = a_{\overline{25}|4\%} + a_{\overline{10}|4\%} v^{25}$$

Substitute values from Table I:

$$= 15.622080 + 8.110896(.375117)$$

Multiply the last two numbers; round to six decimal places:

$$= 15.622080 + 3.042535$$

Add:

$$= 18.664615$$

TWO RATES OF INTEREST. Sometimes it is necessary to find the present value of an annuity over a period of time during which the interest rate changes.

The same principles apply that were shown in Section 4.3 in which accumulated values were calculated using dual interest rates. The value is calculated as being the total of two separate parts.

To Illustrate—How much should an insurance company invest now, if it is to be repaid by seven annual payments of $1,000 each (at the end of each year)? The company desires to earn 6% during the first four years and 5% during the last three years.

Solution—The amount to be invested is equal to the *present value* of the seven payments. The line diagram appears as follows:

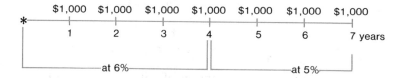

The present value of the first four payments (that is, those made during the time when the interest rate is 6%) is

$$\$1,000 a_{\overline{4}|6\%}$$

The present value of the final three payments, evaluated at the beginning of this final three-year period (that is, at the point in time when the interest rate changes) is

$$\$1,000a_{\overline{3}|5\%}$$

Then, in order to find the present value of these three payments at the beginning of the entire seven-year period, the above value must be discounted for four years, that is, it must be multiplied by v^4 at 6%, using the interest rate in effect for the first four years:

$$\$1,000a_{\overline{3}|5\%}(v^4 \text{ at } 6\%)$$

A line diagram showing just these final three payments should help to make this clear:

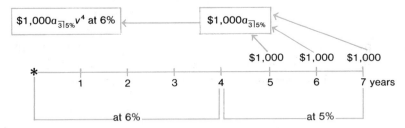

A line diagram showing just the first four payments would appear as follows:

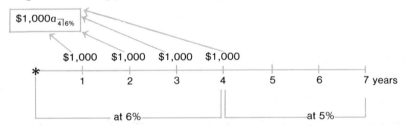

The total present value of the entire series of seven payments will be the two parts added together:

$$\$1,000a_{\overline{4}|6\%} + \$1,000a_{\overline{3}|5\%}(v^4 \text{ at } 6\%)$$

Substituting values from Table I, this becomes:

$$\$1,000(3.465106) + \$1,000(2.723248)(.792094) = \$5,622.17$$

It can be demonstrated that the investment of \$5,622.17 will be exactly repaid by the seven payments of \$1,000 each, including interest at 6% during the first four years and at 5% during the last three years. The following schedule shows the progress of the investment year by year. The schedule is arranged to show the portion of the \$1,000 yearly payment which is needed to pay the yearly interest with the balance of the \$1,000 being applied to reduce the debt owed to the company:

(1)	(2)	(3)	(4)	(5)	(6)
Year	Owed to Company Beginning of Year	Interest for Year (Col. 2 × .06 or .05)	Payment Made End of Year	Amount Applied on Debt (Col. 4 − Col. 3)	Owed After Annual Payment (Col. 2 − Col. 5)
1	$5,622.17	$337.33	$1,000.00	$662.67	$4,959.50
2	4,959.50	297.57	1,000.00	702.43	4,257.07
3	4,257.07	255.42	1,000.00	744.58	3,512.49
4	3,512.49	210.75	1,000.00	789.25	2,723.24
5	2,723.24	136.16	1,000.00	863.84	1,859.40
6	1,859.40	92.97	1,000.00	907.03	952.37
7	952.37	47.62	1,000.00	952.38	− .01

The discrepancy of one cent at the end is simply due to rounding off all figures in the calculations to the nearest cent. Notice particularly in column (3) above that 6% has been used for the first four years, and 5% thereafter.

EXERCISES, SET 10

(Draw line diagrams for all exercises where appropriate)

1. Calculate the value of $a_{\overline{3}|5\%}$ by finding the present value of each payment individually at the evaluation date and totaling them. Check the answer with Table I.

2. Calculate the value of $\$50a_{\overline{14}|4\%}$.

3. The beneficiary of a life insurance policy is to receive $350 at the end of each year for 15 years. What is the present value of these payments, assuming the interest rate used is 6%?

4. How much must a person deposit now in a savings account, which credits interest at a nominal 6% compounded semiannually, in order to withdraw $60 at the end of every half-year for ten years?

5. What is the value, on February 1, 1981, of a series of annual payments of $25 each, if the first payment is due on February 1, 1982 and the last is due on February 1, 2000? Assume 6% interest.

6. A policyowner is repaying a loan to the insurance company by means of payments of $100 at the end of every three months for ten years. If interest on the loan is calculated at a nominal 8% compounded quarterly, calculate the amount of the original loan.

7. Write, in symbolic notation, the expression that shows how to calculate the present value of an annuity immediate of $1,500 per period for 12 periods, assuming that the interest rate is 10% for the first eight periods and 12% thereafter.

8. If $v^4 = .735$, $v^5 = .681$, and $a_{\overline{4}|i} = 3.312$, then $a_{\overline{5}|i}$ equals

    (1) 2.577   (3) 3.993
    (2) 2.631   (4) 4.047

5.6 THE PRESENT VALUE OF AN ANNUITY DUE

In a life insurance company's operations, the calculation of present value very often involves an *annuity due* (that is, payments made at the beginning of each period). This is important because the premiums for a life insurance policy (Chapter 10) are paid at the beginning of each period and *settlement option payments* (Chapter 8) are made at the beginning of each period.

The present value of an annuity due is calculated as of the beginning of the first interval of time. Since payments are made at the beginning of each period, the present value is calculated at the time of the first payment.

The present value at the time of the first payment of a series of payments of 1 each made at the beginning of each period for n periods at interest rate i per period is presented by the symbol

$$\ddot{a}_{\overline{n}|i}$$

The two dots over the a indicate that payments are made at the beginning of each period and that the series of payments constitutes an annuity due.

For example, consider a series of three payments of $1 each made at the beginning of each year at an interest rate of 2% per year. The line diagram appears as follows:

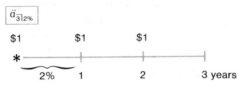

Since the number of payments is three and the interest rate is 2%, the present value (at the beginning of the first year) is

$$\ddot{a}_{\overline{3}|2\%}$$

If each payment had been $25, then the present value of the above annuity due would have been $25 multiplied by the above value, that is,

$$\$25\ddot{a}_{\overline{3}|2\%}$$

This present value can be calculated by finding separately the present value of each payment of $25 as of the evaluation date and then finding the total of these values. The following line diagram illustrates this procedure:

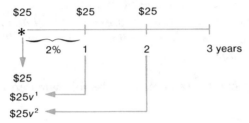

The first $25 payment, made on the evaluation date, is not discounted at all, so its present value is $25. The second $25 payment, made at the beginning of the second year, is discounted for one year. The third $25 payment is discounted for two years. Using the equation for finding present values, $A = Sv^n$, separately for each payment after the first, the total present value is

$$\$25\ddot{a}_{\overline{3}|2\%} = \$25 + \$25v^1 + \$25v^2, \text{ all } v\text{'s at } 2\%$$

The common multiplier ($25) can be factored out, remembering that the first term, $25, can be expressed as $25(1):

$$\$25\ddot{a}_{\overline{3}|2\%} = \$25(1 + v^1 + v^2), \text{ all } v\text{'s at } 2\%$$

The numerical value for each expression inside the parentheses can be found in Table I (2%), column (2).

$$\$25\ddot{a}_{\overline{3}|2\%} = \$25(1.000000 + .980392 + .961169)$$

$$= \$25(2.941561)$$

$$= \$73.54$$

(The expression v^1 in the equations could have been written as v.)

To use general terms: To find the present value at the beginning of n periods of a series of payments of 1 made at the beginning of each period for n periods at interest rate i per period, the first term of the series will be 1. The second term will be v^1, and the succeeding terms will be v with the exponent increasing by one each year. The exponent of the the final term will be $(n - 1)$. The general equation is as follows:

$$\ddot{a}_{\overline{n}|i} = 1 + v + v^2 + \cdots + v^{n-2} + v^{n-1}$$

Assuming that a table of values of v^n is available, this equation can be used to construct a table of present values of an annuity due ($\ddot{a}_{\overline{n}|i}$). The procedure would be similar to that described in Section 5.5, Construction and Use of Tables of $a_{\overline{n}|i}$.

RELATIONSHIP BETWEEN PRESENT VALUES OF ANNUITIES DUE AND IMMEDIATE. Tables of the present value of annuities due ($\ddot{a}_{\overline{n}|i}$) are not shown in this text. They are not frequently found in practice. Any desired value of $\ddot{a}_{\overline{n}|i}$ can readily be calculated from a table of $a_{\overline{n}|i}$ (the present value of an annuity immediate), using one of two relationships.

The first such relationship is that *the present value of an annuity due is equal to the present value of the corresponding annuity immediate, for the same number of periods, multiplied by* $(1 + i)$.

This relationship can be expressed by the following equation:

$$\ddot{a}_{\overline{n}|i} = (1 + i)a_{\overline{n}|i}$$

To Illustrate—Find the present value, at the time of the first payment, of an annuity due of $25 per year for three years at a 2% interest rate.

Solution—The line diagram is as follows:

This is the same annuity due as above. The present value can be calculated more readily by use of the equation

$$\ddot{a}_{\overline{n}|i} = (1 + i)a_{\overline{n}|i}$$

as follows:

Basic equation:

$$\$25\ddot{a}_{\overline{n}|i} = \$25(1 + i)a_{\overline{n}|i}$$

Substitute 3 for n, .02 for i:

$$\$25\ddot{a}_{\overline{3}|2\%} = \$25(1.02)a_{\overline{3}|2\%}$$

Substitute the value from Table I for $a_{\overline{3}|2\%}$:

$$= \$25(1.02)(2.883883)$$

Multiply (1.02)(2.883883); round to six decimal places:

$$= \$25(2.941561)$$

Multiply; round to nearest cent:

$$= \$73.54$$

This answer agrees with the present value calculated above by adding the separate present values of each payment.

A SECOND RELATIONSHIP. A second relationship is that *the present value of an annuity due is equal to the present value of the corresponding annuity immediate for one fewer periods plus the amount of one payment.*

This relationship can be expressed in general terms by the following equation:

$$\ddot{a}_{\overline{n}|i} = a_{\overline{n-1}|i} + 1$$

To Illustrate—Find the present value, at the time of the first payment, of an annuity due of $25 per year for three years at a 2% interest rate.

Solution—This is the same annuity due as in the last illustration. Now the present value can be calculated by using the equation

$$\ddot{a}_{\overline{n}|i} = a_{\overline{n-1}|i} + 1$$

as follows:

Basic equation:

$$\$25\ddot{a}_{\overline{n}|i} = \$25(a_{\overline{n-1}|i} + 1)$$

Substitute 3 for n, 2% for i:

$$\$25\ddot{a}_{\overline{3}|2\%} = \$25(a_{\overline{2}|2\%} + 1)$$

Substitute the value for $a_{\overline{2}|2\%}$ from Table I:

$$= \$25(1.941561 + 1)$$

Add within the parentheses:

$$= \$25(2.941561)$$

Multiply; round to nearest cent:

$$= \$73.54$$

This answer agrees with the present value calculated above by the other two methods.

If the value of $a_{\overline{n-1}|i}$ and $a_{\overline{n}|i}$ are both known, the second relationship

$$\ddot{a}_{\overline{n}|i} = a_{\overline{n-1}|i} + 1$$

is easier to use than the first relationship

$$\ddot{a}_{\overline{n}|i} = (1 + i)a_{\overline{n}|i}$$

because adding 1 is easier than multiplying by $(1 + i)$. It should also be noted that it is not necessary to know the interest rate involved in order to use the equation

$$\ddot{a}_{\overline{n}|i} = a_{\overline{n-1}|i} + 1$$

To Illustrate—An insurance company is paying the beneficiary of a life insurance policy $8.50 at the beginning of each quarter for five years. Interest is calculated at a nominal 10% compounded quarterly. Calculate the present value at the time of the first payment.

Solution—Since payments are made each quarter for five years, there are 20 payments altogether. The rate of interest is equal to $2\frac{1}{2}\%$ (one fourth of 10%). The line diagram appears as follows:

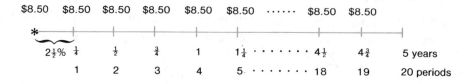

This series of payments constitutes an annuity due, since payments are made at the beginning of each period and the evaluation date is at the time of the first payment. Hence, the present value is $8.50\ddot{a}_{\overline{20}|2\%}$.

Basic equation:

$$\$8.50\ddot{a}_{\overline{n}|i} = \$8.50(a_{\overline{n-1}|i} + 1)$$

Substitute 20 for n, $2\frac{1}{2}\%$ for i:

$$\$8.50\ddot{a}_{\overline{20}|2\frac{1}{2}\%} = \$8.50(a_{\overline{19}|2\frac{1}{2}\%} + 1)$$

Substitute the value for $a_{\overline{19}|2\frac{1}{2}\%}$ from Table I:

$$= \$8.50(14.978891 + 1)$$

Add within parentheses:

$$= \$8.50(15.978891)$$

Multiply; round to nearest cent:

$$= \$135.82$$

To Illustrate Again—The purchasing department of an insurance company wants to acquire a small computing machine. The machine can be purchased for $5,000, or it can be leased for $650 at the beginning of each year for ten years. If the current interest rate is 6%, should the company purchase or lease the machine? (Assume its useful life is ten years.)

Solution—The two choices can be compared if the amounts of outlay are both valued as of the same date, that is, the present value of the lease payments can be compared with the single-sum cost. This present value of the lease payment is $650\ddot{a}_{\overline{10}|6\%}$ and can be calculated as follows:

Basic equation:

$$\$650\ddot{a}_{\overline{n}|i} = \$650(a_{\overline{n-1}|i} + 1)$$

Substitute 10 for n, 6% for i:

$$\$650\ddot{a}_{\overline{10}|6\%} = \$650(a_{\overline{9}|6\%} + 1)$$

Substitute the value for $a_{\overline{9}|6\%}$ from Table I:

$$= \$650(6.801692 + 1)$$

Add within parentheses:

$$= \$650(7.801692)$$

Multiply; round to nearest cent:

$$= \$5,071.10$$

Therefore, the lease payments appear to be slightly more costly than the $5,000 single-sum cost.

DETERMINING WHICH TYPE OF ANNUITY. In calculating the present value of a series of payments, it is sometimes necessary to note where the first payment falls in relation to the evaluation date in order to determine whether the series represents an annuity immediate or an annuity due.

To Illustrate—A couple plans to withdraw $100 from their savings account every July 1, from July 1, 1980 to July 1, 1984, inclusive, exhausting the account with the final withdrawal. If interest is added to the account at 5%, how much must they have in their account on July 1, 1980, just prior to the first withdrawal, in order to provide for all the withdrawals?

Solution—The problem does not specify whether the withdrawals are made at the beginning or the end of each period. When no reference to the evaluation date is made, the line diagram appears as follows:

```
              $100   $100   $100   $100   $100
        ⎧――――――⎫  +      +      +      +      +
        ⎩      ⎭  7-1-80 7-1-81 7-1-82 7-1-83 7-1-84
          5%
```

It is impossible to tell by looking at this diagram whether this series of payments represents an annuity immediate or an annuity due. However, when the evaluation date (July 1, 1980) is added, the line diagram appears as follows:

```
        $100    $100   $100   $100   $100
         *        +      +      +      +
       7-1-80  7-1-81 7-1-82 7-1-83 7-1-84
```

Since the first payment falls upon the evaluation date, this represents an annuity due, that is, payments are made at the begining of each period.

$$\text{Present Value} = \$100\ddot{a}_{\overline{5}|5\%}$$

Substitute $a_{\overline{4}|5\%} + 1$ for $\ddot{a}_{\overline{5}|5\%}$:

$$= \$100(a_{\overline{4}|5\%\%} + 1)$$

Substitute the value of $a_{\overline{4}|5\%}$ from Table I:

$$= \$100(3.545950 + 1)$$

Add within parentheses:

$$= \$100(4.545950)$$

Multiply; round to nearest cent:

$$= \$454.60$$

EXERCISES, SET 11

(Draw line diagrams for all exercises where appropriate)

1. Calculate the value of $\ddot{a}_{\overline{4}|5\%}$ by finding the present value of each payment individually at the evaluation date and totaling them.

2. Calculate the value of $\ddot{a}_{\overline{12}|2\frac{1}{4}\%}$ by using both of the usual equations. Compare the two answers as a check.

3. Calculate the value of $\$40\ddot{a}_{\overline{17}|2\%}$.

4. If a person wishes to make a $150 withdrawal at the beginning of each year for ten years from a savings account which credits 6% interest per year, how much must be in the account just prior to the first withdrawal?

5. If a loan by an insurance company is to be repaid by payments of $25 to the company at the beginning of each quarter for six years, what is the amount of the loan? Assume interest is owed at a nominal 8% compounded quarterly.

6. An insurance company is making annual payments of $100 from May 1, 1984, to May 1, 1998, inclusive. Calculate the present value of the payments on May 1, 1984, and the accumulated value of the payments on May 1, 1998, assuming interest at 5% per year. (Hint: A line diagram is especially helpful for this exercise.)

7. A man is repaying a loan by paying an installment of $1,000 at the beginning of each three months for two years. The interest rate charged on the loan is 8% compounded quarterly. The amount he originally borrowed (to the nearest dollar) was

    (1) $7,325   (3) $8,583
    (2) $7,472   (4) $8,755

CHAPTER SUMMARY

- The *present value* of an amount of money is the amount which must originally be loaned or invested to produce a certain accumulated value at a certain later date.

- The present value, A, is calculated by dividing the accumulated value, S, by $(1 + i)^n$:

$$A = \frac{S}{(1 + i)^n}$$

- This is the same as multiplying by the fraction $\dfrac{1}{(1 + i)^n}$.

- The fraction $\dfrac{1}{(1 + i)^n}$ is often expressed as v^n, so the equation for calculating the present value can be expressed as

$$A = Sv^n$$

- When the number of periods is increased, the present value, v^n, is decreased; when the number of periods is decreased, the present value is increased.

- When the interest rate is increased, the present value, v^n, is decreased; when the interest rate is decreased, the present value is increased.

- The present value of an annuity (series of payments) of 1 each due at the end of each period for n periods at interest rate i per period is represented by the symbol

$$a_{\overline{n}|i}$$

- The value of $a_{\overline{n}|i}$ may be calculated by the equation:

$$a_{\overline{n}|i} = v + v^2 + \cdots + v^{n-1} + v^n$$

- The value of $a_{\overline{n}|i}$ is always less than n (the number of periods).

- A value of $a_{\overline{n}|i}$ may be found where the number of payments is greater than shown in the table. The technique involves splitting the series into segments, each of which contains the maximum number of payments shown in the table (or fewer), and evaluating each segment as of the evaluation date.

- The present value of an annuity due is calculated as of the same time as the first payment.

- This present value for n periods at interest rate i per period is represented by the symbol

$$\ddot{a}_{\overline{n}|i}$$

- This present value can be calculated as the total of the present value of each separate payment:

$$\ddot{a}_{\overline{n}|i} = 1 + v^1 + v^2 + \cdots + v^{n-2} + v^{n-1}$$

- Usually, tables of $\ddot{a}_{\overline{n}|i}$ are not available. Hence, a table of $a_{\overline{n}|i}$ (that is, annuity immediate) must be used and applied to one of these two relationships:

$$\ddot{a}_{\overline{n}|i} = (1 + i)a_{\overline{n}|i}$$

or

$$\ddot{a}_{\overline{n}|i} = a_{\overline{n-1}|i} + 1$$

LEARNING OBJECTIVES

After reading this chapter, the student should know

- What is meant by present value.
- How to calculate present values.
- What is meant by the symbol v^n.
- How to use tables of v^n.
- How to calculate the present value of an annuity by calculating the present value of each individual payment separately.
- What is meant by the symbol $a_{\overline{n}|i}$.
- The general equation defining $a_{\overline{n}|i}$.
- How to use tables of $a_{\overline{n}|i}$.
- How to evaluate annuities having more payments than are shown in an available table.
- How to evaluate annuities where the interest rate changes during the period.
- What is meant by the symbol $\ddot{a}_{\overline{n}|i}$.
- The general equation defining $\ddot{a}_{\overline{n}|i}$.
- Where the first payment falls in relation to the evaluation date for each of the two kinds of annuities.
- The differences between the general equations defining $\ddot{a}_{\overline{n}|i}$ and $a_{\overline{n}|i}$.
- How to use the two equations relating $\ddot{a}_{\overline{n}|i}$ and $a_{\overline{n}|i}$.

More on Present Values

Chapter 5 presented the basic principles of present values and how present values may be used in every-day problems. Chapter 6 will conclude the discussion of present values by taking the student through three specific situations where the calculation of present values is particularly important:

- *Deferred Annuities*—in which the first payment in a series of payments is made several periods after the evaluation date.
- *Amortization Payments*—in which regular, periodic payments are made to repay a debt.
- *Coupon Bonds*—for which the present value must be determined in order to calculate the value of an investment.

Among other topics to be discussed will be annuities payable more frequently than the interest conversion period and the relationship between present value and accumulated value.

6.1 PRESENT VALUE OF A DEFERRED ANNUITY

An annuity which has its first payment postponed for one period or more is known as a *deferred annuity*.

For example, consider an annuity immediate of $10 per year for five years, deferred three years, at 4%. The line diagram appears as follows:

Instead of the first payment being made at the end of the first year, the first payment is made three years later at the end of the fourth year. Each of the five payments falls three years later than it would if the annuity were not deferred.

FIRST METHOD. The present value of the above deferred annuity can be calculated by finding the present value of each payment separately, and then finding the total of these five values. The first $10 payment will be made four years after the evaluation date; hence, its present value is

$10v^4$ at 4%

Similarly, the second payment will be made five years after the evaluation date; the third payment six years after the evaluation date; etc. Hence, the total of the five present values is

Present Value = $10v^4 + $10v^5 + $10v^6 + $10v^7 + $10v^8, all v's at 4%

Factor out the common multiplier:

$$= \$10(v^4 + v^5 + v^6 + v^7 + v^8), \text{ all } v\text{'s at 4\%}$$

Substitute valuesfrom Table I:

$$= \$10(.854804 + .821927 + .790315 + .759918 + .730690)$$

Add inside the parentheses:

$$= \$10(3.957654)$$

Multiply; round to nearest cent:

$$= \$39.58$$

SECOND METHOD. A second method is available which generally requires less calculating. Consider the following line diagram. It is similar to the preceding line diagram, but has additional payments at the end of one, two, and three years (enclosed in brackets):

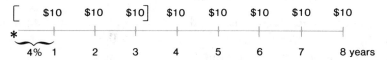

The addition of the three bracketed payments to the original five payments gives a total of eight payments. The entire eight payments constitute an annuity which has a present value of $10a_{\overline{8}|4\%}$.

If the present value of a three-year annuity (the three bracketed payments) is subtracted from the present value of the eight-year annuity described above, the answer is the present value of a five-year annuity deferred three years:

Present Value = $10a_{\overline{8}|4\%} - $10a_{\overline{3}|4\%}

Factor out the common multiplier:

$$= \$10(a_{\overline{8}|4\%} - a_{\overline{3}|4\%})$$

Substitute values from Table I:

$$= \$10(6.732745 - 2.775091)$$

Subtract inside the parentheses:

$$= \$10(3.957654)$$

Multiply; round to nearest cent:

$$= \$39.58$$

This agrees with the answer calculated by the first method.

THIRD METHOD. A third method is also available. Consider the following line diagram. It is the same as the first line diagram for this deferred annuity, except that the evaluation date is shown as three years later:

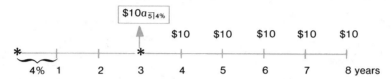

The present value of this annuity, *at a time one year before the first payment*, is

$$\$10a_{\overline{5}|4\%}$$

The true desired evaluation date is actually three years earlier than the evaluation date shown in the above line diagram. Hence, the present value $\$10a_{\overline{5}|4\%}$ can be discounted for those three years of the deferred period.

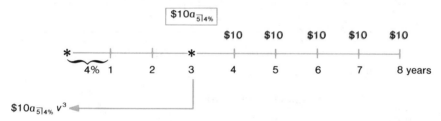

Basic equation for discounting (finding present value):

$$A = Sv^n$$

Substitute $\$10a_{\overline{5}|4\%}$ for S, 3 for n:

$$= \$10a_{\overline{5}|4\%}\, v^3 \text{ at } 4\%$$

Substitute values from Table I:

$$= \$10(4.451822)(.888996)$$

Multiply (4.451822)(.888996); round to six decimal places:

$$= \$10(3.957652)$$

Multiply again; round to nearest cent:

$$= \$39.58$$

This answer agrees with the answers calculated by the first two methods.

The second method above, in which the present value of an annuity for the deferred period is subtracted from the present value of an annuity for the entire period, usually requires the least work. The third method, however, is generally used in cases where the entire period exceeds the period shown in available tables of $a_{\overline{n}|i}$.

To Illustrate—A student now starting four years of college will repay a 6% loan by making three annual payments of $2,000 beginning at the end of the year after graduation. Calculate the present value of repayments by each of the three methods given above.

Solution—The line diagram appears as follows:

The first payment, instead of being made at the end of the first year, is deferred for four years to the end of the fifth year.

Using the first method:

Total the present values of individual payments:

Present Value = $2,000v^5$ + $2,000v^6$ + $2,000v^7$, all v's at 6%

Factor out the common multiplier:

$$= \$2,000(v^5 + v^6 + v^7), \text{ all } v\text{'s at } 6\%$$

Substitute values from Table I:

$$= \$2,000(.747258 + .704961 + .665057)$$

Add inside the parentheses:

$$= \$2,000(2.117276)$$

Multiply; round to nearest cent:

$$= \$4,234.55$$

Using the second method:

Subtract the annuity for the deferred period from the annuity for the entire period:

Present Value = $2,000a_{\overline{7}|6\%}$ − $2,000a_{\overline{4}|6\%}$

Factor out the common multiplier:

$$= \$2,000(a_{\overline{7}|6\%} - a_{\overline{4}|6\%})$$

Substitute values from Table I:

$$= \$2,000(5.582381 - 3.465106)$$

Subtract inside the parentheses:

$$= \$2,000(2.117275)$$

Multiply; round to nearest cent:

$$= \$4,234.55$$

Using the third method:

Discount the present value of a three-year annuity for the four-year deferred period:

$$\text{Present Value} = \$2,000a_{\overline{3}|6\%}\,v^4 \text{ at } 6\%$$

Substitute values from Table I:

$$= \$2,000(2.673012)(.792094)$$

Multiply (2.673012)(.792094); round to six decimal places:

$$= \$2,000(2.117277)$$

Multiply; round to nearest cent:

$$= \$4,234.55$$

The answers are identical with each of the three methods.

These same three methods can also be used in calculating the present value of a *deferred annuity due*. For example, an annuity due of $10 per year for five years, deferred three years, at 4% would appear as follows in line diagram form:

Instead of the first payment being made at the beginning of the first year, the first payment is made *three years later*, at the beginning of the fourth year. Each of the five payments falls three years later than it would if the annuity were not deferred.

Briefly, the present value of such a deferred annuity due could be calculated as follows:

FIRST METHOD:

$$\text{Present Value} = \$10(v^3 + v^4 + v^5 + v^6 + v^7) \text{ all } v\text{'s at } 4\%$$

SECOND METHOD:

$$\text{Present Value} = \$10\ddot{a}_{\overline{8}|4\%} - \$10\ddot{a}_{\overline{3}|4\%}$$

THIRD METHOD:

$$\text{Present Value} = \$10\ddot{a}_{\overline{5}|4\%}\,v^3 \text{ at } 4\%$$

6.2 AMORTIZATION PAYMENTS

To repay a debt by means of regular periodic payments is known as *amortizing* the debt. The payments themselves are known as *amortization payments*. The present value of all the amortization payments must equal the debt.

In the illustrations presented up to this point, the amount of each periodic payment (amortization payment) has been known. The present value had to be calculated. Now the converse problem will be considered. The present value of the payments is known, and the amount of each payment will be calculated.

In a life insurance company's operations, this problem has frequent application. For example, beneficiaries of life insurance policies may elect to receive periodic payments instead of a single sum. The amount of each periodic payment must be calculated so that the present value of the series will equal the single sum to which they are entitled.

CALCULATING AMORTIZATION PAYMENTS. Suppose that amortization payments are being made for n years, and interest is being charged at the rate of i per year. If each amortization payment is made at the end of the year, these payments constitute an annuity immediate. The equation for the present value at the beginning of the first year is

$$(\text{Amortization Payment}) \, a_{\overline{n}|i} = \text{Present Value}$$

The line diagram is as follows:

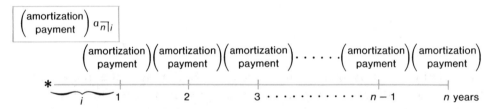

To find the amortization payment, both sides of the equation can be divided by $a_{\overline{n}|i}$, giving

$$(\text{Amortization Payment}) = \frac{\text{Present Value}}{a_{\overline{n}|i}}$$

This equation states that the known present value is divided by $a_{\overline{n}|i}$ to arrive at the desired amortization payment.

To Illustrate—How large an amortization payment must be made at the end of each year for four years to amortize a debt of $600? Assume 6% interest is charged on the debt.

Solution—The line diagram appears as follows:

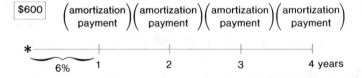

Using the equation for finding amortization payments:

$$(\text{Amortization Payment}) = \frac{\text{Present Value}}{a_{\overline{n}|i}}$$

Substitute $600 for present value, 4 for n, 6% for i:

$$= \frac{\$600}{a_{\overline{4}|6\%}}$$

Substitute the value of $a_{\overline{4}|6\%}$ from Table I:

$$= \frac{\$600}{3.465106}$$

Divide; round to nearest cent:

$$= \$173.15$$

It can be demonstrated that the annual amortization payment of $173.15 in the above illustration will repay the $600 loan plus 6% interest exactly. The following schedule shows the progress of the amortization year by year:

(1)	(2)	(3)	(4)	(5)	(6)
				Amount	*Debt after*
		Interest		*Applied*	*Annual*
	Debt	*for Year*	*Payment*	*on Debt*	*Payment*
	Beginning	*(Col. 2 ×*	*Made*	*(Col. 4 −*	*(Col. 2 −*
Year	*of Year*	*.06)*	*End of Year*	*Col. 3)*	*Col. 5)*
1	$600.00	$36.00	$173.15	$137.15	$462.85
2	462.85	27.77	173.15	145.38	317.47
3	317.47	19.05	173.15	154.10	163.37
4	163.37	9.80	173.15	163.35	.02

The apparent underpayment of 2 cents is due to rounding off all figures to the nearest cent. In actual practice, a final payment of $173.17 would extinguish the debt.

The schedule is arranged to show the portion of the yearly payment which is needed to pay the yearly interest, the balance of the payment being applied on the debt. As the amount of the outstanding debt decreases each year, the interest on the debt decreases, and a greater portion of the yearly payment is applied to reduce the principal of the debt.

It is also important to note that, at the end of any period, the remaining balance of the debt is equal to the present value of the remaining payments, that is, the original debt is

$$\$173.15 \, a_{\overline{4}|6\%} = \$600,$$

the balance at the end of the first year (in column 6) is

$$\$173.15 \, a_{\overline{3}|6\%} = \$462.85,$$

the balance at the end of the second year is

$$\$173.15\, a_{\overline{2}|6\%} = \$317.47,$$

and so forth. Thus, the remaining balance of such a debt can be calculated for any point in time desired without actually constructing an entire table showing the progress down to that point.

AMORTIZATION PAYMENTS AT BEGINNING OF PERIOD. Amortization payments may be made at the beginning of each period instead of at the end. In this case the payments would constitute an annuity due. The equation for the present value, at the time of the first payment, of amortization payments made at the beginning of each year for n years at interest rate i per year, is

$$(\text{Amortization Payment})\, \ddot{a}_{\overline{n}|i} = \text{Present Value}$$

The line diagram is as follows:

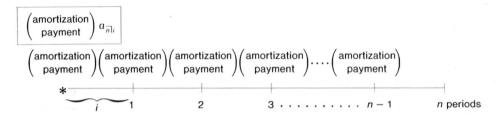

As before, to find the amortization payment, both sides of the equation can be divided by $\ddot{a}_{\overline{n}|i}$, giving

$$(\text{Amortization Payment}) = \frac{\text{Present Value}}{\ddot{a}_{\overline{n}|i}}$$

This equation states that the known present value is divided by $\ddot{a}_{\overline{n}|i}$ to arrive at the desired amortization payment. However, if the value of $\ddot{a}_{\overline{n}|i}$ is not tabulated, it must first be calculated by use of one of the two equations:

$$\ddot{a}_{\overline{n}|i} = (1 + i)a_{\overline{n}|i}$$

or

$$\ddot{a}_{\overline{n}|i} = a_{\overline{n-1}|i} + 1$$

To Illustrate—A person has been granted a lump-sum compensation of $600 for an injury. Instead of the lump-sum payment, the person requests four equal annual payments, the first to be paid immediately. What amount will the person receive each year? Assume an interest rate of 6%.

Solution—The line diagram appears as follows:

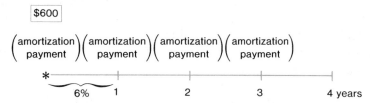

Since the first payment is due on the evaluation date, this series constitutes an annuity due. Using the equation for finding amortization payments which are made at the beginning of each period:

$$\text{(Amortization Payment)} = \frac{\text{Present Value}}{\ddot{a}_{\overline{n}|i}}$$

Substitute $a_{\overline{n-1}|i} + 1$ for $\ddot{a}_{\overline{n}|i}$:

$$= \frac{\text{Present Value}}{a_{\overline{n-1}|i} + 1}$$

Substitute $600 for present value, 4 for n, 6% for i:

$$= \frac{\$600}{a_{\overline{3}|6\%} + 1}$$

Substitute the value of $a_{\overline{3}|6\%}$ from Table I:

$$= \frac{\$600}{2.673012 + 1}$$

Add in the denominator:

$$= \frac{\$600}{3.673012}$$

Divide; round to nearest cent:

$$= \$163.35$$

Comparing the last two illustrations, it will be observed that the amortization payment of $163.35, needed at the beginning of each year, is less than the corresponding payment of $173.15, needed at the end of each year. This is true because the debt has one more year to accrue interest if payments are made at the end of each year. In fact, the exact relationship between the two payments is

$$\$163.35(1.06) = \$173.15$$

6.3 PURCHASE PRICE OF A COUPON BOND

An important application of present value and amortization principles is found in *coupon bonds*, one of the major kinds of investments made by life insurance companies.

A bond is a certificate of indebtedness, issued by a corporation or governmental body, in which the issuer agrees to reimburse the purchaser by paying a certain amount of money, the *par value* of a bond, on a certain date in the future. In addition to repayment of the principal, interest is paid periodically by the issuer. On corporate bonds, the interest due is commonly represented in the form of *coupons* which are detached from the bond by the purchaser and presented for payment as they fall due.

For example, a bond might promise to pay $1,000 on June 1, 1995, plus 8% per year interest prior to that date. This interest would commonly be represented by annual coupons attached to the bond, each bearing a due-date and each worth 8% of $1,000, or $80, when presented. A line diagram of the amounts payable would appear as follows, assuming the bond was first sold on June 1, 1990:

				$1,000
$80	$80	$80	$80	$80
6-1-90	6-1-91	6-1-92	6-1-93	6-1-94	6-1-95

The $80 coupons are payable at the end of each year. The $1,000 itself is payable at the end of the final year. Thus, on June 1, 1995, two amounts are actually payable: the final year's coupon plus the actual amount of the bond itself.

Since most coupon bonds are transferable and can be bought or sold through the bond market, the bond may have a current market value which is greater than or less than the par value. Thus, a prospective buyer may wish to buy a bond that will yield a higher rate of return than that listed for the bond (8% in the example given above). In this case, the buyer can compute a purchase price for the bond that will return the yield desired.

CALCULATING THE PURCHASE PRICE. To earn the rate of interest desired, the amount which a purchaser should pay for a bond will equal the present value of all the amounts the purchaser will receive. For the coupons, this is the present value of an annuity. For the value of the bond itself (its *redemption price*), this is the present value of a single payment.

The interest rate which is used to calculate these present values is the rate which the purchaser wishes to realize on this investment. *This is not necessarily the same rate which is used to calculate the amount of the coupons.* In the above example, 8% was used to calculate the amount of the coupons which the issuer promises to pay. Let us assume that the purchaser wishes the bond to yield 10% as an investment. In that case, the amounts payable would all be discounted at 10%:

$$\binom{\text{Purchase Price}}{\text{on June 1, 1990}} = \binom{\text{Present Value}}{\text{of Coupons}} + \binom{\text{Present Value}}{\text{of Bond Itself}}$$

$$= \$80 a_{\overline{5}|10\%} + \$1,000(v^5 \text{ at } 10\%)$$

Substitute values from Table I (10%):

$$= \$80(3.790787) + \$1,000(.620921)$$

$$= \$303.26 + \$620.92$$

$$= \$924.18$$

To Illustrate—Calculate the purchase price (at the time of issue) of a four-year $1,000 bond, promising to pay 10%, payable semiannually. Assume that the investment will actually yield a nominal 12%, compounded semiannually to the purchaser.

Solution—The coupons are calculated as being 5% each half-year, that is, 5% of $1,000, or $50. The present values are to be calculated using 6% each half-year since the bond is bought to yield 12% compounded semiannually. Hence, the line diagram showing the amounts payable appears as follows:

There are eight coupons payable, and the $1,000 amount of the bond itself is payable eight periods after the evaluation date:

$$\begin{pmatrix} \text{Purchase Price} \\ \text{at Issue} \end{pmatrix} = \begin{pmatrix} \text{Present Value} \\ \text{of Coupons} \end{pmatrix} + \begin{pmatrix} \text{Present Value} \\ \text{of Bond Itself} \end{pmatrix}$$

$$= \$50 a_{\overline{8}|6\%} + \$1,000(v^8 \text{ at } 6\%)$$

$$= \$50(6.209794) + \$1,000(.627412)$$

$$= \$310.49 + \$627.41$$

$$= \$937.90$$

EXERCISES, SET 12

(Draw line diagrams for all exercises where appropriate)

1. Calculate the present value of an annuity of $10 per year for eight years, deferred two years, at 4% interest. Use two different methods.

2. Calculate the present value of an annuity *due* of $10 per year for eight years, deferred two years, at 4% interest. Use two different methods.

3. Calculate the value on January 1, 1987 of a series of four annual payments of $200 each at 3% if the first payment is made on January 1, 1993.

4. What is the general name given to periodic payments which are calculated so that their present value will equal a known amount?

5. The present value of seven equal annual payments due at the end of each year at interest rate 2% is $164.26. Find the amount of each payment.

6. The present value of seven equal annual payments due at the beginning of each year at interest rate 2% is $164.26. Find the amount of each payment.

7. A property purchased for $20,000 requires a down payment of $5,000 and the balance in equal payments at the end of each year for ten years. Assuming an interest rate of 10%, calculate the amount of each annual payment.

8. Instead of a lump-sum payment of $1,200 for a new machine, the purchaser

agrees to pay for it in five equal yearly payments, the first payment on date of purchase. If the interest rate is 5%, what is the amount of each payment?

9. A deposit of $1,000 is made into a fund with the understanding that it may be withdrawn in five equal annual payments, the first payment to be made at the end of three years. If the fund allows 6% interest, what will be the amount of each payment?

10. An injured worker who has been granted $15,000 as disability compensation requests that it be paid in ten equal annual installments, the first installment payable immediately. Find the amount of the annual payment, if the rate of interest used is 5%.

11. An insurance company loans $5,000 to a policyowner who will repay the loan in 20 equal annual payments at the end of each year thereafter. Assuming that 6% interest is charged, what will be the outstanding balance of the loan immediately after the fifth payment?

12. What price should a purchaser pay for a 6% $1,000 bond (coupons payable annually), terminating in five years, if the purchaser wishes to realize 5% per year on the investment?

13. A $5,000 bond with semiannual coupons of $100 terminates in three years. What price should a purchaser pay for this bond in order to realize a nominal 6% compounded semiannually?

14. A woman borrows $1,200 from her aunt who makes the loan at an interest rate of 8% compounded semiannually. To the nearest dollar, the payment that the woman must make at the end of each half-year in order to repay the loan over a three-year period is

    (1) $181   (3) $220
    (2) $187   (4) $229

6.4 ANNUITIES PAYABLE MORE FREQUENTLY THAN THE INTEREST CONVERSION PERIOD

The annuities discussed up to this point have been payable with the same frequency as the interest compoundings. For example, where payments were quarterly, the interest was compounded quarterly. This period of time for the interest compoundings is known as the the *interest conversion period*.

In the operations of a life insurance company, monthly payments are very common, while interest rates are frequently compounded annually or semi-annually. Hence, many instances arise in which there are twelve or six annuity payment periods in one interest conversion period.

One method of calculating the accumulated value or present value of such annuities is to replace all the payments occurring in each interest conversion period with a single equivalent payment due at the end of that period. This single payment equals the accumulated value as of the end of the period of the individual payments during the period. In practice, the accumulated value is found by multiplying the total of the payments in each interest conversion period by a factor which has been calculated and tabulated in advance for various interest rates and numbers of payments within one interest conversion period. (Such factors are not tabulated in this book.)

A second method is to find an interest rate to use for each payment period which will be equivalent to the interest rate which is already known for the compounding period. For example, if interest is compounded annually at 6% and payments are made monthly, a monthly compounded interest rate of .48675% can be used. This rate is equivalent to the annual 6%. The methods for deriving this equivalent rate are beyond the scope of this book.

6.5 CONTINUOUS PAYMENTS

Assuming interest is compounded yearly, there would be 52 payment periods in one interest conversion period when payments are weekly, 365 payment periods in one interest conversion period when payments are daily, etc. As the payments become more and more frequent (every hour, minute, second, etc.), they approach being made continuously. The concept of *continuous payments* means that there is an unlimited number of payments in one interest conversion period.

If the total amount of the payments to be made in a year's time is fixed, but the number of payments in that year is increased, the present value of the annuity increases. For example, suppose $12 is to be paid over a year's time, and interest is at 8% per year (compounded annually). If payments are annual, then $12 is paid at the end of the year (present value = $11.11); if payments are semiannual, then $6 is paid at the end of each half-year (present value = $11.33); if quarterly, then $3 is paid at the end of each quarter (present value = $11.44); if monthly, then $1 is paid at the end of each month (present value = $11.51). As the number of installments becomes very large, the present value increases but approaches a limit. In other words, although there is no limit to the number of installments that may be paid in one interest conversion period, the present value of the installments never exceeds a certain limit. This limit is called the present value of an annuity payable continuously.

In such calculations, the payments in each interest conversion period are replaced by a single equivalent payment at the end of that period (just as described above for annuities payable more frequently than the interest conversion period). A special factor is used for multiplying the total of the payments in each interest conversion period when payments are continuous.

The concept of continuous payments is only theoretical and could not exist in practice. However, there are places where this concept is used by life insurance companies in making calculations. For example, sometimes *reserves* for life insurance policies (to be explained in Chapter 11) are calculated assuming that the policyowner pays the premiums for the policy continuously.

6.6 RELATIONSHIP BETWEEN PRESENT VALUE AND ACCUMULATED VALUE

Calculating the present value of an annuity has the effect of replacing the series of payments with a single amount. This single amount is evaluated as of the beginning of the first period of the series. Similarly, calculating the accumulated value of an annuity has the effect of replacing the series of payments with a single amount, evaluated as of the end of the last period of the series.

The following line diagram illustrates these situations for an n-year annuity of 1 per year:

If $a_{\overline{n}|i}$ and $s_{\overline{n}|i}$ represent the present value and accumulated value, respectively, of the same annuity, then $a_{\overline{n}|i}$ is the present value of the single amount, $s_{\overline{n}|i}$. Similarly, $s_{\overline{n}|i}$ is the accumulated value of the single amount, $a_{\overline{n}|i}$.

In the equation for finding the accumulated value of a single amount:

$$S = A(1 + i)^n$$

the single amount, S, may be replaced by $s_{\overline{n}|i}$. The single amount evaluated at the beginning, A, may be replaced by $a_{\overline{n}|i}$.

Basic equation for accumulating:

$$S = A(1 + i)^n$$

Substitute $s_{\overline{n}|i}$ for S, $a_{\overline{n}|i}$ for A:

$$s_{\overline{n}|i} = a_{\overline{n}|i}(1 + i)^n$$

An example of this relationship may be seen by checking a value shown in Table I. If $n = 5$ and $i = .04$:

Basic equation:

$$s_{\overline{n}|i} = a_{\overline{n}|i}(1 + i)^n$$

Substitute 5 for n, .04 for i:

$$s_{\overline{5}|4\%} = a_{\overline{5}|4\%}(1.04)^5$$

Substitute values from Table I:

$$= (4.451822)(1.216653)$$

Multiply; round to six decimal places:

$$= 5.416323$$

This answer agrees with the value given in Table I for $s_{\overline{5}|4\%}$.

In the basic equation for finding the present value of a single amount

$$A = Sv^n$$

S may be replaced by $s_{\overline{n}|i}$, and A may be replaced by $a_{\overline{n}|i}$.

$$A = Sv^n$$

$$a_{\overline{n}|i} = s_{\overline{n}|i}v^n$$

The relationships shown above are also applicable to annuities due.

To Illustrate—If the accumulated value at the end of 15 years of a yearly annuity due is $412.08, calculate the present value of the same annuity at the time of the first payment. Use $2\frac{1}{2}$% interest.

Solution—The above equation implies that the present value of an annuity (or annuity due) can be found by multiplying the accumulated value by v^n. In this illustration, $412.08 would be multiplied by v^{15} at $2\frac{1}{2}$%:

Basic equations:

Present Value $= Sv^n$

Substitute $412.08 for S, 15 for n:

$$= \$412.08(v^{15} \text{ at } 2\tfrac{1}{2}\%)$$

Substitute value of v^{15} at $2\frac{1}{2}$% from Table I:

$$= \$412.08(.690466)$$

Multiply; round to nearest cent:

$$= \$284.53$$

Postscript. The principles of compound interest, which have been discussed in Chapters 3 through 6, are used extensively in several areas of a life insurance company's operations. In the actuary's work, compound interest is used not only in the way described in the preceding chapters but also combined with the principles of probability. Chapter 7 will describe the basics of the probabilities of living and dying. The chapters that follow will show how compound interest is combined with these probabilities to ensure the conduct of the life insurance business on a financially sound and scientific basis.

EXERCISES, SET 13

(Review Exercises for Chapters 3 through 6)

1. What is the accumulated value of $500 at the end of ten years at $2\frac{1}{2}$% interest?

2. What is the present value of $500 due at the end of ten years at $2\frac{1}{2}$% interest?

3. A deposit of $50 is made at the end of each year into a savings account paying 6% interest. What is the value of the account at the end of eight years?

4. What is the accumulated value of a 14-year annuity of $75, if the interest rate is 4%?

5. What is the present value of a 14-year annuity of $75, if the interest rate is 4%?

6. What is the accumulated value of an eight-year annuity due of $200 at 6%?

7. What is the present value of an eight-year annuity due of $200 at 6%?

8. How much money must be deposited at the beginning of each year for six years at 5% in order to accumulate $1,000 at the end of that period?

9. Payments of $300 are to be made to a beneficiary at the end of each half-year for ten years. If the interest rate is a nominal 6% compounded semiannually, what is the present value of these payments?

10. Find the accumulated value of an annuity due of $75 per month for two years, assuming an interest rate of a nominal 24% compounded monthly.

11. What payment, made at the end of each year for four years into a fund earning 10%, will accumulate to $1,000 at the end of the fourth year?

12. Construct a schedule showing the accumulation of the annuity in Exercise 11 and thus verify the amount of the payment.

13. What effective interest rate is equivalent to a nominal 12% compounded every two months?

14. Calculate the present value of a five-year annuity of $20 per quarter, deferred five years, at a nominal 10% compounded quarterly.

15. Parents deposit $4,000 into an account which is to accumulate for ten years, and the accumulated amount is then to be used to pay their child an equal amount at the beginning of each year for four years to cover college expenses. If interest is earned at 6%, what amount will the child receive each year?

16. According to the terms of an agreement, a person is to receive $1,000, $750, $500, and $250 at the end of one, two, three, and four years, respectively, from the date of the agreement. At the date of the agreement, what is the total present value at 6% of these payments?

17. A life insurance company uses an interest rate of 6% for calculating the present value of premiums paid in advance. On the due date of an annual premium of $84.63, the insured wishes to pay the premium due, and four additional annual premiums in advance. What total amount must the insured pay?

18. A student borrows $1,000 on September 1 each year for four consecutive years. The student agrees to repay the loan in eight equal annual installments, the first payment to be made two years after the date of the last $1,000 loan. Assuming an interest rate of 5% for the entire transaction, what will be the amount of each annual payment?

19. Calculate the price one should pay for a $2,000, five-year bond with 9% interest payable annually in order to earn 6% on the purchase price.

20. The accumulated value of a yearly annuity due is $1,208.15. Calculate the present value of the same annuity due, if the interest rate is 5% and there are 20 payments.

21. At an interest rate of 4% compounded annually, the present value of a ten-year annuity immediate is $405.55. The accumulated value, at the same interest rate, of this annuity at the time of the last payment is

    (1) $273.97   (3) $577.22
    (2) $421.77   (4) $600.31

CHAPTER SUMMARY

- An annuity which has its first payment postponed for one or more periods is known as a *deferred annuity*.

- Its present value may be found by any of three different methods:
  (1) Calculating the present value of each payment separately.

  (Example: $v^4 + v^5 + v^6 + v^7$)

  (2) Calculating the present value as if the "missing" payments were to be paid, then subtracting the present value of the "missing" payments.

  (Example: $a_{\overline{7}|i} - a_{\overline{3}|i}$)

  (3) Calculating the present value as if the evaluation date were at the beginning of the actual payment-period, then discounting this value to the actual evaluation date.

  (Example: $a_{\overline{4}|i}\, v^3$)

- When the present value of an annuity is known and the problem is to find the amount of each payment in the annuity, each such payment is known as an *amortization payment*.

- The amortization payment may be found by dividing the present value by $a_{\overline{n}|i}$:

$$(\text{Amortization Payment}) = \frac{\text{Present Value}}{a_{\overline{n}|i}}$$

- If an *annuity due* is involved, the formula is simply:

$$(\text{Amortization Payment}) = \frac{\text{Present Value}}{\ddot{a}_{\overline{n}|i}}$$

- If a debt with interest is being repaid by equal periodic payments, the outstanding balance of the debt at any point will be equal to the present value, at that time, of the future such amortization payments remaining to be paid.

- A *coupon bond* is a certificate of indebtedness through which the issuer agrees to pay the purchaser a certain amount of money on a specified date in the future. In addition, the issuer pays the purchaser interest on the amount of the bond when the purchaser periodically presents the issuer with coupons detached from the bond.

- To earn a desired rate of interest, the amount which a purchaser should pay for a bond will equal the present value of all amounts the purchaser will receive (coupons plus payment for redemption of the bond itself).

- Annuities are sometimes payable more frequently than the interest compounding period. The value may be calculated by replacing all the payments in one interest period by a single payment, the value of which is calculated by means of a table of factors (not shown in this book). A second method is to find an interest rate (compounded with the same frequency as the annuity payments) which is equivalent to the true rate.

- Payments which are made (theoretically) so frequently that there is an unlimited number of them in each interest period are called *continuous payments*.

- If the total amount of the payments to be made in one period is fixed, as the number of such payments increases, the present value also increases. However, the value reaches a certain limit when the payments are made continuously.

- The present value and the accumulated value of the same annuity are related as follows:

$$s_{\overline{n}|i} = a_{\overline{n}|i}\,(1 + i)^n$$

or

$$a_{\overline{n}|i} = s_{\overline{n}|i}\,v^n$$

LEARNING OBJECTIVES

After reading this chapter, the student should know

- What is meant by deferred annuity.
- The three methods for calculating present value of a deferred annuity.
- What is meant by amortization payments.
- How to calculate amortization payments.
- What is meant by a coupon bond, its par value, and its redemption price.
- How to calculate the purchase price of a coupon bond.
- How to calculate the accumulated value of an annuity if its present value is known.
- How to calculate the present value of an annuity if its accumulated value is known.

7

Mortality Tables

In Chapter 1, it was stated that compound interest and probability are the cornerstones of the life insurance industry. In Chapters 3 through 6, many of the principles of compound interest were explained. Chapter 7 will explain what is meant by probability and how it is used to develop *mortality tables*.

In the life insurance business, probability is used in calculations to predict future deaths based on past experiences. To help actuaries calculate these probabilities of living and dying, mortality tables (like tables of compound interest) have been constructed. Two of the most widely used mortality tables are printed in this book and will be used in the illustrative calculations that are shown.

Because mortality tables form a part of so many life insurance calculations, the principles explained in this chapter will be used throughout the remainder of this book.

7.1 PROBABILITY

The probability, or likelihood, of some event occurring is generally expressed mathematically as a fraction or a decimal. This indicates how many times an event may be expected to occur out of a certain number of opportunities. For example, the probability in one attempt of drawing an ace at random out of a standard deck of 52 playing cards (four of which are aces) is $\frac{4}{52}$ or $\frac{1}{13}$. This means that an ace can be expected to be drawn one time out of every 13 attempts.

If a very large number of such attempts were made, it would actually happen that very nearly $\frac{1}{13}$ of the attempts would produce aces. That statement can be made with certainty, because of the statistical concept known as the *law of large numbers*, which states that if there are a very large number of opportunities for an event to occur, the actual relationship of occurrences to opportunities will be very close to the true probability. In this particular example, the probability given, $\frac{1}{13}$, could be derived either by

1) Exact mathematical calculation, since it is known that $\frac{1}{13}$ of the cards in the deck are aces; or

2) Observing a large number of attempts and calculating the ratio of aces drawn to total draws. This process will generally approximate the $\frac{1}{13}$ figure closely, because of the law of large numbers.

Consider the probability of a person now age 75 dying within the next year. On the basis of past experience accumulated, this probability might be .07337. This decimal may also be expressed as the fraction $\frac{7,337}{100,000}$. This means that approximately 7,337 persons now age 75 out of every 100,000 such persons now alive can be expected to die within the next year. In this particular example, the probability has been derived only by the observation of a large number of persons age 75. It could not have been derived from the kind of prior knowledge involved with the aces in a deck of cards.

To Illustrate—A doctor has attended 5,000 births and observed that on 57 of these 5,000 occasions the birth was a multiple one (twins, triplets, etc.). Calculate the probability of a birth being a multiple one.

Solution—If the event occurs 57 times out of 5,000 opportunities for it to occur, relying on the law of large numbers, the probability is approximated by the fraction

$$\frac{57}{5,000}$$

If 57 is divided by 5,000, the above probability can be expressed as a decimal:

.0114

Note that 5,000 − 57 = 4,943 of the observed births were not multiple. Hence, the probability that a birth will not be multiple can be calculated as

$$\frac{4,943}{5,000}, \text{ or } .9886$$

The total of the two probabilities (.0114 + .9886) is 1.

When an event is certain to occur, the probability of its occurrence is 1. This is evident because, if the event were to occur on every opportunity, the numerator of the fraction would always be the same as the denominator. Any number divided by itself is 1.

The probability of an event which cannot happen under any circumstances is 0.

PROBABILITIES OF MULTIPLE EVENTS. It is often necessary to consider probabilities involving the occurrence of more than one event. One of the two following rules will usually be applicable:

Rule 1. *If there are several possible events, but only one could occur at any one time, the probability that one of such events will actually occur at a given time is the total of the probabilities of each individual event happening at that time.* (This is called the Addition Rule.)

For example, if, in drawing one card from a deck, the "several events" are

1) drawing an ace, or
2) drawing a king,

it will be seen that only one event can occur at any one time. Hence, the probability that one of the events will occur (that the draw will produce either an ace or a king) is the total of the probabilities of each event happening individually:

$$\text{Total Probability} = \begin{pmatrix} \text{Probability of} \\ \text{Drawing an Ace} \end{pmatrix} + \begin{pmatrix} \text{Probability of} \\ \text{Drawing a King} \end{pmatrix}$$

$$= \frac{1}{13} + \frac{1}{13}$$

$$= \frac{2}{13}$$

If the total of two probabilities equals 1, and it is impossible for both to occur in a given situation, the probabilities are said to be *complementary*, that is, it is a certainty that either one or the other event will happen. The most common application of this situation in life insurance is the probabilities of either living or dying. In calculating the probability that a person will either live or die within a certain period, Rule 1 stated above is applicable (because only one of the two events can occur). When the two separate probabilities of living or dying are added, the total equals 1, because it is a certainty that one or the other of the events will occur.

To Illustrate—If the probability that a certain person will die within the next year is given as .0648, calculate the probability that the person will live at least to the end of the year.

Solution—Since only one of the two events can occur, Rule 1 is applicable. Therefore, the probabilities of the individual events are added.

$$\begin{pmatrix} \text{Probability} \\ \text{of Dying} \end{pmatrix} + \begin{pmatrix} \text{Probability} \\ \text{of Living} \end{pmatrix} = \begin{pmatrix} \text{Probability of} \\ \text{Either Living or Dying} \end{pmatrix}$$

In this illustration, the probability of dying is given. Also, it is known that the probability of either living or dying equals 1 because it is a certainty that either one or the other will happen. Hence, the above equation can be solved for the probability of living:

$$\begin{pmatrix} \text{Probability} \\ \text{of Dying} \end{pmatrix} + \begin{pmatrix} \text{Probability} \\ \text{of Living} \end{pmatrix} = \begin{pmatrix} \text{Probability of} \\ \text{Either Living or Dying} \end{pmatrix}$$

Substitute .0648 for probability of dying, 1 for probability of either living or dying:

$$.0648 + \begin{pmatrix} \text{Probability} \\ \text{of Living} \end{pmatrix} = 1$$

Subtract .0648 from each side:

$$\left(\begin{array}{c}\text{Probability}\\\text{of Living}\end{array}\right) = .9352$$

Rule 2. *If several events are independent (that is, the occurrence of any one has no effect on the probability of the occurrence of the others), the probability that all of the events will happen is represented by multiplying the probabilities of the individual events together. (This is called the Multiplication Rule.)*

For example, if the "several events" are

1. Drawing an ace when one card is drawn from a yellow deck, and
2. Drawing a king when one card is drawn from a blue deck,

the occurrence of either one has no effect on the occurrence of the other. The probability that both of the events will occur is represented by multiplying the two individual probabilities together:

$$\left(\begin{array}{c}\text{Probability of}\\\text{Drawing Both}\end{array}\right) = \left(\begin{array}{c}\text{Probability of}\\\text{Drawing an Ace}\\\text{from Yellow Deck}\end{array}\right)\left(\begin{array}{c}\text{Probability of}\\\text{Drawing a King}\\\text{from Blue Deck}\end{array}\right)$$

$$= \left(\frac{1}{13}\right)\left(\frac{1}{13}\right)$$

$$= \frac{1}{169}$$

To Illustrate—Calculate the probability that a newly married couple will live to celebrate their 50th wedding anniversary, if the probability that the husband will live 50 years is .277, and the probability that the wife will live 50 years is .522.

Solution—Assuming that the fact that one person stays alive has no effect on another person's probability of living, Rule 2 is applicable.

$$\left(\begin{array}{c}\text{Probability of}\\\text{Both Living}\\\text{50 Years}\end{array}\right) = \left(\begin{array}{c}\text{Probability of}\\\text{Husband Living}\\\text{50 Years}\end{array}\right)\left(\begin{array}{c}\text{Probability of}\\\text{Wife Living}\\\text{50 Years}\end{array}\right)$$

Substitute the given values for the probabilities:

$$= (.277)(.522)$$

Multiply; round to three decimal places:

$$= .145$$

7.2 DERIVING PROBABILITIES

The most important probability for a life insurance company is the probability that a particular person will die within one year. One of the chief functions of the actuary and the actuarial department is to determine what that probability is, for it will be used in making important calculations. It has been found that while many characteristics affect that probability, the most important characteristic is the person's age. A different probability exists for each age. Chart 7–1 shows examples of such probabilities.

CHART 7–1

Person's Age	Probability That the Person Will Die within One Year
20	.00179
21	.00183
22	.00186
.	.
.	.
.	.
85	.16114

It has been pointed out that probabilities of dying can be derived only by observing a large number of persons. In actual practice, insurance actuaries usually observe all of the persons their company is currently insuring but over a very limited period of time. By this means, persons of all ages are observed within this period, and probabilities of dying within one year are calculated for each age.

Basically, the probability of dying within one year at each age (called the *rate of mortality*) is equal to the ratio of the number dying at that age to the number who are exposed to the risk of dying at that age. (The number dying at a certain age includes those persons who die within the year starting at one birthday and ending before their next birthday.) The rate of mortality for a certain age is calculated by dividing the number dying at that age by the number so exposed. For example, if 910 persons, age 54, are being observed, and 12 of them die during the year of observation, the probability that a person age 54 will die within a year (the rate of mortality at age 54) may be calculated as

$$\frac{12}{910} \text{ or .01319 (rounded off)}$$

To Illustrate—A certain group of insured persons all the same age has been observed over a period of years. If 4,112 persons in this group celebrated their 64th birthday, and it was observed that 87 of the group had died during the previous year, calculate the rate of mortality at age 63.

Solution—Since 87 of the group died the year before, there were actually 4,112 + 87 = 4,199 persons attaining age 63 (one year previous). Hence, the rate of mortality at age 63 may be calculated as

$$\left(\begin{matrix}\text{Rate of Mortality} \\ \text{at Age 63}\end{matrix}\right) = \frac{\text{Number Age 63 Dying Within the Following Year}}{\text{Number Alive at Age 63}}$$

Substitute 87 for number dying, 4,199 for number exposed:

$$= \frac{87}{4,199}$$

$$= .02072$$

METHODS USED IN PRACTICE. Most of the practical problems that actuaries face in deriving these probabilities are associated with the calculation of the number to be considered. For example, while the period of time being observed may be a calender year (from January 1 to December 31), birth dates occur over the entire year. If a particular person became 45 years old on July 1 that year, that person would be exposed to death as a 44-year-old person for half the year and as a 45-year-old person for half the year. Adjustments must also be made for those persons who enter the group or terminate at some time during the observation period. It would be wrong to exclude them completely from the number exposed because, had they died while under observation, they would certainly have been included in the number dying.

The actual rates of mortality for each age experienced by a single insurance company will show considerable fluctuation from year to year. To produce valid and reliable estimates of the mortality rates and to minimize accidental fluctuations, rates of mortality are usually based on the experience of a number of years rather than on the experience of a single year. However, the number of years used must be small enough to reflect current experience. It is also common practice to combine the experience of a number of companies.

Because of accidental fluctuations, the actual rates of mortality will not vary from age to age—even with a large volume of experience—exactly in the manner theoretically expected. Consequently, the observed rates of mortality are adjusted slightly to correct for accidental fluctuations. This adjustment, called *graduation*, is made to obtain a theoretically proper relationship among mortality rates for various ages and thus produce consistent mortality tables.

As an example, suppose that an actuary derives the following rates of mortality from observations of a certain company's own experience on a large number of persons:

Age	Rate of Mortality
61	.0172
62	.0180
63	.0231
64	.0221
65	.0260

The results of these observations would appear as follows in the form of a graph, Figure 7–1:

FIGURE 7–1

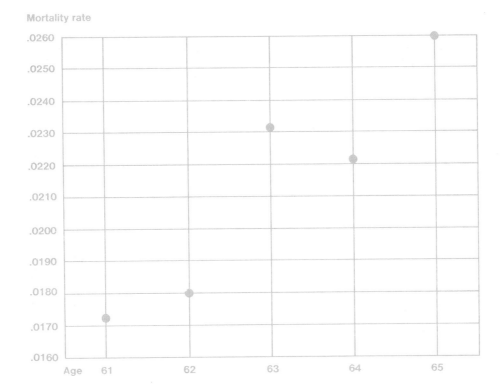

The large dots represent the observed *values* of mortality rates. The ages are shown along the bottom of the graph. For each age, the distance up to the dot indicates the probability of dying or the value of the mortality rate at that age. Values are indicated on the left side of the graph. Graphs of observed data, such as this, are called *scatter diagrams*.

Due to fluctuations in experience, the dots in the diagram do not lie exactly on a smooth curve. To adjust for these fluctuations, a graduation process is used which involves some methods of higher mathematics. The graduation produces a smooth curve which represents the actuary's attempt to display the "true" mortality experience, free from the accidental ups and downs always encountered.

Figure 7–2 shows the smooth curve which the actuary constructs to represent the true mortality experience of the company.

CHARACTERISTICS AFFECTING MORTALITY. In addition to age, there are other important characteristics which affect the probability of dying. For a life insurance company, the most important of these are

1) The person's sex;
2) The person's health status at the time of becoming insured; and
3) The length of time since the person became insured.

FIGURE 7-2

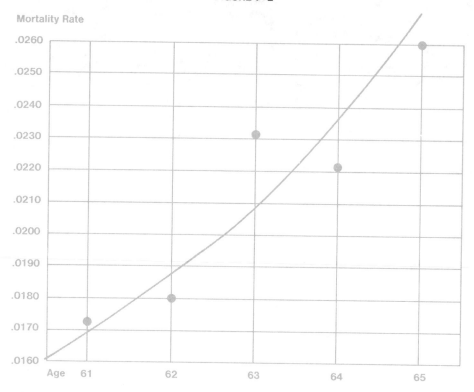

Therefore, separate probabilities of dying within one year (age by age) are often derived for each of these characteristics.

In practice, the actuary usually adds safety margins to the computed rates of mortality before the rates are used for certain insurance calculations, such as setting premiums. These safety margins provide for unpredicted increases in mortality or for temporary adverse mortality fluctuations.

EXERCISES, SET 14

1. What is meant by the probability of an event happening?

2. What are two probabilities called if they have a total equal to 1?

3. If there are a very large number of opportunities for an event to occur, the actual relationship of occurrences to opportunities will be very close to the true probability. By what name is this circumstance called?

4. What is the probability of getting a 3 when one ordinary six-faced die is thrown one time?

5. If a red die and a green die are thrown one time each, what is the probability that the red die will show a 2 and the green die will show a 5?

6. If the probability that a pregnant woman will bear twins is .0114, triplets is .0017, quadruplets is .0003, and quintuplets is virtually 0, what is the probability that a pregnant woman will have a multiple birth?

7. If the probability that a person age 35 will live to age 36 is .9994, and the probability that a person age 36 will die before reaching age 37 is .0008, what is the probability that a person age 35 will live to age 36 and then die before reaching age 37?

8. If the probability that a newborn baby will be a boy is .5039, what is the probability that a newborn baby will be a girl?

9. When mortality rates are calculated using an insurance company's own experience, why are the rates not smooth or consistent from age to age?

10. If a group of 1,000 persons age 25 is observed for one year and two of them die during that year, compute the rate of mortality at age 25.

11. If a group of 1,000 persons age 25 is observed for one year and two of them die during that year, compute the probability that a person age 25 will live at least one year.

12. If an observed group has 100 persons living one year after they all became 88 years old, and 22 persons of that age group died during the year, compute the rate of mortality at age 88.

13. The probability that on a single draw a cardplayer will draw either an ace or a club from a standard deck of playing cards is

$$(1) \ \frac{4}{52} + \frac{13}{52} \qquad (3) \ \frac{4}{52} + \frac{13}{52} - \frac{1}{52}$$

$$(2) \ \frac{4}{52} \times \frac{13}{52} \qquad (4) \ \frac{4}{52} \times \left(\frac{13}{52} - \frac{1}{52}\right)$$

7.3 TYPES OF MORTALITY TABLES

A mortality table, as the name implies, is a tabulation of the probabilities of dying during the year at each age, that is, the rate of mortality. Generally, it also includes related information which can be derived from these rates.

Depending on the origin of the data used to derive the rates of mortality, there are two principal types of mortality tables.

1. Tables derived from population statistics. These are generally prepared by the National Center for Health Statistics, based on registered deaths and data collected during a regular census. An example is the U.S. Life Tables: 1969–71.

2. Tables derived from data on insured lives. These generally represent the pooled experience of a number of life insurance companies. These tables are classified into two types:
   a) Annuity mortality tables, for use with annuity contracts (benefits payable only if the contract-holder is alive). An example is the 1971 Individual Annuity Mortality Table which is printed in the back of this book in Table II.
   b) Insurance mortality tables, for use with life insurance contracts (benefits payable when the contract-holder dies). An example is the Commissioners 1958 Standard Ordinary Mortality Table (called the 1958

C.S.O. Table for short), which is printed in the back of this book in Table III.

Experience has shown that the rates of mortality for persons buying annuity contracts are lower, age by age, than for those buying life insurance contracts. This apparently results from the fact that some persons base their choice of buying either an annuity or an insurance contract on the knowledge that their own probabilities of dying are better or worse than the average. Therefore, actuaries generally construct different mortality tables for life insurance and for annuities.

CONSERVATIVE TABLES. In both annuity and insurance operations, it is important that the rates of mortality assumed be conservative. In life insurance, this means that a table should show higher rates of mortality than will probably be experienced so that the company will not be required to pay death benefits sooner than anticipated. The opposite is true in the selection of a conservative table for use in annuity contracts. Here the rates of mortality assumed should be lower than the expected rates so that the company will not be required to pay annuity benefits for a longer period of time than anticipated.

As a result of economic and medical advances, there has been a general trend over a period of years toward lower mortality rates. Therefore, conservative insurance mortality tables have tended to become even more conservative. On the other hand, conservative annuity mortality tables have tended to become less conservative (because more people are living longer).

DIFFERENCES BY SEX. It was pointed out in Section 7.2 that separate probabilities of dying are often derived for each sex. Experience has shown that mortality rates for females are lower, age by age, than for males. At many ages this difference is very substantial. Therefore, the 1971 Individual Annuity Mortality Table actually consists of two separate tables—one for males and one for females. Both the male and female tables are printed in Table II.

The 1958 C.S.O. Table, which is used in connection with life insurance, was developed from the mortality rates of males and females. However, it is customary (and permitted by law) to assume that the rates of mortality contained in this table apply only to males. When using this table for females, the normal procedure is to subtract a number of years, such as three or six, from the true age of the female. For example, a woman age 25 might be subject to the rate of mortality applicable to a man age 22. This is known as using a three-year setback or a three-year rating down in age. Because of the substantial differences between male and female mortality, various laws which specify allowable bases for calculating *reserves* and *nonforfeiture values* (to be explained in later chapters) provide for as much as a six-year setback for females. In Table III, the label "male" is used as a reminder that it is customary to make an adjustment where a female life is involved. At very young ages an age setback is not appropriate, however, and other types of adjustments are customary.

The 1971 Individual Annuity Mortality Table (Table II) and the 1958 C.S.O. Table (Table III) will be used for all calculations in this text. However, the principles discussed are general and can be applied to any mortality table.

7.4 STRUCTURE OF A MORTALITY TABLE

A mortality table is generally shown with four basic columns. Chart 7–2, taken from the 1958 C.S.O. Table, shows the four columns and will be used throughout this section to help explain their interrelationship.

CHART 7–2
Portions of the 1958 C.S.O. Table

(1) Age x	(2) Number Living at Age x l_x	(3) Number Dying Between Age x and Age $(x + 1)$ d_x	(4) Rate of Mortality q_x
0	10,000,000	70,800	.00708
1	9,929,200	17,475	.00176
2	9,911,725	15,066	.00152
.	.	.	.
.	.	.	.
97	37,787	18,456	.48842
98	19,331	12,916	.66815
99	6,415	6,415	1.00000

COLUMNS FOR AGE AND RATE OF MORTALITY. Column (1) represents age. Ages are very often shown starting with age zero (a person's first year of life).

Column (4) contains the rates of mortality. The rate of mortality shown opposite each age represents the assumed probability of dying within one year for a person who is that particular age. It is customary to select arbitrarily some very high age at which the probability of dying is assumed to be a certainty (equals 1). Thus, 99 is the last age shown in this table.

The rate of mortality, or the probability of dying, at age x is represented by the symbol

$$q_x$$

In this symbol, the letter x, shown to the right and slightly lower than the q, is a subscript. Hence, it is a part of the whole symbol, and q_x does not mean q multiplied by x. The symbol is read q sub x or simply q x. An example would be

$$q_{27}$$

which is read q sub 27 or q 27. It means the rate of mortality at age 27 or the probability that a person age 27 will die within a year (before the person reaches age 28).

This symbol q_x appears at the top of the rate of mortality column in a mortality table. Since the letter x is used as a general representation for age, that letter appears at the top of the age column.

GRAPHIC PRESENTATION OF q_x. Relative values of q_x can be seen on the graph, Figure 7–3.

FIGURE 7–3

Values of q_x

(Solid line is 1971 Individual Annuity Mortality Table; dashed line is 1958 C.S.O. Table)

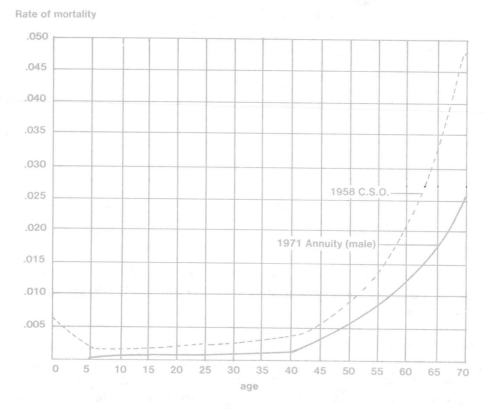

The two curved lines represent values of q_x (for males) from the 1971 Individual Annuity Mortality Table and the 1958 C.S.O. Table. Ages 0 to 70 are shown along the bottom of the graph. For each age, the distance up the vertical lines indicates the value of q_x at that age, as set forth in the particular mortality table. Space limitations make it impossible to show the graph to the highest age in the tables. The value of q_x is 1.000 at age 99 in the 1958 C.S.O. Table and at age 115 in the 1971 Individual Annuity Mortality Table. This gives an indication of how rapidly the death rates increase after age 70. This graph would have to be 20 times as tall as it is to show values for all ages up through the highest age.

It is interesting to note that the rates of mortality actually decrease age by age from age 0 to approximately age 10. From this point, the rates increase very slowly until about age 40. It should also be noted that the graph portrays rates of mortality assumed for those buying annuity contracts as being lower, age by age, than for those buying life insurance contracts.

COLUMNS FOR NUMBER LIVING AND DYING. The other two basic columns of a mortality table are set up to show what happens each year to a large group of people all the same age, starting when they are all at a certain low age, such as age zero. An arbitrary number of people, such as 10,000,000, are assumed to be alive at this time. During the first year, a certain number will die, leaving the remaining persons to begin the second year. In the second year, a certain number of these will die, etc.

Column (2) shows how many persons (out of the original group) are assumed to be alive at each age. The number of this group who are still alive at age x is represented by the symbol

$$l_x$$

that is, l with a subscript x. It is read "l sub x" or simply "l x." An example would be

$$l_{20}$$

which is read "l sub 20" or "l 20." It means the assumed number of the original group still living at age 20.

Column (3) shows how many persons out of this group are expected to die at each age. The number of this group who die in the year they are age x is represented by the symbol

$$d_x$$

that is, d with a subscript x. It is read "d sub x" or simply "d x." An example would be

$$d_{74}$$

which is read "d sub 74" or "d 74." It means the number of the group expected to die while age 74 (in the year after reaching age 74 but before reaching age 75).

In Chart 7–2, the l_x column shows that 10,000,000 persons (in this hypothetical group) start out life together at age zero. This is the same as saying that $l_0 = 10,000,000$. The same column shows that it is assumed that 9,929,200 of these people will still be alive at age one, and 9,911,725 of them will still be alive at age two, that is, $l_1 = 9,929,200$ and $l_2 = 9,911,725$.

The d_x column shows that 70,800 of the persons in this group die while they are age zero (during the year after birth but before reaching age one). This is the same as saying that $d_0 = 70,800$. The same column shows that it is expected that 17,475 of them will die during the year they are age one, and 15,066 will die during the year they are age two, that is $d_1 = 17,475$ and $d_2 = 15,066$.

The probability of dying while age x, that is, during the year between age

x and age $(x + 1)$, is sometimes called the probability of dying at age x. Likewise, the number so dying is sometimes called the number dying at age x.

EQUATIONS FOR INTERRELATIONSHIP. **If the number of dying in a given year (d_x) is subtracted from the number living at the beginning of that year (l_x), the result will represent the number still alive at the next higher age (l_{x+1}). In equation form, this is written:**

$$l_{x+1} = l_x - d_x$$

To Illustrate—Calculate the value of l_{98} for the 1958 C.S.O. Table using the above equation.

Solution—

Basic equation:

$$l_{x+1} = l_x - d_x$$

Substitute 97 for x (the age):

$$l_{98} = l_{97} - d_{97}$$

Substitute the values for l_{97} and d_{97} from the table:

$$= 37{,}787 - 18{,}456$$

$$= 19{,}331$$

This value of l_{98} agrees with that given in the table.

If the number living at a certain age (l_x) is multiplied by the rate of mortality at the age (q_x), the result will represent the number expected to die during the year they are that age (d_x). In equation form, this is written

$$d_x = l_x q_x$$

To Illustrate—Calculate the value of d_{97} for the 1958 C.S.O. Table using the above equation.

Solution—

Basic equation:

$$d_x = l_x q_x$$

Substitute 97 for x (the age):

$$d_{97} = l_{97} q_{97}$$

Substitute the values for l_{97} and q_{97} from the table:

$$= (37{,}787)(.48842)$$

Multiply; round to nearest whole number:

$$= 18,456$$

This value of d_{97} agrees with that given in the table.

If the number of people expected to die during the year at a certain age (d_x) is divided by the number living at that age (l_x), the result will be the rate of mortality at that age (q_x).

The equation, $d_x = l_x q_x$, may be solved for q_x by dividing both sides by l_x, giving this relationship in equation form:

$$\frac{d_x}{l_x} = q_x$$

To Illustrate—Calculate the value of q_2 for the 1958 C.S.O. Table using the above equation.

Solution—

Basic equation:

$$q_x = \frac{d_x}{l_x}$$

Substitute 2 for x (the age):

$$q_2 = \frac{d_2}{l_2}$$

Substitute values for d_2 and l_2 from the table:

$$= \frac{15,066}{9,911,725}$$

$$= .00152$$

This value of q_2 agrees with that given in the table.

It will be observed that the value for q_{99} shown in the 1958 C.S.O. Table is *certainty*, that is, 1. As explained above, this is done arbitrarily for the purpose of conveniently ending the table, and not because it was observed that everybody who reaches age 99 dies before reaching 100.

DOUBLE DECREMENT TABLES. Tables which show persons leaving the group for two different reasons (generally by death or withdrawal) are called *double decrement tables.* Such tables generally show columns for probability of withdrawal each year and for number withdrawing each year, in addition to the regular columns described above. (Withdrawal generally means voluntarily terminating the insurance contract.) The use of double decrement tables will be further referred to in later chapters. They are important in situations where a payment is made upon withdrawal from the group (as well as payment being made upon death).

7.5 CONSTRUCTION OF A MORTALITY TABLE

Once the rates of mortality (q_x) have been established for all ages (usually by observing the number of deaths among one or several companies' insured persons), the numbers in the other two columns can be easily derived. The first age shown should be the youngest age for which the table is to be used. In most cases, this is age zero. The entire mortality table can be constructed by following these steps:

1. Assume an initial value for l_x (at the youngest age in the table). This is usually some large round number, such as 1,000,000 or 10,000,000.
2. Calculate the number of deaths between this age, x, and the next age, $(x + 1)$. This is done using the equation

$$d_x = l_x q_x$$

3. Calculate the number living at the second age $(x + 1)$, using the equation

$$l_{x+1} = l_x - d_x$$

4. Repeat steps 2 and 3, successively, for each higher age.

For example, it can be seen how the columns of the 1958 C.S.O. Table were constructed by this process after the rates of mortality were known. The portions of the table appearing in Section 7.4 indicate that an initial value of l_x was chosen to be 10,000,000 at age zero. In other words,

$$l_0 = 10,000,000$$

The number of deaths between age zero and age one was calculated by applying the basic equation:

$$d_x = l_x q_x$$

Substitute 0 for x:

$$d_0 = l_0 q_0$$

Substitute 10,000,000 for l_0, and the value of q_0 from the table:

$$= (10,000,000)(.00708)$$

Multiply; round to nearest whole number:

$$= 70,800$$

Next, the number living at age one was calculated as follows:

Basic equation:

$$l_{x+1} = l_x - d_x$$

Substitute 0 for x:

$$l_1 = l_0 - d_0$$

Substitute 10,000,000 for l_0, and the value of d_0 calculated above:

$$= 10,000,000 - 70,800$$

$$= 9,929,200$$

By the same process, the number of deaths at age one (between age one and age two) was calculated.

Basic equation:

$$d_x = l_x q_x$$

Substitute 1 for x:

$$d_1 = l_1 q_1$$

Substitute the value of l_1 calculated above, and the value for q_1:

$$= (9,929,200)(.00176)$$

$$= 17,475$$

The number living at age two was then calculated as follows:

Basic equation:

$$l_{x+1} = l_x - d_x$$

Substitute 1 for x:

$$l_2 = l_1 - d_1$$

Substitute the values for l_1 and d_1 calculated above:

$$= 9,929,200 - 17,475$$

$$= 9,911,725$$

All these values agree with those in the portion of the table shown earlier in this chapter. This process was repeated successively until the entire 1958 C.S.O. Table was constructed.

In constructing the 1971 Individual Annuity Mortality Table, age five was chosen as the lowest age for both the male and the female portions.

EXERCISES, SET 15

1. Why do persons holding annuity contracts generally show lower rates of mortality than those holding life insurance contracts?

2. Should a conservative annuity mortality table show mortality rates higher or lower than can actually be expected?

3. According to Table II, what is the probability that a man age 60 will die before reaching age 61?

4. According to Table III, what is the rate of mortality at age 60? Express the answer as a fraction.

5. If the rate of mortality at a certain age is .00742, and the number of persons living at that age is 107,412, how many of them may be expected to die within a year?

6. Using Table III, calculate the probability that a man age 79 will live to age 80.

7. What are two methods used that enable mortality table calculations to be made separately for males and females?

8. Using a six-year setback for females, what is the female rate of mortality at age 29, according to Table III?

9. If a mortality table shows $l_{18} = 994,831$ and $d_{18} = 1,094$, calculate the value of l_{19}.

10. If a mortality table shows $l_{42} = 9,408,108$ and $l_{43} = 9,374,239$, calculate the value of d_{42}.

11. If a mortality table shows $l_{36} = 951,003$ and $q_{36} = .0022$, calculate the value of d_{36}.

12. Using the figures in Exercise 11, calculate the value of l_{37}.

13. If a mortality table shows $l_{75} = 4,940,810$ and $d_{75} = 361,498$, calculate the value of q_{75}.

14. Calculate the missing items in the following portion of a mortality table:

Age x	l_x	d_x	q_x
20	92,637	...	...
21	91,914	...	...
22	91,192	...	...
23	90,471		

15. The mortality rate at age x can correctly be expressed as

(1) $\dfrac{d_{x+1}}{l_x}$ (3) $\dfrac{l_{x+1}}{l_x}$

(2) $\dfrac{l_x - l_{x+1}}{l_x}$ (4) $\dfrac{d_x - d_{x+1}}{l_x}$

7.6 PROBABILITIES OF LIVING AND DYING

It has already been noted that the probability that a person age x will die in the next year is represented by the symbol q_x. The probability that a person age x will live to reach $(x + 1)$ is represented by the symbol

p_x

That is, p with a subscript x. It is read "p sub x" or simply "p x." An example would be

p_{43}

which is read "p sub 43" or "p 43." It means the probability that a person age 43 will live to reach age 44, that is, will be alive for at least one whole year.

In general terms, it may be said that if the number living at age $(x + 1)$ is divided by the number living at age x, the result will be the probability that a person age x will live to reach age $(x + 1)$. In equation form, this is written

$$p_x = \frac{l_{x+1}}{l_x}$$

To Illustrate—Given the following portion of a mortality table, calculate the value of p_{82} (that is, the probability that a person age 82 will live for a least one year):

Age x	l_x
80	2,410
81	2,180
82	1,955
83	1,737
84	1,528

Solution—

Basic equation:

$$p_x = \frac{l_{x+1}}{l_x}$$

Substitute 82 for x:

$$p_{82} = \frac{l_{83}}{l_{82}}$$

Substitute the values for l_{83} and l_{82} from the table:

$$= \frac{1,737}{1,955}$$

$$= .8885$$

The result shows that, according to this particular table, the probability that a person age 82 will live for at least one whole year is .8885.

It is a certainty that a person will either live for one year or die within that year. Since only one of those two events can occur, Rule 1 in Section 7.1 is applicable: the probability that one of the events will happen is the total of the probabilities of each individual event happening.

$$\begin{pmatrix} \text{Probability of} \\ \text{Living 1 Year} \end{pmatrix} + \begin{pmatrix} \text{Probability of} \\ \text{Dying Within} \\ \text{1 Year} \end{pmatrix} = \begin{pmatrix} \text{Probability of} \\ \text{Either Living or} \\ \text{Dying That Year} \end{pmatrix}$$

Symbols can be substituted for each of the above expressions, as follows:

$$\text{Substitute } p_x \text{ for } \begin{pmatrix} \text{Probability of} \\ \text{Living 1 Year} \end{pmatrix}$$

Substitute q_x for $\left(\begin{array}{l}\text{Probability of}\\\text{Dying Within 1 Year}\end{array}\right)$

Substitute 1 (certainty) for $\left(\begin{array}{l}\text{Probability of Either}\\\text{Living or Dying That Year}\end{array}\right)$

Consequently, the equation is

$$p_x + q_x = 1$$

As an example, according to Table III, $q_{21} = .00183$. Expressed as a fraction, this is $\dfrac{183}{100,000}$. This means that, out of 100,000 persons, all age 21, there can be expected to be 183 deaths during the year. If 183 persons out of 100,000 can be expected to die between ages 21 and 22, then $100,000 - 183 = 99,817$ will survive to age 22. Therefore, the probability that a person age 21 will be living at age 22 is

$$\frac{99,817}{100,000}$$

or

.99817

In other words:

$$p_{21} = .99817$$

Using these figures, it can be shown that the equation $p_x + q_x = 1$ is applicable:

Basic equation:

$$p_x + q_x = 1$$

Substitute 21 for x:

$$p_{21} + q_{21} = 1$$

Substitute the values given above for p_{21} and q_{21}:

$$.99817 + .00183 = 1$$

Add; result verifies the equation:

$$1.00000 = 1$$

The equation $p_x + q_x = 1$ can be used to calculate either p_x or q_x when the value of only one of these probabilities is known.

To Illustrate—Given that $p_{46} = .995138$, how many persons age 46 can be expected to die before reaching age 47 out of a group of 1,000,000? out of a group of 100,000?

Solution—

Basic equation:

$$p_x + q_x = 1$$

Substitute 46 for x:

$$p_{46} + q_{46} = 1$$

Substitute the given value for p_{46}:

$$.995138 + q_{46} = 1$$

Subtract .995138 from both sides:

$$q_{46} = .004862$$

This result can also be written:

$$q_{46} = \frac{4,862}{1,000,000}$$

which means that out of 1,000,000 persons age 46, we can expect 4,862 to die before reaching age 47.

To find the number expected to die out of a group of 100,000, divide both the numerator and denominator by ten. This can be done by moving the decimal points one place to the left:

$$q_{46} = \frac{486.2}{100,000.0}$$

The numerator would seem to imply a number of persons dying which is not a whole number. This need not be confusing if it is remembered that such numbers are approximations for the exact number predicted to die or averages based on observations of more than one year. Hence, this expression means that, out of 100,000 persons age 46, approximately 486 can be expected to die in the succeeding year.

PROBABILITIES OF LIVING FOR n YEARS. The concepts presented above can be extended to include the probabilities of a person living for any numbers of years, or dying within any number of years. The probability that a person age x will live at least n more years, or that the person will reach age $(x + n)$, is represented by the symbol

$$_np_x$$

that is, p with subscripts of n preceding and x following. It is read "$n\ p\ x$." An example would be

$$_{15}p_{20}$$

which is read "15 p 20." It represents the probability that a person age 20 will live at least 15 more years, that is, that the person will reach age 35.

The probability that a person age x will live at least n more years ($_np_x$) is found by dividing the number living at age ($x + n$) by the number living at age x. In equation form this is written

$$_np_x = \frac{l_{x+n}}{l_x}$$

To Illustrate—Using the following portion of a mortality table, calculate the probability that a person age 48 will live at least six more years. Show the answer to three decimal places.

Age x	l_x
47	9,015
48	8,920
49	8,817
50	8,707
51	8,590
52	8,465
53	8,332
54	8,192
55	8,043

Solution—

Basic equation:

$$_np_x = \frac{l_{x+n}}{l_x}$$

Substitute 48 for x, 6 for n:

$$_6p_{48} = \frac{l_{48+6}}{l_{48}}$$

$$= \frac{l_{54}}{l_{48}}$$

Substitute the values for l_{54} and l_{48} from the above table:

$$= \frac{8,192}{8,920}$$

$$= .918$$

To Illustrate Again—Using the following portion of a male mortality table and a three-year setback for females, calculate the probability that a woman age 36 will live to reach age 40. Show the answer to three decimal places.

Male Age x	l_x
33	9,209
34	9,173
35	9,135
36	9,094
37	9,049
38	9,001
39	8,948
40	8,891

Solution—Three years must be subtracted from the ages before using the table. This means using the table as if calculating the probability of a male age 33 reaching age 37. The number of years involved, n, is 4.

Basic equation:

$$_n p_x = \frac{l_{x+n}}{l_x}$$

Substitute 33 for x, 4 for n:

$$_4 p_{33} = \frac{l_{33+4}}{l_{33}}$$

$$= \frac{l_{37}}{l_{33}}$$

Substitute values for l_{37} and l_{33} from the above table:

$$= \frac{9,049}{9,209}$$

$$= .983$$

PROBABILITIES OF DYING WITHIN n YEARS. The probability that a person age x will die within n years or will die before reaching age $(x + n)$ is represented by the symbol

$$_n q_x$$

that is, q with subscripts of n preceding and x following. It is read "n q x." An example would be

$$_{12} q_{65}$$

which is read "12 q 65." It means the probability that a person age 65 will die within the next 12 years, that is, that the person will die before reaching age 77.

The probability that a person age x will die within n years ($_n q_x$) is found by dividing the difference between the number living at ages x and $(x + n)$

by the number living at age x. This is expressed in equation form as

$$_n q_x = \frac{l_x - l_{x+n}}{l_x}$$

The numerator equals the number of people who die between ages x and $(x + n)$ because the number living at age x is reduced by all those who die in the interval in order to arrive at the number still living at age $(x + n)$.

To Illustrate—Using the following portion of a mortality table, calculate the probability that a person age 30 will die within the next five years. Show the answer to three decimal places.

Age x	l_x	d_x
30	9,827	13
31	9,814	13
32	9,801	15
33	9,786	16
34	9,770	16
35	9,754	17

Solution—

Basic equation:

$$_n q_x = \frac{l_x - l_{x+n}}{l_x}$$

Substitute 30 for x, 5 for n:

$$_5 q_{30} = \frac{l_{30} - l_{30+5}}{l_{30}}$$

$$= \frac{l_{30} - l_{35}}{l_{30}}$$

Substitute values from the table above:

$$= \frac{9,827 - 9,754}{9,827}$$

$$= \frac{73}{9,827}$$

$$= .007$$

The number in the numerator, 73, is the number of people who die between ages 30 and 35. It is equal to the total of the numbers in the d_x column, beginning with d_{30} and ending with d_{34}.

It is a certainty that a person age x will either live at least n years or else die within n years. Therefore, the total of these two individual probabilities is equal to 1. In equation form, this is written as

$$_n p_x + {_n q_x} = 1$$

This equation is similar to that discussed above for the relationship between the probabilities of living and/or dying for *one* year.

PROBABILITIES INVOLVING MORE THAN ONE EVENT. Probabilities involving more than one event may be calculated using the Addition Rule and Multiplication Rule given in Section 7.1.

To Illustrate—Using the following portion of a mortality table, calculate the probability that a person age 30 will die either at age 50 or at age 51.

Age x	l_x	d_x
30	97,353	198
31	97,155	216
.	.	.
.	.	.
.	.	.
50	84,650	1,325
51	83,325	1,406
52	81,919	1,491

Solution—Since only one of the events can occur, the Addition Rule (Rule 1)—that two individual probabilities are added—is applicable. The probability that a person age 30 will die during the year he or she is age 50 is equal to the number of people dying at age 50 divided by the number living at age 30:

Basic equation:

$$\left(\begin{matrix} \text{Probability of} \\ \text{Dying at Age 50} \end{matrix} \right) = \frac{d_{50}}{l_{30}}$$

Substitute the values for d_{50} and l_{30} from the above table:

$$= \frac{1,325}{97,353}$$

$$= .0136$$

Similarly, the probability that a person age 30 will die during the year he or she is age 51 is

Basic equation:

$$\left(\begin{matrix} \text{Probability of} \\ \text{Dying at Age 51} \end{matrix} \right) = \frac{d_{51}}{l_{30}}$$

Substitute the values for d_{51} and l_{30} from the above table:

$$= \frac{1,406}{97,353}$$

$$= .0144$$

The desired probability equals the total of the two individual probabilities:

Basic equation:

$$\begin{pmatrix} \text{Probability of} \\ \text{Dying at} \\ \text{Age 50 or 51} \end{pmatrix} = \begin{pmatrix} \text{Probability of} \\ \text{Dying at} \\ \text{Age 50} \end{pmatrix} + \begin{pmatrix} \text{Probability of} \\ \text{Dying at} \\ \text{Age 51} \end{pmatrix}$$

Substitute the probabilities calculated above:

$$= .0136 + .0144$$

$$= .0280$$

To Illustrate Again—Using the following portions of a mortality table, calculate the probability that a father, age 50, and his son, age 20, will both live at least 15 more years.

Age x	l_x
19	9,953
20	9,947
21	9,940
.	.
.	.
.	.
34	9,827
35	9,814
36	9,801
.	.
.	.
.	.
49	9,444
50	9,388
51	9,327
.	.
.	.
.	.
64	7,885
65	7,717
66	7,539

Solution—Assuming that one event has no effect on the other, the Multiplication Rule (Rule 2)—that two individual probabilities are multiplied—is applicable. For the father:

Basic equation:

$$_np_x = \frac{l_{x+n}}{l_x}$$

Substitute 50 for x, 15 for n:

$$_{15}p_{50} = \frac{l_{50+15}}{l_{50}}$$

$$= \frac{l_{65}}{l_{50}}$$

Substitute values for l_{65} and l_{50} from the above table:

$$= \frac{7,717}{9,388}$$

$$= .8220$$

For the son:

Basic equation:

$$_{n}p_{x} = \frac{l_{x+n}}{l_{x}}$$

Substitute 20 for x, 15 for n:

$$_{15}p_{20} = \frac{l_{20+15}}{l_{20}}$$

$$= \frac{l_{35}}{l_{20}}$$

Substitute values for l_{35} and l_{20} from the above table:

$$= \frac{9,814}{9,947}$$

$$= .9866$$

The desired probability that both will live at least 15 years equals the two individual probabilities multiplied together:

Basic equation:

$$\begin{pmatrix} \text{Probability} \\ \text{Both Live} \end{pmatrix} = \begin{pmatrix} \text{Probability} \\ \text{Father Lives} \end{pmatrix} \begin{pmatrix} \text{Probability} \\ \text{Son Lives} \end{pmatrix}$$

Substitute the probabilities calculated above:

$$= (.8220)(.9866)$$

$$= .8110$$

7.7 SELECT AND ULTIMATE MORTALITY TABLES

It was stated in Section 7.2 that the time which elapses after a person becomes insured affects that person's probability of dying. At the time a person becomes insured under an individual policy, it is proved if he or she is in good health. Those whose health is not good may be required to pay a higher insurance premium or even be refused a policy. It is customary for mortality tables to be based on the mortality rates of persons in good health.

Experience has shown that mortality rates are lower for persons whose good health has just been proved than for other persons of the same age whose good health was proved in the past. However, as the years go by, differences between the mortality rates of these two groups gradually disappear. The period of years during which there is a significant difference in the mortality rates is known as the *select period*. A mortality table which records mortality rates during the select period is known as a *select mortality table*.

To indicate that mortality rates apply to persons whose good health has just been proved, it is customary to enclose the age in square brackets. Thus, instead of writing q_x, the mortality rate at age x for persons who have just been proved to be in good health is written

$$q_{[x]}$$

that is, q with a subscript $[x]$. The x in brackets is part of the whole symbol, and $q_{[x]}$ does not mean "q multiplied by x." An example would be

$$q_{[35]}$$

which means the mortality rate of persons who are age 35 and who have just been proved to be in good health.

The mortality rates for such persons at the end of one, two, and three years is expressed by

$$q_{[x]+1}$$

$$q_{[x]+2}$$

$$q_{[x]+3}$$

respectively. Thus, the age at which good health was proved remains a part of the symbol, enclosed in brackets. An example would be

$$q_{[24]+4}$$

which means the mortality rate four years after good health was proved, which took place at age 24. In other words, the mortality rate was $q_{[24]}$ at age 24 when good health was just proved. Now, four years later (at age 28), $q_{[24]+4}$ is the mortality rate for such persons.

Beyond the select period, when the effects of the selection have worn off, the mortality rates constitute the *ultimate mortality table*. The combination of these two tables is called a *select and ultimate mortality table*. An example of portions of such a table appears in Chart 7–3. This example shows a five-year select period; however, tables with 10- or 15-year select periods are also common.

The first column shows the ages at which it may be assumed good health has just been proved. The second column records the mortality rate for persons who have just been proved to be in good health at each such age, namely $q_{[x]}$. Starting at any age recorded in the first column, the mortality rate at successive ages is found by reading the table horizontally to the right. It will be seen that these columns to the right are labeled: $q_{[x]+1}$, $q_{[x]+2}$, $q_{[x]+3}$,

CHART 7–3
Portion of a Select and Ultimate Mortality Table
(five-year select period)

Age [x]	$q_{[x]}$	$q_{[x]+1}$	$q_{[x]+2}$	$q_{[x]+3}$	$q_{[x]+4}$	q_{x+5}	Age x + 5
	Select					*Ultimate*	
70	.0175	.0249	.0313	.0388	.0474	.0545	75
71	.0191	.0272	.0342	.0424	.0518	.0596	76
72	.0209	.0297	.0374	.0463	.0566	.0652	77
73	.0228	.0324	.0409	.0507	.0620	.0714	78
74	.0249	.0354	.0447	.0554	.0678	.0781	79
75	.0273	.0387	.0489	.0607	.0742	.0855	80
76	.0298	.0424	.0535	.0664	.0812	.0936	81
77	.0326	.0464	.0586	.0727	.0889	.1024	82
78	.0357	.0508	.0641	.0796	.0973	.1121	83
79	.0391	.0556	.0702	.0871	.1065	.1227	84

$q_{[x]+4}$, and q_{x+5}. There are no brackets on the x in the q_{x+5} column because, in this table, persons still living five years after their good health was proved are considered to be subject to the same rates of mortality as any other person of the same age, that is, in this particular table, the *select period* only lasts for five years. Hence, the q_{x+5} column may be considered by itself to be an *ultimate* mortality table. Accordingly, the ages represented ($x + 5$) are recorded (in the right-hand column) beside the respective values of q_{x+5}.

For example, the $q_{[x]}$ column records a mortality rate of .0209 for persons at age 72 whose good health has just been proved, that is,

$$q_{[72]} = .0209$$

Reading across the table horizontally to the right from there, the table records that the mortality rate is .0297 one year later (at age 73), that is,

$$q_{[72]+1} = .0297$$

Similarly, the mortality rate is .0374 two years later, .0463 three years later, and .0566 four years later. Finally, the q_{x+5} column records that the mortality rate is .0652 for these persons five years later (at age 77). At this point it makes no difference at what age good health was proved. It is only the current age which is used, and therefore, the mortality rates for succeeding years are found by reading down the q_{x+5} column. For example, the mortality rate for persons at age 78 is .0714.

The other columns usually found in a mortality table can also be constructed on a select and ultimate basis. For example, a table of the number of persons living (l_x) can be calculated and would be arranged exactly like the q_x table shown in Chart 7–3. The columns for the number living would be labeled $l_{[x]}$, $l_{[x]+1}$, $l_{[x]+2}$, etc. Using such a table, various probabilities of living and dying in periods of greater than one year can be calculated. For example, the probability that a person whose good health was proved at age

70 would still be alive four years later is

$$\frac{l_{[70]+4}}{l_{[70]}}$$

EXERCISES, SET 16

1. What is meant by the symbol $_8p_{42}$?

2. What symbol can be written to express the probability which is calculated as follows:

$$\frac{l_{65} - l_{75}}{l_{65}}$$

(Use Table III For Exercises 3 to 12)

3. What is the probability that a man age 20 will live for one more year?

4. What is the probability that a man age 20 will live for 25 more years?

5. What is the probability that a man age 30 will be living at age 50?

6. Using a three-year setback for females, calculate the probability that a female age 20 will survive to age 45.

7. Of 10,000 men age 35, how many can be expected to live to age 65?

8. What is the probability that a man age 30 will die before reaching age 65?

9. Using a six-year setback for females, calculate how many of 100,000 females age 27 can be expected to die within ten years.

10. What is the probability that two men, ages 30 and 40, will both survive ten years?

11. What is the probability that two men, ages 30 and 40, will both die in the next ten years?

12. What is the probability that a man age 20 will die either during the year he is age 70 or during the year he is age 80?

13. When a select and ultimate table is used, what is meant by enclosing a number in brackets as part of a symbol?

(Use the select and ultimate table in Section 7.7 for Exercises 14 to 17)

14. What is the mortality rate at age 80 for persons whose good health was proved at age 79?

15. What is the probability that a person age 78, whose good health was proved at age 75, will survive for one year?

16. What is the probability that a person whose good health has just been proved at age 72 and a person age 77, who was proved to be in good health at age 71, will both die during the next year.

17. If a select and ultimate mortality table shows 100,000 persons living at age 70 whose good health has just been proved, what number out of this group would be shown living at age 71?

18. Using symbols, write the expression for calculating the probability that a person now age 26, whose good health was proved one year ago, will die within the next three years.

19. The probability that a person age 32 will live to age 34 can be expressed correctly as

$$(1) \quad \frac{l_{32} - l_{34}}{l_{32}} \qquad (3) \quad \frac{l_{33} + d_{34}}{l_{32}}$$

$$(2) \quad \frac{d_{32} + d_{33}}{l_{32}} \qquad (4) \quad \frac{l_{35} + d_{34}}{l_{32}}$$

CHAPTER SUMMARY

- The *probability* of an event occurring indicates how many times it may be expected to occur out of a certain number of opportunities for it to occur.

- If the probability is known in advance, then a very large number of opportunities will actually produce a number of occurrences very near the number expected.

- If not known in advance, a good approximation to the probability can be derived by observing the actual number of occurrences in a large number of opportunities.

- Two probabilities are called complementary if their total equals 1. (Example: the probabilities of living or dying).

- If there are several possible events, but only one could occur at any one time, the probability that one of these events will actually occur at a given time is the total of the individual probabilities at that time. This is Rule 1, the Addition Rule.

- The probability that all of certain independent events will occur is found by multiplying the individual probabilities. This is Rule 2, the Multiplication Rule.

- The rate of mortality at any age is derived by calculating the ratio of the number dying at that age to the number exposed to the risk of dying at that age.

- Rates of mortality are affected by, among other things, a person's age, sex, and health status.

- Rates of mortality are generally observed to be lower for persons buying annuities than for those buying life insurance.

- Tables of mortality rates are conservative if the rates contained in them are higher than expected for life insurance or lower than expected for annuities.

- Because of the substantial difference in mortality rates between the sexes, separate mortality tables are often constructed for each sex, or else an age set-back is used for females.

- The basic columns of a mortality table are:

   age (x),
   number living at each age (l_x),
   number dying at each age (d_x), and
   rate of mortality at each age (q_x).

- The values in the columns are interrelated as follows:

$$l_{x+1} = l_x - d_x$$

$$d_x = l_x q_x$$

$$q_x = \frac{d_x}{l_x}$$

- The probability that a person age x will live one year is represented by p_x and is derived from a mortality table by either

$$p_x = \frac{l_{x+1}}{l_x}$$

or

$$p_x = 1 - q_x$$

- The probability that a person age x will live for at least n more years is represented by $_np_x$ and is derived from a mortality table as follows:

$$_np_x = \frac{l_{x+n}}{l_x}$$

- The probability that a person age x will die within the next n years is represented by $_nq_x$, and is derived from a mortality table as follows:

$$_nq_x = \frac{l_x - l_{x+n}}{l_x}$$

- It is customary for life insurance mortality tables to be constructed from the experience of persons who were found to be in good health at the time the policy was issued.

- The *select period* is the period of years during which there is a significant difference in mortality rates between persons (the same age) whose good health was recently proved and persons whose good health was proved in the past. The select period is limited to a set number of years after which its differences are no longer significant. The years following the select period are called the *ultimate period*.

- A *select and ultimate* mortality table shows mortality rates not only for each age but also for each number of years since good health was proved.

- When using a select and ultimate mortality table, the age at which good health was proved is enclosed in brackets, and the number of years elapsed since then is shown following. For example:

$$q_{[30]+3}$$

is the mortality rate at age 33, for persons whose good health was proved at age 30. In the ultimate part of the table, the usual notation is used.

LEARNING OBJECTIVES

After reading this chapter, the student should know

- The definition of the probability of an event occurring.
- The ways of expressing a probability.
- The ways of deriving a probability.
- How to use Rule 1 when there are several events.
- How to solve for one probability when another probability and the total of the two are known.
- That a probability of 1 means certainty.
- The definition of complementary probabilties.
- How to use Rule 2 when there are several events.

- How to calculate the probability of dying when the number who died and the number remaining are known.
- What a mortality table is.
- The differences between insurance mortality tables and annuity mortality tables.
- The meaning of "conservative insurance mortality table" and "conservative annuity mortality table."
- The definition of mortality rate.
- What is meant by the symbols q_x, l_x, and d_x.
- The equations showing relationships between q_x, l_x, and d_x.
- What is meant by the symbol p_x.
- The equation for calculating p_x.
- What is meant by the symbols $_np_x$ and $_nq_x$.
- The equations for calculating $_np_x$ and $_nq_x$.
- What is meant by select and ultimate mortality tables.
- How to use a select and ultimate mortality table.

8

Life Annuities

In this Chapter, the student will begin to learn how life insurance companies make important calculations which combine the principles of compound interest (Chapters 3 through 6) and probability (Chapter 7).

It was pointed out in Chapter 7 that, in a life insurance company, *annuity contracts* represent payments being made only if a person is alive, while *life insurance contracts* represent payments being made only when a person dies. In this chapter, we will explain how to calculate the present value and the accumulated value of *life annuity payments*, that is, payments which are contingent on a designated person being alive.

An important practical application of the principles of life annuities is made with *settlement options*. Almost all life insurance policies contain *Tables of Settlement Options*. It will be explained how these tables are created and used, and the student will see that both *annuities certain* and *life annuities* are included in such tables.

In this chapter, life annuities will first be calculated using the values found in mortality tables and interest tables in order to make the principles involved as clear as possible. In actual practice, however, *commutation functions* simplify the work considerably. The student will learn what *commutation functions* are and how to use them.

Certain commutation functions are printed in the back of this book for use in working out some of the illustrations and exercises.

8.1 INTRODUCTION

Present and accumulated values for life annuities can be calculated in a manner quite similar to the method described for annuities certain in earlier chapters. In the same way, we will begin by considering the present value and accumulated value of a single payment.

PAYMENT WITH BENEFIT OF SURVIVORSHIP. Asking the question:

"How much should a person now age 35 pay for the right to receive $100 at age 60 if that person is then alive to receive it?"

is the same thing as asking:

> "What is the present value to a person now age 35 of $100 payable at age 60, calculated with the benefit of survivorship?"

The phrase *with benefit of survivorship* is used to distinguish this situation from one where only rates of interest are involved, as was the case in Chapter 5. If only rates of interest were involved in finding the present value, the answer would be

Basic equation for present value:

$$A = Sv^n$$

Substitute $100 for S, 25 for n because there are 25 years between age 35 and age 60:

$$= \$100v^{25}$$

But now the element of survivorship is also involved because the person must survive in order to receive the payment. Therefore, *with benefit of survivorship* means that payments will be made only if the designated payor or recipient is alive at the time the payment is due.

To begin solving the problem posed above, it is necessary to consult a mortality table. If Table II (male) is used, the number shown as living at each of the two ages involved is

$$l_{35} = 9,829,860$$

$$l_{60} = 8,735,824$$

This means that if there is a group of 9,829,860 people alive at age 35, then 8,735,824 of this group will still be alive at age 60. In order to solve the problem, we must assume that all of these people are individually involved, that is, each one still alive at age 60 will receive $100. We wish to know the present value of this money to these people when they are age 35 (calculated with benefit of survivorship).

Since $100 is to be paid to each of the l_{60} people, the total amount that will be paid out is

$$\$100(l_{60}) = (\$100)(8,735,824)$$

$$= \$873,582,400$$

Twenty-five years earlier, l_{35} people will pay money in. The original question now may be stated: "How much will each pay?" The total amount paid in is

$$\left(\begin{array}{c}\text{Amount Each} \\ \text{Pays In}\end{array}\right)(l_{35}) = \left(\begin{array}{c}\text{Amount Each} \\ \text{Pays In}\end{array}\right)(9,829,860)$$

$$\left(\begin{array}{c}\text{amount each} \\ \text{pays in}\end{array}\right)(l_{35}) \qquad\qquad \$100(l_{60})$$

*————————————————————————|

age 35   age 60

The money paid in will earn interest over the 25-year period. For this example, the rate will be assumed to be 6%. The basic equation for finding present value can be used to show that *all the money paid in equals the present value of all the money to be paid out 25 years later.* The amount each pays in can then be found:

$$A = Sv^n$$

Substitute $\left(\dfrac{\text{Amount Each}}{\text{Pays In}}\right)$(9,829,860) for A, \$873,582,400 for S, and the value of v^{25} at 6% from Table I:

$$\left(\dfrac{\text{Amount Each}}{\text{Pays In}}\right)(9{,}829{,}860) = (\$873{,}582{,}400)(.232999)$$

$$\left(\dfrac{\text{Amount Each}}{\text{Pays In}}\right)(9{,}829{,}860) = \$203{,}543{,}826$$

$$\left(\dfrac{\text{Amount Each}}{\text{Pays In}}\right) = \$20.71$$

This \$20.71 is less than the present value calculated at interest only. The latter would be

$$A = \$100(v^{25} \text{ at } 6\%)$$

$$= (\$100)(.232999)$$

$$= \$23.30$$

\$23.30 is the amount each person would pay in if all were to receive \$100 25 years later (dead or alive). The \$20.71 payment with benefit of survivorship is smaller because in that case only those who survive are to receive their \$100.

It can be proved that \$20.71 is the desired present value, with benefit of survivorship, at age 35 of \$100 payable at age 60 as follows:

Total amount paid in $= \$20.71(l_{35})$

$$= (\$20.71)(9{,}829{,}860)$$

$$= \$203{,}576{,}400.60$$

Total amount accumulated at 6% for 25 years

$$= (\$203{,}576{,}400.60)(1.06)^{25}$$

$$= (\$203{,}576{,}400.60)(4.291871)$$

$$= \$873{,}723{,}650.02$$

Amount payable to each survivor at age 60 (the accumulated fund divided by the number of survivors)

$$= \$873{,}723{,}650.02 \div l_{60}$$

$$= \$873{,}723{,}650.02 \div 8{,}735{,}824$$

$$= \$100.02$$

(The extra two cents is due to the fact that \$20.71 was rounded off to the nearest cent instead of using more decimal places.)

EQUATION FOR PRESENT VALUE. **The present value, with benefit of survivorship, at age 35 of $100 payable at age 60 can be written as**

$$\text{Present Value} = \$100\left(\frac{l_{60}}{l_{35}}\right)v^{25}$$

or as

$$\text{Present Value} = \frac{(\$100)(l_{60}v^{25})}{l_{35}}$$

Both these expressions permit interesting verbal interpretations. In the first, $\left(\frac{l_{60}}{l_{35}}\right)$ equals the probability that a person age 35 will live to age 60. Hence, the first expression says that the $100 is multiplied by the probability of surviving and also by the regular discounting factor for finding present values at interest. The second expression says that the $100 payable to each of l_{60} persons is discounted at interest for 25 years, and this amount is divided among the l_{35} persons to find out how much each must pay in.

In the numerical example given above, we have shown how compound interest and probability are combined in calculating contingent payments. Using more general terms, the equation is

$$\begin{pmatrix} \text{Present Value of } \$1 \\ \text{Due in } n \text{ Years to a} \\ \text{Life Now Age } x, \text{ with} \\ \text{Benefit of Survivorship} \end{pmatrix} = \$1\left(\frac{l_{x+n}v^{n}}{l_{x}}\right)$$

To Illustrate—Using Table III and 3% interest, calculate the present value at age 20 of $400 due in 15 years if the person is still alive; then determine the present value if the same amount is due in 25 years.

Solution—

Due in 15 Years

Basic equation:

$$\text{Present Value} = \$400\left(\frac{l_{x+n}v^{n}}{l_{x}}\right)$$

Substitute 20 for x (the evaluation age), 15 for n (the number of years):

$$= \$400\left(\frac{l_{35}v^{15}}{l_{20}}\right)$$

Substitute the values for the l's from Table III, for v^{15} from Table I (3%):

$$= \$400\left[\frac{(9,373,807)(.641862)}{9,664,994}\right]$$

$$= \$400\left(\frac{6,016,691}{9,664,994}\right)$$

$$= \$249.01$$

Due in 25 Years

Basic equation:

$$\text{Present Value} = \$400\left(\frac{l_{x+n}v^n}{l_x}\right)$$

Substitute 20 for x, 25 for n:

$$= \$400\left(\frac{l_{45}v^{25}}{l_{20}}\right)$$

Substitute the values for the l's from Table III, for v^{25} from Table I (3%):

$$= \$400\left[\frac{(9{,}048{,}999)(.477606)}{9{,}664{,}994}\right]$$

$$= \$400\left(\frac{4{,}321{,}856}{9{,}664{,}994}\right)$$

$$= \$178.87$$

As the number of years increases before the payment is to be made, the present value decreases. This is true because, first, there is a smaller probability that it will have to be paid and because, second, there are more years in which to earn interest.

CHOICE OF TABLES. It should also be understood that the present value of such contingent payments depends on the particular mortality table and interest rate used in the calculation. In general, mortality tables which show higher mortality rates will result in lower present values of payments which are contingent upon a person being alive (because fewer persons will be assumed to be alive to receive the payment). Similarly, the use of a higher rate of interest will result in lower present values, in the same manner as for payments certain.

Before making important calculations in actual practice, the actuary must plan carefully what mortality tables and interest rates to use. For example, in calculating an amount which the insurance company would charge if it were actually going to make contingent payments, a conservative approach would be desirable. This would call for use of fairly low mortality rates and low interest rates. On the other hand, in calculations where the insurance company would be receiving contingent payments, conservatism would indicate the opposite (higher mortality and interest rates). In forecasting for the insurance company's management the results actually expected from such arrangements, it would be desirable to use a mortality table and interest rate which the actuary feels will most nearly represent the company's own experience in the future. Mortality tables and interest rates are often imposed by governmental bodies in connection with certain calculations. Most commonly, reserves for annuity and insurance contracts (to be described in Chapters 11 and 12) must be calculated using certain mortality tables, plus a rate of interest no higher than that prescribed by law. The particular mortality tables and interest rates shown in the examples in this book are intended to be typical of those used in many life insurance companies today.

8.2 PRESENT VALUE OF A LIFE ANNUITY

CALCULATION OF PRESENT VALUES. As stated earlier, an annuity is a series of payments, and the present value of the annuity is the total of the present values of each of the individual payments. To find the present value of a series of payments where each payment is made only if the designated payor or recipient is alive to pay or receive it, we can now use the method explained above for calculating the present value of a single payment.

For example, the present value at age 25 of a life annuity of $100 per year for three years (with the first payment due at age 26) can be represented by the following line diagram:

The present value of each of the three payments can be calculated individually, as follows:

The Payment Due at Age 26

Basic equation:

$$\text{Present Value} = \$100\left(\frac{l_{x+n}v^{n}}{l_{x}}\right)$$

Substitute 25 for x, 1 for n (exponent 1 need not be written):

$$= \$100\left(\frac{l_{26}v}{l_{25}}\right)$$

The Payment Due at Age 27

Basic equation:

$$\text{Present Value} = \$100\left(\frac{l_{x+n}v^{n}}{l_{x}}\right)$$

Substitute 25 for x, 2 for n:

$$= \$100\left(\frac{l_{27}v^{2}}{l_{25}}\right)$$

The Payment Due at Age 28

Basic equation:

$$\text{Present Value} = \$100\left(\frac{l_{x+n}v^{n}}{l_{x}}\right)$$

Substitute 25 for x, 3 for n:

$$= \$100\left(\frac{l_{28}v^3}{l_{25}}\right)$$

The present value at age 25 of this annuity is the total of these three expressions. The common multiplier (\$100) can be factored out. The fractions to be added together have a common denominator (l_{25}). Hence, the present value of the annuity can be expressed as

$$\text{Present Value} = \$100\left(\frac{l_{26}v + l_{27}v^2 + l_{28}v^3}{l_{25}}\right)$$

The numerator of this expression represents the total to be paid out to the survivors at each age, with each such amount being discounted at interest to the evaluation date. The denominator represents the number of persons alive on the evaluation date, among whom this total present value to be paid in must be allocated.

If, for example, Table III and 3% interest were used, the present value of the annuity would be calculated as follows:

From above:

$$\text{Present Value} = \$100\left(\frac{l_{26}v + l_{27}v^2 + l_{28}v^3}{l_{25}}\right)$$

Substitute the values for the l's from Table III, for the v's from Table I (3%):

$$= \$100\left[\frac{\begin{array}{l}(9,557,155)(.970874)\\+ (9,538,423)(.942596)\\+ (9,519,442)(.915142)\end{array}}{9,575,636}\right]$$

$$= \$100\left(\frac{9,278,793 + 8,990,879 + 8,711,641}{9,575,636}\right)$$

$$= \$100\left(\frac{26,981,313}{9,575,636}\right)$$

$$= \$281.77$$

It can be verified that the payment of \$281.77 by each of the persons age 25 will provide \$100 to each of the survivors at ages 26, 27, and 28, as follows (using the 1958 C.S.O. Table at 3%):

If each of the l_{25}, or 9,575,636, persons contributes \$281.77, a fund is provided of

$$(\$281.77)(9,575,636) = \$2,698,126,955.72$$

During one year it will earn interest of

$$(\$2,698,126,955.72)(.03) = \$80,943,808.67$$

The total amount of money in the fund at the end of one year is then

$$\$2,698,126,955.72 + \$80,943,808.67 = \$2,779,070,764.39$$

Payments of $100 to each of the l_{26}, or 9,557,155, survivors will require

$$(\$100)(9,557,155) = \$955,715,500$$

This leaves a balance in the fund at the end of one year of

$$\$2,779,070,764.39 - \$955,715,500 = \$1,823,355,264.39$$

The continued progress of the fund can be traced in Chart 8–1.

CHART 8–1

(1) Year	(2) Fund at Beginning of Year	(3) Interest for One Year (Col. 2 × .03)	(4) Total Fund at End of Year before Annuity Payments Are Made (Col. 2 + Col. 3)	(5) Annuity Payments to Survivors	(6) Balance in Fund after Annuity Payments Are Made (Col. 4 − Col. 5)
1	$2,698,126,955.72	$80,943,808.67	$2,779,070,764.39	$955,715,500.00	$1,823,355,264.39
2	1,823,355,264.39	54,700,657.93	1,878,055,922.32	953,842,300.00	924,213,622.32
3	924,213,622.32	27,726,408.67	951,940,030.99	951,944,200.00	(−4,169.01)

The shortage of $4,169.01 represents less than one twentieth of a cent for each of the survivors and results from rounding off the individual contribution, $281.77, to two decimal places. If all calculations had been carried to more decimal places, the balance in the fund at the end of the third year would have been even closer to zero.

To Illustrate—Using Table II (female) and 6% interest, calculate the present value at age 40 of a life annuity of $25 per year for four years, first payment due at age 41.

Solution—The line diagram for this life annuity appears as follows:

The expression for the present value will have a numerator representing the total to be paid out to the survivors at each age, with each such amount being discounted at interest to the evaluation date:

$$\$25(l_{41}v + l_{42}v^2 + l_{43}v^3 + l_{44}v^4)$$

The denominator is the number living on the evaluation date (l_{40}):

Basic equation:

$$\text{Present Value} = \$25\left(\frac{l_{41}v + l_{42}v^2 + l_{43}v^3 + l_{44}v^4}{l_{40}}\right)$$

Substitute values for the l's from Table II (female), for the v's from Table I (6%):

$$= \$25\left[\frac{\begin{array}{l}(9,865,399)(.943396)\\ + (9,855,406)(.889996)\\ + (9,844,624)(.839619)\\ + (9,832,948)(.792094)\end{array}}{9,874,662}\right]$$

$$= \$25\left(\frac{9,306,978 + 8,771,272 + 8,265,733 + 7,788,619}{9,874,662}\right)$$

$$= \$86.41$$

TEMPORARY LIFE ANNUITIES. Life annuities may be either temporary life annuities or whole life annuities. Both kinds have many practical uses in actuarial calculations, as this book will show. In a *temporary life annuity*, each payment is made only if a designated person is then alive, but the payments are limited to a fixed number of years. In a *whole life annuity*, the payments continue for the entire lifetime of a designated person.

The three-year and four-year life annuities calculated above are examples of temporary life annuities. Each payment is made only if a designated person is then alive, but the number of such payments is limited to a definite number. The first payment is made one period after the date on which the present value is calculated.

There are also temporary life annuities in which the first payment is made at the beginning, that is, on the same date on which the present value is calculated. These are known as *temporary life annuities due*. The use of the word "due" is comparable to its use in annuities certain. This type of annuity is important in life insurance calculations, because premiums payable for a life insurance policy represent an annuity due, as will be explained in Chapter 10.

The line diagrams of two five-payment life annuities, one immediate and one due, look like this:

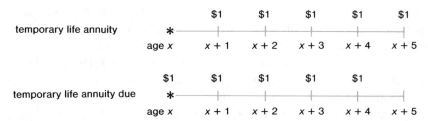

To Illustrate—Using Table III and 3% interest, calculate the present value at age 25 of a three-year life annuity due of $100 per year.

Solution—The line diagram for this life annuity due appears as follows:

The expression for the present value will have a numerator representing the total to be paid out to the survivors at each age, with each such amount being discounted at interest to the evaluation date. The first payment is due upon the evaluation date. Hence, its present value is simply $100($l_{25}$)$; it is not multiplied by any discounting factor. The denominator is the number living at the evaluation date:

Basic equation:

$$\text{Present Value} = \$100 \left(\frac{l_{25} + l_{26}v + l_{27}v^2}{l_{25}} \right)$$

Substitute values of the l's from Table III, for the v's from Table I (3%):

$$= \$100 \left[\frac{\begin{array}{l} (9{,}575{,}636) \\ + (9{,}557{,}155)(.970874) \\ + (9{,}538{,}423)(.942596) \end{array}}{9{,}575{,}636} \right]$$

$$= \$100 \left(\frac{9{,}575{,}636 + 9{,}278{,}793 + 8{,}990{,}879}{9{,}575{,}636} \right)$$

$$= \$290.79$$

The present value of a three-year life annuity identical to this one, except that the first payment was made at the end of the first year, was calculated earlier in this section to be $281.77. This value is less than the present value of the life annuity due ($290.79), because each payment in the annuity immediate is paid one year later than its counterpart in the annuity due. Hence, there is a smaller probability that it will have to be paid, and there is a greater number of years in which interest is earned.

WHOLE LIFE ANNUITIES. Life annuities wherein the payments continue for the entire lifetime of a designated person are known as *whole life annuities*. Without the word "due," this name implies that the first payment is made one period after the date on which the present value is calculated. Whole life annuities in which the first payment is made at the beginning, that is, on the same date on which the present value is calculated, are known as *whole life anuities due*. As mentioned above, premiums payable for a life insurance policy are an important example of this.

The present value of whole life annuities is calculated by exactly the same procedure as that shown above for temporary life annuities. In the case of whole life annuities, the payments are included to the end of the mortality table. It is thus assumed that all will die before a certain age; therefore, the number of payments to include in the calculation is actually a limited number, just as for temporary life annuities.

When calculating the value of benefits extending for the whole of life in this book, we will generally use extremely high ages as the ages at which such benefits begin. This may be unrealistic, but it serves better to show the principles involved, because the calculations can be kept shorter.

To Illustrate—Using Table II (female) and 6% interest, calculate the present value at age 112 of a whole life annuity of $50 per year.

Solution—The first payment is due one year after age 112 (at age 113). Payments will continue for the person's entire lifetime. However, Table II assumes that no one lives beyond age 115. Hence, the line diagram for this annuity appears as follows:

$$
\begin{array}{ccccc}
 & \$50 & \$50 & \$50 \\
* & \vdash & \vdash & \vdash \\
\text{age 112} & 113 & 114 & 115 \\
 & 1 & 2 & 3 \text{ years}
\end{array}
$$

The expression for the present value will have a numerator representing the total to be paid out to the survivors at each age, with each such amount being discounted at interest to the evaluation date. The denominator is the number living on the evaluation date:

Basic equation:

$$\text{Present Value} = \$50 \left(\frac{l_{113}v + l_{114}v^2 + l_{115}v^3}{l_{112}} \right)$$

Substitute the values for the *l*'s from Table II (female), for the *v*'s from Table I (6%):

$$= \$50 \left[\frac{\begin{array}{c} (83)(.943396) \\ + (21)(.889996) \\ + (4)(.839619) \end{array}}{269} \right]$$

$$= \$50 \left(\frac{78.3019 + 18.6899 + 3.3585}{269} \right)$$

$$= \$18.65$$

There is no rule for the number of decimal places to keep in rounding the answers obtained by the actual multiplications in the numerator. It is desirable to keep only a sufficient number of digits to have a meaningful answer. In the above illustration, each multiplication answer was rounded to four decimal places. In previous illustrations (involving much larger numbers for the *l*'s), each multiplication answer was rounded to the nearest whole number.

The present value of the annuity calculated in the above illustration ($18.65) is less than the amount of one year's payment ($50). This is a phenomenon encountered when only the very high ages are being used. This illustration indicates that a considerable portion of those paying for the annuity at age 112 will die before receiving even one payment.

The calculation of the present value of whole life annuities at the younger ages would become very laborious if calculations were made manually and the above procedure were followed. Therefore, in actual practice this calculation is done by using *commutation functions*, explained in Section 8.5.

DEFERRED LIFE ANNUITIES. A *deferred life annuity* is a life annuity in which the first payment is postponed one or more periods. Once payments commence, they may continue for the remaining lifetime of the designated person, or they may be limited to a specified number of payments. In a life insurance company, this type is particularly important in connection with *settlement options*, which will be explained in Section 8.4.

As an example of a deferred life annuity, consider the problem of finding the present value at age 65 of a whole life annuity of $100 per year, the first payment being made 44 years after the evaluation date. This means that the first payment is due at age $65 + 44 =$ age 109 (if the person is then alive). Using Table II, the final payment would be made at age 115, because this table shows no one living after that age:

$$
\begin{array}{ccccccc}
\$100 & \$100 & \$100 & \$100 & \$100 & \$100 & \$100 \\
\end{array}
$$

*							
age 65 · · · · · · · ·109	110	111	112	113	114	115
· · · · · · · · 44	45	46	47	48	49	50 years

The total amount to be paid out to the survivors at age 109 would be

$$\$100\,(l_{109})$$

The present value is calculated as of a time 44 years prior to the date of this payment. Hence, the present value is this total multiplied by the factor for finding present value:

$$\$100\,(l_{109}\,v^{44})$$

The present value of each of the payments is similarly calculated, and the total is divided by the number living at age 65 to derive the amount each must pay in. The expression for the present value of this deferred life annuity is

$$\$100\left(\frac{l_{109}v^{44} + l_{110}v^{45} + l_{111}v^{46} + l_{112}v^{47} + l_{113}v^{48} + l_{114}v^{49} + l_{115}v^{50}}{l_{65}}\right)$$

To Illustrate—Using Table II (male) and 6% interest, calculate the present value at age 40 of a temporary life annuity of $1,500 per year, first payment at age 50 and the last payment at age 53.

Solution—The line diagram for this life annuity appears as follows:

$$
\begin{array}{cccc}
\$1,500 & \$1,500 & \$1,500 & \$1,500 \\
\end{array}
$$

*				
age 40 · · · · · · · · · 50	51	52	53
· · · · · · · · · · 10	11	12	13 years

The amount payable at age 50 is due ten years after the evaluation date; the amount payable at age 51 is due 11 years after the evaluation date; etc. Following the above procedure of expressing the present value as the total of the present values of the individual payments:

Basic equation:

$$\text{Present Value} = \$1{,}500\left(\frac{l_{50}v^{10} + l_{51}v^{11} + l_{52}v^{12} + l_{53}v^{13}}{l_{40}}\right)$$

Substitute the value for the l's from Table II (male), for the v's from Table I (6%):

$$= \$1{,}500\left[\frac{\begin{array}{l}(9{,}484{,}249)(.558395)\\ + (9{,}434{,}125)(.526788)\\ + (9{,}378{,}841)(.496969)\\ + (9{,}318{,}244)(.468839)\end{array}}{9{,}765{,}867}\right]$$

$$= \$1{,}500\left(\frac{5{,}295{,}957 + 4{,}969{,}784 + 4{,}660{,}993 + 4{,}368{,}756}{9{,}765{,}867}\right)$$

$$= \$2{,}963.71$$

TWO RATES OF INTEREST. Sometimes it is desirable to discount future contingent payments using a currently-earned interest rate for only a limited number of years in the calculation. Then, because of the uncertainty of rates to be earned in the future, a more conservative rate is used for the later years. If the interest rate to be used changes over the period that life annuity payments are to be made, then the payments can be discounted in the manner shown in Section 5.5, where payments certain were shown discounted using dual interest rates.

For example, consider a four-year life annuity of $1 per year at age 60, where the interest rate is assumed to be 6% for the first two years and 4% for the final two years. The line diagram appears as follows:

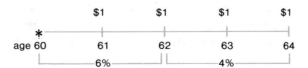

The present value of the payments due at ages 61 and 62 is found by discounting at 6%, since the interest rate is 6% during the entire period (from evaluation date to payment date):

$$l_{61}(v \text{ at } 6\%) + l_{62}(v^2 \text{ at } 6\%)$$

The payment due at age 63 is discounted for one year at 4% (which produces its present value at the beginning of the 4% period), and this result is then discounted for two years at 6% (which produces its present value at the evaluation date):

$$l_{63}(v \text{ at } 4\%)(v^2 \text{ at } 6\%)$$

Similarly, the payment due at age 64 is discounted for two years at 4% and for two years at 6%:

$$l_{64}(v^2 \text{ at } 4\%)(v^2 \text{ at } 6\%)$$

The total present value is then divided by the number living on the evaluation date:

$$\text{Present Value} = \frac{l_{61}(v \text{ at } 6\%) + l_{62}(v^2 \text{ at } 6\%) + l_{63}(v \text{ at } 4\%)(v^2 \text{ at } 6\%) + l_{64}(v^2 \text{ at } 4\%)(v^2 \text{ at } 6\%)}{l_{60}}$$

If Table II (female) were used, this present value would be $3.45.

RELATIONSHIPS AMONG LIFE ANNUITIES. There are certain relationships among types of annuities which are important. The use of these relationships helps to simplify many of the calculations made by the actuarial department.

The first of these is the relationship between a *whole life annuity* and a *whole life annuity due*. The following line diagrams show a whole life annuity and a whole life annuity due, both evaluated at age x:

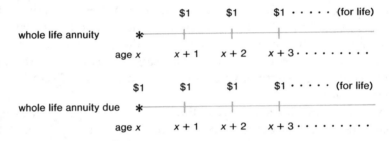

The diagrams show that the only difference between the two types is the one payment at age x in the second annuity. This illustrates that the *present value of the whole life annuity due is equal to the present value of the whole life annuity plus the amount of one payment*. In equation form, this is

$$\left(\begin{array}{c}\text{Present Value at Age } x \\ \text{of Whole Life Annuity Due}\end{array}\right) = \left(\begin{array}{c}\text{Present Value at Age } x \\ \text{of Whole Life Annuity}\end{array}\right) + 1$$

For a payment of $10 per year, the equation would be

$$\$10\left(\begin{array}{c}\text{Present Value at Age } x \\ \text{of Whole Life Annuity Due}\end{array}\right) = \$10\left[\left(\begin{array}{c}\text{Present Value at Age } x \\ \text{of Whole Life Annuity}\end{array}\right) + 1\right]$$

$$= \$10\left(\begin{array}{c}\text{Present Value at Age } x \\ \text{of Whole Life Annuity}\end{array}\right) + \$10$$

To Illustrate—Using Table II (female) and 6% interest, calculate the present value at age 112 of a whole life annuity due of $50 per year.

Solution—The line diagram for this life annuity due appears as follows (with 115 being the highest age in this particular mortality table):

```
        $50         $50         $50         $50
         *           +           +           +
      age 112       113         114         115
                     1           2         3 years
```

In the illustration on page 165, the present value at age 112 of a whole life annuity of $50 per year (first payment made one year after age 112) was calculated to be $18.65. Hence, the above relationship can be used, with $18.65 substituted in the calculation.

Basic equation:

$$\$50\left(\begin{array}{c}\text{Present Value at Age 112}\\\text{of Whole Life Annuity Due}\end{array}\right) = \$50\left[\left(\begin{array}{c}\text{Present Value at Age 112}\\\text{of Whole Life Annuity}\end{array}\right) + 1\right]$$

$$= \$50\left(\begin{array}{c}\text{Present Value at Age 112}\\\text{of Whole Life Annuity}\end{array}\right) + \$50$$

$$= \$18.65 + \$50$$

$$= \$68.65$$

This desired present value could also have been calculated by using the other procedure, as follows (remembering that since the first payment is due on the evaluation date, it is not multiplied by any present value factor):

Basic equation:

$$\text{Present Value} = \$50\left(\frac{l_{112} + l_{113}v + l_{114}v^2 + l_{115}v^3}{l_{112}}\right)$$

Substitute the values for the l's from Table II (female), for the v's from Table I (6%):

$$= \$50\left[\frac{\begin{array}{c}(269)\\+ (83)(.943396)\\+ (21)(.889996)\\+ (4)(.839619)\end{array}}{269}\right]$$

$$= \$50\left(\frac{269.0000 + 78.3019 + 18.6899 + 3.3585}{269}\right)$$

$$= \$68.65$$

This answer agrees with that obtained by using the relationship between a whole life annuity and a whole life annuity due.

The second important relationship is that between *temporary life annuities* and *temporary life annuities due*. The following line diagrams show, as a specific example, a $500 19-year life annuity and a $500 20-year life annuity due, both evaluated at age 30:

The only difference between them is the one payment of $500 on the evaluation date. This example illustrates that *the present value of a temporary life annuity due is equal to the present value of a temporary life annuity having one fewer total periods plus the amount of one payment.* In equation form, this is

$$\left(\begin{array}{c} \text{Present Value at Age } x \\ \text{of } n\text{-Year Life Annuity Due} \end{array} \right) = \left(\begin{array}{c} \text{Present Value at Age } x \\ \text{of } (n-1)\text{-Year Life Annuity} \end{array} \right) + 1$$

To Illustrate—Using Table III and 3% interest, calculate the present value at age 25 of a four-year life annuity due of $100 per year.

Solution—The line diagram for this temporary life annuity due appears as follows:

In the example on pages 160–162, the present value at age 25 of a three-year life annuity of $100 per year (first payment due one year following age 25) was calculated to be $281.77. Using the above relationship and substituting $281.77, gives

Basic equation:

$$\$100 \left(\begin{array}{c} \text{Present Value at Age } x \\ \text{of } n\text{-Year Life Annuity Due} \end{array} \right) = \$100 \left[\left(\begin{array}{c} \text{Present Value at Age } x \\ \text{of } (n-1)\text{-Year Life Annuity} \end{array} \right) + 1 \right]$$

Substitute 25 for x, 4 for n:

$$\$100 \left(\begin{array}{c} \text{Present Value at Age 25} \\ \text{of 4-Year Life Annuity Due} \end{array} \right) = \$100 \left[\left(\begin{array}{c} \text{Present Value at Age 25} \\ \text{of 3-Year Life Annuity} \end{array} \right) + 1 \right]$$

$$= \$100 \left(\begin{array}{c} \text{Present Value at Age 25} \\ \text{of 3-Year Life Annuity} \end{array} \right) + \$100$$

Substitute present value calculated above:

$$= \$281.77 + \$100$$

$$= \$381.77$$

This desired present value could have been calculated by using the other procedure, as follows:

Basic equation:

$$\text{Present Value} = \$100 \left(\frac{l_{25} + l_{26}v + l_{27}v^2 + l_{28}v^3}{l_{25}} \right)$$

Substitute the values for the l's from Table III, for the v's from Table I (3%):

$$= \$100 \left[\frac{\begin{array}{l} (9,575,636) \\ + (9,557,155)(.970874) \\ + (9,538,423)(.942596) \\ + (9,519,442)(.915142) \end{array}}{9,575,636} \right]$$

$$= \$100 \left(\frac{9,575,636 + 9,278,793 + 8,990,879 + 8,711,641}{9,575,636} \right)$$

$$= \$381.77$$

This answer agrees with that obtained by using the relationship between an n-year life annuity due and an $(n - 1)$-year life annuity.

The third important relationship involves whole life annuities, temporary life annuities, and deferred life annuities. This relationship is as follows: *A temporary life annuity plus a deferred life annuity (deferred the same number of years for which the temporary annuity runs) equals a whole life annuity.* The reasoning here is the same as that for annuities certain in Section 6.1 (second method). In equation form, this is

$$\left(\begin{array}{c} \text{Present Value} \\ \text{at Age } x \text{ of} \\ n\text{-Year Temporary} \\ \text{Life Annuity} \end{array} \right) + \left(\begin{array}{c} \text{Present Value} \\ \text{at Age } x \text{ of} \\ \text{Life Annuity} \\ \text{Deferred } n \text{ Years} \end{array} \right) = \left(\begin{array}{c} \text{Present Value} \\ \text{at Age } x \text{ of} \\ \text{Whole Life} \\ \text{Annuity} \end{array} \right)$$

For example, a five-year temporary life annuity plus a life annuity deferred five years equals a whole life annuity. This is shown in the following line diagram:

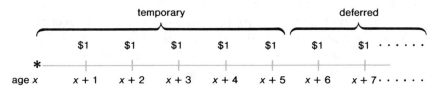

It is useful to know this relationship because published tables of life annuity values usually show only whole life annuities and temporary life annuities. The values of deferred life annuities must be obtained by some other means.

To Illustrate—If a published table gives the present value of a whole life annuity of $1 per year to a person age 40 as $18.80, and the present value of a 15-year temporary life annuity of $1 per year to a person age 40 as $12.84, find the present value of a $100 life annuity deferred for 15 years to a person age 40.

Solution—Using the present value relationship above:

Basic equation:

$$\$100\left(\begin{array}{c} n\text{-Year} \\ \text{Temporary} \end{array}\right) + \$100\left(\begin{array}{c} \text{Deferred} \\ n \text{ Years} \end{array}\right) = \$100(\text{Whole Life})$$

Substitute 15 for n:

$$\$100\left(\begin{array}{c} 15\text{-Year} \\ \text{Temporary} \end{array}\right) + 100\left(\begin{array}{c} \text{Deferred} \\ 15 \text{ Years} \end{array}\right) = \$100(\text{Whole Life})$$

Substitute the present values given:

$$\$100(12.84) + \$100\left(\begin{array}{c} \text{Deferred} \\ 15 \text{ Years} \end{array}\right) = \$100(18.80)$$

Substract $100(12.84) from each side:

$$\$100\left(\begin{array}{c} \text{Deferred} \\ 15 \text{ Years} \end{array}\right) = \$100(18.80) - \$100(12.84)$$

$$= \$100(18.80 - 12.84)$$

$$= \$100(5.96)$$

$$= \$596$$

PRACTICAL USES. Both life annuities (first payment at the end of one period) and life annuities due (first payment at the beginning of the first period) have considerable practical use in life insurance company operations. For example, annuities are widely sold for which the buyer pays a lump sum to the insurance company, and the company then pays back a periodic income as long as the buyer lives. Here, the first payment is usually made to the buyer at the end of the first period. Hence, this is an example of a life annuity. In fact, such contracts are generally named *Immediate Annuities* in the company's rate manuals, as well as on the face of the contract itself. The actual amount which the buyer pays for such a contract is calculated by the company's actuary as being equal to the present value of the payments to be made (with benefit of survivorship), plus amounts needed to cover certain of the company's expenses. In calculating the present value of the annuity, the actuary uses mortality and interest rates which can reasonably be expected to be actually experienced over the years ahead.

Life annuity contracts are also sold by life insurance companies for which the buyer pays either a lump sum or a series of payments, but then actual annuity payments back to the purchaser do not begin until some time in the future. In the meantime, the amounts paid to the company by the purchaser are generally accumulated (after first subtracting amounts needed to cover certain of the company's expenses). Such an accumulation is made with interest, but not with benefit of survivorship. At the time the company is to begin making payments back to the purchaser, the amount that has accumulated is used to provide life annuity payments, that is, the present value of the life annuity at that time equals the amount that has accumulated. Such contracts are generally called *Retirement Annuities* or *Deferred Annuities*. However, they should not be confused with the deferred annuities described in Section 6.1 (which involve interest but not benefit of survivorship), nor with the deferred life annuities described earlier in Section 8.2 (which involve benefit of survivorship throughout, even during the deferred period).

A common example of a life annuity due would be the payment of premiums on a life insurance policy. They constitute a life annuity due because money changes hands only if a designated person is alive at the time each premium is payable, this premium being payable at the beginning of each period. These calculations will be thoroughly explained in Chapter 10.

EXERCISES, SET 17

1. Which would be expected to have a larger present value (if the same interest rate were used): $100 to be paid 15 years from now certain, or $100 to be paid 15 years from now with benefit of survivorship?

2. Write an expression (using symbols) for the present value at age ten of $250 due in 25 years with benefit of survivorship.

3. Write an expression (using symbols) for the present value at age 65 of a four-year temporary life annuity due of $50 per year.

4. Write an expression (using symbols) for the present value at age 20 of a deferred life annuity having three payments of $750 each, the first one of which is payable at age 42.

5. Write an expression (using symbols) for the present value at age 96 of a whole life annuity of $1,000 per year, assuming the mortality table which will be used is the 1958 C.S.O. Table.

(Use Table II, male, and 6% interest for exercises 6 and 7.)

6. Calculate the present value at age 70 of a $40 payment due at age 80 with benefit of survivorship.

7. Calculate the amount that a person age 22 should pay for the right to receive $10 per year, first payment due at age 30 and last payment due at age 32.

8. Using Table II (female) and 6% interest, calculate the present value at age 106 of a deferred life annuity of $1,000 per year, first payment at age 113 (payments continue for life).

9. Using Table III and 3% interest, calculate the present value at age 97 of a whole life annuity due of $100 per year.

10. Calculate the present value at age 40 of a whole life annuity, deferred for ten years, of $15 per year, using the following present value factors for 1 per year:

   Present Value at Age 40 of Whole Life Annuity = 18.713
   Present Value at Age 40 of 10-year Life Annuity = 8.509

11. If the present value of a whole life annuity of $20 per year is $461.12, what is the present value (at the same age) of a whole life annuity due of $20 per year?

12. The present value of a three-year temporary life annuity of $100 per year for a person now age 25 is represented by the expression

   (1) $\$100\left(\dfrac{l_{26} + l_{27}v + l_{28}v^2}{l_{25}}\right)$

   (3) $\$100\left(\dfrac{l_{25} + l_{26}v + l_{27}v^2}{l_{25}}\right)$

   (2) $\$100\left(\dfrac{l_{25}v + l_{26}v^2 + l_{27}v^3}{l_{25}}\right)$

   (4) $\$100\left(\dfrac{l_{26}v + l_{27}v^2 + l_{28}v^3}{l_{25}}\right)$

8.3 ACCUMULATED VALUE OF LIFE ANNUITIES

In insurance practice the accumulated value of a life annuity is much less frequently used than the present value. However, accumulated value is a useful tool in the calculation of reserves, as will be seen later in Chapter 11.

The present value of a life annuity is, in general, the amount which must be paid at the beginning to provide future payments, with benefit of survivorship. On the other hand, the accumulated value of a life annuity refers, in general, to the total amount payable at the end to a surviving person (that is, the accumulated value of past payments, which have been made with benefit of survivorship). In actual practice, such an arrangement is generally illegal. However, as stated above, we will see that the concept is important as being a part of the calculation of reserves.

The procedure used in calculating accumulated values is similar to the one discussed for present values. To begin an illustration by accumulating a single payment, the question can be asked:

If a person deposited $1 at age 35, how much money would that person receive at age 60 if that person must be alive to receive it?

If Table II (male) is used, the number shown as living at each of the two ages is

   $l_{35} = 9,829,860$

   $l_{60} = 8,735,824$

Since $1 is to be paid in by each of the l_{35} people, the total amount that will be paid in altogether is

   $\$1(l_{35}) = \$9,829,860$

Twenty-five years later, l_{60} people will receive the money. The original question now may be stated: "How much will each receive?" The money paid in will earn interest over the 25-year period. If the rate of interest is 6%, then the original $9,829,860 will accumulate as follows:

Basic equation for accumulating:

$$S = A(1 + i)^n$$

Substitute $9,829,860 for A, .06 for i, 25 for n:

$$= \$9,829,860(1.06)^{25}$$

Substitute the value of $(1.06)^{25}$ from Table I:

$$= (\$9,829,860)(4.291871)$$

$$= \$42,188,491.07$$

This sum is then divided among the l_{60} people:

$$\frac{\$42,188,491.07}{l_{60}} = \frac{\$42,188,491.07}{8,735,824}$$

$$= \$4.83$$

This $4.83 is greater than the accumulated value calculated at interest only. The latter would be

$$S = \$1(1.06)^{25}$$

$$= \$1(4.291871)$$

$$= \$4.29$$

$4.29 is the amount each person would receive at the end of the 25 years if all those who contributed originally were to share at the end. The $4.83 payment with benefit of survivorship is larger because in that case only those who survive are to share in the accumulation.

EQUATION FOR ACCUMULATED VALUE. In general terms, if x is the age when the deposit is made, and n is the number of years elapsed until the payment is returned to the survivors, then each survivor will receive

$$\$1\left[\frac{l_x(1 + i)^n}{l_{x+n}}\right]$$

This expression states that $1 deposited by each of the l_x persons accumulates at interest for n years, and the total is then divided among the l_{x+n} persons still alive. In equation form, this is written:

$$\begin{pmatrix}\text{Accumulated Value of \$1} \\ \text{at End of } n \text{ Years to a} \\ \text{Life Age } x \text{ at the Beginning} \\ \text{with Benefit of Survivorship}\end{pmatrix} = \$1\left[\frac{l_x(1 + i)^n}{l_{x+n}}\right]$$

This accumulation factor modifies the $(1 + i)^n$ used in Chapter 3 to provide for the fact that now *contingent* payments are being considered.

The respective factors for calculating the present value and accumulated value of a single payment, both with interest only and with benefit of survivorship, are summarized in Chart 8–2. In each case, n is the number of years involved, x is the age at the beginning of the time, and $x + n$ is the age at the end of the time:

CHART 8-2

	With Interest Only	With Benefit of Survivorship
Present Value Factor	$\dfrac{1}{(1 + i)^n}$ or v^n	$\left(\dfrac{l_{x+n}}{l_x}\right)\left[\dfrac{1}{(1 + i)^n}\right]$ or $\dfrac{l_{x+n}v^n}{l_x}$
Accumulation Factor	$(1 + i)^n$	$\dfrac{l_x(1 + i)^n}{l_{x+n}}$

The present value factor and the accumulation factor are the inverse of each other (that is, numerator and denominator are switched). This is true when dealing with benefit of survivorship or when dealing with interest only.

A SERIES OF PAYMENTS. The accumulated value of a series of payments can be determined to totaling the accumulated values of each of the individual payments. For example, suppose it is desired to know the accumulated value, with benefit of survivorship, at age 65 for a three-year annuity due of $1. This means that $1 was deposited at the beginning of each of the last three years, and the accumulation will be paid to a designated person (at age 65) only if that person is alive to receive it. If that person is alive, how much will he or she receive? The deposits were made at ages 62, 63, and 64:

```
      $1          $1          $1
   ├───────────┼───────────┼───────────*
 age 62        63          64          65
```

The accumulated value of each of the three payments can be calculated individually, as follows:

The Payment Due at Age 62

Basic equation:

$$\text{Accumulated Value} = \$1\left[\frac{l_x(1 + i)^n}{l_{x+n}}\right]$$

Substitute 62 for x (that is, the age at the beginning), 3 for n (that is, number of years), and .06 for i:

$$= \$1\left[\frac{l_{62}(1.06)^3}{l_{65}}\right]$$

The Payment Due at Age 63

Basic equation:

$$\text{Accumulated Value} = \$1\left[\frac{l_x(1+i)^n}{l_{x+n}}\right]$$

Substitute 63 for x, 2 for n, and .06 for i:

$$= \$1\left[\frac{l_{63}(1.06)^2}{l_{65}}\right]$$

The Payment Due at Age 64

Basic equation:

$$\text{Accumulated Value} = \$1\left[\frac{l_x(1+i)^n}{l_{x+n}}\right]$$

Substitute 64 for x, 1 for n, and .06 for i:

$$= \$1\left[\frac{l_{64}(1.06)}{l_{65}}\right]$$

The accumulated value at age 65 of this annuity is the total of the three above expressions. The common multiplier, $1, can be factored out. The fractions to be added together have a common denominator, l_{65}. Hence, the accumulated value of the annuity can be expressed as

$$\text{Accumulated Value} = \$1\left[\frac{l_{62}(1.06)^3 + l_{63}(1.06)^2 + l_{64}(1.06)}{l_{65}}\right]$$

The numerator of this expression represents the total amount paid in by the survivors at each age, with each such amount being accumulated at interest to the evaluation date. The denominator represents the number of persons still alive on the evaluation date, among whom this total accumulated value will be allocated to be paid out.

To Illustrate—Using Table II (female) and 6% interest, calculate the accumulated value at age 40 of a life annuity of $15 per year for four years, first payment due at age 36.

Solution—The line diagram for this life annuity appears as follows:

The expression for the accumulated value will have a numerator representing the total amount paid in by the survivors at each age, with each such amount being accumulated at interest to the evaluation date:

$$\$15[l_{36}(1+i)^4 + l_{37}(1+i)^3 + l_{38}(1+i)^2 + l_{39}(1+i)]$$

The denominator is the number living on the evaluation date (l_{40}).

Basic equation:

$$\text{Accumulated Value} = \$15\left[\frac{l_{36}(1+i)^4 + l_{37}(1+i)^3 + l_{38}(1+i)^2 + l_{39}(1+i)}{l_{40}}\right]$$

Substitute values for the l's from Table II (female), for the $(1 + i)$'s from Table I (6%):

$$= \$15\left[\frac{\begin{array}{l}(9,905,571)(1.262477)\\+ (9,898,657)(1.191016)\\+ (9,891,233)(1.123600)\\+ (9,883,250)(1.060000)\end{array}}{9,874,662}\right]$$

$$= \$15\left(\frac{\begin{array}{l}12,505,556 + 11,789,459\\+ 11,113,789 + 10,476,245\end{array}}{9,874,662}\right)$$

$$= \$69.70$$

In this section on accumulated values of annuities, we have dealt only with the accumulations of temporary life annuities, because the accumulations of whole life or deferred life annuities have no application in practice.

8.4 TABLES OF SETTLEMENT OPTIONS

At the time a settlement is made under a life insurance policy, as when a death claim is paid, the person who receives the proceeds may be entitled to receive the proceeds in the form of an annuity, that is, in periodic payments rather than in one sum. In such a case, the present value of these periodic payments must be equal to the one-sum proceeds.

Life insurance policies contain provisions which spell out the alternative types of periodic payments available and include either the mortality and interest assumptions to be used, or tables which incorporate these assumptions or both. These *Tables of Settlement Options* include options for periodic payments figured at interest only (*payments certain*) and also for periodic payments figured with benefit of survivorship (*contingent payments*).

INVOLVING INTEREST ONLY. Commonly, the options involving interest only are the following:

1. *Interest Option*—which means the company holds the proceeds and periodically pays out the interest thereon.

For example, the policy might specify that this option pays 4%. If the recipient of $1,000 of proceeds chooses this option, then the company would keep the $1,000 and pay $40 per year ($1000 × .04 = $40). The recipient could also then choose to terminate the option and take the $1,000 at any time thereafter.

2. *Fixed Period Option*—which means the company pays out a series of equal payments for a designated period of time only, such as for ten years with no consideration of life contingencies. The recipient chooses the period of time, and the amount of the periodic payment is then so calculated that the present value of the series equals the proceeds.

For example, the Tables of Settlement Options may provide that for each $1,000 of proceeds, the recipient may elect to receive instead $123.29 at the end of each year for ten years. The $123.29 was calculated so that the present value of the ten payments certain will equal $1,000 (using 4% interest). This can be verified by multiplying $123.29 by the factor for $a_{\overline{10}|4\%}$ from Table I, which is 8.110896. Calculating such tables is a common practical application of the principles of Section 6.2, Amortization Payments.

3. *Fixed Payment Option*—which means the company pays out a series of equal payments of a certain amount, such as $500 per year, with no consideration of life contingencies. The recipient chooses the amount of the periodic payment, then the period of time over which payments will be made is calculated so the present value of the series equals the proceeds.

For example, the recipient may elect to receive $100 at the end of each year instead of proceeds of $1,000. If the Table of Settlement Options provides that 4% interest is allowed on the *fixed payment option*, then the $100 annual payments will be made for 13 years, plus a final payment of $2.49 made at the end of the 14th year. Using factors from Table I, it can be verified that these payments have a present value of $1,000.

$$\text{Present Value} = \$100\,a_{\overline{13}|4\%} + \$2.49\,v^{14} \text{ at } 4\%$$

$$= \$100(9.985648) + \$2.49(.577475)$$

$$= \$998.56 + \$1.44$$

$$= \$1,000.00$$

The *fixed payment option* will not generally provide payments for an exact number of periods; hence, a final payment of a smaller amount is necessary (as the $2.49 in the above example).

These options must be calculated at fairly low interest rates, because the company, by printing these tables in the policy, is actually guaranteeing that it will pay this rate of interest to somebody at some time many years in the future (if the recipient then wishes it). The actual interest rate which the company will be able to pay many years in the future is unknown at the time these guaranteed figures are printed in the policy. However, it is common for companies to pay additional amounts (often called *excess interest*) to recipients who are receiving settlement option payments during periods when the interest rates that the company is actually earning are very high.

INVOLVING CONTINGENT PAYMENTS. Commonly, the options involving contingent payments are the following:

1. *Life Income Option*—which means the company pays out a series of equal payments for as long as the recipient lives.

For example, the table may show that for a female age 65, annual payments of $85.81 would be payable for each $1,000 of proceeds. The first payment would be made at the beginning of the first year, and payments would be made each year thereafter as long as the recipient was alive. The present value of this life annuity due, calculated using the particular mortality and interest bases the company has chosen to figure these payments, would be $1,000. It is also common for Tables of Settlement Options to provide for selecting monthly payments in addition to annual payments.

2. *Life Income Option with Period Certain*—which means the company pays out a series of equal payments for a designated period of time (such as 10 years or 20 years), these payments being certain and not contingent. Thereafter, payments will continue for as long as the recipient lives.

The *life income option with period certain* represents a combination of a *temporary annuity certain* and a *deferred life annuity*. An example would be annual payments for five years certain and as long thereafter as the recipient lives (payments at the beginning of each period, that is, an annuity due):

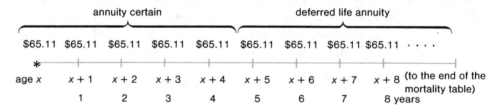

The present value of the first five payments illustrated above, which are $65.11 each, is

$$\$65.11\,\ddot{a}_{\overline{5}|i}$$

using interest only, because they are payments certain. The present value of the remainder of the payments is

$$\$65.11\left(\frac{l_{x+5}v^5 + l_{x+6}v^6 + l_{x+7}v^7 + \cdots \quad \text{to the end of the mortality table}}{l_x}\right)$$

The payments represent a deferred life annuity (first payment due at age $x + 5$). The total of these two present values, then, must be equal to the proceeds which the person is entitled to receive at age x.

3. *Life Income Option with Refund*—which may use either one of the following approaches:

a) *Installment Refund*—wherein payments are certain until the total of the payments equals the proceeds. Thereafter, payments continue as long as the recipient lives. For example, assume the proceeds are $1,000 and payments are $8.00 per month. The payments would be made for 125 months certain (since 125 payments at $8.00 each totals $1,000). Thereafter, the $8.00 per month would continue as long as the recipient lives.

b) *Cash Refund*—wherein a special single payment is made if the recipient dies before receiving total payments equal to the proceeds. The amount of the special single payment is equal to the amount needed to make total payments equal to the proceeds. For example, assume the proceeds are $1,000 and payments are $5.00 per month. If the recipient dies after receiving 150 monthly payments, the total received before death is $5.00 × 150 = $750. In that case, a special single payment of $250 is made, so that the total paid equals the proceeds ($750 + $250 = $1,000). However, if this recipient dies after payments have already totaled $1,000, nothing more is paid upon death.

In order to calculate the amount of the payments for a *life income option with refund*, very complex mathematics is needed. Under either the *installment refund* or *cash refund* approach, the period during which payments are certain depends on the size of each payment. Conversely, the size of each payment depends on the period of time during which payments are certain. This is because the present value of all the payments must equal the proceeds, and the number of payments which are certain affects this present value. Since the certain period and payment amount are interdependent, the calculation of a table of amounts payable under such an option requires the use of methods of higher mathematics.

Under the *installment refund* approach, if a table has already been calculated showing the size of each payment, then the period for which payments are certain is found by dividing the proceeds by the amount of each payment. For example, if such a table showed payments of $8.00 per month for proceeds of $1,000 available beginning at age 70, then the certain period would be:

$$\$1,000.00 \div \$8.00 = 125$$

that is, 125 months. Payments would continue after the 125 months only as long as the recipient is alive. In most cases under the *installment refund option*, the certain period will not turn out to provide an exact number of payments, such as the above example does.

CURRENT SETTLEMENT OPTION RATES. As with the options involving interest only, it is also common to use fairly low rates of interest to figure the payments for options involving contingent payments. Conservative annuity mortality tables are also generally used. However, during periods of time when interest rates actually being earned by the company are very high, companies will often quote *special* settlement option figures for recipients who elect to begin receiving payments involving life contingencies. These are usually called *current options*, and the amounts quoted are changed frequently. They are not printed in the policy.

For example, the whole life annuity option for a male age 65 which is printed in the policy may be $6.68 per month for each $1,000 of proceeds. This was calculated using 3% interest plus a mortality table. If the interest rates which the company can earn are currently very high, the company may quote a *current option* figure of $8.06 per month. This would be available only for new recipients beginning to receive payments within the next few months but would then remain at that figure for the remainder of that recipient's life. It was calculated using 7% interest plus a mortality table.

COMPARISON OF PAYMENTS. Since the present value of a certain payment is greater than the present value of a contingent payment, it follows that the amount of each payment will be smaller under options providing for more certain payments. For example, a typical Settlement Option Table might show the following monthly payments available at a certain age per $1,000 of proceeds:

$6.68 Life Income (no payments certain)

$6.22 Life Income with 120 months certain

$5.15 Life Income with 240 months certain

As the number of certain payments increases, the amount of each payment decreases. In addition, the above table might show:

$5.78 Life Income with Installment Refund

The period during which these $5.78 payments are certain is found as follows:

$1,000 ÷ $5.78 = approximately 173

that is, in 173 months the $1,000 proceeds will have been "refunded." This also follows the above pattern, since the $5.78 falls between $6.22 (the 120-month payment) and $5.15 (the 240-month payment).

To Illustrate—Which of the following available settlement options should the recipient choose in order to receive the largest regular payments:

    a) a monthly annuity due for 15 years certain and as long thereafter as the recipient lives,
    b) a monthly annuity due for 15 years certain,
    c) a monthly annuity for 15 years certain,
    d) monthly interest on the proceeds, or
    e) a monthly whole life annuity?

Solution—The interest option (d) would give the smallest payment, because none of the proceeds is being paid, only the interest. The options (a) and (e), which involve payments being made for life, would provide smaller payments than either of the two certain-only options (b) and (c), because payments must be spread over a much longer period. In comparing the two 15-year annuities certain, the proceeds will provide for larger installments if installments are paid at the *end* of each month, since there is a longer time for the money to earn interest. Hence, (c) is the correct choice.

CALCULATION OF PAYMENTS. It is well to remember that in the complete array of alternative amounts printed in a Table of Settlement Options, every figure shares the common characteristic that the present value of all the payments called for equals $1,000 (because the tables show figures per $1,000 of proceeds). In actual practice, companies are usually willing to set up payments in almost any manner the recipient desires, as long as the present value equals the proceeds available.

To Illustrate—Using Table II (female) and 6% interest, calculate the amount of annual payment for age 98, per $1,000 of proceeds, in a settlement option which provides payments for 15 years certain and for life thereafter.

Solution—If it is assumed that the first payment is made at the beginning, then the line diagram appears as follows:

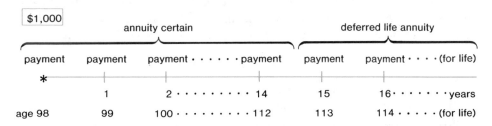

The present value of the 15 payments certain is

Basic equation:

$$\text{Present Value} = (\text{Payment})\ddot{a}_{\overline{15}|6\%}$$

Use the equation $\ddot{a}_{\overline{n}|i} = a_{\overline{n-1}|i} + 1$:

$$= (\text{Payment})\,(a_{\overline{14}|6\%} + 1)$$

Substitute the value for $a_{\overline{14}|6\%}$ from Table I:

$$= (\text{Payment})(9.294984 + 1)$$

$$= (\text{Payment})(10.294984)$$

The present value of the life annuity due, deferred 15 years (first payment at age 113), is

Basic equation (age 115 is highest age in Table II):

$$\text{Present Value} = (\text{Payment})\left(\frac{l_{113}v^{15} + l_{114}v^{16} + l_{115}v^{17}}{l_{98}}\right)$$

Substitute the values for the l's from Table II (female), for the v's from Table I (6%):

$$= (\text{Payment}) \left[\frac{\begin{array}{l}(83)(.417265) \\ + (21)(.393646) \\ + (4)(.371364)\end{array}}{450{,}890} \right]$$

$$= (\text{Payment}) \left(\frac{34.6330 + 8.2666 + 1.4855}{450{,}890} \right)$$

$$= (\text{Payment})(.000098)$$

The total of the two present values must equal $1,000:

$$(\text{Payment})(10.294984) + (\text{Payment})(.000098) = \$1{,}000$$

Factor out the common multiplier, (Payment):

$$(\text{Payment})(10.294984 + .000098) = \$1{,}000$$

$$(\text{Payment})(10.295082) = \$1{,}000$$

$$\text{Payment} = \$97.13$$

In addition to the settlement options already described in this section, options are sometimes available which are even more complicated, such as life annuities depending on one or more of several persons being alive.

EXERCISES, SET 18

1. Write an expression (using symbols) for the accumulated value at age 65 of $1,000 paid in at age 20 with benefit of survivorship.

2. Write an expression (using symbols) for the accumulated value at age 25 of a four-year life annuity of $25 per year, first payment at age 21.

3. A man deposits $100 with an insurance company at age 65. What amount should the company pay him five years later if the payment is conditioned on his being alive to receive it? (Use Table II and 6% interest.)

4. If the beneficiary of a life insurance policy elects to receive the proceeds in yearly payments of $565 each (first payment at once) for five years certain, find the amount of the proceeds. (Use 3%.)

5. The proceeds of a life insurance policy amount to $5,000. How much would the recipient receive each year if the option were selected to have these proceeds payable in yearly payments for ten years certain (first payment at end of one year)? (Use 4%.)

6. It is given that the present value at age 33 of a whole life annuity (immediate) of 1 per year is 24.764575. Calculate the amount of annual payment which would then be shown in a Table of Settlement Options for the whole life annuity due option at age 33 (first payment at beginning).

7. In periods of time when the company can earn very high rates of interest on the money it invests, what are two different methods it can use to make up for the fact that the Tables of Settlement Options in the policy are calculated using fairly low rates of interest?

8. How many payments are certain if the recipient chooses an *installment refund* settlement option which specifies $5.00 per month for each $1,000 of proceeds?

9. Why are settlement option payments that are payable for 20 years certain and for life thereafter *smaller* than payments that are to be made for 20 years certain?

10. The accumulated value at age 33 of a three-year temporary life annuity of $1,000 per year, issued at age 30, is

(1) $\$1,000\left[\dfrac{l_{30} + l_{31}v + l_{32}v^2}{l_{33}}\right]$ (3) $\$1,000\left[\dfrac{l_{31}(1 + i)^2 + l_{32}(1 + i) + l_{33}}{l_{33}}\right]$

(2) $\$1,000\left[\dfrac{l_{31} + l_{32}v + l_{33}v^2}{l_{33}}\right]$ (4) $\$1,000\left[\dfrac{l_{30}(1 + i) + l_{31}(1 + i)^2 + l_{32}(1 + i)^3}{l_{33}}\right]$

8.5 COMMUTATION FUNCTIONS—A SIMPLER METHOD OF CALCULATION

The actual calculation of annuity values by using the numerical values for l's, v's, and $(1 + i)$'s, as we have done in the first part of this chapter, can be very laborious. This is especially true for annuities involving payments for a person's entire lifetime. Many of the actuarial department's calculations are made easier by the use of *commutation functions*. *Commutation functions* (sometimes called *commutation symbols*) are derived by combining l's or d's (from a mortality table) and v's (from an interest table). Tables of values for these various commutation functions are thus prepared.

We will now see how the use of commutation functions simplifies the work that has been shown earlier in this chapter in calculating the present value of life annuities. In this chapter, those particular commutation functions which are applicable to such annuity calculations will be introduced.

In succeeding chapters (dealing with calculations of life insurance premiums and reserves), we will again explain elementary principles first, using the basic figures from mortality tables and interest tables. Then we will demonstrate how the chore of calculating is simplified by commutation functions. At that time those particular commutation functions which are applicable to life insurance premium and reserve calculations will be introduced.

EVALUATING A SINGLE PAYMENT   When dealing with payments certain, the tabulated values for the present value and accumulated value factors (such as in Table I) provide aid in performing calculations. However, when benefit of survivorship is involved, these factors are much more complicated. For example, the factor for the present value of a payment of 1 with benefit of survivorship

$$\frac{l_{x+n}v^n}{l_x}$$

is different for each separate age (x) and number of years (n). While tabulated values for this particular factor, as well as factors for the present values of temporary and whole life annuities, are generally published, such tabulations are quite voluminous. Therefore, in practice, commutation functions are widely used as an aid in performing calculations.

To see how commutation functions are used and how they simplify the work, consider again the expression for finding present values of a contingent payment due in n years to a life now age x:

$$\frac{l_{x+n} v^n}{l_x}$$

As will be seen later, it will be very useful to have the numerator and denominator look similar to each other. This is accomplished by multiplying both the numerator and denominator by v^x:

$$\frac{(l_{x+n} v^n)(v^x)}{(l_x)(v^x)} = \frac{l_{x+n} v^{x+n}}{l_x v^x}$$

The value of the fraction is unchanged by multiplying both the numerator and the denominator by the same amount. In the numerator, v^n multiplied by v^x equals v^{x+n} (adding exponents when multiplying). The numerator and denominator above now look similar to each other, since in each case the subscript of the l is the same as the exponent of the v.

Obviously, it would be extremely useful to have $l_x v^x$ already calculated for all values of x (based on a desired mortality table and interest rate). This value of l_x multiplied by v^x is represented by the commutation symbol

$$D_x$$

The following, then, is the definition of the D_x symbol:

$$D_x = l_x v^x$$

In Table II and Table IV, columns of D_x are shown for the 1971 Individual Annuity Mortality Table (male and female) at 6% and for the 1958 C.S.O. Table at 3%, respectively.

As an example, using age 20 in Table IV, the value of D_{20} can be verified by multiplying l_{20} (from Table III) by v^{20} at 3% (from Table I):

Basic equation:

$$D_x = l_x v^x$$

Substitute 20 for x:

$$D_{20} = l_{20} v^{20}$$

Substitute the values for l_{20} and v^{20} from the tables:

$$= (9,664,994)(.553676)$$
$$= 5,351,275$$

The values of D_x in Table IV were derived using more decimal places of v^x. Nevertheless, the above answer is very close to that shown in the Table for D_{20}.

Recall that the factor for finding present values of a contingent payment due in n years to a life now age x was finally expressed as

$$\frac{l_{x+n} v^{x+n}}{l_x v^x}$$

It has already been noted that the denominator is equal to D_x. Similarly, the numerator is equal to D_{x+n}, since the definition of a D is l multiplied by v (the subscript of the l being the same as the exponent of the v and this then being the subscript of the D). Hence, the factor for finding present values may be expressed

$$\begin{pmatrix} \text{Present Value of \$1} \\ \text{Due in } n \text{ Years to a} \\ \text{Life Now Age } x, \text{ with} \\ \text{Benefit of Survivorship} \end{pmatrix} = \$1\left(\frac{D_{x+n}}{D_x}\right)$$

In the above expression, the subscript of D in the numerator is the age when the contingent payment is to be made. The subscript of D in the denominator is the age at which the present value is being evaluated.

The value of this factor

$$\frac{D_{x+n}}{D_x}$$

is the same as the value of the factor used previously

$$\frac{l_{x+n} v^n}{l_x}$$

but the D's are easier to use in making calculations.

In the example given in Section 8.1 (pp. 155–157), the present value at age 35 of $100 payable at age 60 with benefit of survivorship would be

$$\$100\left(\frac{D_{60}}{D_{35}}\right)$$

Using values of D from Table II (male), this becomes

$$\$100\left(\frac{264,821}{1,278,916}\right) = \$20.71$$

The answer is the same as before, but the calculation is simplified.

To Illustrate—Using Table IV, calculate the present value at age 20 of $400 due in 15 years if the person is then still alive.

Solution—This is the same problem as shown in the illustration on page 158. The solution will now be given using commutation functions.

Basic equation:

$$\text{Present Value} = \$400\left(\frac{D_{x+n}}{D_x}\right)$$

Substitute 20 for x, 15 for n:

$$= \$400\left(\frac{D_{35}}{D_{20}}\right)$$

Substitute the values for D_{35} and D_{20} from Table IV:

$$= \$400\left(\frac{3{,}331{,}295}{5{,}351{,}273}\right)$$

$$= \$249.01$$

The answer agrees with that calculated on page 158.

The factor for calculating the accumulated value of a single payment by using commutation functions is the *inverse* of the present value factor (that is, numerator and denominator are switched):

$$\begin{pmatrix} \text{Accumulated Value of \$1} \\ \text{at End of } n \text{ Years to a} \\ \text{Life Age } x \text{ at the Beginning} \\ \text{with Benefit of Survivorship} \end{pmatrix} = \$1\left(\frac{D_x}{D_{x+n}}\right)$$

Note that in this expression, it is still true that the subscript of D in the numerator is the age when the contingent payment is to be made. The subscript of D in the denominator is the age at which the accumulated value is being evaluated.

EVALUATING AN ANNUITY. The present value at age x of a whole life annuity due at \$1 per year may be expressed as the total of the present values of the individual payments. Therefore, expressed in commutation symbols:

$$\text{Present Value} = \$1\left(\frac{D_x}{D_x}\right) + \$1\left(\frac{D_{x+1}}{D_x}\right) + \$1\left(\frac{D_{x+2}}{D_x}\right) + \cdots \quad \begin{array}{l}\text{to the end of the} \\ \text{mortality table}\end{array}$$

The common multiplier (\$1) can be factored out. The fractions to be added together all have a common denominator (D_x). Hence, the present value of the annuity can be expressed as follows:

$$\text{Present Value} = \$1\left(\frac{D_x + D_{x+1} + D_{x+2} + \cdots \text{ to the end of the mortality table}}{D_x}\right)$$

To avoid the necessity of adding together all the D's to the end of the mortality table, this total has also been calculated and put into tables. This total of the D's to the end of the mortality table is represented by the commutation symbol

$$N_x$$

with subscript of the N being the same as that of the first D in the series.

The following, then, is the definition of the N_x symbol:

$$N_x = (D_x + D_{x+1} + D_{x+2} + \cdots \text{ to the end of the mortality table})$$

In Table II and Table IV, columns of N_x are shown for the 1971 Individual Annuity Mortality Table (male and female) at 6% and for the 1958 C.S.O. Table at 3%, respectively.

As an example, using age 108 in Table II (female), the value of N_{108} can be verified by adding the D's starting with D_{108} to the end of the mortality table:

Basic equation:

$$N_x = (D_x + D_{x+1} + D_{x+2} + \cdots \text{ to the end of the mortality table})$$

Substitute 108 for x:

$$N_{108} = D_{108} + D_{109} + D_{110} + D_{111} + D_{112} + D_{113} + D_{114} + D_{115}$$

Substitute the values for the D's from Table II (female):

$$= 13 + 6 + 3 + 1 + 1 + 0 + 0 + 0$$
$$= 24$$

This value agrees with that shown in Table II for N_{108}.

The commutation function N_x can also be used to simplify the calculation of temporary life annuities. In the example given in Section 8.2 (pp. 160–162), the present value at age 25 of a life annuity of $100 per year for three years, the first payment due at age 26, would be

$$\$100\left(\frac{D_{26} + D_{27} + D_{28}}{D_{25}}\right)$$

Here the total of the D's to the end of the mortality table is not needed, only the total for three years. This can be found by taking N_{26} (the total of the D's from age 26 to the end of the table) and subtracting N_{29} (the total of the D's from age 29 to the end of the table). What remains after the subtraction is $D_{26} + D_{27} + D_{28}$, that is,

$$\$100\left(\frac{D_{26} + D_{27} + D_{28}}{D_{25}}\right) = \$100\left(\frac{N_{26} - N_{29}}{D_{25}}\right)$$

Using values of N and D from Table IV, this becomes

$$\$100\left(\frac{108{,}616{,}223 - 95{,}729{,}800}{4{,}573{,}377}\right) = \$281.77$$

The answer is the same as that calculated on pages 161–162.

The annuity just examined is a three-year annuity immediate—evaluation at age 25, first payment at age 26. The expression for this same three-year annuity, if it had been an annuity due (first payment at age 25), would have been $100\left(\dfrac{N_{25} - N_{28}}{D_{25}}\right)$.

THE GENERAL FORM. A general statement may be made that the factor to use in evaluating a life annuity will be of the form $\dfrac{N - N}{D}$, where (1) the subscript of the first N is the age when the first payment is due, (2) the subscript of the second N is the first age when there are no more payments due, that is, one greater than the age when the last payment is due, and (3) the subscript of the D is the age at which the annuity is being evaluated or paid for. Also, the difference between the subscripts of the two N's equals the actual number of payments. If the payments are to be made for life, the second N does not appear.

To Illustrate—Using Table II (male), calculate the present value at age 40 of a deferred temporary life annuity of $1,500 per year, first payment at age 50 and last payment at age 53.

Solution—This is the same problem as shown in an illustration (pp. 166–167) in Section 8.2. The solution will now be given by using commutation functions:

Basic equation: subscript of first N is age at first payment; subscript of second N is one age greater than when last payment is due; subscript of D is evaluation age:

$$\text{Present Value} = \$1,500\left(\frac{N_{50} - N_{54}}{D_{40}}\right)$$

Substitute the values for N_{50}, N_{54}, and D_{40} from Table II (male):

$$= \$1,500\left(\frac{7,003,039 - 5,127,089}{949,459}\right)$$

$$= \$2,963.71$$

This answer agrees with that calculated on pages 166–167.

MORE ABOUT COMMUTATION FUNCTIONS. One commutation symbol standing by itself has no useful purpose. When commutation functions are used for calculations, they must be employed in a fraction; that is, one or more commutation functions must be divided by one or more other commutation functions. The reason underlying this is the fact that present values or accumulated values (with benefit of survivorship) always involve probabilities of living or dying. Such probabilities are calculated by dividing some number of persons living (or dying) by some number of persons living.

If the interest rate changes during the period of a life annuity, the calculation of commutation functions becomes considerably more complicated. In effect, when using dual interest rates, separate complete tables of commutation functions must be produced for every age at which an annuity is to be evaluated; that is, the calculation of a life annuity evaluated at age 20 will require a completely separate table of commutation functions from that needed for a life annuity evaluated at age 21. (The equation used to calculate values of D_x when dual interest rates are used is beyond the scope of this book.) Although it may seem to require an inordinate amount of effort to prepare so many tables, it is no problem at all with the use of modern-day computers.

EXERCISES, SET 19

(Use Table II, male, and 6% interest, unless specified differently)

1. Write an expression (using commutation functions) for the present value at age 24 of $1,000 payable at age 62 (if alive). Calculate the value.

2. Write an expression (using commutation functions) for the accumulated value, with benefit of survivorship, at age 63 of $500 deposited with an insurance company when a person is age 21. Calculate the value.

3. Calculate the values of $\dfrac{D_x}{D_{25}}$ for $x = 35, 40, 45,$ and 50. Compare the results with the corresponding values of the present value factor, v^n, for $n = 10, 15, 20,$ and 25 at 6% using Table I.

4. Instead of using the female table, if it is assumed that females will exhibit the same mortality as males who are five years younger, calculate the amount which a woman now age 30 would receive back 20 years later if she deposits $100 now to accumulate with benefit of survivorship.

5. Write expressions (using commutation functions) for the present value at age 23 of a whole life annuity of $1 per year, with the first payment at age 23; age 24; and age 55. Calculate the values.

6. Write an expression (using commutation functions) for the present value at age 36 of a deferred ten-year life annuity of $100 per year, first payment due at age 46. Calculate the value.

7. Calculate the value at age 35 of a whole life annuity due of $1,500 per year.

8. Calculate the amount a person age 45 should pay for a life annuity due of $1,000 per year, which has payments for ten years only.

9. What is the present value to a person age 64 of a temporary life annuity of $100 per year for three years?

10. Construct a schedule showing that the value found in Exercise 9 will provide the benefits specified.

11. An insurance company has sold a life insurance policy to a person age 25 with premiums of $18.09 payable every year for life. What is the present value at the time the policy is sold of all future premiums the company will receive?

12. State in words what each of the following expressions represents:

$$\$100\left(\frac{N_{69}}{D_{20}}\right)$$

$$\$100\left(\frac{N_{69} - N_{79}}{D_{20}}\right)$$

13. The expression $\$100\left(\dfrac{N_{26} - N_{35}}{D_{25}}\right)$ represents the value of a

    (1) nine-year life annuity of $100 per year, issued at age 25
    (2) ten-year life annuity of $100 per year, issued at age 25
    (3) nine-year life annuity due of $100 per year, issued at age 25
    (4) ten-year life annuity due of $100 per year, issued at age 25

CHAPTER SUMMARY

- A payment *with benefit of survivorship* is made only if a designated person is alive on the payment date. This is also referred to as a *contingent payment*.

- The present value of such a payment is the amount which each person must pay in at the beginning in order to have the right to receive the payment (if living) when the designated date arrives. The present value of such a payment, to be made n years from now to a person now age x, is found by multiplying the payment amount by the factor

$$\frac{l_{x+n}v^n}{l_x}$$

- This is the same as discounting (at interest) the total amount payable to l_{x+n} persons and dividing that present value by the number who will have to pay it (l_x). An alternative view is that this is the same as multiplying the payment amount by the interest-discount factor (v^n) and also by the probability of living for n years $\left(\dfrac{l_{x+n}}{l_x}\right)$.

- A *life annuity* is a series of such contingent payments (payments not made after the person's death).

- The present value of a life annuity can be calculated as the total of the present values of the individual payments. (All these fractions already have a common denominator.) For example:

$$\frac{l_{x+1}v^1 + l_{x+2}v^2 + l_{x+3}v^3 + \text{etc.}}{l_x}$$

- A *temporary life annuity* involves only a limited number of contingent payments. For example, $100 a year as long as a person now age 65 is alive but no more than ten such payments.

- A *whole life annuity* involves contingent payments continuing for a person's entire lifetime. The present value is calculated as the present value of payments to the end of the particular mortality table being used.

- A *deferred life annuity* involves contingent payments where the first payment in the series is postponed for one or more periods. (Payments may then be limited in number or continue for the person's entire lifetime.)

- In each of the above three types, payments may be made at the end of each period (*annuity immediate*, or simply, *annuity*) or at the beginning of each period (*annuity due*). In any case, the person must be alive on the exact *payment date* in order for the payment to be made.

- The present value of a whole life annuity due is equal to the present value of a whole life annuity plus the amount of one payment. For example, the present value of a whole life annuity due of $500 per year is equal to the present value of a whole life annuity (immediate) plus $500.

- The present value of a temporary life annuity due is equal to the present value of a temporary life annuity having one fewer total periods plus the amount of one payment. For example, the present value of a ten-year life annuity due of $25 per year is equal to the present value of a nine-year annuity (immediate) plus $25.

- The present value of a temporary life annuity plus a deferred life annuity (deferred the same number of years as the temporary annuity runs) equals the present value of a whole life annuity. For example, the present value of a ten-year life annuity of $100 per year, plus the present value of a whole life annuity of $100 per year deferred for ten years, equals the present value of a whole life annuity of $100 per year.

- The accumulated value of a payment with benefit of survivorship is the amount paid to each survivor on a designated date from amounts paid in at an earlier date. The accumulated value of such a payment at the end of n years to a person age x at the beginning is found by multiplying the amount originally paid in by the factor

$$\frac{l_x(1 + i)^n}{l_{x+n}}$$

- The accumulated value of a life annuity can be calculated as the total of the accumulated values of the individual payments. (All these fractions already have a common denominator.) For example:

$$\frac{l_x(1 + i)^2 + l_{x+1}(1 + i)^1 + l_{x+2}}{l_{x+2}}$$

- *Tables of Settlement Options* included in life insurance policies spell out the alternative types of periodic payments available to a person who is entitled to receive the proceeds of the policy.

- The amount of the periodic payments specified in all of the various settlement options are calculated so their present value equals the amount of the proceeds available to the recipient.

- Commonly, these options include payments *certain*:

  Interest Option—proceeds are held and periodic interest is paid.
  Fixed Period Option—payments are made for a designated period only.
  Fixed Payment Option—payments are made for a designated amount.

- Commonly, the options also include *contingent* payments:

  Life Income Option—payments continue for as long as the recipient lives.
  Life Income with Period Certain Option—payments are made for a period certain and then continue for as long as the recipient lives.
  Life Income with Refund Option—payments are certain until the total paid equals the original proceeds, then payments continue for as long as the recipient lives.

- Under the *Life Income with Refund Option*, if the recipient dies before the total paid equals the original proceeds, the remaining amount owed by the company can be paid either (1) by continuing the payments until the amount owed is paid (known as *Installment Refund*) or (2) by paying the amount owed in one sum (known as *Cash Refund*).

- The *Life Income with Period Certain Option* is a combination of an annuity certain plus a deferred whole life annuity. For example, a "ten years certain and life thereafter option" would be a combination of a ten-year annuity certain plus a whole life annuity deferred for ten years.

- Since payments that are certain have a larger present value than contingent payments, it follows that the amount of each payment will be smaller under settlement options providing for more certain payments. For example, the twenty years certain and life thereafter option would provide smaller payments than the ten years certain and life thereafter option.

- Since payments extending for the whole of life are spread out much longer than payments for a certain period only, it follows that the amount of each payment will be smaller under settlement options providing for lifetime payments. For example, the twenty years certain and life thereafter option would provide smaller payments than the twenty years certain option.

- In times when interest rates earned by the company are very high, it is common for companies to make additional payments (called *excess interest*) to recipients of settlement options *involving interest only*. It is also common in such times to offer better payments than are printed in the Table of Settlement Options to recipients who are beginning new settlement options *involving contingent payments*. (These better payments are called *current options*.)

- *Commutation functions* or *commutation symbols* simplify the actuary's calculations by combining mortality table values with interest table values.

- The commutation symbol D_x is defined as:

$$D_x = l_x v^x$$

For example, $D_{25} = l_{25} v^{25}$.

- Using commutation functions, the present value of a contingent payment due n years in the future to a person now age x is found by multiplying the payment by the factor

$$\frac{D_{x+n}}{D_x}$$

This gives the same result as using the factor

$$\frac{l_{x+n} v^n}{l_x}$$

- The factor for finding the accumulated value of a payment with benefit of survivorship is the inverse:

$$\frac{D_x}{D_{x+n}}$$

- The commutation symbol N_x is equal to the total of the D's to the end of the mortality table:

$$N_x = D_x + D_{x+1} + D_{x+2} + \cdots \text{ to the end of the table.}$$

- The value of a life annuity can be calculated using commutation functions:

$$\frac{N - N}{D}$$

The subscript of the first N is age at first payment; the subscript of the second N is age when no more payments are due; and the subscript of the D is age on the evaluation date. The difference between the subscripts of the two N's equals the number of payments. If payments continue for life, the second N does not appear.

LEARNING OBJECTIVES

After reading this chapter, the student should know

- The meaning of life annuity.
- How to calculate the present value of a contingent payment.
- The meaning of "with benefit of survivorship."
- How to calculate the present value of a life annuity.
- What is meant by temporary life annuity, whole life annuity, and deferred whole life annuity.
- What is meant by life annuities due.
- The relationship between the present value of whole life annuity and whole life annuity due.
- The relationship between temporary, deferred, and whole life annuities.
- How to calculate the accumulated value of a life annuity.
- How settlement options work.
- The various types of settlement options.
- How to tell which options will provide larger or smaller periodic payments than other options.
- What is meant by commutation functions or commutation symbols.
- How the values of D_x are calculated.
- How to calculate the present value of a contingent payment using commutation functions.
- How the values of N_x are calculated.
- How to calculate the present value of a life annuity using commutation functions.

Life Insurance: Net Single Premiums

In the last chapter we discussed life annuity payments, which are made by a life insurance company only if a designated person is still alive.

In this chapter and the next, we will discuss the actuarial principles involved in determining premiums on life insurance policies, that is, where payment is made only when a designated person dies.

The amount of such a payment is called the face amount of insurance or the death benefit. It is common practice to base all figures quoted in connection with such insurance on a death benefit of $1,000.

This chapter deals with the *net single premium*, which is the same as the present value of the future benefits offered by a particular insurance policy. As with life annuities, calculations require the use of a designated mortality table and a specified interest rate. The net single premium does not include any amount for expenses or profits, and it does not take into account any withdrawals.

The first section below describes how the net single premium is determined for one year of life insurance. Succeeding sections explore the basic procedures for calculating net single premiums for various other types of policies: *term*, *whole life*, and *endowment insurance*. Section 9.6 gives the procedures used to figure the accumulated cost of insurance, while Section 9.7 explains how commutation functions are used to simplify the job of calculating a net single premium for the different kinds of insurance.

9.1 NET SINGLE PREMIUM FOR ONE YEAR OF LIFE INSURANCE

We will start an account of the net single premium by illustrating how the calculation is done for one year of life insurance.

It may be desired, for example, to calculate the net single premium that a person age 25 should pay for $1,000 of life insurance covering a one-year period. Under such insurance, if the person dies before reaching age 26, $1,000 will be paid to the beneficiary. To begin solving the problem, it is necessary to consult a mortality table. If Table III is used, the numbers shown living and dying at age 25 are

$$l_{25} = 9{,}575{,}636$$

$$d_{25} = 18{,}481$$

This means that if there is a group of 9,575,636 people alive at age 25, then 18,481 of this group may be expected to die during the year (before reaching age 26). In order to find the net single premium, it is assumed that all of these people are individually involved, that is, that each one who dies that year will receive $1,000 (to be paid to the recipient designated). In actual practice, such payments are made very soon after death occurs. However, for purposes of simplifying some of the calculations, it is customary to assume that all such payments are made at the end of the year in which death occurs.

Since a $1,000 benefit is to be paid for each of the d_{25} people, the total amount that will be paid out as benefits is

$$\$1{,}000 d_{25} = (\$1{,}000)(18{,}481)$$

$$= \$18{,}481{,}000$$

One year earlier, l_{25} people will pay the money in. The original problem may now be stated: "How much will each pay?" The total amount paid in is

$$\left(\begin{array}{c}\text{Amount Each}\\\text{Pays In}\end{array}\right)(l_{25}) = \left(\begin{array}{c}\text{Amount Each}\\\text{Pays In}\end{array}\right)(9{,}575{,}636)$$

$\left(\begin{array}{c}\text{amount each}\\\text{pays in}\end{array}\right)(9{,}575{,}636)$ \qquad $\begin{array}{c}(\$1{,}000)(18{,}481)\\ = \$18{,}481{,}000\end{array}$

```
 *————————————————————|
 age 25              age 26
```

The money paid in will earn interest over the one-year period. For this example, the rate will be assumed to be 3%. The basic equation for finding present value can be used to show that *all the money paid in equals the present value of all the money to be paid out one year later.* The "amount each pays in" can then be solved for:

$$A = Sv^n$$

Substitute $\left(\begin{array}{c}\text{Amount Each}\\\text{Pays In}\end{array}\right)(9{,}575{,}636)$ for A, $\$18{,}481{,}000$ for S and the value of v^1 at 3% from the table:

$$\left(\begin{array}{c}\text{Amount Each}\\\text{Pays In}\end{array}\right)(9{,}575{,}636) = (\$18{,}481{,}000)(.970874)$$

$$\left(\begin{array}{c}\text{Amount Each}\\\text{Pays In}\end{array}\right)(9{,}575{,}636) = \$17{,}942{,}722$$

$$\left(\begin{array}{c}\text{Amount Each}\\\text{Pays In}\end{array}\right) = \$1.87$$

It can be demonstrated that $1.87 is the desired net single premium at age 25 to provide $1,000 of insurance for a one-year period, as follows:

$$\text{Total amount paid in } = \$1.87(l_{25})$$

$$= \$1.87(9,575,636)$$

$$= \$17,906,439.32$$

Total amount accumulated at 3% to the end of the year

$$= \$17,906,439.32(1 + i)$$

$$= \$17,906,439.32(1.03)$$

$$= \$18,443,632.50$$

Amount payable for each person who dies during the year (the accumulated fund divided by the number who die)

$$= \$18,443,632.50 \div d_{25}$$

$$= \$18,443,632.50 \div 18,481$$

$$= \$998 \text{ approximately}$$

(The missing $2 results from rounding off $1.87 to the nearest cent, instead of using more decimal places.)

This net single premium for one year of life insurance at age 25 could be written as

$$\$1,000\left(\frac{d_{25}}{l_{25}}\right)v$$

or as

$$\frac{\$1000d_{25}v}{l_{25}}$$

Both these expressions for this net single premium permit interesting verbal interpretations. In the first, $\left(\frac{d_{25}}{l_{25}}\right)$ equals the probability that a person age 25 will die before reaching age 26, that is, q_{25}. The first expression says that the $1,000 is multiplied by the probability of dying and also by the regular factor for finding present values at interest. The second expression says that the $1,000 payable for each of d_{25} persons is discounted at interest for one year, and this amount is divided among the l_{25} persons to find out how much each must pay in.

Using more general terms, the equation for this net single premium is

$$\begin{pmatrix}\text{Net Single Premium for}\\ \text{\$1,000 Death Benefit}\\ \text{to a Life Age } x, \text{ for}\\ \text{One Year of Insurance}\end{pmatrix} = \$1,000\left(\frac{d_x v}{l_x}\right)$$

To Illustrate—Using Table III and 3% interest, calculate the net single premium for one year of life insurance of $1,000 at age 40; at age 60; at age 80.

At Age 40

Basic equation:

$$\begin{pmatrix} \text{Net Single} \\ \text{Premium} \end{pmatrix} = \$1,000 \left(\frac{d_x v}{l_x} \right)$$

Substitute 40 for x:

$$= \$1,000 \left(\frac{d_{40} v}{l_{40}} \right)$$

Substitute values from the tables:

$$= \$1,000 \left[\frac{(32,622)(.970874)}{9,241,359} \right]$$

$$= \$3.43$$

At Age 60

Basic Equation:

$$\begin{pmatrix} \text{Net Single} \\ \text{Premium} \end{pmatrix} = \$1,000 \left(\frac{d_x v}{l_x} \right)$$

Substitute 60 for x:

$$= \$1,000 \left(\frac{d_{60} v}{l_{60}} \right)$$

Substitute values from the tables:

$$= \$1,000 \left[\frac{(156,592)(.970874)}{7,698,698} \right]$$

$$= \$19.75$$

At Age 80

Basic equation

$$\begin{pmatrix} \text{Net Single} \\ \text{Premium} \end{pmatrix} = \$1,000 \left(\frac{d_x v}{l_x} \right)$$

Substitute 80 for x:

$$= \$1,000 \left(\frac{d_{80} v}{l_{80}} \right)$$

Substitute values from the tables:

$$= \$1,000 \left[\frac{(288,848)(.970874)}{2,626,372} \right]$$

$$= \$106.78$$

It can be seen that the net single premium for one year of insurance increases sharply at the older ages. This is similar to the age-by-age increase in the values of q_x (the probability of dying within one year) shown in Chapter 7.

CHOICE OF TABLES. When calculating net single premiums, the actuary must plan carefully which particular mortality tables and interest rates to use, as was pointed out in Section 8.1 dealing with annuities. In general, mortality tables which show higher mortality rates will result in higher net single premiums. (The effect is opposite for life annuity values.)

In calculating net single premiums, the use of a higher interest rate will result in lower net single premium values. This is the same effect as that for life annuity present values, and also for the present value of payments certain.

Many considerations enter decisions when choosing the bases to use the calculation. For example, in calculating the amount which the insurance company would charge if it were going to provide insurance coverage, a conservative approach would be desirable. This would call for use of fairly high mortality rates and low interest rates. However, in forecasting for the insurance company's management the results actually expected from selling insurance coverage, it would be desirable to use a mortality table and interest rate which the actuary expects will most nearly represent the company's own future experience. For some net single premium calculations, mortality and interest bases are prescribed by law. This will be explained in later chapters.

9.2 NET SINGLE PREMIUMS FOR TERM INSURANCE

Life insurance which provides a benefit if death occurs during a specified period of years is known as *term insurance*. The one-year insurance considered in the above section is one-year term insurance.

To determine the net single premiums for term life insurance for longer periods, the procedure is basically the same. For example, it may be desired to find the net single premium at age 25 for $1,000 of insurance during a period of three years (between ages 25 and 28), that is, for three-year term insurance. The total amount to be paid out for those who die during the first year is

$$\$1,000d_{25}$$

Assuming such payments are made at the *end of the year*, the present value at age 25 of those payments is

$$\$1,000d_{25}v$$

The total amount to be paid out for those who die during the second year is

$$\$1,000d_{26}$$

Assuming such payments are made at the end of the year, the present value at age 25 of those payments is

$$\$1,000d_{26}v^2$$

The total amount to be paid out for those who die during the third year is

$1,000d_{27}$

Assuming such payments are made at the end of the year, the present value at age 25 of those payments is

$1,000d_{27}v^3$

(In each case the exponent of the v is the number of years between age 25 and the date when the death benefit is paid.)

The present value at age 25 of all the death benefits paid during the three-year period is the total of the three individual present values. The common multiplier ($1,000) can be factored out:

$$\text{Present value} = \$1,000(d_{25}v + d_{26}v^2 + d_{27}v^3)$$

This amount is paid in at age 25 by the l_{25} persons. Hence, the above expression should be divided by l_{25} to find out how much each must pay in (the net single premium):

$$\binom{\text{Net Single}}{\text{Premium}} = \$1,000\left(\frac{d_{25}v + d_{26}v^2 + d_{27}v^3}{l_{25}}\right)$$

The *numerator* of this expression represents the total to be paid out for those who die in each of the three years, with each such amount being discounted at interest from the end of the year of death to the evaluation date. The *denominator* represents the number of persons alive on the evaluation date, among whom this total present value to be paid in must be allocated.

If, for example, Table III and 3% interest are used, the value of this net single premium can be calculated as follows.

From above:

$$\binom{\text{Net Single}}{\text{Premium}} = \$1,000\left(\frac{d_{25}v + d_{26}v^2 + d_{27}v^3}{l_{25}}\right)$$

Substitute values from the tables:

$$= \$1,000\left[\frac{\begin{array}{c}(18,481)(.970874)\\+(18,732)(.942596)\\+(18,981)(.915142)\end{array}}{9,575,636}\right]$$

$$= \$1,000\left(\frac{17,943 + 17,657 + 17,370}{9,575,636}\right)$$

$$= \$5.53$$

It can be demonstrated that if each of the l_{25} persons pays $5.53, the resulting fund will provide $1,000 (at the end of the year of death) for all who die before age 28. At the beginning of the first year, the amount paid in is

$$\$5.53l_{25} = (\$5.53)(9,575,636)$$

$$= \$52,953,267.08$$

At the end of one year, interest earned on the fund is equal to

$$(\$52,953,267.08)(.03) = \$1,588,598.01$$

Hence, the total fund at that time is

$$\$52,953,267.08 + \$1,588,598.01 = \$54,541,865.09$$

From this total fund, $1,000 is deducted for each person who has died during the first year:

$$\$1,000d_{25} = (\$1,000)(18,481)$$

$$= \$18,481,000$$

This leaves a balance in the fund of

$$\$54,541,865.09 - \$18,481,000 = \$36,060,865.09$$

The continued operation of the fund for succeeding years may be traced in the accompanying schedule (Chart 9–1). The final shortage in the fund represents less than $1 for each person dying the final year and results from rounding off the net single premium to two decimal places.

CHART 9–1

(1)	(2)	(3)	(4)	(5)	(6)
			Total Fund at End of Year	*Claims Paid at End of*	*Balance of Fund at End of Year After*
	Fund at Beginning of Year (Col. 6 of	*Interest for One Year (Col. 2 ×*	*Before Payment of Death Claims (Col. 2 +*	*Year (Number of Deaths ×*	*Payment of Claims (Col. 4 −*
Year	*Previous Year)*	*.03)*	*Col. 3)*	*$1,000)*	*Col. 5)*
1	$52,953,267.08	$1,588,598.01	$54,541,865.09	$18,481,000	$36,060,865.09
2	36,060,865.09	1,081,825.95	37,142,691.04	18,732,000	18,410,691.04
3	18,410,691.04	552,320.73	18,963,011.77	18,981,000	−17,988.23

To Illustrate—Using Table III and 3% interest, calculate the net single premium at age 50 for $5,000 of two-year term insurance.

Solution—The line diagram for this life insurance appears as follows:

The expression for the net single premium is a fraction with a numerator equal to the total of the amounts to be paid out for those who die in each of the two years, discounted at interest from the end of each year of death to the evaluation date:

$$\$5,000 d_{50} v + \$5,000 d_{51} v^2$$

or

$$\$5,000 (d_{50} v + d_{51} v^2)$$

The denominator of the fraction is the number living on the evaluation date at age 50:

Basic equation:

$$\binom{\text{Net Single}}{\text{Premium}} = \$5,000 \left(\frac{d_{50} v + d_{51} v^2}{l_{50}} \right)$$

Substitute values from the tables:

$$= \$5,000 \left[\frac{(72,902)(.970874) + (79,160)(.942596)}{8,762,306} \right]$$

$$= \$5,000 \left(\frac{70,779 + 74,616}{8,762,306} \right)$$

$$= \$82.97$$

9.3 NET SINGLE PREMIUMS FOR WHOLE LIFE INSURANCE

Under whole life insurance, the death benefit will be paid whenever death occurs; that is, the period of years covered by the insurance extends to the end of the mortality table. Thus, whole life insurance may be looked upon as term insurance covering a period of years equal to those remaining in the mortality table.

The calculation of the net single premium for whole life insurance follows exactly the same procedure as that shown above for term insurance. In the case of whole life insurance, the years included extend to the end of the mortality table.

To Illustrate—Using Table III and 3% interest, calculate the net single premium at age 96 for $1,000 of whole life insurance.

Solution—The period of years covered by this insurance extends for the person's entire lifetime. However, since Table III assumes that no persons live beyond the age of 100, it is assumed that the insurance ends at age 100. The line diagram for this whole life insurance appears as follows:

The expression for the net single premium is a fraction with a numerator representing the total to be paid out for those who die in each of the years, with each such amount being discounted at interest from the end of the year of death to the evaluation date. The denominator of the fraction is the number living on the evaluation date:

Basic equation:

$$\left(\begin{matrix} \text{Net Single} \\ \text{Premium} \end{matrix}\right) = \$1,000 \left(\frac{d_{96}v + d_{97}v^2 + d_{98}v^3 + d_{99}v^4}{l_{96}}\right)$$

Substitute values from the tables:

$$= \$1,000 \left[\frac{\begin{array}{l}(25,250)(.970874) \\ + (18,456)(.942596) \\ + (12,916)(.915142) \\ + (\ 6,415)(.888487)\end{array}}{63,037}\right]$$

$$= \$1,000 \left(\frac{24,515 + 17,397 + 11,820 + 5,700}{63,037}\right)$$

$$= \$942.81$$

In actual practice, it could happen that a few of the persons insured under whole life insurance coverage might still be alive at the age when the particular mortality table used shows that all have died. In this case, the insurance company would make payment to them when the final age is reached.

The calculation of net single premiums for whole life insurance at the younger ages would become very laborious if the above procedure were used. Therefore, in actual practice this calculation is usually done by using commutation functions. The commutation functions which apply in net single premium calculations will be explained in Section 9.7.

9.4 NET SINGLE PREMIUMS FOR A PURE ENDOWMENT

A *pure endowment* is an amount which is paid on a certain date only if a designated person is then alive to receive it. It is, therefore, the opposite of life insurance. It is, in fact, the same as a payment which is made with benefit of survivorship, as described in Chapter 8. In practice it is generally illegal to establish a pure endowment arrangement. Such prohibitions were enacted because the arrangements are viewed as being against the public good. However, pure endowments are often combined with life insurance, as will be shown in Section 9.5. In that context, the term, *net single premium for a pure endowment*, is used instead of *present value of a single payment with benefit of survivorship*.

Since the principles and equations for such a payment were presented earlier in Section 8.1, the following equation will be given here without further explanation:

$$\begin{pmatrix} \text{Net Single Premium for} \\ \text{\$1,000 Pure Endowment to} \\ \text{a Life Age } x, \text{ Due at the} \\ \text{End of } n \text{ Years} \end{pmatrix} = \$1,000 \left(\frac{l_{x+n} v^n}{l_x} \right)$$

To Illustrate—Using Table III and 3% interest, calculate the net single premium for a female age 34 for a \$5,000 pure endowment due in 25 years, using a three-year setback for females.

Solution—The line diagram for this pure endowment appears as follows:

```
                                    $5,000
        *————————————————————————————|
     age 34  · · · · · · · · · · · · age 59
                                  25 years
```

The female's age at the date the pure endowment is due is $34 + 25 = 59$. The use of a three-year setback means that three years must be subtracted from the age before using the Table. The problem must be treated as if the age were $34 - 3 = 31$, and the pure endowment were payable at age $59 - 3 = 56$:

Basic equation:

$$\begin{pmatrix} \text{Net Single} \\ \text{Premium} \end{pmatrix} = \$5,000 \left(\frac{l_{x+n} v^n}{l_x} \right)$$

Substitute 31 for x, 25 for n:

$$= \$5,000 \left(\frac{l_{56} v^{25}}{l_{31}} \right)$$

Substitute values from the tables:

$$= \$5,000 \left[\frac{(8,223,010)(.477606)}{9,460,165} \right]$$

$$= \$2,075.73$$

9.5 NET SINGLE PREMIUMS FOR ENDOWMENT INSURANCE

Endowment insurance means that the benefit will be paid if death occurs during a specified number of years, or the benefit will be paid at the end of that period if the person is then alive. Although the endowment insurance is actually a single contract, it can be thought of as consisting of two parts: term insurance and pure endowment. The payment on death constitutes term insurance, while the payment on survival constitutes a pure endowment. Thus, calculating the net single premium requires combining the calculations discussed above for those two separate types.

To Illustrate—Using Table III and 3% interest, calculate the net single premium at age 62 for a $7,500 endowment-at-age-65 insurance policy.

Solution—The policy provides that $7,500 will be paid if death occurs during the period between ages 62 and 65. It also provides that $7,500 will be paid at age 65 if the person is then alive. The line diagram for this endowment insurance policy appears as follows:

$$
\begin{array}{ccccc}
 & & & & \$7{,}500l_{65} \\
 & \$7{,}500d_{62} & & \$7{,}500d_{63} & \$7{,}500d_{64} \\
 & + & & + & + \\
* & \rule{3cm}{0.4pt} & & & \\
\text{age 62} & 63 & & 64 & 65 \\
 & 1 & & 2 & 3\ \text{years}.
\end{array}
$$

The expression for the net single premium for the term insurance part has a numerator representing the total to be paid out for those who die each year, with each such amount being discounted at interest from the end of the year of death to the evaluation date. The denominator is the number living on the evaluation date. The common multiplier ($7,500) can be factored out:

$$
\binom{\text{Net Single Premium for}}{\text{Term Insurance Part}} = \$7{,}500 \left(\frac{d_{62} v + d_{63} v^2 + d_{64} v^3}{l_{62}} \right)
$$

The expression for the net single premium for the pure endowment part follows from the equation given in Section 9.4:

$$
\binom{\text{Net Single Premium for}}{\text{Pure Endowment Part}} = \$7{,}500 \left(\frac{l_{x+n} v^n}{l_x} \right)
$$

$$
= \$7{,}500 \left(\frac{l_{65} v^3}{l_{62}} \right)
$$

The expression for the net single premium for the entire endowment insurance policy is the total of the above two expressions. The two expressions can be readily added, since they already have a common denominator (l_{62}). The common multiplier ($7,500) can be factored out:

Add the above expressions:

$$
\binom{\text{Net Single}}{\text{Premium}} = \$7{,}500 \left(\frac{d_{62} v + d_{63} v^2 + d_{64} v^3 + l_{65} v^3}{l_{62}} \right)
$$

Substitute values from the tables:

$$
= \$7{,}500 \left[\frac{
\begin{array}{l}
(179{,}271)(.970874) \\
+ (191{,}174)(.942596) \\
+ (203{,}394)(.915142) \\
+ (6{,}800{,}531)(.915142)
\end{array}
}{7{,}374{,}370} \right]
$$

$$
= \$7{,}500 \left(\frac{174{,}050 + 180{,}200 + 186{,}134 + 6{,}223{,}452}{7{,}374{,}370} \right)
$$

$$
= \$6{,}879.06
$$

It should be noted that the exponents on the last two v's are the same in the expression above. (d_{64} and l_{65} are both multiplied by v^3.) This is done because the two benefits are payable on the same date: the death benefit for those who die during the final year, and the pure endowment benefit for those still alive at the end of the final year.

COMPARISON OF THE TWO PARTS. The two separate parts of the net single premium for endowment insurance (term insurance and pure endowment) can be calculated separately if it is desired to know the relative contribution of each to the total net premium. For example, Chart 9–2 shows such figures (according to the 1958 C.S.O. Table at 3%) for 20-year endowment insurance issued at ages 20, 40, and 60.

CHART 9–2

Net Single Premiums per $1,000

	Age 20	Age 40	Age 60
20-Year Term	$ 31.77	$115.08	$474.22
20-Year Pure Endowment	529.41	461.25	188.88
TOTAL = 20-Year Endowment Policy	$561.18	$576.33	$663.10

It is evident that, for the older ages, a much greater proportion of the net single premium is used to provide term insurance rather than pure endowment, since the likelihood of dying during the period is greater for the older ages.

It is also important to understand that the two parts are affected differently when higher or lower mortality rates are used. If a mortality table is used which shows higher mortality rates, then the net single premium for the term insurance part will be higher, as described earlier in Section 9.1. On the other hand, the use of higher mortality rates will produce a lower net single premium for the pure endowment part, in a manner similar to that described for annuity payments.

TWO RATES OF INTEREST. If the interest rate to be used changes over the period of the life insurance coverage, then the net single premium can be calculated by discounting the benefit payments in the manner shown in Section 5.5, where payments certain were discounted using dual interest rates, or in Section 8.2, where life annuity payments were discounted using dual interest rates.

For example, consider a $1,000 three-year term insurance policy issued at age 55, where the interest rate is assumed to be 4% for the first year and 3% thereafter. The line diagram appears as follows:

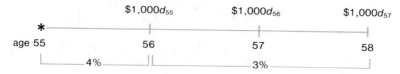

The present value of the death benefits payable at the end of the first year is calculated entirely at 4%:

$$\$1,000d_{55}(v \text{ at } 4\%)$$

The death benefits payable at the end of the second year are discounted for one year at 3% and for one year at 4%:

$$\$1,000d_{56}(v \text{ at } 3\%)(v \text{ at } 4\%)$$

The death benefits payable at the end of the third year are discounted for two years at 3%, which produces their present value at the beginning of the 3% period. This result is then discounted for one year at 4% which produces its present value on the evaluation date:

$$\$1,000d_{57}(v^2 \text{ at } 3\%)(v \text{ at } 4\%)$$

The total present value is then divided by the number living on the evaluation date (with the common multiplier $1,000 being factored out):

$$\begin{pmatrix} \text{Net} \\ \text{Single} \\ \text{Premium} \end{pmatrix} = \$1,000 \left[\frac{\begin{array}{c} d_{55}(v \text{ at } 4\%) + d_{56}(v \text{ at } 3\%)(v \text{ at } 4\%) \\ + d_{57}(v^2 \text{ at } 3\%)(v \text{ at } 4\%) \end{array}}{l_{55}} \right]$$

If Table III were used, the value would be $39.30.

9.6 THE ACCUMULATED COST OF INSURANCE

The net single premium, which would have to be paid by each of the survivors at the end of the term of coverage to provide the death benefits for those in the group who had died during the term, is called the *accumulated cost of insurance*. The only practical use for the accumulated cost of insurance is as a part of the calculation of reserves, which will be explained in Chapter 11.

It may be desired, for example, to calculate the accumulated cost of insurance at age 28 for $1,000 of insurance during a period of three years (that is, between ages 25 and 28). The total amount to be paid out for those who die during the first year is

$$\$1,000d_{25}$$

Assuming the payments are made at the end of the year, these payments, accumulated at interest to the evaluation date (two years later at age 28), would amount to

$$\$1,000d_{25}(1 + i)^2$$

The total amount to be paid for those who die during the second year is

$$\$1,000d_{26}$$

Accumulated at interest from the end of the year to the evaluation date (one year later at age 28), this would amount to

$$\$1,000d_{26}(1 + i)$$

The total amount to be paid for those who die during the third year is

$$\$1,000d_{27}$$

Assuming such payments are made at the end of the year, the value at age 28 of those payments is

$$\$1,000d_{27}$$

because payment would be made on the evaluation date (at age 28). In each case the exponent of the $(1 + i)$ is the number of years between the date when the death benefit is paid and age 28.

The accumulated value at age 28 of all the death benefits paid during the three-year period is the total of the three individual accumulated values. The common multiplier ($1,000) can be factored out.

$$\text{Accumulated Value} = \$1,000[d_{25}(1 + i)^2 + d_{26}(1 + i) + d_{27}]$$

This amount is paid in at age 28 by the survivors. Hence, the above expression should be divided by l_{28} to find out how much each must pay in (the accumulated cost of insurance):

$$\begin{pmatrix} \text{Accumulated Cost} \\ \text{of Insurance} \end{pmatrix} = \$1,000\left[\frac{d_{25}(1 + i)^2 + d_{26}(1 + i) + d_{27}}{l_{28}}\right]$$

The numerator of this expression represents the total to be paid out for those who die in each of the years, with each such amount being accumulated at interest from the end of the year of death to the evaluation date. The denominator represents the number of persons alive on the evaluation date, among whom this total accumulated cost must be allocated to be paid in.

If, for example, Table III and 3% interest are used, the value of this accumulated cost can be calculated as follows:

Equation above:

$$\begin{pmatrix} \text{Accumulated Cost} \\ \text{of Insurance} \end{pmatrix} = \$1,000\left[\frac{d_{25}(1 + i)^2 + d_{26}(1 + i) + d_{27}}{l_{28}}\right]$$

Substitute values from the tables:

$$= \$1,000\left[\frac{\begin{array}{l}(18,481)(1.060900) \\ + (18,732)(1.030000) \\ + (18,981)\end{array}}{9,519,442}\right]$$

$$= \$1,000\left(\frac{19,606 + 19,294 + 18,981}{9,519,442}\right)$$

$$= \$6.08$$

In Section 9.2, the net single premium (payable at age 25) for this same term insurance was calculated to be $5.53. The accumulated cost calculated above (payable at age 28) can be verified by multiplying the net single premium by the factor for accumulating with benefit of survivorship (described in Section 8.3):

Basic equation:

$$\left(\begin{array}{c}\text{Accumulated Cost}\\ \text{of Insurance}\end{array}\right) = \left(\begin{array}{c}\text{Net Single}\\ \text{Premium}\end{array}\right)\left[\frac{l_x(1+i)^n}{l_{x+n}}\right]$$

Substitute 25 for x, 3 for n:

$$= \left(\begin{array}{c}\text{Net Single}\\ \text{Premium}\end{array}\right)\left[\frac{l_{25}(1+i)^3}{l_{28}}\right]$$

Substitute $5.53 for net single premium and values from the tables:

$$= \$5.53\left[\frac{(9{,}575{,}636)(1.092727)}{9{,}519{,}442}\right]$$

$$= \$6.08$$

These two calculations agree.

To Illustrate—Using Table III and 3% interest, calculate the accumulated cost of insurance at age 65 for $15,000 of two-year term insurance.

Solution—The line diagram for this life insurance appears as follows:

$15,000d_{63}$ $15,000d_{64}$

|————————————|————————————*

age 63   64   65

The expression for the accumulated cost will have a numerator representing the total to be paid out for those who die in each of the years, with each such amount being accumulated at interest from the end of the year of death to the evaluation date:

$$\$15{,}000d_{63}(1+i) + \$15{,}000d_{64}$$

The common multiplier ($15,000) can be factored out. The denominator is the number living on the evaluation date (l_{65}).

Basic equation:

$$\left(\begin{array}{c}\text{Accumulated Cost}\\ \text{of Insurance}\end{array}\right) = \$15{,}000\left[\frac{d_{63}(1+i) + d_{64}}{l_{65}}\right]$$

Substitute values from the tables:

$$= \$15{,}000\left[\frac{(191{,}174)(1.030000) + (203{,}394)}{6{,}800{,}531}\right]$$

$$= \$15{,}000\left(\frac{196{,}909 + 203{,}394}{6{,}800{,}531}\right)$$

$$= \$882.95$$

EXERCISES, SET 20

1. What name is given to the amount which represents the total value of all the benefits of a life insurance policy if evaluated (a) at the beginning of the period of coverage or (b) at the end of the period of coverage?

2. When calculating the value of life insurance coverage, at what point in time is it assumed that the death benefits are paid out each year?

3. What are the benefits provided by an endowment insurance contract?

4. When calculating the net single premium for an endowment insurance contract, what two parts of the benefit are considered to be paid on the same date?

(Use Table III and 3% interest for all of the following)

5. Write an expression (using symbols) for the net single premium at age 25 for $4,000 of one-year term insurance. Calculate this premium.

6. Write an expression (using symbols) for the net single premium at age 45 for $1,000 of three-year term insurance. Calculate this premium.

7. Write an expression (using symbols) for the net single premium at age 97 for $10,000 of whole life insurance. Calculate this premium.

8. Write an expression (using symbols) for the net single premium at age 50 for a $1,000 pure endowment payable at age 65. Calculate this premium.

9. Write an expression (using symbols) for the net single premium at age 20 for a $5,000 three-year endowment insurance policy. Calculate this premium.

10. Calculate separately the term insurance part and the pure endowment part of the answer to Exercise 9.

11. Write an expression (using symbols) for the accumulated cost of insurance at age 22 for $1,000 of three-year term insurance. Calculate this cost.

12. The accumulated cost of insurance at age 51 for a $1,000 two-year term policy issued at age 49 is equal to

$$(1)\ \$1,000\left[\frac{d_{49}(1 + i) + d_{50}}{l_{51}}\right] \qquad (3)\ \$1,000\left[\frac{d_{49}(1 + i)^2 + d_{50}(1 + i)}{l_{51}}\right]$$

$$(2)\ \$1,000\left[\frac{l_{49}(1 + i) + l_{50}}{l_{51}}\right] \qquad (4)\ \$1,000\left[\frac{l_{49}(1 + i)^2 + l_{50}(1 + i)}{l_{51}}\right]$$

9.7 COMMUTATION FUNCTIONS

FOR ONE-YEAR TERM INSURANCE. In actual practice, actuaries make considerable use of commutation functions in calculating net single premiums. To see how commutation functions are used for that purpose, consider again the expression for the net single premium for a death benefit of 1 to a life age x if death occurs in one year:

$$\frac{d_x v^1}{l_x}$$

The same procedure is followed here as was shown in Chapter 8, namely, both the numerator and the denominator are multiplied by v^x:

$$\frac{(d_x v^1)(v^x)}{(l_x)(v^x)} = \frac{d_x v^{x+1}}{l_x v^x}$$

The value of the fraction is unchanged by multiplying both the numerator and the denominator by the same amount. In the numerator, v^1 multiplied by v^x equals v^{x+1} (adding exponents when multiplying).

Looking at the numerator, it is seen that it would be useful to have $d_x v^{x+1}$ already calculated for all values of x (based on a desired mortality table and interest rate). This value of d_x multiplied by v^{x+1} is represented by the commutation symbol:

$$C_x$$

The following, then, is the definition of the C_x symbol:

$$C_x = d_x v^{x+1}$$

In Table IV, columns of C_x are shown for the 1958 C.S.O. Table at 3%.

As an example, using age 20 in Table IV, the value of C_{20} can be verified by multiplying d_{20} (from Table III) by v^{21} at 3% (from Table I):

Basic equation:

$$C_x = d_x v^{x+1}$$

Substitute 20 for x:

$$C_{20} = d_{20} v^{21}$$

Substitute values from the tables:

$$= (17,300)(.537549)$$
$$= 9,300$$

This agrees with the value given in Table IV.

Above, the factor for finding the net single premium for one year of insurance to a life age x was finally expressed as

$$\frac{d_x v^{x+1}}{l_x v^x}$$

The numerator is equal to C_x because C_x is defined as d_x multiplied by v^{x+1}. The denominator is equal to D_x because D_x is defined as l_x multiplied by v^x. Hence, the factor for finding the net single premium for one-year term insurance may be expressed

$$\begin{pmatrix} \text{Net Single Premium for} \\ \text{\$1,000 Death Benefit} \\ \text{to a Life Age } x, \text{ If} \\ \text{Death Occurs in 1 Year} \end{pmatrix} = \$1,000 \left(\frac{C_x}{D_x} \right)$$

The value of this factor

$$\frac{C_x}{D_x}$$

is the same as the value of the factor for the net single premium used previously:

$$\frac{d_x v^1}{l_x}$$

but the commutation functions are easier to use in making calculations.

In the example given in Section 9.1, the net single premium at age 25 for $1,000 of one-year term insurance would be

$$\$1,000\left(\frac{C_{25}}{D_{25}}\right)$$

Using values for the commutation functions from Table IV, this becomes

$$\$1,000\left(\frac{8,570}{4,573,377}\right) = \$1.87$$

The answer is the same as before, but the calculation is simplified.

To Illustrate—Using Table IV, calculate the net single premium at age 40 for one year of life insurance of $1,000.

Solution—This problem is the same at the one shown in the illustration in Section 9.1. The solution will now be calculated using commutation functions:

Basic equation:

$$\left(\begin{array}{c}\text{Net Single}\\\text{Premium}\end{array}\right) = \$1,000\left(\frac{C_x}{D_x}\right)$$

Substitute 40 for x:

$$= \$1,000\left(\frac{C_{40}}{D_{40}}\right)$$

Substitute values from Table IV:

$$= \$1,000\left(\frac{9,709}{2,833,002}\right)$$

$$= \$3.43$$

The answer agrees with that calculated in Section 9.1.

FOR OTHER TYPES OF POLICIES. The net single premium at age x for $1,000 of *whole life insurance* may be expressed as the following total of the net single premiums for the individual years' insurance, with the subscripts of the D's all being the age at the evaluation date:

$$\binom{\text{Net Single}}{\text{Premium}} = \$1{,}000 \left(\frac{C_x}{D_x}\right) + \$1{,}000 \left(\frac{C_{x+1}}{D_x}\right)$$

$$+ \$1{,}000 \left(\frac{C_{x+2}}{D_x}\right) + \cdots \quad \begin{array}{l}\text{to the end of the}\\\text{mortality table}\end{array}$$

The common multiplier ($\$1{,}000$) can be factored out. The fractions to be added together all have a common denominator, D_x. Accordingly, the net single premium for the whole life insurance can be expressed as

$$\binom{\text{Net Single}}{\text{Premium}}$$

$$= \$1{,}000 \left[\frac{C_x + C_{x+1} + C_{x+2} + \cdots \text{ to the end of the mortality table}}{D_x}\right]$$

In order to avoid the necessity of adding together all the C's to the end of the mortality table, this total is also tabulated. The total of the C's to the end of the mortality table is represented by the commutation symbol

$$M_x$$

The subscript of the M being the same as that of the first C in the series.

The following, then, is the definition of the M_x symbol:

$$M_x = (C_x + C_{x+1} + C_{x+2} + \cdots \text{ to the end of the mortality table})$$

In Table IV, columns of M_x are shown for the 1958 C.S.O. Table at 3%.

The commutation function M_x can also be used to simplify the calculation of net single premiums for term insurance and endowment insurance. In the example given in Section 9.2, the net single premium at age 25 for $\$1{,}000$ of three-year term insurance is

$$\$1{,}000 \left(\frac{C_{25} + C_{26} + C_{27}}{D_{25}}\right)$$

Here the total of the C's to the end of the mortality table is not needed, but only the total for three years. This total can also be found by taking M_{25} (the total of the C's from age 25 to the end of the table) and subtracting M_{28} (the total of the C's from age 28 to the end of the table). What remains after the subtraction is $C_{25} + C_{26} + C_{27}$, that is,

$$\$1{,}000 \left(\frac{C_{25} + C_{26} + C_{27}}{D_{25}}\right) = \$1{,}000 \left(\frac{M_{25} - M_{28}}{D_{25}}\right)$$

Using values of M and D from Table IV, this becomes

$$\$1,000 \left(\frac{1,276,590 - 1,251,291}{4,573,377} \right) = \$5.53$$

The answer is the same as that calculated in Section 9.2.

THE GENERAL FORM. A general statement may be made to cover all situations: When using commutation functions, the factor to use in calculating a net single premium or an accumulated cost of insurance will be of the form $\dfrac{M - M + D}{D}$, where (1) the subscript of the first M is the age when the insurance coverage begins, (2) the subscript of the second M is the age at which the insurance coverage stops, that is, one greater than the last age covered, (3) the subscript of the D in the numerator is the age at which a pure endowment would be paid, and (4) the subscript of the D in the denominator is the age at which this net single premium or accumulated cost of insurance is paid. The difference between the subscripts of the M's equals the actual number of years of insurance coverage. If there is no pure endowment involved, the D in the numerator does not appear. If the insurance is for the whole of life, the second M does not appear.

To Illustrate—Using Table IV, calculate the net single premium at age 50 for $5,000 of two-year term insurance.

Solution—This problem is the same as the problem shown in the illustration in Section 9.2. The solution will now be calculated using commutation functions. In the general expression given above, the D in the numerator will not appear, because there is no pure endowment involved:

Basic equation (subscripts of the M's define the period of coverage; subscript of D is the evaluation age):

$$\left(\begin{matrix} \text{Net Single} \\ \text{Premium} \end{matrix} \right) = \$5,000 \left(\frac{M_{50} - M_{52}}{D_{50}} \right)$$

Substitute values from Table IV:

$$= \$5,000 \left(\frac{1,028,986 - 995,821}{1,998,744} \right)$$

$$= \$82.96$$

The answer is only one cent different from that calculated in Section 9.2.

To Illustrate Again—Using Table IV, calculate the net single premium at age 96 for $1,000 of whole life insurance.

Solution—This problem is the same as the one shown in the illustration in Section 9.3. The solution will now be calculated using commutation functions. In the general expression for net single premiums, the second M will not appear, because the insurance is for the whole of life. Furthermore, the D in the numerator will not appear, because there is no pure endowment involved:

Basic equation:

$$\left(\begin{array}{c}\text{Net Single} \\ \text{Premium}\end{array}\right) = \$1000\left(\frac{M_{96}}{D_{96}}\right)$$

Substitute values from Table IV:

$$= \$1,000\left(\frac{3,481}{3,692}\right)$$

$$= \$942.85$$

This answer is only four cents different from that calculated in Section 9.3.

To Illustrate Again—Using Table IV, calculate the net single premium at age 62 for a $7,500 endowment-at-age-65 insurance policy.

Solution—This problem is the same as the one shown in the illustration in Section 9.5. The solution will now be calculated using commutation functions:

Basic equation (subscripts of the M's define the period of coverage; subscript of D in the numerator is the age of pure endowment; subscript of D in the denominator is the evaluation age):

$$\left(\begin{array}{c}\text{Net Single} \\ \text{Premium}\end{array}\right) = \$7,500\left(\frac{M_{62} - M_{65} + D_{65}}{D_{62}}\right)$$

Substitute values from Table IV:

$$= \$7,500\left(\frac{773,206 - 686,750 + 995,688}{1,179,823}\right)$$

$$= \$6,879.07$$

This answer is only one cent different from that calculated in Section 9.5.

The form $\dfrac{M - M + D}{D}$ is also used to compute the accumulated cost of insurance. However, the evaluation date for the accumulated cost of insurance is at the *end* of the term of coverage, whereas the net single premium is evaluated at the *beginning*. This is because the accumulated cost of insurance represents the amount that would have to be paid by the survivors at the end of the term of coverage, while the net single premium is the amount to be paid by those living at the beginning of the term of coverage. Therefore, when the accumulated cost is computed, the subscript of the D in the denominator is the highest age.

To Illustrate—Using Table IV, calculate the accumulated cost of insurance at age 28 for $1,000 of three-year term insurance.

Solution—This is the same three-year term policy for which the net single premium was calculated in a previous illustration to be $5.53. There the denominator used in the calculation was D_{25} because the net single premium is evaluated at the beginning of the insurance. Now, to calculate the accumulated cost of insurance, the denominator is D_{28} because the evaluation date is at the end. (The D in the numerator will not appear, because there is no pure endowment involved.)

Basic equation (subscripts of the M's define the period of coverage; subscript of D is the evaluation age):

$$\begin{pmatrix} \text{Accumulated Cost} \\ \text{of Insurance} \end{pmatrix} = \$1,000 \left(\frac{M_{25} - M_{28}}{D_{28}} \right)$$

Substituting values from Table IV:

$$= \$1,000 \left(\frac{1,276,590 - 1,251,291}{4,160,727} \right)$$

$$= \$6.08$$

This answer agrees with that calculated in Section 9.6 for the same policy without the use of commutation functions.

It should be noted that the accumulated cost of insurance ($6.08) is higher than the net single premium ($5.53). This is as expected since the number of persons paying in at the beginning of the term of coverage is greater than the number of survivors who would pay at the end.

TWO RATES OF INTEREST. The commutation functions C_x and M_x can be calculated using dual interest rates. It was pointed out in Section 8.5 (in connection with the D_x and N_x functions) that when the interest rate changes over the period being considered, separate complete tables of commutation functions must be produced for every age at which the present value is being calculated. The same is true for the C_x and M_x functions. For example, the calculation of a net single premium evaluated at age 35 will require a completely separate table of commutation functions from that needed for a net single premium evaluated at age 36. (The equation used to calculate values of C_x when dual interest rates are used is beyond the scope of this book). The tables can be produced by computers, however, and once they are available they are used in the same way as the tables shown in this book.

In the next chapter, premiums will be explained which are payable annually for a life insurance policy. First, the calculations will be shown based only on a mortality table and interest rate, in the same manner as the net single premiums in this chapter. Then, the calculation of the annual premiums which are actually paid by the policyowner will be explained.

EXERCISES, SET 21

(Use Table IV for all of the following.)

1. Write an expression (using commutation functions) for the net single premium at age ten for $10,000 of one-year term insurance. Calculate the value.

2. Write an expression (using commutation functions) for the net single premium at age ten for $10,000 of term-to-age-40 insurance. Calculate the value.

3. Write an expression (using commutation functions) for the net single premium at age 65 for $1,000 of whole life insurance. Calculate the value.

4. Write an expression (using commutation functions) for the net single premium at age five for a $2,000 pure endowment due 25 years thereafter. Calculate the value.

5. Write an expression (using commutation functions) for the net single premium at age 40 for a $5,000 30-year endowment insurance policy. Calculate the value.

6. Write an expression (using commutation functions) for the accumulated cost at age 30 for a $10,000 12-year term insurance policy. Calculate the value.

7. Describe what type of policy is represented by each of the following expressions:

a) $1,000\left(\dfrac{C_{43}}{D_{43}}\right)$

d) $5,000\left(\dfrac{M_{62}}{D_{62}}\right)$

b) $1,000\left(\dfrac{C_{43} + C_{44} + C_{45} + C_{46}}{D_{43}}\right)$

e) $15,000\left(\dfrac{M_{25} - M_{50} + D_{50}}{D_{25}}\right)$

c) $1,000\left(\dfrac{M_{43} - M_{47}}{D_{43}}\right)$

f) $1,500\left(\dfrac{D_{65}}{D_{25}}\right)$

8. The net single premium at age 32 for a three-year endowment insurance policy of $4,000 is expressed in commutation functions as

(1) $4,000\left(\dfrac{M_{35} - M_{32} + D_{32}}{D_{32}}\right)$

(3) $4,000\left(\dfrac{M_{32} - M_{35} + D_{35}}{D_{32}}\right)$

(2) $4,000\left(\dfrac{M_{32} - M_{35} + D_{32}}{D_{32}}\right)$

(4) $4,000\left(\dfrac{M_{32} - M_{35} + D_{35}}{D_{35}}\right)$

CHAPTER SUMMARY

- A *net single premium* is defined as the present value of the future benefits of a life insurance policy, calculated using a mortality table and interest rate (but without consideration for expenses or profit or withdrawals).

- Unless specified otherwise, net single premiums generally are calculated assuming that death benefits are paid at the end of the year of death.

- The net single premium for one year of life insurance, with $1,000 of death benefit, is calculated as follows:

$$1,000\left(\frac{d_x v}{l_x}\right)$$

- This expression shows that $1,000 paid for all persons who die in that year is discounted back to the beginning of the year, and this value is divided among all living at the beginning of the year. It may also be looked upon as the death benefit ($1,000) being multiplied by the probability of dying in the year $\left(\dfrac{d_x}{l_x}\right)$ and also multiplied by the factor for finding present value at interest (v).

- *Term insurance* provides a benefit if death occurs during a specified period of years.

- The net single premium for term insurance is calculated (1) by multiplying each year's death benefit by the number dying that year, (2) by further multiplying each such amount by the factor for discounting at interest to the evaluation date, and (3) by dividing this total amount by the number living on the evaluation date. For example, for $1,000 three-year term insurance at age 25 the net single premium is:

$$\$1,000\left(\frac{d_{25}v + d_{26}v^2 + d_{27}v^3}{l_{25}}\right)$$

- *Whole life insurance* provides a benefit whenever death occurs, that is, coverage extends to the end of the mortality table.

- The net single premium for whole life insurance is calculated the same way as term insurance, except that the calculation extends to the end of the mortality table.

- A *pure endowment* is an amount paid on a certain date if a certain person is then alive.

- The net single premium for a $1,000 pure endowment due at the end of n years to a person age x at the beginning is

$$\$1,000\left(\frac{l_{x+n}v^n}{l_x}\right)$$

This is the same as the present value of a payment with benefit of survivorship described in Chapter 8.

- *Endowment insurance* provides a benefit if death occurs during a specified period of years, or the benefit will be paid at the end of that period if the person is then alive.

- The net single premium for endowment insurance is calculated as a combination of term insurance plus a pure endowment. For example, for $1,000 three-year endowment insurance at age 25, the net single premium is:

$$\$1,000\left(\frac{d_{25}v + d_{26}v^2 + d_{27}v^3 + l_{28}v^3}{l_{25}}\right)$$

The exponent is the same on the last two v's, because the benefit is paid on the same date for those who die in the final year and those still alive at the end of that year.

- The use of higher mortality rates results in higher net single premiums, which is the opposite effect from the present value of life annuities. An exception is the net single premium for a pure endowment (and for the pure endowment part of endowment insurance).

- The use of a higher interest rate results in lower net single premiums, which is similar to the present value of life annuities.

- The *accumulated cost of insurance* is the amount each survivor would pay at the end of a period of years to provide death benefits for those who died during the period. It has useful application in the calculation of reserves.

- The accumulated cost of insurance is calculated (1) by multiplying each year's death benefit by the number dying that year, (2) by further multiplying each such amount by the factor for accumulating at interest to the evaluation date, and (3) by dividing this total amount by the number living on the evaluation date. For example, for $1,000 three-year term insurance beginning at age 25, the accumulated cost of insurance (at age 28) is:

$$\$1,000\left(\frac{d_{25}(1 + i)^2 + d_{26}(1 + i)^1 + d_{27}}{l_{28}}\right)$$

- The accumulated cost of insurance is related to the net single premium for the same benefits as follows:

$$\begin{pmatrix}\text{Accumulated Cost} \\ \text{of Insurance}\end{pmatrix} = \begin{pmatrix}\text{Net Single} \\ \text{Premium}\end{pmatrix}\left[\frac{l_x(1 + i)^n}{l_{x+n}}\right]$$

where x is the age at the beginning, and n is the period of years covered.

- The commutation symbol C_x is defined as:

$$C_x = d_x v^{x+1}$$

For example, $C_{25} = d_{25} v^{26}$.

- Using commutation functions, the net single premium for one-year term insurance at age x is found by multiplying the death benefit by the factor

$$\frac{C_x}{D_x}$$

This gives the same result as using the factor

$$\frac{d_x v^1}{l_x}$$

- The commutation symbol M_x is equal to the total of the C's to the end of the mortality table:

$$M_x = C_x + C_{x+1} + C_{x+2} \cdots \text{ to the end of the table.}$$

- A net single premium or an accumulated cost of insurance can be calculated using commutation functions:

$$\frac{M - M + D}{D}$$

The subscript of the first M is the age when the insurance coverage begins; the subscript of the second M is the age at which the insurance coverage stops (that is, one greater than the last age covered); the subscript of the D in the numerator is the age at which a pure endowment would be paid; and the subscript of the D in the denominator is the age at which this net single premium or accumulated cost of insurance is paid. The difference between the subscripts of the M's equals the actual number of years of insurance coverage. If there is no pure endowment involved, the D in the numerator does not appear. If the insurance is for the whole of life, the second M does not appear.

LEARNING OBJECTIVES

After reading this chapter, the student should know

- The meaning of net single premium.
- How to calculate the net single premium for one year of insurance.
- The meaning of term insurance.
- How to calculate the net single premium for term insurance.
- The meaning of whole life insurance.
- How to calculate the net single premium for whole life insurance.
- The meaning of pure endowment.
- How to calculate the net single premium for a pure endowment.
- The meaning of endowment insurance.
- How to calculate the net single premium for endowment insurance.
- The meaning of accumulated cost of insurance.
- How to calculate the accumulated cost of insurance.
- How the values of C_x are calculated.
- How to calculate the net single premium for one year of insurance using commutation functions.
- How the values of M_x are calculated.
- How to calculate net single premiums and accumulated cost of insurance using commutation functions.

Life Insurance: Annual Premiums

In this chapter, we will describe how actuaries calculate the premiums which are paid for life insurance policies.

First, in explaining the underlying principles, we will use basic mortality and interest tables so that the student can better understand the theory on which premium calculations are based. Such calculations will be explained for various kinds of life insurance policies: term, whole life, and endowment.

Practical methods which simplify premium calculation will also be explained, namely, the use of published tables of *life annuities* and *net single premiums* and the use of commutation functions to calculate annual premiums.

We will explain the important differences between *net annual premiums* and *gross annual premiums* and the separate purposes served by each, as well as the differences between calculating premiums for *participating* and *nonparticipating* life insurance.

The student will learn how a company's expenses are analyzed and used to calculate the premiums which a policyowner actually pays. The total of annual premiums plus interest thereon must be adequate to cover the company's death claims plus its expenses and profit.

Finally, this chapter will introduce the subject of *modified* premiums, a method which life insurance companies use to vary the amount they have available to cover their expenses without varying the premiums which the policyowner pays.

10.1 INTRODUCTION

Purchasing life insurance by paying a single premium when the policy is issued is relatively uncommon, because few people are financially able to make such a payment. A more acceptable procedure has been devised for paying premiums whereby the premium is paid in equal annual amounts. In effect, these premiums constitute an annuity as described in earlier chapters. Instead of paying the premium in a single sum, payments are made in equal amounts over a number of years. This can be thought of as comparable to paying off a loan by periodic payments, where the loan is equal to the net single premium. The calculation of such a premium is based on the following principle: *At the date the policy is issued, the present value of all the annual level premiums must be equal to the present value of the benefits.*

The premium so calculated is called a *net annual premium.* The word "net" here means that the premium calculation involves only rates of interest and mortality with no consideration for expenses or profits. (The annual premium which does include an amount for expenses and profits is called the *gross annual premium.* It will be considered in Section 10.7.)

Life insurance policies may be issued on any date during a calendar year. The first annual premium is due on that date, the second annual premium is due one year later, etc. The period of time between such anniversaries is known as a *policy year,* to distinguish it from a calendar year (that is, January 1 to December 31). In this book, references to years in connection with insurance policies will mean policy years. (It should also be noted that premiums can be paid more frequently than annually, such as monthly. This topic will be explained in Section 10.8.)

Annual premiums are always paid at the beginning of the policy year, such payments taking place each year only if the person insured is then alive to pay. Thus, they constitute an example of a *contingent annuity.* More specifically annual premiums for a policy constitute a *life annuity due.* Such premiums may be paid either for the same number of years as the insurance benefit covers or for a fewer number of years. Thus, they may constitute either a *whole life annuity due* or a *temporary life annuity due.* In describing a certain policy, if the premium-paying period is not specified, it is generally understood that premiums are payable for as long as there is life insurance coverage.

CHOICE OF TABLES. Because the calculation of net premiums has many uses, it is important that the actuary plan carefully which particular mortality tables and interest rates to use when calculating these net premiums. For instance, if a net annual premium is used to calculate reserves, compliance with legal requirements may be paramount; but if a net annual premium is used as the basis of a nonparticipating gross premium calculation, then conformity to true experienced mortality and interest may be most important.

In this chapter, the illustrations are based on the 1958 C.S.O. Table, which is usually employed in practice to calculate reserves or participating gross premiums.

In general, mortality tables which show higher mortality rates result in higher net annual premiums, as noted in Chapter 9 for net single premiums.

The use of a higher interest rate will result in lower net annual premiums. This is the same effect as for net single premiums, life annuity present values, and the present value of payments certain.

10.2 NET ANNUAL PREMIUMS FOR TERM INSURANCE

A term life insurance policy which covers a stated number of years normally requires an annual premium payable at the beginning of each of those years. The calculation of the net annual premiums is based on the principle stated above: *At the date the policy is issued, the present value of the net premiums must be equal to the present value of the benefits.*

For example, it may be desired to calculate the net annual premium (per $1,000 of insurance) for a four-year term insurance policy issued to a person age 25. Since no premium-paying period is specified, it is understood that these premiums are payable for four years. In line diagram form, this series of net annual premiums appears as follows:

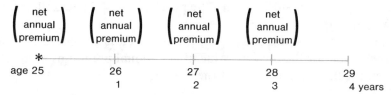

The net annual premiums constitute a *temporary life annuity due.* Their present value, at the date the policy is issued, may be calculated by consulting a mortality table and assuming that all persons enumerated therein will be making payments. Therefore, at age 25, their present value is

$$\begin{pmatrix} \text{Present Value of} \\ \text{Net Annual Premiums} \end{pmatrix} = \begin{pmatrix} \text{Net Annual} \\ \text{Premium} \end{pmatrix} (l_{25} + l_{26}v + l_{27}v^2 + l_{28}v^3)$$

This equation shows that the present value of the net annual premiums equals the total of each of the net annual premiums paid by survivors at each age, with each such amount being discounted at interest to the evaluation date. The first item inside the parentheses, namely l_{25}, is not multiplied by any v factor because it represents those net annual premiums which are payable on the evaluation date.

To find the present value per person (as was done in Chapter 8), the above expression would be divided by the number living on the evaluation date (l_{25}). However, this step is not necessary here since we will need to use only the total present value for all l_{25} persons to find the net annual premium per person.

In like manner, the present value of the benefits may be calculated. In line diagram form, the death benefits to be paid appear as follows:

	$1,000d_{25}$	$1,000d_{26}$	$1,000d_{27}$	$1,000d_{28}$
*age 25	26	27	28	29
	1	2	3	4 years

At age 25, the present value is

$$\left(\begin{array}{c}\text{Present Value of}\\ \text{Benefits}\end{array}\right) = \$1{,}000(d_{25}v + d_{26}v^2 + d_{27}v^3 + d_{28}v^4)$$

that is, the $1,000 death benefit is paid for those who die at each age, with each such amount being discounted at interest from the end of the year of death to the evaluation date.

The above expression would be divided by the number living on the evaluation date (l_{25}) to find this present value per person, that is, the net single premium (as was done in Chapter 9). Again, however, this step is not necessary since the expression which represents a total net single premium for all the l_{25} persons is sufficient for the purpose of calculating the net annual premium per person.

We can now express the equality of the two factors considered above, that is, the expression for the present value of net annual premiums is equal to the expression for the present value of the benefits:

$$\left(\begin{array}{c}\text{Present Value of}\\ \text{Net Annual Premiums}\end{array}\right) = \left(\begin{array}{c}\text{Present Value of}\\ \text{Benefits}\end{array}\right)$$

$$\left(\begin{array}{c}\text{Net Annual}\\ \text{Premium}\end{array}\right)\left(\begin{array}{c}l_{25} + l_{26}v\\ + l_{27}v^2 + l_{28}v^3\end{array}\right) = \$1{,}000\left(\begin{array}{c}d_{25}v + d_{26}v^2\\ + d_{27}v^3 + d_{28}v^4\end{array}\right)$$

The equation can be solved for the net annual premium, which will be the net annual premium per person. If, for example, Table III and 3% interest were used to calculate the above net annual premiums, the present value of the net annual premiums (the left side) would be evaluated as follows:

From above:

$$\left(\begin{array}{c}\text{Present Value of}\\ \text{Net Annual Premiums}\end{array}\right) = \left(\begin{array}{c}\text{Net Annual}\\ \text{Premium}\end{array}\right)(l_{25} + l_{26}v + l_{27}v^2 + l_{28}v^3)$$

Substitute values for the l's from Table III, for the v's from Table I (3%):

$$= \left(\begin{array}{c}\text{Net Annual}\\ \text{Premium}\end{array}\right)\left[\begin{array}{l}(9{,}575{,}636)\\ + (9{,}557{,}155)(.970874)\\ + (9{,}538{,}423)(.942596)\\ + (9{,}519{,}442)(.915142)\end{array}\right]$$

$$= \left(\begin{array}{c}\text{Net Annual}\\ \text{Premium}\end{array}\right)\left(\begin{array}{c}9{,}575{,}636 + 9{,}278{,}793\\ + 8{,}990{,}879 + 8{,}711{,}641\end{array}\right)$$

$$= \left(\begin{array}{c}\text{Net Annual}\\ \text{Premium}\end{array}\right)(36{,}556{,}949)$$

The same mortality table and interest rate used to calculate the present value of the net annual premiums are used to calculate the present value of the benefits. The right side of the equation would be evaluated as follows:

From above:

$$\left(\begin{array}{c}\text{Present Value of}\\ \text{Benefits}\end{array}\right) = \$1{,}000\,(d_{25}v + d_{26}v^2 + d_{27}v^3 + d_{28}v^4)$$

Substitute values for the d's from Table III, for the v's from Table I (3%):

$$= \$1{,}000 \left[\begin{array}{c}(18{,}481)(.970874)\\ + (18{,}732)(.942596)\\ + (18{,}981)(.915142)\\ + (19{,}324)(.888487)\end{array}\right]$$

$$= \$1{,}000(17{,}943 + 17{,}657 + 17{,}370 + 17{,}169)$$

$$= \$70{,}139{,}000$$

The net annual premium per person can now be found:

Basic equation:

$$\left(\begin{array}{c}\text{Present Value of}\\ \text{Net Annual Premiums}\end{array}\right) = \left(\begin{array}{c}\text{Present Value of}\\ \text{Benefits}\end{array}\right)$$

Substitute values calculated above:

$$\left(\begin{array}{c}\text{Net Annual}\\ \text{Premium}\end{array}\right)(36{,}556{,}949) = \$70{,}139{,}000$$

$$\left(\begin{array}{c}\text{Net Annual}\\ \text{Premium}\end{array}\right) = \frac{\$70{,}139{,}000}{36{,}556{,}949}$$

$$= \$1.91862$$

$$= \$1.92$$

In line diagram form, this series of net annual premiums appears as follows:

PROOF BY ACCUMULATING A FUND. It can be demonstrated that the payment of these net annual premiums will provide $1,000 (at the end of the year of death) for all who die between ages 25 and 29. Using Table III, the amount of premium paid in at the beginning of the first year is

$$\$1.92\,(l_{25}) = \$1.92\,(9{,}575{,}636)$$

$$= \$18{,}385{,}221.12$$

At the end of one year, the accumulated value of this amount is

$$(\$18{,}385{,}221.12)(1.03) = \$18{,}936{,}777.75$$

From this fund is deducted $1,000 for each who have died during the first year:

$$\$1,000\,(d_{25}) = \$1,000\,(18,481)$$
$$= \$18,481,000$$

This leaves a balance in the fund of

$$\$18,936,777.75 - \$18,481,000 = \$455,777.75$$

The continued operation of the fund for succeeding years may be traced in the accompanying schedule (Chart 10–1). The final excess in the fund represents less than $3 for each person dying the final year and results from rounding off the net annual premium to two decimal places. If more decimal places had been used, the final balance in the fund would be shown as nearly equal to zero.

CHART 10–1

(1) Year	(2) Premiums Paid at Beginning of Year (Number Living × $1.92)	(3) Total Fund at Beginning of Year (Col. 6, Previous Year, plus Col. 2)	(4) Fund Accumulated for One Year (Col. 3 × 1.03)	(5) Claims Paid at End of Year (Number of Deaths × $1,000)	(6) Balance in Fund at End of Year after Payment of Claims (Col. 4 − Col. 5)
1	$18,385,221.12	$18,385,221.12	$18,936,777.75	$18,481,000	$455,777.75
2	18,349,737.60	18,805,515.35	19,369,680.81	18,732,000	637,680.81
3	18,313,772.16	18,951,452.97	19,519,996.56	18,981,000	538,996.56
4	18,277,328.64	18,816,325.20	19,380,814.96	19,324,000	56,814.96

To Illustrate—Using Table III and 3% interest, calculate the net annual premium (per $1,000) for a two-year term insurance policy issued at age 60.

Solution—In line diagram form, the *net annual premiums* for this policy appear as follows:

$$\left(\begin{array}{c}\text{net}\\\text{annual}\\\text{premium}\end{array}\right) \qquad \left(\begin{array}{c}\text{net}\\\text{annual}\\\text{premium}\end{array}\right)$$

```
    *----------------+----------------+
  age 60            61               62
                     1              2 years
```

The total present value of the net annual premiums is equivalent to the net annual premiums paid by the survivors at each age, with each such amount being discounted at interest to the evaluation date.

Basic equation:

$$\left(\begin{array}{c}\text{Present Value of}\\\text{Net Annual Premiums}\end{array}\right) = \left(\begin{array}{c}\text{Net Annual}\\\text{Premium}\end{array}\right)(l_{60} + l_{61}v)$$

Substitute values from the tables:

$$= \left(\begin{array}{c}\text{Net Annual}\\ \text{Premium}\end{array}\right)\left[\begin{array}{c}(7,698,698)\\ +\ (7,542,106)(.970874)\end{array}\right]$$

$$= \left(\begin{array}{c}\text{Net Annual}\\ \text{Premium}\end{array}\right)(7,698,698 + 7,322,435)$$

$$= \left(\begin{array}{c}\text{Net Annual}\\ \text{Premium}\end{array}\right)(15,021,133)$$

In line diagram form, the benefits for this policy appear as follows:

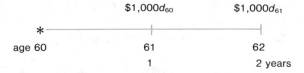

The total present value of the benefits is equivalent to the amounts paid for those who die at each age, with each amount being discounted at interest from the end of the year of death to the evaluation date.

Basic equation:

$$\left(\begin{array}{c}\text{Present Value of}\\ \text{Benefits}\end{array}\right) = \$1,000\,(d_{60}v + d_{61}v^2)$$

Substitute values from the tables:

$$= \$1,000\left[\begin{array}{c}(156,592)(.970874)\\ +\ (167,736)(.942596)\end{array}\right]$$

$$= \$1,000\,(152,031 + 158,107)$$

$$= \$310,138,000$$

The net annual premium is then found by substituting these values in the basic equation:

$$\left(\begin{array}{c}\text{Present Value of}\\ \text{Net Annual Premiums}\end{array}\right) = \left(\begin{array}{c}\text{Present Value of}\\ \text{Benefits}\end{array}\right)$$

$$\left(\begin{array}{c}\text{Net Annual}\\ \text{Premium}\end{array}\right)(15,021,133) = \$310,138,000$$

$$\left(\begin{array}{c}\text{Net Annual}\\ \text{Premium}\end{array}\right) = \$20.65$$

10.3 NET ANNUAL PREMIUMS FOR WHOLE LIFE INSURANCE

The net annual premiums for a whole life insurance policy may be paid

$$\boxed{\text{either}}$$

for the entire lifetime of the person insured. They thus constitute a *whole life annuity due*. This kind of insurance policy is known as *ordinary life* or *continuous payment life* or *straight life* policy.

$$\boxed{\text{or}}$$

for a number of years which is *less* than the entire lifetime, say for *n* years. They thus constitute a *temporary life annuity due*. This kind of insurance is known as an *n-payment life* policy.

To Illustrate—Using Table III and 3% interest, first calculate the net annual premium (per $1,000) for an ordinary life insurance policy issued at age 96, then for a two-payment life policy issued at that age.

Solution—The present value of the benefits will be the same for both policies because both provide insurance coverage for the whole of life. The line diagram for these benefits appears as follows. (Remember, according to the 1958 C.S.O. Table, all persons die before age 100.):

	$1,000d_{96}$	$1,000d_{97}$	$1,000d_{98}$	$1,000d_{99}$
*				
age 96	97	98	99	100
	1	2	3	4 years

Once again, the total present value is equivalent to the amounts of benefits paid for those who die at each age, with each such amount being discounted at interest from the end of the year of death to the evaluation date.

Basic equation:

$$\left(\begin{array}{c}\text{Present Value of}\\ \text{Benefits}\end{array}\right) = \$1,000(d_{96}v + d_{97}v^2 + d_{98}v^3 + d_{99}v^4)$$

Substitute values from the tables:

$$= \$1,000\left[\begin{array}{c}(25,250)(.970874)\\ +(18,456)(.942596)\\ +(12,916)(.915142)\\ +(\ 6,415)(.888487)\end{array}\right]$$

$$= \$1,000(24,515 + 17,397 + 11,820 + 5,700)$$

$$= \$59,432,000$$

The line diagrams for the net annual premiums for these two policies appear as follows:

Ordinary Life

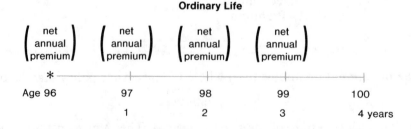

	$\left(\begin{array}{c}\text{net}\\ \text{annual}\\ \text{premium}\end{array}\right)$	$\left(\begin{array}{c}\text{net}\\ \text{annual}\\ \text{premium}\end{array}\right)$	$\left(\begin{array}{c}\text{net}\\ \text{annual}\\ \text{premium}\end{array}\right)$	$\left(\begin{array}{c}\text{net}\\ \text{annual}\\ \text{premium}\end{array}\right)$
*				
Age 96	97	98	99	100
	1	2	3	4 years

Two-Payment Life

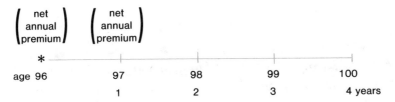

In each case their total present value is equivalent to the net annual premiums paid by the survivors at each age, with each such amount being discounted at interest to the evaluation date.

Ordinary Life

Basic equation:

$$\left(\begin{array}{c}\text{Present Value of}\\\text{Net Annual Premiums}\end{array}\right) = \left(\begin{array}{c}\text{Net Annual}\\\text{Premium}\end{array}\right)(l_{96} + l_{97}v + l_{98}v^2 + l_{99}v^3)$$

Substitute values from the tables:

$$= \left(\begin{array}{c}\text{Net Annual}\\\text{Premium}\end{array}\right)\left[\begin{array}{l}(63,037)\\ +(37,787)(.970874)\\ +(19,331)(.942596)\\ +(\ 6,415)(.915142)\end{array}\right]$$

$$= \left(\begin{array}{c}\text{Net Annual}\\\text{Premium}\end{array}\right)\left(\begin{array}{c}63,037 + 36,686\\ +18,221 + 5,871\end{array}\right)$$

$$= \left(\begin{array}{c}\text{Net Annual}\\\text{Premium}\end{array}\right)(123,815)$$

Two-Payment Life

Basic equation:

$$\left(\begin{array}{c}\text{Present Value of}\\\text{Net Annual Premiums}\end{array}\right) = \left(\begin{array}{c}\text{Net Annual}\\\text{Premium}\end{array}\right)(l_{96} + l_{97}v)$$

Substitute values from the tables:

$$= \left(\begin{array}{c}\text{Net Annual}\\\text{Premium}\end{array}\right)\left[\begin{array}{l}(63,037)\\ +(37,787)(.970874)\end{array}\right]$$

$$= \left(\begin{array}{c}\text{Net Annual}\\\text{Premium}\end{array}\right)(63,037 + 36,686)$$

$$= \left(\begin{array}{c}\text{Net Annual}\\\text{Premium}\end{array}\right)(99,723)$$

The net annual premium for each policy is then solved for, as follows:

Ordinary Life

Basic equation:

$$\begin{pmatrix} \text{Present Value of} \\ \text{Net Annual Premiums} \end{pmatrix} = \begin{pmatrix} \text{Present Value of} \\ \text{Benefits} \end{pmatrix}$$

Substitute values calculated above:

$$\begin{pmatrix} \text{Net Annual} \\ \text{Premium} \end{pmatrix}(123{,}815) = \$59{,}432{,}000$$

$$\begin{pmatrix} \text{Net Annual} \\ \text{Premium} \end{pmatrix} = \$480.01$$

Two-Payment Life

Basic equation:

$$\begin{pmatrix} \text{Present Value of} \\ \text{Net Annual Premiums} \end{pmatrix} = \begin{pmatrix} \text{Present Value of} \\ \text{Benefits} \end{pmatrix}$$

Substitute values calculated above:

$$\begin{pmatrix} \text{Net Annual} \\ \text{Premium} \end{pmatrix}(99{,}723) = \$59{,}432{,}000$$

$$\begin{pmatrix} \text{Net Annual} \\ \text{Premium} \end{pmatrix} = \$595.97$$

As the premium-paying period is shortened, the amount of the net annual premium for the same benefits increases. This can be seen by comparing the net annual premium for the ordinary life policy above ($480.01) with the net annual premium for the two-payment life policy ($595.97).

The calculation of net annual premiums for whole life insurance at the younger ages would become very laborious if the procedure described had to be used. In actual practice, calculations for all kinds of net annual premiums are usually simplified by using commutation functions, as will be explained in Section 10.6.

10.4 NET ANNUAL PREMIUMS FOR ENDOWMENT INSURANCE

The net annual premiums for an endowment insurance policy may be paid

either

for the same number of years as the insurance covers, say for *n* years. They thus constitute a *temporary life annuity due for n years*. This kind of insurance policy is known as an *n-year endowment* policy. An example would be a ten-year endowment policy, where premiums and insurance coverage are both for a ten-year period.

or

for a number of years which is less than the period that the insurance covers, say for *m* years (with the insurance coverage for *n* years). They thus constitute a *temporary life annuity due for m years*. This kind of insurance policy is known as an *m-payment n-year endowment* policy. An example would be a twenty-payment endowment-at-age-65 policy. If the policy were issued at age 35, it would be a twenty-payment thirty-year endowment policy.

TWO RATES OF INTEREST. If the interest rate to be used changes over the period of the life insurance coverage, the net annual premiums can be calculated using the methods shown in Chapters 8 and 9 for dual interest situations.

In using the equation

$$\begin{pmatrix} \text{Present Value of} \\ \text{Net Annual Premiums} \end{pmatrix} = \begin{pmatrix} \text{Present Value of} \\ \text{Benefits} \end{pmatrix}$$

the annuity factor used to evaluate the left-hand side is calculated as shown in Section 8.2, where life annuity payments were shown discounted using dual interest rates. The right-hand side is calculated as shown in Section 9.5, where net single premiums were shown using dual interest rates.

10.5 RELATIONSHIPS BETWEEN NET PREMIUMS AND LIFE ANNUITIES

The derivation of all the net annual premiums discussed in this chapter has followed the principle: *At the date the policy is issued, the present value of the net annual premiums must be equal to the present value of the benefits.* The calculations above were made on a total basis, that is, the total present values for all persons living on the evaluation date.

Net premiums can also be calculated on a per person basis. The present value of the net annual premiums may be expressed as the net annual premium multiplied by the present value at age *x* of a temporary life annuity due of 1. This latter present value is known as the *annuity factor*. This relationship can be expressed by the following equation:

$$\begin{pmatrix} \text{Net Annual} \\ \text{Premium} \end{pmatrix} \begin{pmatrix} \text{Annuity} \\ \text{Factor} \end{pmatrix} = \begin{pmatrix} \text{Present Value of Net} \\ \text{Annual Premiums} \end{pmatrix}$$

Since the present value of the benefits is the same as the net single premium, the basic statement of equality may be written:

$$\begin{pmatrix} \text{Net Annual} \\ \text{Premium} \end{pmatrix} \begin{pmatrix} \text{Annuity} \\ \text{Factor} \end{pmatrix} = \begin{pmatrix} \text{Net Single} \\ \text{Premium} \end{pmatrix}$$

From this equation, the value of any one of the items in the equation can be calculated if the values of the other two are known. Most importantly, the net annual premium can be expressed as follows (solving the above equation for the net annual premium):

$$\left(\begin{array}{c} \text{Net Annual} \\ \text{Premium} \end{array} \right) = \dfrac{\left(\begin{array}{c} \text{Net Single} \\ \text{Premium} \end{array} \right)}{\left(\begin{array}{c} \text{Annuity} \\ \text{Factor} \end{array} \right)}$$

Since tables of net single premiums and annuity factors are published and are usually available in the actuarial department, this relationship provides a convenient means to calculate net annual premiums per person per $1,000 of insurance.

   To Illustrate—The following annuity factors and net single premiums (Chart 10–2) are taken from published tables based on the 1958 C.S.O. Table and $3\frac{1}{2}\%$ interest. These values are calculated at age 55. The particular values shown are for 10, 15, 20, and 45 years, that is, the first annuity factor is for a ten-year annuity, the first net single premium for term insurance is for ten years of term insurance, and the first net single premium for a pure endowment is for a pure endowment due ten years in the future. The second value in each column is for a 15-year benefit, etc.

CHART 10-2

Number of years (n)	Present value of an n-year temporary life annuity due of 1 per year	Net single premium for $1,000 term insurance for n years	Net single premium for $1,000 pure endowment payable at end of n years
10	8.03	$149.82	$578.66
15	10.56	242.34	400.64
20	12.24	336.80	249.13
45(or rest of life)	13.99	527.07	0

Based on these values, calculate the net annual premium for a $1,000 policy issued at age 55 for each of the following kinds of policies.
   (a) ordinary life
   (b) whole life with premiums stopping at age 70
   (c) ten-payment 20-year endowment

Solution—

(a) For an ordinary life policy, the benefit is equivalent to term insurance to the end of the mortality table, and the premiums are payable for the rest of life.

Basic equation:

$$\left(\begin{array}{c}\text{Net Annual}\\\text{Premium}\end{array}\right)=\frac{\left(\begin{array}{c}\text{Net Single}\\\text{Premium}\end{array}\right)}{\left(\begin{array}{c}\text{Annuity}\\\text{Factor}\end{array}\right)}$$

Substitute values from the table:

$$=\frac{\$527.07}{13.99}$$

$$=\$37.67$$

(b) For a whole life policy with premiums stopping at age 70, the benefit is also equivalent to term insurance to the end of the mortality table. The annuity factor would be for 15 years, since there are 15 years of premiums $(70 - 55 = 15)$.

Basic equation:

$$\left(\begin{array}{c}\text{Net Annual}\\\text{Premium}\end{array}\right)=\frac{\left(\begin{array}{c}\text{Net Single}\\\text{Premium}\end{array}\right)}{\left(\begin{array}{c}\text{Annuity}\\\text{Factor}\end{array}\right)}$$

Substitute values from the table:

$$=\frac{\$527.07}{10.56}$$

$$=\$49.91$$

(c) For a ten-payment 20-year endowment policy, it should be remembered that the benefit consists of two parts: term insurance for 20 years and a pure endowment due at the end of 20 years. Therefore, the total net single premium is equal to these two net single premiums added together. The annuity factor would be for ten years, since there are ten years of premiums.

Basic equation:

$$\left(\begin{array}{c}\text{Net Annual}\\\text{Premium}\end{array}\right)=\frac{\left(\begin{array}{c}\text{Net Single}\\\text{Premium}\end{array}\right)}{\left(\begin{array}{c}\text{Annuity}\\\text{Factor}\end{array}\right)}$$

Substitute values from the table:

$$= \frac{\$336.80 + \$249.13}{8.03}$$

$$= \frac{\$585.93}{8.03}$$

$$= \$72.97$$

To Illustrate Again—Calculate the present value at age 40 of a ten-year life annuity due of 1 per year (the annuity factor), given the following values:

$57.84 = Net Annual Premium per $1,000 at Age 40 for a Ten-Payment Life Policy

$502.64 = Net Single Premium per $1,000 at Age 40 for Whole Life Insurance

Solution—

Basic equation:

$$\begin{pmatrix} \text{Net Annual} \\ \text{Premium} \end{pmatrix} \begin{pmatrix} \text{Annuity} \\ \text{Factor} \end{pmatrix} = \begin{pmatrix} \text{Net Single} \\ \text{Premium} \end{pmatrix}$$

Substitute values given:

$$\$57.84 \begin{pmatrix} \text{Annuity} \\ \text{Factor} \end{pmatrix} = \$502.64$$

$$\begin{pmatrix} \text{Annuity} \\ \text{Factor} \end{pmatrix} = 8.69$$

To Illustrate Again—Calculate the net single premium per $1,000 at age 40 for a ten-year pure endowment, given the following values:

$90.68 = Net Annual Premium per $1,000 at Age 40 for a Ten-Year Endowment Policy

$70.90 = Net Single Premium per $1,000 at Age 40 for a Ten-Year Term Insurance Policy

8.69 = Present Value at Age 40 of a Ten-Year Life Annuity Due of 1 per Year (Annuity Factor)

Solution—It must be remembered that the net single premium for a ten-year endowment policy consists of two parts:

Net single premium for term insurance

and

Net single premium for a pure endowment

The value of the first part is given; the value of the second part must be solved for.

Basic equation, showing net single premium in two parts:

$$\left(\begin{array}{c}\text{Net Annual}\\\text{Premium}\end{array}\right)\left(\begin{array}{c}\text{Annuity}\\\text{Factor}\end{array}\right) = \left(\begin{array}{c}\text{Net Single Premium}\\\text{for Term Insurance}\end{array}\right) + \left(\begin{array}{c}\text{Net Single Premium}\\\text{for Pure Endowment}\end{array}\right)$$

Substitute values given:

$$(\$90.68)(8.69) = \$70.90 + \left(\begin{array}{c}\text{Net Single Premium}\\\text{for Pure Endowment}\end{array}\right)$$

$$(\$90.68)(8.69) - \$70.90 = \left(\begin{array}{c}\text{Net Single Premium}\\\text{for Pure Endowment}\end{array}\right)$$

$$\$717.11 = \left(\begin{array}{c}\text{Net Single Premium}\\\text{for Pure Endowment}\end{array}\right)$$

EXERCISES, SET 22

1. Explain the difference between a net annual premium and a gross annual premium.

2. What kind of an annuity is represented by the premiums for a ten-year term insurance policy?

3. Will a policy's net annual premium be higher or lower if a higher interest rate is used in the calculation?

4. Write an equation (using symbols) showing the present value of the net annual premiums as equal to the present value of the benefits for each of the following $1,000 policies (on a total basis, not per person). Using Table III and 3% interest, solve each equation for the net annual premium per person.

   a) A one-year term insurance policy issued at age 75
   b) A three-year term insurance policy issued at age 69
   c) An ordinary life policy issued at age 97
   d) A two-payment life policy issued at age 97
   e) A three-year endowment insurance policy issued at age 10
   f) A four-year endowment insurance policy issued at age 25, wherein premiums stop at age 27, that is, last premium is payable at age 26

5. Given the following annuity factors and net single premiums at age 40,

Number of years (n)	Present value of an n-year temporary life annuity due of 1 per year	Net single premium for $1,000 term insurance for n years	Net single premium for $1,000 pure endowment payable at end of n years
10	8.621	$ 43.37	$705.52
20	14.546	115.07	461.25
30	18.180	221.20	249.30
60(or rest of life)	20.374	406.58	0

calculate the net annual premium for each of the following $1,000 policies issued at age 40:

a) ordinary life
b) 20-payment life
c) ten-year endowment
d) 20-payment endowment-at-age-70

6. Given the following values, calculate the present value of a 20-year life annuity due of 1 per year.

$808.41 = Net Single Premium per $1,000 at Age 69 for Whole Life Insurance

$102.15 = Net Annual Premium per $1,000 at Age 69 for a 20-Payment Life Insurance Policy

7. If the following values are given, calculate the net single premium per $1,000 at age 30 for endowment-at-age-65 insurance

$21.18 = Net Annual Premium per $1,000 at Age 30 for an Endowment-at-Age-65 policy

19.47 = Present Value at Age 30 of a 35-Year Life Annuity Due of 1 per Year

8. If the net annual premium for a $5,000 two-year term life insurance policy issued at age 22 is $Z, then the present value of net annual premiums for this policy is equal to

(1) $Z[l_{21}(1 + i) + l_{22}]$ (3) $Z[d_{22}v + d_{23}v^2]$
(2) $Z[l_{22} + l_{23}v]$ (4) $Z[l_{22}v + l_{23}v^2]$

10.6 COMMUTATION FUNCTIONS

The commutation functions which were explained in Chapters 8 and 9 can be used to calculate net annual premiums and will generally simplify the work.

The basis for the calculation is the equation given in Section 10.5:

$$\left(\begin{array}{c}\text{Net Annual}\\\text{Premium}\end{array}\right)\left(\begin{array}{c}\text{Annuity}\\\text{Factor}\end{array}\right) = \left(\begin{array}{c}\text{Net Single}\\\text{Premium}\end{array}\right)$$

The $1,000 four-year term insurance policy issued at age 25, discussed in Section 10.2, will be used as an example. The left-hand side of the above equation may be written

$$\left(\begin{array}{c}\text{Net Annual}\\\text{Premium}\end{array}\right)\left(\frac{N_{25} - N_{29}}{D_{25}}\right)$$

This follows from the general statement made in Chapter 8 that the factor to use in evaluating a *life annuity* will be of the form $\frac{N - N}{D}$, where (1) the subscript of the first N is the age when the first payment is due, (2) the subscript of the second N is the first age when there are no more payments due, and (3) the subscript of the D is the age at which the annuity is being evaluated.

The right-hand side of the above equation (Net Single Premium) may be written

$$\$1,000\left(\frac{M_{25} - M_{29}}{D_{25}}\right)$$

This follows from the general statement made in Chapter 9 that the factor to use in calculating a *net single premium* will be of the form $\dfrac{M - M + D}{D}$, where (1) the subscript of the first M is the age when the insurance coverage begins, (2) the subscript of the second M is the age at which the insurance coverage stops, (3) the subscript of the D in the numerator is the age at which a pure endowment would be paid, and (4) the subscript of the D in the denominator is the age at which this net single premium is evaluated. (In this particular case, D in the numerator does not appear, because no pure endowment is involved.)

The entire equation then appears as follows:

$$\left(\begin{array}{c}\text{Net Annual} \\ \text{Premium}\end{array}\right)\left(\frac{N_{25} - N_{29}}{D_{25}}\right) = \$1,000\left(\frac{M_{25} - M_{29}}{D_{25}}\right)$$

The commutation symbol D_{25} appears in the denominator on both sides of the equation. If both sides are multiplied by D_{25}, the denominators are eliminated. The equation can then be solved for (Net Annual Premium) by dividing both sides by $(N_{25} - N_{29})$. The result is

$$\left(\begin{array}{c}\text{Net Annual} \\ \text{Premium}\end{array}\right) = \$1,000\left(\frac{M_{25} - M_{29}}{N_{25} - N_{29}}\right)$$

Using values of M and N from Table IV, this becomes

$$\left(\begin{array}{c}\text{Net Annual} \\ \text{Premium}\end{array}\right) = \$1,000\left(\frac{1,276,590 - 1,243,091}{113,189,600 - 95,729,800}\right)$$

$$= \$1.92$$

The answer is the same as that calculated in Section 10.2.

THE GENERAL FORM. A general statement can be made that the factor to use in calculating a *net annual premium* will be of the form $\dfrac{M - M + D}{N - N}$, where the subscripts in the numerator define the ages at which the benefits begin and end, following the rule given in Chapter 9 for calculating net single premiums, and where the subscripts of the N's in the denominator define the premium-paying period and follow the rule given in Chapter 8 for calculating life annuity factors.

To Illustrate—Using Table IV, calculate the net annual premium (per $1,000) for a two-year term insurance policy issued at age 60.

Solution—This problem is the same as the one illustrated in Section 10.2. The solution will now be calculated using commutation functions. The D in the numerator of the general expression will not appear, because again there is no pure endowment involved.

Basic equation; subscripts of the M's define the period of coverage; subscripts of the N's define the premium-paying period:

$$\left(\begin{array}{c}\text{Net Annual}\\ \text{Premium}\end{array}\right) = \$1,000\left(\frac{M_{60} - M_{62}}{N_{60} - N_{62}}\right)$$

Substitute values from Table IV:

$$= \$1,000\left(\frac{825,847 - 773,206}{16,510,076 - 13,960,493}\right)$$

$$= \$1,000\left(\frac{52,641}{2,549,583}\right)$$

$$= \$20.65$$

This answer agrees with that calculated in Section 10.2.

To Illustrate Again—Using Table IV, calculate the net annual premium (per $1,000) for an ordinary life policy issued at age 96.

Solution—This problem is the same as the one illustrated in Section 10.3. The solution will now be calculated using commutation functions. In this case, the second M in the numerator of the general expression will not appear, because the insurance is for the whole of life. Furthermore the D in the numerator will not appear, because there is no pure endowment involved. In the denominator, the second N will not appear, because the premium payments are to be made for life.

Basic equation:

$$\left(\begin{array}{c}\text{Net Annual}\\ \text{Premium}\end{array}\right) = \$1,000\left(\frac{M_{96}}{N_{96}}\right)$$

Substitute values from Table IV:

$$= \$1,000\left(\frac{3,481}{7,251}\right)$$

$$= \$480.07$$

This answer is only six cents different from that calculated in Section 10.3. The difference is due to the fact that the commutation functions as shown in the tables are rounded off to the nearest whole number.

To Illustrate Again—Using Table IV, calculate the net annual premium for a $1,000 two-payment endowment-at-age-65 policy issued to a person age 61.

Solution—The solution will now be calculated by using commutation functions.

Basic equation; subscripts of the M's define the period of coverage; subscript of D is the age of pure endowment; subscripts of the N's define the premium-paying period:

$$\binom{\text{Net Annual}}{\text{Premium}} = \$1,000\left(\frac{M_{61} - M_{65} + D_{65}}{N_{61} - N_{63}}\right)$$

Substitute values from Table IV:

$$= \$1,000\left(\frac{800,042 - 686,750 + 995,688}{15,203,352 - 12,780,670}\right)$$

$$= \$1,000\left(\frac{1,108,980}{2,422,682}\right)$$

$$= \$457.75$$

EXERCISES, SET 23

(Use Table IV for all of the following.)

1. Write an expression (using commutation functions) for the net annual premium (per $1,000) for each of the following policies. (If you wish, complete the calculations for the value of each.)

   a) A 20-year term insurance policy issued at age 25
   b) A one-year term insurance policy issued at age 65
   c) A term-to-age-65 insurance policy issued at age 40
   d) An ordinary life policy issued at age 0
   e) A 30-payment life policy issued at age 21
   f) A whole life insurance policy issued at age 30, wherein premiums stop at age 70 (that is, the last premium is payable at age 69)
   g) A 25-year endowment insurance policy issued at age 28
   h) A 20-payment 30-year endowment insurance policy issued at age 15
   i) A 30-payment endowment-at-age-70 policy issued at age 22

2. Calculate the net annual premium for a $20,000 ordinary life insurance policy issued to a girl age 15. Use a three-year setback for females.

3. State in words what each of the following represents:

   a) $\$1,000\left(\dfrac{M_5 - M_{35} + D_{35}}{N_5 - N_{25}}\right)$

   b) $\$1,000\left(\dfrac{M_{60}}{N_{60} - N_{80}}\right)$

   c) $\$1,000\left(\dfrac{M_{14} - M_{24}}{N_{14} - N_{19}}\right)$

4. The net annual premium for a $7,000 20-payment whole life policy issued at age 35 may be expressed in commutation functions as

   (1) $\$7,000\left(\dfrac{N_{35}}{M_{35} - M_{55}}\right)$ (3) $\$7,000\left(\dfrac{M_{35}}{N_{35} - N_{55}}\right)$

   (2) $\$7,000\left(\dfrac{M_{35} - M_{55}}{N_{35}}\right)$ (4) $\$7,000\left(\dfrac{N_{35} - N_{55}}{M_{35}}\right)$

10.7 GROSS ANNUAL PREMIUMS

The net annual premiums dealt with above are calculated by taking account of assumed mortality and interest rates to provide the benefits guaranteed in the policy. However, they make no provision for the life insurance company's expense for conducting business. The net annual premium, which is used in the calculation of reserves and nonforfeiture values (to be explained in later chapters), is calculated by using the particular mortality tables and interest rates which are specified by law.

COMPARISON OF GROSS AND NET PREMIUMS. The premium which the policyowner actually pays to the insurance company is called the *gross premium.* It differs from the *net premium* in two important ways:

1. Gross premiums include amounts intended to provide for expenses, profits, and the possibility of unforeseen adversities.
2. Gross premiums do not have to be calculated by using the particular mortality tables and interest rates specified by law, that is, those used to calculate reserves and nonforfeiture values.

The gross premium for a policy is usually larger than the net premium, even if the two are calculated using different mortality and interest rates. The amount by which the gross premium exceeds the net premium is called the *loading.* Therefore:

Gross Premium − Net Premium = Loading

or

Net Premium + Loading = Gross Premium

When the policy is *participating* (receives policy dividends), it is not necessary to employ great refinement in the calculation of the gross premium. Savings from operations can be returned to the owners of participating policies in the form of dividends, and the dividend calculations can be changed when necessary to meet changing conditions. (Dividend calculations will be explained in Chapter 14.) Therefore, gross premiums for participating policies are generally calculated by adding a loading to the net premium, this loading being derived by a fairly simple formula. The principal concern is that the amount of the gross premium be conservative.

When a policy is *nonparticipating*, however, no policy dividends are returned to the policyowner. Therefore, the insurance company has no means of adjusting its income to allow for changes in mortality, interest rates, or expenses subsequent to issue of the policy. Such premiums are based on a very detailed analysis of the mortality, interest, and expenses which the company expects to experience. The actual premium calculations become highly complex and will not be covered in this book.

Gross premiums are calculated by a wide variety of methods in practice. This book will illustrate some of the simpler formulas.

DETERMINING THE COMPANY'S EXPENSES. The area of greatest complexity has to do with that portion of the gross premium which provides for expenses. For this reason, the company's accountants and actuaries generally make careful analyses of the actual expenses which the company incurs. When such analyses are made, it is often found that the company's expenses can be classified into three principal categories. Each of the three types can be taken account of separately, if desired, in the calculation of the actual gross premium. These categories are:

1. Those expenses which are relatively *constant for each policy* regardless of the amount of the policy. These include the cost of issuing the policy, collecting the premiums, paying the claims, etc.
2. Those expenses which *vary with the amount of the premium*. These include state premium taxes and agents' commissions.
3. Those expenses which *vary with the amount of insurance*, that is, those expenses which are usually higher for larger amount policies. These include costs of proving whether applicants are in good health (such as medical examiners' fees), drawing up directions for payment of proceeds, etc.

In deriving these expense amounts for their company, the accountants and actuaries must employ a certain amount of judgment. It is often difficult to decide exactly which category certain expenditures should be assigned to. Thus, this particular part of the work sometimes reflects the experience and outlook of the persons making the analyses. However, the total expenses assigned to all categories will always equal the company's total actual expenses incurred.

As an example of the method used, suppose that the accountant or actuary is finding the cost of issuing each new policy. The total of all expenditures involved in issuing policies includes (1) the salaries of persons in the departments which evaluate the health of the applicants and issue the new policies, (2) the costs of medical examinations and other reports obtained, and (3) a portion of the rent the company pays for the space it occupies, that is, the portion occupied by the departments named above.

However, when allotting expenses, a certain amount of judgment is needed to decide how much should be allotted to "the issuing of new policies" out of the expenditures made for such things as recruiting new agents (who will sell the new policies), purchasing computers (which will calculate the premiums on the new policies), or the salaries of managers (who direct the activities of several departments, including the policy issue departments).

If, for example, the total expenditures in one year that are believed attributable to issuing new policies is $9,076,413, and the company has issued

85,202 new policies in that year, then the cost of issuing each new policy would be calculated as:

$$\$9,076,413 \div 85,202 = \$106.53$$

If the company had issued more or fewer new policies in that year, the $9,076,413 in the example would probably have been only modestly different, because much of the expense would be the same (salaries, rent, etc.). For this reason, the cost per policy is difficult to predict in advance and will probably be larger if fewer policies are actually issued and smaller if more policies are issued. It is also difficult to predict how inflation will affect this cost in future years.

The expenses are generally much larger in a policy's first year than in subsequent years. In Section 10.9 we will explain some methods used to provide more loading for expenses in a policy's first year. However, if the amount of loading is the same each year (as is the case when the gross premium and the net premium are level each year), then it is customary for the actuary to arrive at a level annual amount to use for expenses. Such an amount is generally calculated so that the present value (at time of issue) of all such level amounts of loading equals the present value of the actual expenses which it is assumed will be incurred in the future.

ACCOUNTING FOR EXPENSES IN CALCULATING GROSS PREMI-UMS. Expenses which are relatively constant regardless of policy size (category 1 above) are frequently provided for by adding a certain charge for each policy, regardless of the amount of the policy. This is known as a *policy charge* or *policy fee*. This method became widespread about 1957.

The method of calculation which was used before 1957 was based on determining the amount of an average-size policy. The gross premiums per $1,000 were so calculated that such an average-size policy w uld yield the amount needed to pay for these particular expenses. The result was that large policies yielded more than enough to cover their expenses, while small policies yielded an insufficient amount. In total, however, approximately the correct amount was collected.

A compromise between the pre-1957 and post-1957 methods is sometimes used to provide for these relatively constant expenses. Under this method, gross premiums per $1,000 are quoted which vary according to the size group into which the policy falls. For example, these groups might be

> Policies of less than $5,000 face amount
> Policies of $5,000 to $9,999 face amount
> Policies of $10,000 to $24,999 face amount
> Policies of $25,000 to $99,999 face amount
> Policies of $100,000 and over face amount

Within each such size group, an average-sized policy is used to calculate the gross premium per $1,000 for that group, so that the premium for this average-sized policy will cover the particular expenses referred to in category

1. The result is that the smaller policies require a larger gross premium per $1,000 than the larger policies. This method is known as *band grading* or simply *banding.*

In providing for those expenses which vary with the amount of the premium (category 2 above), a simple method is to add a percentage of the gross annual premium per $1,000 to the net annual premium. In equation form, this would be

> Gross = Net + Percent of Gross

To Illustrate—Calculate the gross annual premium per $1,000 for a policy for which the net annual premium per $1,000 is $12.49, assuming that a loading of 25% of the gross annual premium is needed for expenses. What gross annual premium would the policyowner pay for a $5,000 policy, assuming a charge is also made of $7.50 per policy?

Solution—Before computing the premium which the policyowner pays, it is necessary to find the gross premium per $1,000 of insurance. Then, the policyowner's total gross premium is this gross premium per $1,000 multiplied by the number of thousands of insurance plus any policy charge which is added by the company.

The calculation is first made to find the gross annual premium per $1,000:

Basic equation:

$$\text{Gross} = \text{Net} + \text{Percent of Gross}$$

Substitute $12.49 for net, .25 for percent:

$$\text{Gross} = \$12.49 + (.25)(\text{Gross})$$

Begin solving for "Gross" by subtracting (.25)(Gross) from each side:

$$\text{Gross} - (.25)(\text{Gross}) = \$12.49$$

$$\text{Gross}(1 - .25) = \$12.49$$

$$\text{Gross}(.75) = \$12.49$$

$$\text{Gross} = \$16.65$$

For the $5,000 policy, the gross annual premium would be five times $16.65 plus the $7.50 charge:

$$\left(\begin{array}{c}\text{Gross Premium} \\ \text{for } \$5,000\end{array}\right) = (5)(\$16.65) + \$7.50$$

$$= \$90.75$$

A common method of providing for those expenses which vary with the amount of insurance (category 3 above) is to use a constant amount per $1,000 of insurance. The expenses referred to in category 2, which vary with the amount of the premium, are then provided for by a percentage of the gross annual premium. In equation form, this total would be

Gross = Net + Constant + Percent of Gross

To Illustrate—Calculate the gross annual premium per $1,000 for a policy for which the net annual premium per $1,000 is $31.28, if it is to be loaded $3 per $1,000 plus 20% of the gross annual premium. What would the gross annual premium be for a $15,000 policy, assuming a charge is also made of $10 per policy?

Solution—The calculation is first made to find the gross annual premium per $1,000:

Basic equation:

$$Gross = Net + Constant + Percent of Gross$$

Substitute $31.28 for net, $3 for constant, and .20 for percent:

$$Gross = \$31.28 + \$3.00 + (.20)(Gross)$$

Solve the equation for "Gross":

$$Gross - (.20)(Gross) = \$31.28 + \$3.00$$

$$Gross(1 - .20) = \$31.28 + \$3.00$$

$$Gross(.80) = \$34.28$$

$$Gross = \$42.85$$

For the $15,000 policy, the gross annual premium paid by the policyowner would be 15 times $42.85 plus the $10 charge:

$$\left(\begin{array}{c}\text{Gross Premium} \\ \text{for } \$15,000\end{array}\right) = (15)(\$42.85) + \$10.00$$

$$= \$652.75$$

In this case, the total $652.75 gross annual premium which the policyowner pays is made up of the net annual premium plus loading, as follows:

$$\left(\begin{array}{c}\text{Net Annual} \\ \text{Premium}\end{array}\right) = (15)(\$31.28) \qquad = \$469.20$$

$$\left(\begin{array}{c}\text{Expenses Constant} \\ \text{per Policy}\end{array}\right) = \$10.00 \qquad\qquad = \quad 10.00$$

$$\left(\begin{array}{c}\text{Expenses Varying} \\ \text{with Premium}\end{array}\right) = (15)(.20)(\$42.85) = \quad 128.55$$

$$\left(\begin{array}{c}\text{Expenses Varying} \\ \text{with Amount} \\ \text{of Insurance}\end{array}\right) = (15)(\$3.00) \qquad = \quad 45.00$$

$$\overline{\qquad\qquad}$$
$$\$652.75 \quad \text{Total}$$

Since each insurance company determines its own methods for calculating the loading, not all insurance companies use loading formulas which add loadings of each of the types described above. Companies sometimes use loading methods involving only one or two of the types of additions described, rather than all three, or they may use very complex methods of loading which are not given in this book.

10.8 FRACTIONAL PREMIUMS

Instead of paying for life insurance by annual premiums, many people prefer to pay premiums in installments during the year—semiannually, quarterly, or monthly. These installments are known as *fractional premiums.* When premiums are paid in this manner, the company cannot invest the premium income as quickly as it can with annual premiums, and it thereby loses some interest. This method of payment also makes the company incur additional expenses for postage, clerical work, etc. The company's loss of interest income and additional expenses incurred should properly be borne by the policyowners who pay such fractional premiums. Therefore, the semiannual premium charged will be more than one half of the annual premium, and the quarterly and monthly premiums will likewise be more than one fourth or one twelfth, respectively, of the annual premium. The amount of the additional charges vary by company.

One way of calculating the gross *semiannual premium* is to increase the total gross annual premium (including any policy charge) by some percentage of itself and then divide the result by 2.

To determine the quarterly premium, the gross annual premium may be increased by some larger percentage, such as 5%, and the result is divided by 4.

To Illustrate—If the gross annual premium for a certain policy is $34.89, calculate the quarterly premium. Assume that it is one quarter of the gross annual premium increased by 5%.

Solution—The gross annual premium increased by 5% is

($34.89)(1.05) = $36.63

The quarterly premium is one quarter of this:

$$\text{Quarterly Premium} = \frac{1}{4}(\$36.63)$$

$$= \$9.16$$

Or, if 1.05 is divided by 4, the factor .2625 is obtained. The gross annual premium can be multiplied by this factor:

$$\text{Quarterly Premium} = (\$34.89)(.2625)$$

$$= \$9.16$$

The answer is the same by both methods.

To determine the *monthly premium*, the gross annual premium may be increased by a still greater percentage, such as 8%, and the result divided by 12.

EXERCISES, SET 24

1. What is meant by the *loading* in a premium?

2. Why are participating gross premiums generally calculated by using fairly simple formulas?

3. How can a level amount of annual loading be arrived at when it is known that actual expenses will vary considerably from year to year?

4. What is meant by the *banding* of premiums?

5. The net annual premium for a certain policy is $12.05 per $1,000. Calculate the gross annual premium per $1,000 by loading the net premium 20% of the gross premium.

6. Using the answer to Exercise 5, calculate the gross annual premium for a $10,000 policy, assuming an $8 policy charge is added to the premium.

7. Calculate the gross annual premium per $1,000 for a certain policy, given the following:

Net annual premium per $1,000 = $21.05
Loading (Except policy charge) = $2.50 per $1,000 plus 10% of gross premium

8. Using the answer to Exercise 7, calculate the gross annual premium for a $15,000 policy, assuming a charge of $12 per policy is added.

9. Calculate the gross annual premium for a $10,000 policy for which the net annual premium per $1,000 (that is, $49.20) is to be loaded $5 per $1,000 plus 15% of the gross premium, and finally, $20 per policy is added.

10. A certain company does not make an additional charge per policy but instead charges a different gross annual premium per $1,000 for different-sized policies, as follows:

20-Payment Life; Age 30

Amount of Policy	Gross Premium per $1,000
Less than $10,000	$33.28
$10,000 to $49,999	32.02
$50,000 and over	31.86

What would be the gross annual premium for a $25,000 20-payment life policy issued at age 30?

11. If the gross annual premium for a certain policy is $314.95, calculate the monthly premium. Assume that it is $\frac{1}{12}$ of the gross annual premium increased by 5%.

12. If the gross annual premium for a certain policy is $14.10 per $1,000, plus a charge of $5 per policy, calculate the semiannual premium for a $10,000 policy. Assume that it is half of the gross annual premium increased by 4%.

13. A life insurance company determines the premium which a policyowner must

pay for a particular type of policy by adding a loading of $6 per $1,000 of insurance plus 12% of the gross annual premium. If the net annual premium per $1,000 is $34.17, the gross annual premium for a $5,000 policy is

(1) $179.33   (3) $224.95
(2) $204.95   (4) $228.24

10.9 MODIFIED NET PREMIUMS

The availability of the loading over and above the net premium to provide for an insurance company's operating expenses was discussed in Section 10.7. However, the actual expenses incurred by the insurance company are not the same for each policy year but will be much heavier during the first year than in subsequent years.

The problem that heavy first-year expenses create for the insurance company can be demonstrated by considering a typical 20-payment life policy issued at age 30. The following figures apply to each $1,000 of insurance provided by this policy. The net level annual premium is $21.15 (based on the 1958 C.S.O. Table and 3% interest), and the gross annual premium is $30.04. Assume an agent's first-year commission is 45% of the gross annual premium, taxes are 2% of the gross annual premium, and expenses of issuing and administering a policy the first-year are $10.00 per $1,000 of insurance. The total expenses per $1,000 the first year are

$$
\begin{array}{ll}
\text{Agent's commission (45\% of \$30.04)} & \$13.52 \\
\text{Taxes (2\% of \$30.04)} & .60 \\
\text{Issue and administration expenses} & \underline{10.00} \\
\text{Total first-year expenses} & \$24.12
\end{array}
$$

The entire *net premium* of $21.15 is needed to pay death claims and provide reserves. None of this net premium is available to help pay expenses. The available loading is the difference between the gross premium and the net premium:

$$\text{Gross Premium} - \text{Net Premium} = \$30.04 - \$21.15$$

$$= \$8.89$$

Therefore, the loading is deficient in the first year by

$$\text{Expenses} - \text{Loading} = \$24.12 - \$8.89$$

$$= \$15.23$$

If a life insurance company has considerable surplus funds, this first-year deficiency in the loading may be met by drawing upon such surplus funds. However, for companies with relatively small surplus funds, such as young companies or rapidly growing companies, this procedure may not be practical.

For this reason, a number of other approaches to alleviating the problem have been developed which permit a larger portion of the first-year gross premium to be used for expenses. In effect, such methods provide for a first-year net premium which is smaller than the net level premium and, to compensate, net premiums for subsequent years which are larger than the net level premium. Net premiums which are changed or modified to release more money for first-year expenses are known as *modified net premiums*. Figure 10-1 will make this easier to see.

FIGURE 10–1

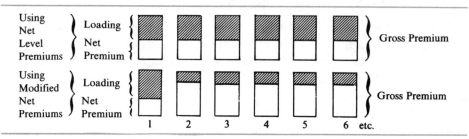

The premiums shown at the bottom part of the chart have had the net premiums modified so that the first net premium is smaller and the rest are larger.

It is important to remember that the policyowner pays a *gross* premium each year throughout the policy's premium-paying period. The policyowner is generally unaware of the amount of the net premiums used by the company or of the methods of calculation which are employed.

This book will present three of the different modified net premium methods which have been developed:

- Full Preliminary Term Method
- Commissioners Method
- Canadian Method

FULL PRELIMINARY TERM METHOD. The net premium for one-year term insurance is exactly sufficient to pay the death claims in that year. When a company uses the Full Preliminary Term Method of calculating net premiums, the modified first-year net premium is equal to this net premium for one-year term insurance.

The modified net premiums for all subsequent years are the same as the net level annual premium for a policy with the same benefits but issued one age older and with a premium-paying period which is one year less.

For example, the 20-payment life policy issued at age 30, which was discussed in the above section, has a net level annual premium of $21.15 (per $1,000). However, if the Full Preliminary Term Method were being used to calculate modified net premiums, then it would have a modified first-year net premium per $1,000 equal to the net premium for one-year term insurance at age 30, which is $2.07. The modified net premium for the remaining 19 years would then be the same as the net level annual premium for a 19-payment life policy issued at age 31, which is $22.51.

It will be instructive to compare this method with the net level method, examining the amount of loading which is made available to pay expenses under each method.

Net Level Method

For all 20 years,

> Loading = Gross Premium − Net Premium
> = $30.04 − $21.15
> = $8.89

Full Preliminary Term Method

For the first year,

> Loading = Gross Premium − Net Premium
> = $30.04 − $2.07.
> = $27.97

For years 2 through 20,

> Loading = Gross Premium − Net Premium
> = $30.04 − $22.51
> = $7.53

Thus, the use of the Full Preliminary Term Method makes available sufficient loading the first year ($27.97) to pay for the first-year expenses of $24.12 which were shown earlier. (Any excess may be available to return to the policyowner as part of a dividend. Dividends will be dicussed in Chapter 14.)

If the Full Preliminary Term Method is used for policies having large premiums per $1,000, an overly large amount is made available for expenses in the first year. This is so because the first-year modified net premium is only the one-year term insurance net premium, although the gross premium for the policy is large. Because of this undesirable situation for high-premium policies, other less extreme modified net premium methods have been developed.

To distinguish it from Full Preliminary Term, any other modified net premium method is called a *modified preliminary term method*. The two remaining methods to be explained are both modified preliminary term methods.

COMMISSIONERS METHOD. The full name of this method is the *Commissioners Reserve Valuation Method*, but it is usually referred to as the *Commissioners Method* or sometimes CRVM.

Under the Commissioners Method, policies are divided into two classes—those with small premiums per $1,000 of insurance and those with larger premiums per $1,000 of insurance.

The policies with smaller premiums per $1,000 have their modified net premiums calculated by the Full Preliminary Term Method. The policies with larger premiums per $1,000 have their modified net premiums calculated in a special way, which is itself usually called the Commissioners Method.

As an example of a higher premium policy, let us look at a 30-year endowment policy issued at age 30 and calculated using the 1958 C.S.O. Table and 3% interest. The modified net premiums per $1,000 (using the Commissioners Method) are as follows:

First year .... $ 3.44
Years 2–30 .... 23.88

Note how these compare with this policy's net level annual premiums, which are $22.82 for all years 1 through 30.

CANADIAN METHOD. The full name of this method is the *New Canadian Modified Reserve Method*, but it will be referred to in this book simply as the Canadian Method.

Under the Canadian Method, the modified net annual premiums are calculated the same for all policies; that is, there is no separation into policies with small or large premiums, such as is done under the Commissioners method. The calculations are made in a manner specified by law, using tables specified in the law.

It is interesting to note that in the Commissioners Method and the Full Preliminary Term Method the present value of the modified net premiums (at the time of issue) must be equal to the present value of the policy's benefits (at the time of issue). On the other hand, however, the Canadian Method provides for modified net annual premiums with a present value (at the time of issue) which exceeds the present value of the policy's benefits.

In this chapter, we have shown how net annual premiums are calculated and how they can serve as the basis for calculating gross premiums. In the next chapter, we will begin the explanation of how net annual premiums are also used as the foundation for calculating reserves for life insurance policies.

EXERCISES, SET 25

1. Which method of calculating modified net annual premiums releases the largest amount of loading to cover expenses for the policy's first year?

2. Which method provides for modified net annual premiums that have a present value (at time of issue) which exceeds the present value of the policy's benefits?

3. Why is it generally easy to calculate the first-year modified net premium for a policy under the Full Preliminary Term Method, even for a policy which provides complex benefits?

4. Using Table III and 3% interest, calculate the first-year modified net premium for a $5,000 17-year endowment policy issued at age 40, using the Full Preliminary Term Method.

5. Using Table IV, calculate the modified net premium for years subsequent to the

first year for a $1,000 three-year term insurance policy issued at age 60, using the Full Preliminary Term Method.

6. If the Commissioners Method is used instead of the net level method, what amount is made available for first-year expenses in addition to the regular loading, assuming the following:

Net level annual premium $84.36
First-year modified net premium (Commissioners) 33.75
Subsequent years' modified net annual premium (Commissioners) 87.42

7. The following figures relate to a $1,000 life insurance in the first policy year:

Net annual premium $21.25
Gross annual premium 30.60
Issue and administration expenses 7.35
First-year commission expense .... 40% of gross annual premium
Premium taxes .... 3% of gross annual premium

According to the net level premium method, the loading for this policy in the first policy year is deficient by

(1) $3.81   (3) $11.16
(2) $9.35   (4) $20.51

CHAPTER SUMMARY

• Net annual premiums are calculated using only mortality and interest.

• When net annual premiums are level, they constitute a life annuity due.

• The present value of net annual premiums as of the date of issue must equal the present value of the benefits.

• Premiums may be required for as long as there is insurance coverage or for a shorter period of time. If it is not specified, then it is assumed that premiums are required as long as there is coverage.

• Use of a higher interest rate will produce lower net annual premiums.

• The net level annual premium of any policy can be calculated using l's, d's, and v's by writing an equation showing the present value of net premiums equal to the present value of benefits for all persons in the mortality table and solving for the unknown net annual premium. For example (a three-year term policy):

$$\left(\begin{array}{c}\text{Net Annual} \\ \text{Premium}\end{array}\right)(l_{25} + l_{26}v + l_{27}v^2) = \$1,000(d_{25}v + d_{26}v^2 + d_{27}v^3)$$

• If published tables are available of annuity factors (present value of life annuity of 1 per year), and net single premiums (present value of a policy's benefits) are available, then net annual premiums can be calculated as follows:

$$\left(\begin{array}{c}\text{Net Annual} \\ \text{Premium}\end{array}\right) = \frac{\left(\begin{array}{c}\text{Net Single} \\ \text{Premium}\end{array}\right)}{\left(\begin{array}{c}\text{Annuity} \\ \text{Factor}\end{array}\right)}$$

The annuity factor would be for a life annuity due for the same number of years as the policy's premium-paying period.

- If commutation functions are to be used, net level annual premiums can be calculated by multiplying the amount of insurance by $\dfrac{M - M + D}{N - N}$. The subscripts in the numerator define the ages at which benefits begin and end, following the rules given in Chapter 9 for net single premiums. The subscripts in the denominator define the ages at which premium payments begin and end, following the rules given in Chapter 8 for life annuity factors.

- The premium which the policyowner actually pays is called the *gross premium*.

- The amount by which the gross premium exceeds the net premium is called the *loading* (generally considered to be the part of the premium available for expenses and profit).

- Net premiums are generally calculated using mortality tables and interest rates specified by law (mainly because net premiums are used to calculate reserves).

- Gross premiums for participating policies need not be calculated with great refinement, since any savings can be returned to policyowners in the form of dividends. Therefore, they are often calculated by adding a simple loading to the net premium.

- Gross premiums for nonparticipating policies must be calculated with very great refinement and using actually expected rates of mortality, interest, and expenses.

- Three principal categories of a company's expenses are:

  1. those which are constant for each policy;
  2. those which vary with the amount of the premium;
  3. those which vary with the amount of insurance.

- Category 1 expenses can be provided for by charging a policy fee or by banding premium rates. (Banding means quoting premiums per $1,000 which vary according to size groups.)

- Category 2 expenses can be provided for by including a percentage of the gross premium in the loading.

- Category 3 expenses can be provided for by including a constant amount per $1,000 of insurance in the loading.

- Actual expenses are much larger in a policy's first year than in subsequent years. However, if the loading is the same each year, that is, if net level premiums are used, then a level amount is generally used for expenses in the calculations. Such level amounts have the same present value as the actual expenses expected.

- Gross premiums which are paid more frequently than yearly (such as semiannually, quarterly, or monthly) must include amounts to cover additional expenses incurred plus interest lost because the company cannot invest the money quickly.
  A common way to calculate such semiannual, quarterly, and monthly premiums is to increase the gross annual premium by a percentage of itself and then divide by the number of payments to be made in a year.

- *Modified net premiums* are smaller for the first year than for subsequent years, thus making more loading available in the first year for the heavy expenses. This book explains three methods of calculating such modified net premiums.

- Under the Full Preliminary Term Method, the first-year net premium is the one-year term insurance net premium; the net premiums for the subsequent years are the same as the net level annual premium for a policy with the same benefits but issued one age older and with a one-year shorter premium-paying period.
  Of any method, the Full Preliminary Term Method releases the largest amount of loading in the first year.
- Under the Commissioners Method, policies are divided into those with smaller premiums per $1,000 and those with larger premiums per $1,000. Policies with smaller premiums per $1,000 have modified net premiums calculated by the Full Preliminary Term Method. Policies with larger premiums per $1,000 have modified net premiums calculated by a special method.

- Under the Canadian Method, one formula is used to determine modified net premiums for all policies. The Canadian method is the only method presented for calculating net annual premiums where the present value of all the net annual premiums at time of issue exceeds the present value of the benefits.

LEARNING OBJECTIVES

After reading this chapter, the student should know

- What is meant by net annual premiums.
- The general principle for calculating net annual premiums:

  Present Value of Net Annual Premiums = Present Value Benefits

- How to describe a policy by describing both the benefits and the premium-paying period.
- That if the premium-paying period is not described, then it is the same as the benefit period.
- What is meant by an ordinary life policy.
- How to find the amount of the net annual premium by setting the present value of premiums equal to the present value of benefits and solving the equation for the amount of the net annual premium.
- That when two policies have the same benefits, the policy with the shorter premium period has the larger premium.
- How to calculate net annual premiums when given the net single premiums and life annuity factors.
- How to calculate net annual premiums using commutation functions.
- What is meant by loading.
- What is meant by gross premium.
- That Gross Premium = Net Premium + Loading.
- Three kinds of expenses: Those that

  1. remain constant for each policy.
  2. vary with the amount of the premium.
  3. vary with the amount of the insurance.

- What a typical formula for calculating a gross annual premium looks like.
- What is meant by a policy fee and by banding.
- How to calculate the gross premium when it appears on both sides of the equation.
- What is meant by fractional premiums or installments.
- How fractional premiums are commonly calculated.

- How actual expenses compare with loading available in the first and subsequent years.
- How net premiums are modified to allow for larger first-year loading.
- That gross premiums are unaffected by modifying the net premiums.
- How the first-year and subsequent net premiums are calculated under the Full Preliminary Term Method.
- Why the Full Preliminary Term Method is inappropriate for high-premium policies.

11

Introduction to Life Insurance Reserves

In the last chapter, it was pointed out that net annual premiums for a life insurance policy, in addition to serving as a base from which gross premiums can be calculated, are also used to calculate policy reserves.

In this chapter and the next, we will be concerned with the calculation of reserves, one of the most important responsibilities of the actuarial department.

Since the aggregate of the "reserves" for all of a company's policies typically is one of the largest factors in a life company's financial picture, the methods and bases used to calculate reserves directly affect the company's profit or loss figures, its tax burden, and even whether it is healthy or insolvent. Consequently, the methods and bases of calculating reserves are strictly regulated by state laws in the United States and by provincial and federal laws in Canada.

This chapter will describe various possible approaches for calculating life insurance reserves. It will acquaint the student with the general patterns reserves follow, what level of reserve figures is typical, how typical reserves appear graphically, and the effect alternate choices of mortality tables and interest rates have on the results.

11.1 TERMINAL RESERVES

It was pointed out in Section 9.1 that the net premium for one-year term insurance increases each year with the age of the insured. In Chapter 10 we described methods of calculating net premiums so that the premium will remain uniform throughout the premium-paying period (or for certain portions of the premium-paying period). In a calculation using a hypothetical, large group of policyowners and the same mortality and interest assumptions as used to calculate such uniform premiums, the total premiums paid in the early years exceed the amounts required to pay death claims in those years. The excess accumulates from year to year to produce a fund known as the *reserve*. Because this fund will be used to help pay benefits in later years and thus represents a major future outgo, the total of the reserves for all the individual policies in force at any time represents the principal liability of a life insurance company. Since the insurance company invests the premium income, it owns assets which will have a value at least large enough to provide for this liability.

A reserve fund is calculated by using net premiums, not gross premiums. The same mortality table and interest rate on which the reserves are based are used to calculate these net premiums. The bases to be used are strictly regulated by law. Throughout most of this chapter and the next, the principles given will be based on net level premiums. In Section 12.5 the use of modified net premiums to calculate reserves will be discussed.

EXAMPLES OF THE CALCULATION. In Chapter 10, a schedule (Chart 10–1) was shown which illustrated the year-by-year accumulation of a reserve fund. The fund shown at the end of each year could be divided by the number of persons living at the end of that year to determine a reserve per person (per $1,000 of insurance). In this way, a reserve is actually determined each year for an individual policy.

Such reserves are calculated as of the end of each policy year, after payment of the year's death claims. They are, therefore, known as *terminal reserves.*

As an example, consider a five-payment ten-year endowment policy for $1,000 issued to a person age 21. The net level annual premium per $1,000 is $158.752, rounding off to three decimal places for this example, instead of the customary two. Using Table III and 3% interest, and assuming that each person in the Table has $1,000 of such insurance, we can construct the schedule shown in Chart 11–1.

The premium income for each of the first five years, shown in column (3), is calculated by multiplying $158.752 by the number living. The death claims each year, shown in column (6), are calculated by multiplying $1,000 by the number dying. It can then be seen how the total fund accumulates year by year. Column (8) of the schedule is the reserve per person (per $1,000 of insurance). It is calculated each year by dividing the total fund at the end of the year by the number of persons living at the end of the year, that is, by the number living at the beginning of the following year.

An inspection of the figures in column (8) shows that the reserve per person grows year by year until it reaches exactly $1,000 on the date when the $1,000 pure endowment is payable. It is also interesting to note that each person pays a premium the first year of $158.752 and that the reserve at the end of that year is $161.98. Since 3% interest is being credited, the $158.752 premium would have accumulated to

$$\$158.752(1.03) = \$163.51$$

using interest only. The difference represents the contribution which each person makes to pay that year's death claims:

$$\$163.51 - \$161.98 = \$1.53$$

CHART 11-1

Age 21 Five-Pay Ten-Year Endowment (1958 C.S.O., 3%)

(1) Age x	(2) l_x	(3) Premium Income (Premium × l_x)	(4) Total Fund Beginning of Year (Col. 3 + Col. 7 Previous Yr.)	(5) Fund Accumulated for 1 year (Col. 4 × 1.03)	(6) Death Claims ($1,000 d_x)	(7) Total Fund at End of Year (Col. 5 − Col. 6)	(8) Reserve per Person (Col. 7 ÷ Col. 2 Following Yr.)
21	9,647,694	$1,531,590,718	$1,531,590,718	$1,577,538,440	$17,655,000	$1,559,883,440	$ 161.98
22	9,630,039	1,528,787,951	3,088,671,391	3,181,331,533	17,912,000	3,163,419,533	329.11
23	9,612,127	1,525,944,386	4,689,363,919	4,830,044,837	18,167,000	4,811,877,837	501.55
24	9,593,960	1,523,060,338	6,334,938,175	6,524,986,320	18,324,000	6,506,662,320	679.50
25	9,575,636	1,520,151,366	8,026,813,686	8,267,618,097	18,481,000	8,249,137,097	863.14
26	9,557,155	0	8,249,137,097	8,496,611,210	18,732,000	8,477,879,210	888.81
27	9,538,423	0	8,477,879,210	8,732,215,586	18,981,000	8,713,234,586	915.31
28	9,519,442	0	8,713,234,586	8,974,631,624	19,324,000	8,955,307,624	942.65
29	9,500,118	0	8,955,307,624	9,223,966,853	19,760,000	9,204,206,853	970.87
30	9,480,358	0	9,204,206,853	9,480,333,059	20,193,000	9,460,140,059	1000.00
31	9,460,165						

To Illustrate—Using the 1958 C.S.O. Table and 3% interest, calculate the terminal reserve per $1,000 at the end of each year for a four-year term insurance policy issued at age 25.

Solution—This is the same policy which was considered in Section 10.2. In that section, the year-by-year fund was calculated, and the schedule is repeated in Chart 11–2. This schedule assumes that each person has $1,000 of insurance. To derive the terminal reserve per $1,000, the balance in the fund at the end of each year is divided by the number living at the end of that year, that is, by the number living at the beginning of the following year.

CHART 11–2

Age 25 Four-Year Term Insurance (1958 C.S.O., 3%)

(1) Year	(2) Premiums Paid at Beginning of Year (Number Living × 1.92)	(3) Total Fund at Beginning of Year (Col. 6 Previous Year + Col. 2)	(4) Fund Accumulated for One Year (Col. 3 × 1.03)	(5) Claims Paid at End of Year (Number of Deaths × $1,000)	(6) Balance in Fund at End of Year After Payment of Claims (Col. 4 − Col. 5)
1	$18,385,221.12	$18,385,221.12	$18,936,777.75	$18,481,000	$455,777.75
2	18,349,737.60	18,805,515.35	19,369,680.81	18,732,000	637,680.81
3	18,313,772.16	18,951,452.97	19,519,996,56	18,981,000	538,996.56
4	18,277,328.64	18,816,325.20	19,380,814.96	19,324,000	56,814.96

(Note: The final balance in the fund would be even closer to zero if the net annual premium were rounded off to more decimal places.)

At the End of First Year

Balance in Fund = $455,777.75

Age at That Time = 26

Number Living at That Time = l_{26}

= 9,557,155

$$\text{Terminal Reserve per } \$1{,}000 = \frac{\text{Balance in Fund}}{\text{Number Living}}$$

$$= \frac{\$455{,}777.75}{9{,}557{,}155}$$

$$= \$.05$$

At the End of Second Year

Balance in Fund = $637,680.81

Age at That Time = 27

Number Living at That Time = l_{27}

= 9,538,423

$$\text{Terminal Reserve per \$1,000} = \frac{\text{Balance in Fund}}{\text{Number Living}}$$

$$= \frac{\$637,680.81}{9,538,423}$$

$$= \$.07$$

At the End of Third Year

Balance in Fund = $538,996.56

Age at That Time = 28

Number Living at That Time = l_{28}

$$= 9,519,442$$

$$\text{Terminal Reserve per \$1,000} = \frac{\text{Balance in Fund}}{\text{Number Living}}$$

$$= \frac{\$538,996.56}{9,519,442}$$

$$= \$.06$$

At the End of Fourth Year

Balance in Fund = $56,814.96

Age at That Time = 29

Number Living at That Time = l_{29}

$$= 9,500,118$$

$$\text{Terminal Reserve per \$1,000} = \frac{\text{Balance in Fund}}{\text{Number Living}}$$

$$= \frac{\$56,814.96}{9,500,118}$$

= $.01, but would be zero if net annual premium were rounded off to more decimal places

The terminal reserves on this term policy are much smaller than those calculated above on the endowment policy. The final reserve on this term policy is zero. This is logical because, at the end of the term, all of the net premium income should have been used to pay death claims. The company owes nothing further in benefits.

WHOLE LIFE POLICY. It is interesting to consider the accumulation of such a fund on a policy where the insurance extends for the whole of life. All mortality tables are constructed to show the number dying in the final year equal to the number living at the beginning of that year, leaving none living at the end. The accumulated fund will normally provide, therefore, exactly enough money in that final year to pay all these death claims, leaving no balance in the fund. From this viewpoint, a whole life insurance policy can be considered as a term-to-age-100 policy, when based on the 1958 C.S.O. Table, which ends at age 100. If, as sometimes happens, an insured person actually lives to age 100, it is customary for the insurance company to pay the amount of insurance at that time.

11.2 THE RETROSPECTIVE METHOD

The method explained above for calculating terminal reserves requires that a year-by-year accumulation be performed. To find the terminal reserve for any year, the actuary must know the accumulations for all the preceding years. However, by another method, reserves may be calculated for any year desired without such a requirement. This second method follows the principle that the terminal reserve, at any specified time, is equal to the accumulated value of all the net premiums which have been received, less the accumulated cost of the insurance which has been provided.

This method is known as the *retrospective method* (looking backwards), because it involves the use of past happenings. In equation form it may be written:

$$\begin{pmatrix} \text{Terminal} \\ \text{Reserve} \end{pmatrix} = \begin{pmatrix} \text{Accumulated Value} \\ \text{of Net Premiums} \\ \text{Received} \end{pmatrix} - \begin{pmatrix} \text{Accumulated} \\ \text{Cost of} \\ \text{Insurance} \end{pmatrix}$$

The two items on the right side of the equation make direct use of principles previously presented. As discussed in Section 8.3, the Accumulated Value of Net Premiums Received represents the accumulated value of a temporary life annuity due (since premium payments are made each year only if the person insured is then alive). The Accumulated Cost of Insurance was presented in Section 9.6.

11.3 THE PROSPECTIVE METHOD

Actuaries can also calculate terminal reserves by looking into the future of a life insurance policy. This method of calculating reserves is known as the *prospective method* (looking ahead).

At any particular time during the life of a policy, the actuary may look ahead at the benefits the company will have to pay on that policy in the future. The money necessary to pay those future benefits will come from two sources: the reserve currently being held and the future net premiums. The following equation may be written to express this fact:

$$\begin{pmatrix} \text{Present Value} \\ \text{of Future Benefits} \end{pmatrix} = \begin{pmatrix} \text{Terminal} \\ \text{Reserve} \end{pmatrix} + \begin{pmatrix} \text{Present Value of} \\ \text{Future Net Premiums} \end{pmatrix}$$

Solving for the terminal reserve results in the following equation which expresses the prospective method:

$$\begin{pmatrix} \text{Terminal} \\ \text{Reserve} \end{pmatrix} = \begin{pmatrix} \text{Present Value} \\ \text{of Future Benefits} \end{pmatrix} - \begin{pmatrix} \text{Present Value of} \\ \text{Future Net Premiums} \end{pmatrix}$$

This is equivalent to the equation:

$$\begin{pmatrix} \text{Terminal} \\ \text{Reserve} \end{pmatrix} = \begin{pmatrix} \text{Net Single Premium} \\ \text{at Attained Age} \end{pmatrix} - \begin{pmatrix} \text{Present Value of} \\ \text{Future Net Annual} \\ \text{Premiums at} \\ \text{Attained Age} \end{pmatrix}$$

The reserve calculated by the prospective method is equal to that calculated by the retrospective method.

It should be stressed that the two items on the right side of the equation for the terminal reserve are calculated at the attained age and take into account only those benefits and premiums, respectively, which will be in effect after the date of the particular reserve which is being calculated. Both make direct use of principles previously presented. The Present Value of Future Benefits is the net single premium presented in Chapter 9. In this case, it is the net single premium at the attained age for those benefits then remaining. The Present Value of Future Net Premiums represents the present value of a life annuity due. The present value is calculated at the attained age, and includes only those premiums still to be paid. These principles were presented in Chapter 8.

For example, if the third terminal reserve were being calculated for a 20-payment 30-year endowment insurance policy issued at age 25, the attained age would be $25 + 3 = 28$. The future benefits at age 28 would be the same as for a 27-year endowment insurance policy at that age. The future net premiums at age 28 would be 17 in number, three premiums having already been collected.

RESERVE AT TIME OF ISSUE. It is interesting to consider the result of applying this equation for the terminal reserve at the end of *zero years*, that is, at the time the policy is issued. The equation, as before, is

$$\begin{pmatrix} \text{Terminal} \\ \text{Reserve} \end{pmatrix} = \begin{pmatrix} \text{Present Value} \\ \text{of Future Benefits} \end{pmatrix} - \begin{pmatrix} \text{Present Value of} \\ \text{Future Net Premiums} \end{pmatrix}$$

However, at the time the policy is issued, the two items on the right side are equal to each other, because the calculation of net annual premiums follows the principle that, at the time the policy is issued

$$\begin{pmatrix} \text{Present Value} \\ \text{of Future Benefits} \end{pmatrix} = \begin{pmatrix} \text{Present Value of} \\ \text{Future Net Premiums} \end{pmatrix}$$

This equality is true only at the time the policy is issued; hence, at that time the value of the terminal reserve is zero. (This is often referred to as the reserve at *duration zero* being equal to zero.)

WHICH METHOD TO USE. Having two different methods for calculating terminal reserves (retrospective and prospective) enables the actuary to choose the method which is simpler for the case at hand. Where the future benefits are complicated, it is often simpler to use the retrospective method (provided the net premium is known). On the other hand, if the reserve is desired at a date when there are no more premiums due (such as the 25th reserve on a 20-payment life policy), the prospective method is usually simpler because the Present Value of Future Net Premiums is then zero. Two other situations where the prospective method is preferable would be a policy in which benefits in the early policy years are complicated or one in which net annual premiums in the early policy years are not uniform year by year.

If published tables of net single premiums and life annuity factors are available, as is generally the case, the prospective method involves less work.

To Illustrate—Given the following table, calculate the fifth terminal reserve per $1,000 on an endowment-at-age-65 policy issued at age 20.

Age	Net Single Premium for $1,000 Endowment at Age 65	Present Value of a Temporary Life Annuity Due of 1 per Year to Age 65
20	$304.75129	23.870206
21	312.66351	23.598552
22	320.80051	23.319182
23	329.17678	23.031596
24	337.80052	22.735515
25	346.68674	22.430421
26	355.84412	22.116018
27	365.27538	21.792211
28	374.98991	21.458679
29	384.99117	21.115303

The values in this table are given to several decimal places, in order to provide greater accuracy in the answer.

Solution—The first step is to calculate the net annual premium. The present value of the net premiums is a temporary life annuity due to age 65.

Basic equation:

$$\left(\begin{array}{c} \text{Present Value of Future} \\ \text{Benefits at Time of Issue} \end{array} \right) = \left(\begin{array}{c} \text{Present Value of Future Net} \\ \text{Premiums at Time of Issue} \end{array} \right)$$

Express this equation in equivalent form:

$$(\text{Net Single Premium}) = \left(\begin{array}{c} \text{Net Annual} \\ \text{Premium} \end{array} \right)(\text{Annuity Factor})$$

Substitute values given:

$$\$304.75129 = \left(\begin{array}{c}\text{Net Annual}\\\text{Premium}\end{array}\right)(23.870206)$$

$$\frac{\$304.75129}{23.870206} = \left(\begin{array}{c}\text{Net Annual}\\\text{Premium}\end{array}\right)$$

$$\$12.76702 = \left(\begin{array}{c}\text{Net Annual}\\\text{Premium}\end{array}\right)$$

The second step is to determine the attained age. If the 5th terminal reserve is to be calculated, the attained age is $20 + 5 = 25$.

In the equation for finding the terminal reserve, the Present Value of Future Benefits will then be the net single premium at attained age 25 for endowment-at-age-65 insurance. The Present Value of Future Net Premiums will be the present value at attained age 25 of a temporary life annuity due of the remaining net annual premiums to age 65.

Basic equation:

$$\left(\begin{array}{c}\text{Terminal}\\\text{Reserve}\end{array}\right) = \left(\begin{array}{c}\text{Present Value of}\\\text{Future Benefits}\end{array}\right) - \left(\begin{array}{c}\text{Present Value of}\\\text{Future Net Premiums}\end{array}\right)$$

Express this equation in equivalent form:

$$= \left(\begin{array}{c}\text{Net Single Premium}\\\text{at Attained Age 25}\end{array}\right) - \left(\begin{array}{c}\text{Net Annual}\\\text{Premium}\end{array}\right)\left(\begin{array}{c}\text{Annuity Factor}\\\text{at Attained Age 25}\end{array}\right)$$

Substitute values given:

$$= \$346.68674 - \$12.76702(22.430421)$$

$$= \$346.68674 - \$286.36963$$

$$= \$60.32$$

TWO RATES OF INTEREST   When a policy's reserves are calculated using dual interest rates, the net annual premium is first calculated as described in Chapter 10 for dual interest rate situations. Then, either the retrospective or the prospective method may be used to calculate the reserves; the result will be the same from either method.

The value of benefits at the attained age (either the net single premium or the accumulated cost of insurance) can be calculated as described in Chapter 9 when using dual interest rates. The value of the net annual premiums at the attained age (either present value of future net premiums or accumulated value of past net premiums) can be calculated as shown in Chapter 8 for life annuities when using dual interest rates. It should be remembered that the net annual premium does not change in amount at the time the interest rate changes.

The use of dual interest rates in calculating reserves allows the company to use an interest rate which is closer to that actually being earned at the time the policy is issued without the necessity of guaranteeing that rate for a long period of time into the future. For example, at a time when the interest rates being earned on the company's investments are quite high, the company may specify in its new policies that reserves will be calculated at $4\frac{1}{2}\%$ for the first 20 years and at 3% thereafter. In that way, if interest rates actually earned on the company's investments at sometime in the future should fall to lower levels, there is a margin of safety, because only 3% is needed to add to the reserves after 20 years.

RELEASE OF RESERVES. At the time a life insurance policy is terminated, there is often a settlement under which the company pays money to the policyowner or the beneficiary. If the termination occurs because of a death claim, the amount of insurance is paid to the beneficiary. If the termination occurs because the policyowner voluntarily terminates the policy, then an amount called the policy's *nonforfeiture value* is payable to the policyowner. (Nonforfeiture values will be fully explained in Chapter 13.)

After such a settlement is made, the company no longer has a reserve (liability) for that policy. The reserves have been *released* for that policy.

The company accumulates assets which, in total, are at least as large as its total liabilities. When a settlement is made on termination of a policy, both assets and liabilties are decreased, that is, assets are paid out and reserves are released.

In the case of a death claim, the amount of assets paid out is greater than the reserve released. Hence, a part of the amount paid out is derived from assets equal in amount to the policy's reserve, and the remainder is from assets which, up to that time, can be thought of as belonging to other policies. (This latter amount will be explained in more detail in Section 12.3, Tabular Cost of Insurance.)

As an example, refer to Chart 11–1. In this theoretical illustration, it may be assumed that the assets and liabilities are equal to each other, that is, that the fund shown in the chart represents the total assets and also the total reserves (liabilities) associated with this group of policies. The reserve per person at the end of the first year is $161.98. For each of the persons who died during the first year, the $1,000 paid out is composed of $161.98 of assets which correspond to the reserve, plus $838.02 additional amount to be deducted from the total fund.

In the case of a voluntary termination of a policy, the amount of assets paid out (representing the policy's nonforfeiture value) is always equal to or less than the policy's reserve released. Therefore, there is generally either an equal decrease in the company's assets and liabilities in such a situation, or else there are *excess assets* no longer needed to offset liabilities. In calculating reserves by carrying forward a fund, however, as was demonstrated in Section 11.1, the effects of such possible voluntary terminations are not taken into account. On the other hand, the calculations of *GAAP reserves* (to be explained in Section 12.6) and *asset shares* (to be explained in Section 12.7) do take into account the effects of such terminations.

EXERCISES, SET 26

1. What name is given to a reserve that is calculated as of the end of a policy year?

2. What is the amount of the terminal reserve on a $1,000 policy in each of the following situations?

   a) at the time of issue, for a 20-year endowment policy
   b) at the end of 20 years, for a 20-year endowment policy
   c) at the end of ten years, for a ten-year term insurance policy

3. Which method of calculating reserves (retrospective or prospective) would generally be simpler in each of the following situations?

   a) at the end of 30 years, for a ten-payment life policy
   b) at the end of two years, for a policy with a complicated schedule of death benefits
   c) at the end of five years, for a policy which has net annual premiums that increase each year for the first three years and remain level thereafter
   d) at the end of ten years, for an ordinary life policy, if published tables of net single premiums and life annuity factors are available

4. Using the following information, calculate the fifth terminal reserve, using both the retrospective and prospective methods. Compare the answers obtained by the two methods.

   Present value (at end of five years) of future net premiums   = $412.77
   Accumulated cost of insurance (at end of five years)   = 181.33
   Present value (at end of five years) of future benefits   = 816.04
   Accumulated value (at end of five years) of net premiums received = 584.60

5. The net annual premium on a certain policy issued at age 19 is $19.92. Calculate the seventh terminal reserve, using the following information:

Attained Age	Present Value of Future Benefits	Present Value of Future Premiums (per $1)
19	$406.17	$20.39
20	417.36	20.00
21	428.86	19.61
22	440.70	19.20
23	452.90	18.78
24	465.48	18.35
25	478.45	17.91
26	491.82	17.45
27	505.61	16.97
28	519.82	16.49
29	534.47	15.98

6. Using the following table, calculate the 38th terminal reserve on a $1,000 ordinary life policy issued at age ten.

Age	Net Single Premium for $1,000 Whole Life Insurance	Present Value of Whole Life Annuity Due of 1 per Year
10	$351.30	33.083
11	357.06	32.790
12	362.99	32.488
.	.	.
.	.	.
.	.	.
47	634.69	18.631
48	643.86	18.163
49	653.04	17.695

7. Using the retrospective method of calculating terminal reserves, the terminal reserve at any time is equal to

(1) $\left(\begin{array}{c}\text{Accumulated Value}\\\text{of Net Premiums}\\\text{Received}\end{array}\right) + \left(\begin{array}{c}\text{Present Value}\\\text{of Future}\\\text{Benefits}\end{array}\right)$

(2) $\left(\begin{array}{c}\text{Accumulated Value}\\\text{of Net Premiums}\\\text{Received}\end{array}\right) - \left(\begin{array}{c}\text{Accumulated}\\\text{Cost of}\\\text{Insurance}\end{array}\right)$

(3) $\left(\begin{array}{c}\text{Accumulated}\\\text{Cost of}\\\text{Insurance}\end{array}\right) - \left(\begin{array}{c}\text{Accumulated Value}\\\text{of Net Premiums}\\\text{Received}\end{array}\right)$

(4) $\left(\begin{array}{c}\text{Present Value}\\\text{of Future}\\\text{Benefits}\end{array}\right) - \left(\begin{array}{c}\text{Present Value}\\\text{of Net Annual}\\\text{Premiums}\end{array}\right)$

11.4 COMMUTATION FUNCTIONS

The commutation functions explained in Chapters 8, 9, and 10 can be used to calculate terminal reserves by either the retrospective or prospective method, and will generally simplify the work.

Regardless of which method is being used, commutation functions are first used to calculate the net annual premium. The procedure was described in Section 10.6.

USING THE RETROSPECTIVE METHOD. In the equation for the retrospective method, namely,

$$\left(\begin{array}{c}\text{Terminal}\\\text{Reserve}\end{array}\right) = \left(\begin{array}{c}\text{Accumulated Value}\\\text{of Net Premiums}\\\text{Received}\end{array}\right) - \left(\begin{array}{c}\text{Accumulated}\\\text{Cost of}\\\text{Insurance}\end{array}\right)$$

the items on the right side make use of principles previously presented. The Accumulated Value of Net Premiums Received represents the accumulated value of a temporary life annuity due. Such a calculation, using commutation functions, was described in Section 8.5. The use of commutation functions to calculate the Accumulated Cost of Insurance was described in Section 9.7.

USING THE PROSPECTIVE METHOD. In the equation for the prospective method, namely,

$$\begin{pmatrix} \text{Terminal} \\ \text{Reserve} \end{pmatrix} = \begin{pmatrix} \text{Present Value} \\ \text{of Future Benefits} \end{pmatrix} - \begin{pmatrix} \text{Present Value of} \\ \text{Future Net Premiums} \end{pmatrix}$$

the items on the right side make use of principles previously presented. The Present Value of Future Benefits is the net single premium at the attained age for those benefits then remaining. Such a calculation, using commutation functions, was described in Section 9.7. The Present Value of Future Net Premiums represents the present value of a life annuity due. The use of commutation functions to calculate life annuities was described in Section 8.5.

TWO RATES OF INTEREST. Commutation functions can be used to calculate reserves for a policy when dual interest rates are specified. As explained in earlier chapters, a separate complete table of commutation functions must be produced for each issue-age. For example, if terminal reserves are to be calculated for a policy issued at age 35, using 4% for the first ten years and 3% thereafter, a complete table of commutation functions must first be produced for issue-age 35. (Such a table would contain columns of D_x, N_x, C_x, and M_x for all ages 35 and higher.)

This particular table would first be used to calculate the net annual premium for the policy, and then the same table would be used to calculate the reserves (by either the retrospective or prospective method) exactly as shown above.

EXERCISES, SET 27

(Use Table IV for all of the following.)

1. Write an expression (using commutation functions) for each of the following terminal reserves, using both the retrospective and prospective methods. (If the student wishes to practice, the value of each reserve can be calculated.)

   a) Tenth terminal reserve on a $1,000 15-year term insurance policy issued at age 40 (net annual premium = $6.308)

   b) Terminal reserve at age 65 on a $1,000 ordinary life policy issued at age 25 (net annual premium = $11.278)

   c) Fifth terminal reserve on a $1,000 20-payment life policy issued at age 30 (net annual premium = $21.145)

   d) Eighth terminal reserve on a $1,000 20-year endowment insurance policy issued at age 0 (net annual premium = $37.266)

2. Calculate the tenth terminal reserve for a $1,000 term-to-age-65 insurance policy issued at age 35.

3. The net annual premium per $1,000 for a 30-payment life insurance policy issued at age 25 is $14.32. Calculate the 15th terminal reserve per $1,000 using the prospective method.

4. Calculate the fifth terminal reserve for a $1,000 20-payment 35-year endowment policy issued at age 30. What would this reserve be for a $3,000 policy?

5. In order to use the prospective method to calculate the seventh-year terminal reserve for a $10,000 ten-year term insurance policy, issued at age 40, an actuary must first determine the present value of future benefits. Expressed in commutation functions, this present value is equal to

(1) $\$10,000\left(\dfrac{M_{47} - M_{50}}{D_{47}}\right)$ (3) $\$10,000\left(\dfrac{M_{47} - M_{49}}{D_{49}}\right)$

(2) $\$10,000\left(\dfrac{N_{47} - N_{50}}{D_{47}}\right)$ (4) $\$10,000\left(\dfrac{M_{48} - M_{50}}{D_{49}}\right)$

11.5 PATTERNS OF TERMINAL RESERVES

The reserve at any particular time for any particular policy is the amount which the company is required by law to have on hand for that policy. From this statement, it follows that there are some special conditions, described previously in this chapter, which can be stated as follows:

1. *For any policy*, the terminal reserve at the end of zero years (at the time the policy is issued) equals zero.
2. *For term insurance policies*, the final terminal reserve (at the end of the term) equals zero. This is because all of the net premiums have been used to pay death claims. The company owes nothing further in benefits.
3. *For endowment insurance policies*, the final terminal reserve (on the date the pure endowment is payable) is equal to the amount of the pure endowment. This provides the exact amount which the company will have to pay on that date.
4. *For whole life insurance policies*, the final terminal reserve (at the end of the mortality table) equals zero. This is because, according to the mortality table, none are then living; hence, the company should owe nothing further in benefits. However, the terminal reserve one year prior is nearly equal to the full amount of the death benefit. This helps to provide for payment of the full death benefit to everybody that final year (when all are presumed to die).

GRAPHIC PRESENTATION OF RESERVES. Typical patterns of terminal reserves, on the common types of policies, can be seen in the graphs that follow. The number of years since the policy was issued is shown along the bottom of each graph. For each such year, the distance up to the line indicates the size of the reserve at the end of that year.

For a term insurance policy, the reserve rises to a high-point near the middle of the term and then decreases back to zero. The size of the reserve never gets very large compared to the amount of insurance. (See Figure 11–1.)

For an endowment insurance policy, the reserve rises to equal the amount of the pure endowment on the date the pure endowment is payable. (See Figure 11–2.)

For a whole life insurance policy, the reserve rises to nearly equal the amount of insurance one year before the end of the mortality table. One year

FIGURE 11–1

**Terminal Reserves per $1,000—50-Year Term Insurance—Age 15
(1958 C.S.O., 3%)**

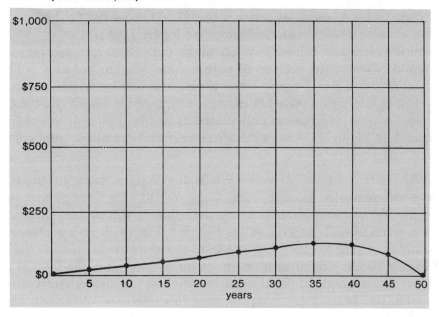

FIGURE 11–2

**Terminal Reserves per $1,000—50-Year Endowment Insurance—Age 15
(1958 C.S.O., 3%)**

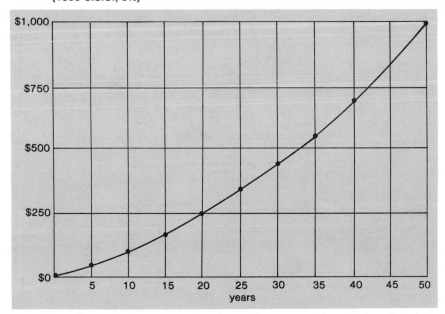

later, at the end of the table, the reserve is zero. It was pointed out earlier that it is customary for the company to pay the amount of insurance to persons who are still alive at the end of the mortality table. For this reason, some published tables of terminal reserves per $1,000 show the final whole life reserve as being $1,000 instead of zero. (See Figure 11–3.)

Some life insurance policies have premiums payable for a shorter time than the period of insurance, such as 20-payment life policies. For such policies, the reserve will increase much faster during the time premiums are being paid than in later years. Another example would be the reserve for the five-payment ten-year endowment policy used as an illustration in this chapter. The graph in Figure 11–4 shows this reserve, using the values from column (8) of Chart 11–1.

TWO RATES OF INTEREST. When dual interest rates are used, the reserve will generally increase faster from year to year during those years when the higher interest rate is being used than it will in the other years. Thus, a graph of such reserves will not show a line which always progresses smoothly from year to year (such as we see in Figure 11–2). Instead, the line will have a bending-point in it (at the point-in-time when the interest rate changes). For example, if the interest rate used in calculating reserves were lower after five years, a graph representing this reserve would appear somewhat like the graph in Figure 11–4.

FIGURE 11–3

Terminal Reserves per $1,000—Ordinary Life—Age 50
(1958 C.S.O., 3%)

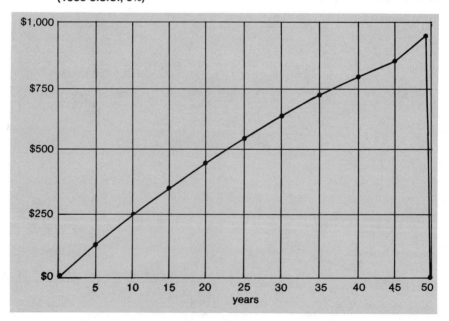

FIGURE 11-4

Terminal Reserves per $1,000—Five-Pay Ten-Year Endowment—Age 21
(1958 C.S.O., 3%)

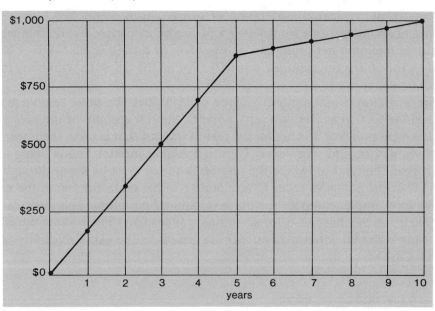

11.6 EFFECTS OF CHANGING MORTALITY OR INTEREST ASSUMPTIONS

The particular mortality tables and interest rates used to calculate net premiums and reserves are referred to as the assumptions on which those net premiums and reserves are based. It is very important for the actuary to choose assumptions which are appropriate for the policy.

The assumptions on which a policy's reserves are based are generally printed in the policy itself, and therefore, the company is obligated to use those assumptions (or assumptions producing a higher reserve but not lower) for the entire lifetime of the policy. For a whole life policy issued at age 0, this could mean a period of 100 years. It is, therefore, important that the actuary select conservative assumptions.

EFFECT OF INTEREST ASSUMPTION USED. Usually, determining what interest rate to use in reserve calculations is more of a problem for the actuary than determining mortality rates; therefore, determining an interest rate requires more care and study. While over the years, mortality rates have usually changed only in one direction (lower) and have proved to be more predictable, the interest rates that companies have been able to earn on their investments have fluctuated a great deal and are much less predictable. When a company adopts a certain interest rate for calculating a policy's reserve, it obligates itself to add that amount of interest to the reserve fund every year the policy will be in force. Hence, the interest rate a company selects must be conservative enough to ensure that the income actually earned from its investments will always be adequate to cover the interest that is committed to its liabilities (reserves).

Besides the typical consideration of conservatism mentioned above, the choice of an interest rate for reserves will also be motivated by the company's desire to maintain net premiums and reserves at certain levels (high or low), and by the effects the assumed rate will have on the taxes that company must pay.

Since whatever assumption is made will produce the same reserve at the end of the final year (zero on term policies, the full amount of the policy on endowment policies), the higher the rate of interest that is used, the lower the reserves will be and vice-versa. Thus, if a higher interest rate is being used each year, the fund on which the interest is added must be lower throughout the life of the policy in order to accumulate to the same amount at the end.

As an example, compare the net level annual premiums and reserves per $1,000 given in Chart 11–3 for an ordinary life policy. These show the effect of using different interest rates. All are based on the same mortality table (1958 C.S.O.):

CHART 11–3
Ordinary Life, 1958 C.S.O., Age 30

Interest Rate	Net Annual Premium	10th Reserve	20th Reserve	30th Reserve
2%	$16.28	$156.50	$330.16	$506.22
2½%	14.80	143.86	309.76	483.66
3%	13.47	132.20	290.48	461.84
3½%	12.28	121.47	272.30	440.82
4%	11.21	111.63	255.24	420.64

It is obvious from the table that higher interest rates produce lower net premiums and lower reserves.

EFFECT OF MORTALITY ASSUMPTION USED. Similarly, the table below (Chart 11–4) shows the effect of using different mortality rates. All are based on the same interest rate, but the values are calculated using a very old mortality table, a later one, a recent one, and finally, a very recent table (1980 C.S.O.), which will soon be used commonly to calculate reserves for new policies.

CHART 11–4
Ordinary Life, Age 30, 3%

Mortality Table	Net Annual Premium	10th Reserve	20th Reserve	30th Reserve
American Experience	$18.28	$120.10	$276.02	$457.51
1941 C.S.O.	15.90	140.27	302.66	475.44
1958 C.S.O.	13.47	132.20	290.48	461.84
1980 C.S.O.	12.38	123.69	272.76	440.21

The later the mortality table, the lower will be the overall mortality rates and, hence, the net annual premiums. This is true because as persons live longer, more are living to pay the premiums each year, and therefore, each of the premiums can be lower. However, the size of the reserves will not necessarily be smaller when using a mortality table that has lower overall mortality rates. Rather, it is the relationship of the mortality rates to each other in a table (how much of an increase from one age to the next in the same table) that determines, in general, whether use of that table produces smaller or larger reserves than some other table. Notice that in Chart 11–4, the later mortality tables do not necessarily produce lower reserves.

CHAPTER SUMMARY

- In a policy's early years, the net annual premium exceeds the amount needed to pay death claims (the one-year term net premium) each year. The excess accumulates from year to year to produce the *reserve*.

- The total reserves for all policies in force is typically the company's principal liability. The company will have accumulated assets at least as large as this liability.

- A reserve is calculated using net premiums and the same mortality and interest tables that are used to calculate the net premium.

- For any policy, reserves can be derived by calculating the accumulation of a fund involving all persons shown in the mortality table. Each year, total net premiums and interest are added to the fund, and death claims are subtracted from the fund. The fund shown at the end of each year can be divided by the number shown as living to derive the reserve per person (or per $1,000 of insurance).

- Reserves calculated as of the end of a policy year are called *terminal reserves*.

- Such a calculation, when applied to a whole life policy, will produce a terminal reserve of zero at the end of the final year, because the mortality table shows that all remaining persons die in the final year. If an insured person actually lives to that age, however, it is customary to pay the amount of insurance at that time.

- The *retrospective method* provides for calculating any terminal reserve as follows:

$$\binom{\text{Terminal}}{\text{Reserve}} = \binom{\text{Accumulated Value}}{\text{of Net Premiums Received}} - \binom{\text{Accumulated}}{\text{Cost of Insurance}}$$

- On the right-hand side, the first expression represents the accumulated value of a life annuity due (which was explained in Chapter 8), and the second expression represents the accumulated cost of insurance (which was explained in Chapter 9).

- The *prospective method* provides for calculating any terminal reserve as follows:

$$\binom{\text{Terminal}}{\text{Reserve}} = \binom{\text{Present Value}}{\text{of Future Benefits}} - \binom{\text{Present Value of}}{\text{Future Net Premiums}}$$

On the right-hand side, the first expression represents a net single premium (which was explained in Chapter 9), and the second expression represents the present value of a life annuity due (which was explained in Chapter 8).

- In both of the two methods (retrospective and prospective), it is necessary to calculate the net annual premium as the first step. In addition, all the values are calculated in both methods as of the attained age. The retrospective and prospective methods both yield the same answer for any particular reserve.

- The terminal reserve at the time a policy is issued (at duration zero) is always zero.

- In certain instances, either one of the two methods given above may be easier to use than the other one. The prospective method, in particular, will involve less work if published tables of net single premiums and life annuity factors are available.

- Dual interest rates are often specified for calculating reserves on new policies in periods when interest rates being earned are high, because a higher rate is thus guaranteed for only a limited number of years, and a lower rate for later years provides a safety margin.

- A policy's reserve is *released* (no longer needed) when the policy terminates. Upon a death claim, the assets paid out are partly those corresponding to the policy's reserve and partly other assets. Upon a voluntary termination, the assets paid out are equal to (or less than) those corresponding to the policy's reserve.

- Commutation functions may be used to calculate terminal reserves by either the retrospective or prospective method.
  First, the net annual premium can be calculated by commutation functions (as explained in Section 10.6).
  If using the retrospective method, the accumulated value of net premiums can be calculated by commutation functions (that is, a life annuity, as explained in Section 8.5) and the accumulated cost of insurance (as explained in Section 9.7).
  If using the prospective method, the present value of future benefits can be calculated by commutation functions (that is, a net single premium, as explained in Section 9.7) and the present value of future net premiums (that is, a life annuity, as explained in Section 8.5).

- The final terminal reserve for a term policy is zero; for an endowment policy, it is equal to the amount of insurance.

- The mortality table and interest rate used to calculate a policy's reserve are generally specified in the policy itself; therefore, the company is obligating itself, and these assumptions must be conservative.

- The higher the rate of interest that is used, the lower the reserves will be.

- Later published mortality tables show lower mortality rates than earlier ones. However, the reserves will not necessarily be lowered by using a table with lower mortality rates.

LEARNING OBJECTIVES

After reading this chapter, the student should know

- How net premiums and interest coming in and benefits going out build up a fund.
- That the fund is exactly depleted at the end of a term policy.
- That the total fund divided by persons still living equals the reserve.
- That the final reserve is equal to the amount of pure endowment for an endowment policy.
- The definition of terminal reserve.

- How to calculate terminal reserves by the retrospective method.
- How to calculate terminal reserves by the prospective method.
- How to calculate terminal reserves using published net single premiums and life annuity factors.
- How to calculate terminal reserves by using commutation functions.
- How the use of higher or lower interest or mortality assumptions affects the size of a policy's reserves.

12

More on Life Insurance Reserves

In the last chapter, we described life insurance reserves at the end of each policy year (terminal reserves). In this chapter, we will see how to find the amount of a policy's legally prescribed reserve at other points in time throughout the year. In actual practice, this is quite important. The reserve amounts which (in total) comprise a major liability on a life insurance company's financial statement are calculated as of these other points-in-time.

In addition, we will explore more of the details of how a policy's reserves are actually carried forward from one year to the next. This should give the student a better understanding of the nature of reserves, and more insight into their calculation and uses.

Certain special types of reserves, often very important in practice, will also be explained. These include *premium deficiency reserves* and *modified reserves*. The latter are calculated using the modified net premiums introduced in Section 10.9. They are important because of the role they play in helping insurance companies meet legal requirements in the United States and Canada.

Another special type of reserve to be described is the *GAAP reserve*, which features several interesting and unique aspects that set it apart from the other reserves described in this book. For instance, insurance companies' expenses which are attributable to a particular policy are included in the GAAP reserve calculation, which is in contrast to the reserves described in Chapter 11.

Finally, *asset shares* will be described at the end of this chapter. In many ways, asset share calculations are similar to reserve calculations. The important role that asset shares play in the functions of the actuarial department will be explained, and some of the methods used to calculate them will be demonstrated.

12.1 INITIAL AND MEAN RESERVES

The premiums for a life insurance policy are paid at the beginning of each year. The terminal reserves for a life insurance policy are calculated as of the end of each year after that year's death benefits are paid. It is assumed that the end of any year falls on the same date as the beginning of the following year. For example, for a policy issued on August 17, 1981, the fifth terminal reserve would be the amount of liability the insurance company would have on August 17, 1986. Also, the premium for the sixth year would be due on August 17, 1986.

INITIAL RESERVES. The *initial reserve* for a policy is the amount that the company has at the beginning of a given year. It equals the terminal reserve at the end of the previous year plus the net premium collected at the beginning of the current year. In the example given in the preceding paragraph, the initial reserve for the sixth year would be the amount on August 17, 1986 after the collection of the net annual premium due on that date.

To Illustrate—Using Table III and 3% interest, calculate the initial reserves per $1,000 for each year for a five-payment ten-year endowment policy issued at age 21.

Solution—This is the same policy for which terminal reserves were calculated in Section 11.1. The net annual premium was given as $158.752, which will be rounded off to $158.75. The terminal reserves appear in column (8) of Chart 11.1. Each year's initial reserve equals the terminal reserve at the end of the previous year, plus the net premium for the current year:

1st Initial Reserve = 0 Terminal Reserve + 1st Year Net Premium

$$= 0 + \$158.75$$
$$= \$158.75$$

2nd Initial Reserve = 1st Terminal Reserve + 2nd Year Net Premium

$$= \$161.98 + \$158.75$$
$$= \$320.73$$

3rd Initial Reserve = 2nd Terminal Reserve + 3rd Year Net Premium

$$= \$329.11 + \$158.75$$
$$= \$487.86$$

4th Initial Reserve = 3rd Terminal Reserve + 4th Year Net Premium

$$= \$501.55 + \$158.75$$
$$= \$660.30$$

5th Initial Reserve = 4th Terminal Reserve + 5th Year Net Premium

$$= \$679.50 + \$158.75$$
$$= \$838.25$$

6th Initial Reserve = 5th Terminal Reserve + 6th Year Net Premium

$$= \$863.14 + 0$$

$$= \$863.14$$

7th Initial Reserve = 6th Terminal Reserve + 7th Year Net Premium

$$= \$888.81 + 0$$

$$= \$888.81$$

8th Initial Reserve = 7th Terminal Reserve + 8th Year Net Premium

$$= \$915.31 + 0$$
$$= \$915.31$$

9th Initial Reserve = 8th Terminal Reserve + 9th Year Net Premium

$$= \$942.65 + 0$$

$$= \$942.65$$

10th Initial Reserve = 9th Terminal Reserve + 10th Year Net Premium

$$= \$970.87 + 0$$

$$= \$970.87$$

The first initial reserve always equals the first year net premium, because there is no previous year's terminal reserve to add to it. It should also be observed that in a year in which no premiums are payable (after the fifth year in the above illustration), the initial reserve is equal to the previous year's terminal reserve.

MEAN RESERVES. In actual practice, life insurance companies are required by government regulatory authorities to determine the total reserves for all policies each December 31. To make this calculation, it is usually convenient to assume that all policies are issued in the middle of the calendar year. For example, all policies issued in 1982 are assumed to be issued in the middle of 1982 (July 1, 1982). This assumption is reasonably accurate, with policies issued before July 1 each year counterbalancing those issued after July 1. Therefore, on December 31 all policies which were issued in the calendar year just ended are assumed to have been in effect for half a year. All policies issued in the calendar year before the calendar year just ended are assumed to have been in effect one and a half years; and so forth.

For the legally required December 31 reserve, *mean reserves* are very often used. The mean reserve for a policy is the amount that the company has on hand in the middle of a given policy year. It equals one half of the total of the initial and terminal reserves for that policy year:

$$\text{Mean Reserve} = \frac{\text{Initial Reserve} + \text{Terminal Reserve}}{2}$$

The answer is generally rounded off to two decimal places. It should be noted that this calculation will often result in answers having a 5 in the third decimal place, such as $148.725. The rule given in Section 2.3 would require that the 5 be dropped off and that 1 be added to the digit which is then in last place, that is, $148.725 would be rounded off to $148.73. However, published tables sometimes round off mean reserves to the nearest dollar.

To Illustrate—Using Table III and 3% interest, calculate the mean reserves per $1,000 for each year for a five-payment ten-year endowment policy issued at age 21.

Solution—This is the same policy for which terminal reserves were calculated in Section 11.1 and initial reserves were calculated in the illustration above. For convenience, these figures are repeated here:

Policy Year	Initial Reserve	Terminal Reserve
1	$158.75	$ 161.98
2	320.73	329.11
3	487.86	501.55
4	660.30	679.50
5	838.25	863.14
6	863.14	888.81
7	888.81	915.31
8	915.31	942.65
9	942.65	970.87
10	970.87	1,000.00

Each year's mean reserve equals one half of the total of the initial and terminal reserves for that policy year:

$$\text{1st Mean Reserve} = \frac{\text{1st Initial Reserve} + \text{1st Terminal Reserve}}{2}$$

$$= \frac{\$158.75 + \$161.98}{2}$$

$$= \frac{\$320.73}{2}$$

$$= \$160.37$$

$$\text{2nd Mean Reserve} = \frac{\text{2nd Initial Reserve} + \text{2nd Terminal Reserve}}{2}$$

$$= \frac{\$320.73 + \$329.11}{2}$$

$$= \frac{\$649.84}{2}$$

$$= \$324.92$$

The remaining mean reserves, calculated in the same manner, are as follows:

3rd Mean Reserve = $494.71

4th Mean Reserve =   669.90

5th Mean Reserve =   850.70

6th Mean Reserve =   875.98

7th Mean Reserve =   902.06

8th Mean Reserve =   928.98

9th Mean Reserve =   956.76

10th Mean Reserve =   985.44

It should be noted that mean reserves can be calculated if the net premium and appropriate terminal reserves are known, because the Initial Reserve in the equation can be replaced by Net Premium + Previous Terminal Reserve:

$$\text{Mean Reserve} = \frac{\text{Net Premium + Previous Terminal Reserve + Terminal Reserve}}{2}$$

To Illustrate—Calculate the reserve used on December 31, 1985, for a policy issued in 1982. The following values are given:

Net level annual premium . . . . $ 27.65
Terminal reserve
  1st year 22.42
  2nd year 49.99
  3rd year 78.67
  4th year 108.30
  5th year 138.92

Solution—If this policy is assumed to have been issued in the middle of 1982, then on December 31, 1985, it has been in effect for three and a half years, that is, it completed three policy years in the middle of 1985 and is half-way through its fourth policy year. The fourth mean reserve is therefore required.

$$\text{4th Mean Reserve} = \frac{\text{Net Premium + 3rd Terminal Reserve + 4th Terminal Reserve}}{2}$$

$$= \frac{\$27.65 + \$78.67 + \$108.30}{2}$$

$$= \frac{\$214.62}{2}$$

$$= \$107.31$$

12.2 NET AMOUNT AT RISK

As explained before, each policy has its own reserve, which is the amount the company has on hand at any particular time for that policy. Therefore, for each death claim paid at the end of the year, a certain portion of the claim payment is available from that policy's terminal reserve. The remainder of the claim payment, known as the *net amount at risk*, is that portion which must be paid from the funds of the other policies on which benefits have not been paid out. A policy's net amount at risk for any year is, therefore, the amount of insurance less the terminal reserve for that year:

$$\begin{pmatrix} \text{Net Amount} \\ \text{at Risk} \end{pmatrix} = \begin{pmatrix} \text{Amount of} \\ \text{Insurance} \end{pmatrix} - \begin{pmatrix} \text{Terminal} \\ \text{Reserve} \end{pmatrix}$$

To Illustrate—Calculate the net amount at risk for each year for a $1,000 five-year term insurance policy issued at age 60, given that the policy's terminal reserves are as follows:

End of Year 1 = $4.01

End of Year 2 = 6.30

End of Year 3 = 6.61

End of Year 4 = 4.63

End of Year 5 =   0

Solution—Each year's net amount at risk equals $1,000 less the terminal reserve for that year:

1st Year Net Amount at Risk = $1,000 − 1st Terminal Reserve

= $1,000 − $4.01

= $995.99

2nd Year Net Amount at Risk = $1,000 − 2nd Terminal Reserve

= $1,000 − $6.30

= $993.70

Continuing such calculations for the remaining years gives the following figures:

3rd Year Net Amount at Risk = $ 993.39

4th Year Net Amount at Risk =   995.37

5th Year Net Amount at Risk =   1,000.00

For the final year of any *term insurance* policy, such as the one just illustrated, the net amount at risk is always equal to the amount of insurance since the final year terminal reserve is always zero.

For the final year of an endowment policy, the net amount at risk is always zero since the final year terminal reserve is the same as the amount of insurance. In the final year of an endowment insurance policy, it makes no difference financially to the company whether the person insured lives or dies. The full amount is paid at the end of the year in either instance.

When actuaries calculate the rates of mortality which are actually observed in a group of insured persons, they generally use the net amount at risk to represent the amount of insurance for each policy. The financial impact on the company caused by a death is best measured by the net amount at risk rather than the face amount of the policy, since the reserve (which is paid in addition to the net amount at risk) represents funds which the company already has on hand for each policy anyway.

12.3 TABULAR COST OF INSURANCE

The progress of the reserve for a policy, for any one-year period, can be described as follows: The initial reserve (at the beginning of the year) accumulates at interest for one year. At the end of the year, an amount necessary to help pay death claims on other policies is deducted. The amount remaining is the terminal reserve.

The amount so deducted to pay such death claims is called the *tabular cost of insurance*. The word "tabular" means that this cost is calculated using the same mortality table and interest rate as used in the calculation of net premiums and reserves.

For all those policies where the persons insured die during this one-year period, the amount necessary to pay these total death claims is made up of the terminal reserves for those particular policies plus the tabular cost of insurance from all policies.

The progress of the reserve for one year, as described above, can be written in equation form:

$$\left(\begin{array}{c} \text{Initial} \\ \text{Reserve} \end{array} \right)(1 + i) - \left(\begin{array}{c} \text{Tabular Cost} \\ \text{of Insurance} \end{array} \right) = \left(\begin{array}{c} \text{Terminal} \\ \text{Reserve} \end{array} \right)$$

When the above equation is solved for the tabular cost of insurance, the following equation results:

$$\left(\begin{array}{c} \text{Tabular Cost} \\ \text{of Insurance} \end{array} \right) = \left(\begin{array}{c} \text{Initial} \\ \text{Reserve} \end{array} \right)(1 + i) - \left(\begin{array}{c} \text{Terminal} \\ \text{Reserve} \end{array} \right)$$

This equation can be used to calculate tabular costs of insurance, provided initial and terminal reserves are known.

To Illustrate—Given the following reserves and using Table III and 3% interest, calculate the tabular cost of insurance for each of the first two years for a $1,000 ordinary life policy issued at age 60.

	Initial Reserve	Terminal Reserve
First Year	$50.02	$31.83
Second Year	81.85	63.48

Solution—The calculation is as follows, using the basic equation given above:

$$\begin{pmatrix} \text{1st Year} \\ \text{Tabular Cost} \\ \text{of Insurance} \end{pmatrix} = \begin{pmatrix} \text{1st Year} \\ \text{Initial} \\ \text{Reserve} \end{pmatrix}(1 + i) - \begin{pmatrix} \text{1st Year} \\ \text{Terminal} \\ \text{Reserve} \end{pmatrix}$$

$$= \$50.02(1.03) - \$31.83$$

$$= \$51.52 - \$31.83$$

$$= \$19.69$$

$$\begin{pmatrix} \text{2nd Year} \\ \text{Tabular Cost} \\ \text{of Insurance} \end{pmatrix} = \begin{pmatrix} \text{2nd Year} \\ \text{Initial} \\ \text{Reserve} \end{pmatrix}(1 + i) - \begin{pmatrix} \text{2nd Year} \\ \text{Terminal} \\ \text{Reserve} \end{pmatrix}$$

$$= \$81.85(1.03) - \$63.48$$

$$= \$84.31 - \$63.48$$

$$= \$20.83$$

For the final year of any endowment policy, the tabular cost of insurance is always zero. This would be expected, since, as mentioned in the previous section, it then makes no financial difference to the company whether the insured lives or dies; that is, for endowment policies, the final year initial reserve accumulates at interest to the final year terminal reserve without subtracting anything for the tabular cost of insurance.

It should be noted that the above equation can also be used if only the net premium and appropriate terminal reserves are given, because the Initial Reserve in the equation can be replaced by Net Premium + Previous Terminal Reserve:

$$\begin{pmatrix} \text{Tabular Cost} \\ \text{of Insurance} \end{pmatrix}$$
$$= \left[\begin{pmatrix} \text{Net} \\ \text{Premium} \end{pmatrix} + \begin{pmatrix} \text{Previous} \\ \text{Terminal Reserve} \end{pmatrix} \right](1 + i) - \begin{pmatrix} \text{Terminal} \\ \text{Reserve} \end{pmatrix}$$

SECOND METHOD OF CALCULATION. Tabular cost of insurance is sometimes referred to as the *tabular cost of insurance based on the net amount at risk*. This description refers to a second method of calculation for this cost, which is as follows: *The tabular cost of insurance for a policy, for any one-year period, equals the net amount at risk multiplied by the rate of mortality for that year.* In equation form, this may be written

$$\left(\begin{array}{c}\text{Tabular Cost}\\ \text{of Insurance}\end{array}\right) = \left(\begin{array}{c}\text{Net Amount}\\ \text{at Risk}\end{array}\right) q_x$$

where x is the attained age at the beginning of the year.

To Illustrate—Using the second method, verify the tabular cost of insurance calculated in the above illustration for the first and second years. The net amount at risk for these years is:

First Year Net Amount at Risk = $968.17

Second Year Net Amount at Risk = $936.52

Solution—For the first year, the attained age is 60 (beginning of the year), and $q_{60} = .02034$ from Table III:

$$\left(\begin{array}{c}\text{1st Year}\\ \text{Tabular Cost}\\ \text{of Insurance}\end{array}\right) = \left(\begin{array}{c}\text{1st Year}\\ \text{Net Amount}\\ \text{at Risk}\end{array}\right) q_x$$

$$= (\$968.17)(.02034)$$

$$= \$19.69$$

For the second year, the attained age is 61, and $q_{61} = .02224$ from Table III.

$$\left(\begin{array}{c}\text{2nd Year}\\ \text{Tabular Cost}\\ \text{of Insrance}\end{array}\right) = \left(\begin{array}{c}\text{2nd Year}\\ \text{Net Amount}\\ \text{at Risk}\end{array}\right) q_x$$

$$= (\$936.52)(.02224)$$

$$= \$20.83$$

These agree with the answers obtained in the first illustration in this section.

As mentioned above, the tabular cost is always zero for the final year of any endowment policy. According to the second method, this results from the fact that the final year net amount at risk is always zero. Multiplying zero by any rate of mortality yields an answer of zero.

It should be noted that this second method can be used when only the mortality rates and appropriate terminal reserves are known. This is because the Net Amount at Risk in the equation can be replaced by Amount of Insurance − Terminal Reserve:

$$\left(\begin{array}{c}\text{Tabular Cost}\\ \text{of Insurance}\end{array}\right) = \left[\left(\begin{array}{c}\text{Amount of}\\ \text{Insurance}\end{array}\right) - \left(\begin{array}{c}\text{Terminal}\\ \text{Reserve}\end{array}\right)\right] q_x$$

To Illustrate—Using Table III, calculate the sixth year tabular cost of insurance on a $5,000 policy issued at age ten, if the sixth terminal reserve is $107.82 per $1,000.

Solution—Since the amount of insurance is $5,000, the total sixth terminal reserve is

$$(5)(\$107.82) = \$539.10$$

Since the policy was issued at age 10, the attained age at the beginning of the sixth year is 15.

$$\begin{pmatrix} \text{Tabular Cost} \\ \text{of Insurance} \end{pmatrix} = \left[\begin{pmatrix} \text{Amount of} \\ \text{Insurance} \end{pmatrix} - \begin{pmatrix} \text{Terminal} \\ \text{Reserve} \end{pmatrix} \right] q_x$$

Substitute values calculated:

$$= (\$5,000 - \$539.10)q_{15}$$

Substitute values from Table III:

$$= (\$5,000 - \$539.10)(.00146)$$

$$= (\$4,460.90)(.00146)$$

$$= \$6.51$$

COMPARING ACTUAL AND EXPECTED MORTALITY. The tabular cost of insurance is sometimes also referred to as the *expected cost of insurance* or the *expected mortality*. Actuaries often evaluate the mortality results in their own company by comparing the mortality actually experienced (based upon the net amount at risk) with the expected cost of insurance. For example, suppose that for all the persons insured in a certain company who were age 35 last year, the expected mortality (as measured by the 1958 C.S.O. Table) was $1,000,000. Further, suppose that the actual mortality at age 35 (that is, amounts paid upon death, less the terminal reserves on those policies where the insured died) amounted to $825,000. In this case, the company's ratio of actual to expected mortality at age 35 last year was

$$\$825,000 \div \$1,000,000 = .825 \text{ or } 82\tfrac{1}{2}\%$$

It would be expected that such a ratio would be less than 100% when the 1958 C.S.O. Table is the basis for the expected mortality. The reason is that overall mortality rates actually experienced by life insurance companies have decreased considerably since the 1958 C.S.O. Table was published. Another reason is that the mortality rates in the 1958 C.S.O. Table contain some extra margins for safety (that is, they have been increased over the rates actually observed at the time the table was published).

Such ratios, however, are very useful when they are compared from year to year. When the same table, such as the 1958 C.S.O. Table, is used each year to calculate the company's total expected mortality, then the ratios of actual to expected mortality will show whether the company's overall mortality experience is improving, worsening, or fluctuating over a period of years.

Another approach often used is to calculate the company's expected mortality using mortality rates which are approximately the same as those which the company's true rates are thought to be. For example, the rates might be the same as those used in calculating the nonparticipating gross premiums. In such a case, ratios of actual to expected mortality of less than 100% would probably mean that the mortality experience was profitable for the company and vice versa.

12.4 PREMIUM DEFICIENCY RESERVES

As mentioned in Chapter 11, the money necessary to pay future benefits on a policy will come from the reserve currently being held and the future net premiums. In most cases, the policy's future gross premiums to be collected are larger than the net premiums which will be needed. However, it occasionally happens that a policy's gross annual premium is less than its net annual premium (that is, has a *negative loading*).

This would generally happen only on nonparticipating policies where the legally prescribed mortality table used to calculate reserves exhibits mortality rates considerably larger than the company expects it will actually experience. This situation is most likely to occur when the mortality table is one which has been used for a considerable number of years. The existence of a number of policies being offered for sale with gross premiums less than the legally calculated net premiums is usually regarded as evidence of the need to establish a new mortality table for calculating reserves.

Special requirements are set forth in the state laws for calculating reserves on policies which have such very low gross premiums. Formerly, an extra reserve was required in addition to the policy's regular reserve. This extra reserve was called a *premium deficiency reserve*. Presently, state laws set forth a special way to calculate such a policy's reserve without any additional amount. The reserves on such policies are sometimes called premium deficiency reserves, although this name is not actually a true description of reserves calculated by the present method.

To determine if the special requirements for calculating reserves apply, a comparison must be made between the policy's actual gross annual premium and its net annual premium calculated using the mortality table and interest rate which are specified in the law. This specified mortality table and interest rate are called *minimum standards* and produce quite low net premiums. If the gross premium is less than the net premium calculated using these minimum standards, then the special requirements apply.

In general, if a policy is subject to the special requirements, then its reserve at any time must be at least as large as that calculated using the minimum standards and the gross premium in the calculation instead of the net premium.

For example, if the prospective method is used, such a policy must have a reserve at least as large as

$$\begin{pmatrix} \text{Present Value of} \\ \text{Future Benefits} \end{pmatrix} - \begin{pmatrix} \text{Present Value of} \\ \text{Future Gross Premiums} \end{pmatrix}$$

where the net single premium and annuity factors are calculated using the minimum standards for mortality and interest.

EXERCISES, SET 28

1. Which type of reserve is generally used to represent the December 31 reserves for all of a company's policies?

2. What name is given to the difference between a policy's amount of insurance and its terminal reserve?

3. What amount is generally used to represent the amount of insurance for each policy when a study is made of a company's actual mortality experience?

4. In calculating a company's ratio of actual to expected mortality, what amount is generally used to represent each policy's expected mortality?

5. In the area of premium deficiency reserves, what is meant by *minimum standards*?

(For Exercises 6 through 9, use the following
information concerning a $10,000 policy.)

Net annual premium	$1,107.65
Terminal Reserve	
1st year	439.40
2nd year	870.60
3rd year	1,291.30
4th year	1,698.30
5th year	2,089.70

6. Calculate the first year initial reserve.

7. Calculate the sixth year initial reserve.

8. Calculate the first year mean reserve.

9. Calculate the net amount at risk for the third year.

10. Given the following information, calculate this year's tabular cost of insurance for a certain policy.

Reserve basis = 1979 United Mortality Table at $3\frac{1}{2}\%$
This year's terminal reserve = $8,401.40
This year's initial reserve = $8,502.00

11. Using Table III, calculate the first year tabular cost of insurance for a policy issued at age 21. The first year net amount at risk is $5,100.

12. Using Table III, calculate the fifth year tabular cost of insurance for a $10,000 policy issued at age 32. The fifth year terminal reserve is $112.40 per $1,000.

13. Assume a whole life policy was issued in April 1982. The reserve liability for this policy which the insurance company would include in its December 31, 1984 annual statement would most likely be the

   (1) third-year mean reserve
   (2) third-year initial reserve
   (3) second-year terminal reserve
   (4) second-year mean reserve

12.5 MODIFIED RESERVES

When a policy's net annual premiums are calculated by a modified premium method, as explained in Section 10.9, the reserves which result from using those modified net premiums are called *modified reserves*.

Modified reserves are calculated by the same methods for calculating reserves explained in Chapter 11, except that modified net premiums are used instead of net level premiums.

FULL PRELIMINARY TERM RESERVES. When a company uses the Full Preliminary Term Method of calculating net premiums, the modified first-year net premium is equal to the net premium for one-year term insurance. The first-year terminal reserve, therefore, is zero. The modified net premiums for all subsequent years are the same as the net level annual premium for a policy with the same benefits but issued one age older and with a premium-paying period which is one year less. The same rule applies to the reserves. For example, a 20-payment life policy issued at age 30 would have modified net premiums (after the first year) the same as the net level annual premium for a 19-payment life policy issued at age 31. This policy's eighth terminal reserve, for example, would then be the same as the seventh year net level terminal reserve for a 19-payment life policy issued at age 31.

Again, consider a policy using the Full Preliminary Term Method which has a first-year modified net premium of $1.81 (the one-year term insurance net premium) and net annual premiums for all subsequent years equal to $10.54. Using the first-year modified net premium, the initial reserve for the first year for this policy would be

$$\begin{pmatrix} \text{First} \\ \text{Initial} \\ \text{Reserve} \end{pmatrix} = \begin{pmatrix} \text{First-Year} \\ \text{Modified} \\ \text{Net Premium} \end{pmatrix}$$

$$= \$1.81$$

The initial reserve for the second year (remembering that the terminal reserve at the end of the first year is zero when using the Full Preliminary Term Method) would be

$$\begin{pmatrix} \text{Second} \\ \text{Initial} \\ \text{Reserve} \end{pmatrix} = \begin{pmatrix} \text{First-Year} \\ \text{Terminal Reserve} \end{pmatrix} + \begin{pmatrix} \text{Second-Year} \\ \text{Modified} \\ \text{Net Premium} \end{pmatrix}$$

$$= 0 + \$10.54$$

$$= \$10.54$$

The mean reserve for the first year, using the first year's modified net premium and remembering that the first-year terminal reserve is zero, would be

$$\left(\begin{array}{c}\text{Mean}\\\text{Reserve}\end{array}\right) = \frac{\begin{array}{c}\text{Modified Net Premium + Previous Terminal Reserve}\\ + \text{ Terminal Reserve}\end{array}}{2}$$

$$= \frac{\$1.81 + 0 + 0}{2}$$

$$= \$.91$$

COMMISSIONERS RESERVES. As explained in Chapter 10, when the *Commissioners Method* is used, policies with relatively small net annual premiums per $1,000 will use the Full Preliminary Term Method, and the others will use a special method to calculate net annual premiums.

Under this special method (also called the *Commissioners Method*), a first-year modified net premium is calculated, and a different modified net annual premium is calculated for years after the first year. Since the present value of all these modified net premiums is equal to the present value of the benefits at the time of issue, the terminal reserve at the time of issue (that is, duration zero) will be equal to zero. It was pointed out in Chapter 11 that the terminal reserve at time of issue is also zero on any policy that uses the net level method.

The terminal reserve at the end of a policy's final year will always be equal to the amount then owed to the policyowner when the Commissioners Method is used, that is, it will be zero for a term insurance policy or equal to the amount of the pure endowment for an endowment insurance policy. This is also the same as in the case of the net level method.

When the Commissioners Method is used, the terminal reserves for all years after issue but before the final year are larger than Full Preliminary Term reserves but smaller than net level reserves.

CANADIAN RESERVES. It was explained in Chapter 10 that, under the Canadian Method, the present value of the policy's modified net premiums at the time the policy is issued is not equal to the present value of future benefits. This is the only reserve method shown in this book where that is true.

The terminal reserve at the end of a policy's final year will always be equal to the amount then owed to the policyowner when the Canadian Method is used. In this regard, all of the reserve methods are the same.

COMPARISON OF METHODS. It is instructive to compare the modified reserves which are produced by the methods discussed in this section. For this purpose, a 25-year endowment policy issued at age 25 will be used.

Chart 12–1 shows some of the modified terminal reserves for this policy produced by each of the methods. In practice, the Canadian Method is generally used with more current assumptions than the 1958 C.S.O. Table at 3%, but this basis is used for all methods in Chart 12–1 for uniformity.

CHART 12-1

Modified Terminal Reserves, $1,000 25-Year Endowment, Age 25
(1958 C.S.O. at 3%)

Policy Year	Net Level Method	Full Preliminary Term Method	Commissioners Method	Canadian Method
1	$ 27.08	$ 0	$ 9.68	$ −16.44
2	55.00	28.70	38.10	12.73
3	83.79	58.29	67.40	42.80
4	113.46	88.79	97.60	73.80
5	144.05	120.22	128.73	105.75
.	.	.	.	.
.	.	.	.	.
.	.	.	.	.
10	311.68	292.52	299.36	280.88
.	.	.	.	.
.	.	.	.	.
15	506.49	492.75	497.66	484.41
.	.	.	.	.
.	.	.	.	.
.	.	.	.	.
20	733.03	725.60	728.25	721.08
.	.	.	.	.
.	.	.	.	.
.	.	.	.	.
24	942.76	941.16	941.73	940.20
25	1,000.00	1,000.00	1,000.00	1,000.00

The following points should be noted:

1. All methods produce a final terminal reserve of $1,000. This is the amount of pure endowment which the company must pay at that time.
2. Except for the Canadian Method (which starts with a negative terminal reserve when the policy is issued), the smaller the first-year modified net premium, the smaller the first-year modified reserve will be. The Full Preliminary Term first-year modified net premium equals the one-year term net premium, and hence, its terminal reserve is zero.
3. The modified reserves by the Commissioners Method will be intermediate between the Full Preliminary Term and the net level reserves.
4. The modified reserves by the Canadian Method are usually negative in the policy's first year.
5. The chart does not show terminal reserves at the time the policy is issued, that is, at duration zero, but all methods have a reserve of zero at that time except the Canadian Method. This reserve is negative under the Canadian Method.

MINIMUM RESERVE REQUIREMENTS. In the United States, the National Association of Insurance Commissioners, composed of the insurance commissioners of every state, has been instrumental in preparing model legislation prescribing minimum reserve standards. Their Standard Valuation Law is in effect (with few modifications) in all states. This law prescribes a mortality table, rate of interest, and modified reserve method as being the *minimum standards.* (These are the same minimum standards referred to in Section 12.4 in connection with premium deficiency reserves.)

Total reserves must be at least as large as those produced by using the minimum standards. A company is free to use other bases for calculating its reserves, provided higher reserves are produced.

The Standard Valuation Law has been amended several times (to prescribe a new mortality table and interest rate for the minimum standards), and the amendments have generally been enacted in all of the states. In such cases, the minimum standards applicable to any particular policy are those that were in effect at the time that policy was issued. The minimum standards in effect in any particular state at any particular time may be ascertained by checking with that state's department or division of insurance. Due to the fact that a recently submitted amendment may not yet be enacted in all states, it is also possible that different standards may be in effect in different states at any one time.

In 1980, the Standard Valuation Law was amended again. Instead of stating the actual interest rate to be used in calculating the minimum standards, the law now states a method by which the interest rate is determined once a year and is tied to the average yield on certain corporate bonds. In addition, the interest rate will be different for policies with longer benefit periods than for those with shorter benefit periods. The purpose of the 1980 amendment is to eliminate the need for amendments whenever interest rates change; the one enactment allows the rate to be changed automatically. However, when calculating the minimum reserve standards for policies issued during any one time period, the interest rate in effect during that time applies for the entire life of those policies.

The 1980 amendment also specifies the 1980 C.S.O. Table for calculating the minimum standards. And in order to eliminate the need for states to enact frequent amendments in the future, this amendment empowers the insurance commissioners themselves to approve new mortality tables for calculating minimum reserve standards in the future.

In Canada, the Canadian Method is presently prescribed as a minimum standard for reserves. This applies to companies which are registered with the Canadian Department of Insurance.

12.6 GAAP RESERVES

Reserves which are reported to state government authorities in the United States or to federal or provincial authorities in Canada are called *statutory reserves.* They are called this because statutes (or laws) govern their calculation. For example, the Standard Valuation Law described above prescribes minimum reserve standards.

However, many persons (particularly owners of the stock of life insurance companies) have felt that these government standards do not produce reserve liabilities which are in accordance with generally accepted accounting principles (GAAP). Therefore, in 1972 the American Institute of Certified Public Accountants set forth guidelines for calculating reserves on a basis which would be considered in accordance with generally accepted accounting principles (GAAP). Such reserves are usually called *GAAP reserves.*

GAAP reserves appear on the balance sheet of a stock life insurance company whenever that balance sheet must be accompanied by a certified public accountant's opinion as to its "fairness." This would be the case, for example, when a company's stock is registered with the Securities and Exchange Commission and is sold and traded by the public. (Besides the reserves, there are also other items on the balance sheet which are handled differently on a GAAP annual statement.) In such a case, the company is also required by statute to report *statutory reserves* to the appropriate governmental authorities. Hence, such a company must compute reserves on two different bases for reporting to two different interested parties.

Statutory annual statements are primarily concerned with the financial strength of the company, that is, the extent to which its assets exceed its liabilities. The primary concern of GAAP annual statements is to reflect the incidence of profits of the company.

THE CALCULATION. In the calculation of GAAP reserves, it is first necessary to calculate a net annual premium, just as is the case for statutory reserves described in the first part of this chapter. In the case of GAAP reserves, this premium is called the *GAAP valuation premium.* Such a premium is always calculated on a *net level* basis, that is, it is the same percentage of the gross premium every year. Since most policies have gross premiums that are level (the same amount each year), in most cases the valuation premiums are also the same amount each year.

These GAAP valuation premiums are calculated to be sufficient to pay the policy's benefits and the regular annual expenses of maintaining the policy, based on the GAAP assumptions. At the time the policy is issued, the present value of the GAAP valuation premiums must be equal to the present value of the benefits plus the present value of these maintenance expenses associated with the policy.

Furthermore, these calculations are all made by using the rates of interest, mortality, and expenses which it is assumed will actually be experienced in the future. Thus, the difference between the gross annual premium (actually charged to the policyowner) and the GAAP valuation premium is equal to the profit which the company would anticipate each year if the GAAP assumptions were realized exactly. This anticipated profit amount is level (the same amount each year) for any one policy and is not included in calculating the GAAP valuation premium.

In addition to the policy's regular maintenance expenses, there are the large additional expenses (excess first-year expenses or acquisition expenses) incurred in connection with placing the policy in force originally. On a GAAP annual statement, such acquisition expenses are generally treated as an asset. This asset is reduced (*amortized*) each year thereafter over the life of the policy. These reductions partially offset the yearly profit mentioned in the last paragraph. However, in this book we will describe only the reserve (liability) side of the GAAP annual statement.

The GAAP reserves themselves are then calculated by essentially the same process as was demonstrated for statutory reserves in Chart 11–1, namely by accumulating a fund. The GAAP valuation premiums and interest actually expected to be received are added to the fund. The benefits and maintenance expenses actually expected to be paid are subtracted from the fund each year. At the end of each policy year, if the fund is divided by the number of persons then living, the result is the GAAP reserve per person (per $1,000 of insurance).

To Illustrate—Given the following rates of mortality, interest, and expenses which a company actually expects to experience, calculate the GAAP terminal reserve per $1,000 for a five-year term insurance policy issued at age 40.

$$q_{40} = .00164$$

Mortality . . . . $q_{40} = .00164$
$$q_{41} = .00176$$
$$q_{42} = .00194$$
$$q_{43} = .00221$$
$$q_{44} = .00257$$

Interest . . . . 6% per year
Acquisition
    Expenses . . . . $ 9.02 per $1,000
Maintenance
    Expenses . . . . $ 1.12 per $1,000 each year

Assume the gross annual premium is $5.21 per $1,000.

Solution—The first step is to produce a table of l's and d's, using the given mortality rates, in the same manner as explained in Section 7.5. If it is arbitrarily assumed that 100,000 persons are living at age 40 (the first age to appear in this segment of the table), this table will appear as follows:

Age x	l_x	d_x
40	100,000	164
41	99,836	176
42	99,660	193
43	99,467	220
44	99,247	255
45	98,992	etc.

The next step is to calculate the GAAP valuation premium. This can be done by finding the present value of both benefits and maintenance expenses and dividing by the present value of a five-year life annuity due of 1 per year, as shown in Chapter 10.

The present value of the benefits (five-year term insurance beginning at age 40) may be calculated in the same manner as was shown in Chapter 9 for net single premiums, except that now we are using the company's own mortality and interest rates.

$$\binom{\text{Present Value}}{\text{of Benefits}} = \$1,000\left(\frac{d_{40}v + d_{41}v^2 + d_{42}v^3 + d_{43}v^4 + d_{44}v^5}{l_{40}}\right)$$

$$= \$1,000\left[\frac{\begin{array}{l}(164)(.943396)\\+(176)(.889996)\\+(193)(.839619)\\+(220)(.792094)\\+(255)(.747258)\end{array}}{100,000}\right]$$

$$= \$1,000\left(\frac{154.7 + 156.6 + 162.0 + 174.3 + 190.6}{100,000}\right)$$

$$= \$1,000\left(\frac{838.2}{100,000}\right)$$

$$= \$8.382$$

To calculate the present value of the expected maintenance expenses, each year's expected expenses per $1,000 are provided for as if they were a pure endowment at the beginning of each year, that is, the expenses will only be incurred by the company each year for any one policy provided the insured person is then alive. Their present value, therefore, is calculated in the same manner as was shown in Chapter 8 for life annuities and payments involving life contingencies, except that now we are using the company's own mortality and interest rates.

$$\binom{\text{Present Value of}}{\text{Maintenance Expenses}} = \$1.12\left(\frac{l_{40} + l_{41}v + l_{42}v^2 + l_{43}v^3 + l_{44}v^4}{l_{40}}\right)$$

$$= \$1.12\left[\frac{\begin{array}{l}100,000\\+(99,836)(.943396)\\+(99,660)(.889996)\\+(99,467)(.839619)\\+(99,247)(.792094)\end{array}}{100,000}\right]$$

$$= \$1.12\left(\frac{\begin{array}{c}100,000 + 94,185 + 88,697\\+ 83.514 + 78,613\end{array}}{100,000}\right)$$

$$= \$1.12\left(\frac{445,009}{100,000}\right)$$

$$= \$4.984$$

As was explained above, these present values must be divided by the present value of a five-year life annuity due of 1 per year, as was shown in Chapter 10, in order to produce the annual valuation premium. This life annuity due is also calculated using the company's own mortality and interest rates.

$$\begin{pmatrix} \text{Present Value of} \\ \text{Life Annuity Due} \\ \text{of 1 per Year} \end{pmatrix} = \frac{l_{40} + l_{41}v + l_{42}v^2 + l_{43}v^3 + l_{44}v^4}{l_{40}}$$

$$= \begin{bmatrix} 100,000 \\ + (99,836)(.943396) \\ + (99,660)(.889996) \\ + (99,467)(.839619) \\ + (99,247)(.792094) \\ \hline 100,000 \end{bmatrix}$$

$$= \frac{100,000 + 94,185 + 88,697 + 83,514 + 78,613}{100,000}$$

$$= \frac{445,009}{100,000}$$

$$= 4.45009$$

The annual valuation premium is then found by dividing the present value of both benefits and maintenance expenses by the above five-year annuity value

$$\text{Valuation Premium} = \frac{\$8.382 + \$4.984}{4.45009}$$

$$= \frac{\$13.366}{4.45009}$$

$$= \$3.0035$$

(Here we are rounding the answer to four decimal places instead of the usual two places in order to give greater accuracy to the calculation of the GAAP reserves, which follow.) The gross annual premium per $1,000 was given as being $5.21. Hence, it can be seen that this policy's premium is set to yield a profit each year that the policy is in force of $5.21 − $3.00 = $2.21. However, as mentioned earlier, a portion of the policy's acquisition expenses offsets this profit each year. In this example, this offsetting amount is found by dividing the $9.02 acquisition expenses by the annuity factor derived above (4.45009):

$$\$9.02 \div 4.45009 = \$2.03$$

Therefore, out of each year's $5.21 gross premium received, $3.00 represents the valuation premium (to be used for that year's benefits, maintenance expenses, and increase in the GAAP reserve), and $2.03 is used to repay the company for the acquisition expenses. The remaining 18 cents each year is for profit.

Next, the GAAP reserves are calculated by an accumulation process, as was explained above. Chart 12–2 shows the progress of this fund. Using the table of l's calculated above, and assuming that each person in the table has $1,000 of insurance, the premium income (GAAP valuation premiums) for each of the five years is calculated by multiplying $3.0035 by the number living. The maintenance expenses each year are calculated by multiplying $1.12 by the number living. The death claims each year are calculated by multiplying $1,000 by the number dying, that is, by d_x for the appropriate age using the company's own mortality experience given above. It can then be seen how the total fund accumulates each year (using the company's experienced interest rate of 6%).

Column (9) of the schedule is the GAAP reserve per person (per $1,000 of insurance). It is calculated by dividing the total fund at the *end* of the year by the number of persons living at the *end* of the year (that is, at the *beginning* of the *following* year). These figures in column (9) are properly called *GAAP reserve factors*, and in practice they would be multiplied by the amount of insurance actually then in force at each such corresponding issue-age and duration-since-issue to determine the company's actual over-all GAAP reserve.

The final GAAP reserve will always be zero on term policies or equal to the amount of insurance on endowment policies, just as with statutory reserves.

The above illustration is considerably simpler than most GAAP reserve calculations dealt with in actual practice. For instance, it is common to take into account the incidence of expected voluntary terminations of policies and consequent payments of nonforfeiture values. (Nonforfeiture values will be discussed in Chapter 13.) In addition, dividends expected to be paid on certain policies may enter the calculation. (Dividends will be discussed in Chapter 14.)

12.7 ASSET SHARES

All of the reserves discussed in this and the previous chapter constitute *liabilities* for the life insurance company. To offset (provide for) these liabilities, the same policies for which the reserves are established will accumulate *assets*, that is, the premiums received by the company, plus interest received from investing the premiums, less the benefits and expenses paid out, will normally accumulate into assets owned by the company. At any point in time, the assets accumulated from any particular policy (or from a group of similar policies issued at the same time) may be less than, more than, or equal to the liability (reserve) for that policy.

At the time a policy is issued, it is desirable for the actuary to forecast the assets which it will accumulate in the future from that policy. Such amounts

CHART 12–2
Age 40, Five-Year Term, Company Experience Mortality and Expenses, 6% Interest.

(1) Policy Year	(2) l_x	(3) GAAP Valuation Premiums ($\$3.0035 \times l_x$)	(4) Maintenance Expenses ($\$1.12 \times l_x$)	(5) Beginning of Year Fund (Col. 8 Previous Yr. + Col. 3 − Col. 4)	(6) Fund Accumulated For 1 Year (Col. 5 × 1.06)	(7) Death Claims ($\$1,000 \times d_x$)	(8) End of Year Fund (Col. 6 − Col. 7)	(9) GAAP Reserve Per Person (Col. 8 ÷ Col. 2 Following Year)
1	100,000	$300,350	$112,000	$188,350	$199,651	$164,000	$35,651	$0.36
2	99,836	299,857	111,816	223,692	237,114	176,000	61,114	.61
3	99,660	299,329	111,619	248,824	263,753	193,000	70,753	.71
4	99,467	298,749	111,403	258,099	273,585	220,000	53,585	.54
5	99,247	298,088	111,157	240,516	254,947	255,000	−53	0
6	98,992							

are called the policy's *asset shares*. Naturally, it is important that such forecasts be made by using the best possible estimates of future income and outgo, because a comparison of asset shares with reserves at each point in the future will show whether the company will be expected to make a profit or lose money on the policy up to that point.

Since asset shares represent forecasts of actual happenings, it follows that the calculations must be made using the presumed actual rates of mortality, interest, expenses, dividends, and voluntary terminations which are expected. This makes them very different from statutory reserve calculations, which use only those rates of mortality and interest that have been narrowly prescribed by law.

USES FOR ASSET SHARES. Besides forecasting the future profitability of a policy, the asset share technique can also be a very useful actuarial tool for testing the general adequacy and appropriateness of the gross premiums, nonforfeiture values, and dividends. (Nonforfeiture values and dividends will be discussed in later chapters.) By initially calculating asset shares in a number of different ways, each making different underlying assumptions, the actuary can, for example, determine the financial effects of using a higher or lower gross premium or set of dividends. All of these tests are particularly important in the highly competitive atmosphere of life insurance today. Asset share calculations can be used to determine exactly how far a company can safely go in pricing its policies to "meet the competition."

Likewise, by recalculating asset shares based on assumptions of higher or lower rates of mortality, interest, or expenses to be experienced in the future, the actuary can see the financial effects which would be produced by favorable or unfavorable turns of events over which the company has little control.

THE CALCULATION. Although computers can perform the actual asset share calculations quickly and easily, we will show a hand-calculation so the student can better understand the method and principles. The following is a simplified example. It assumes that $10,000,000 of five-year term insurance, with an annual gross premium of $7.00 per $1,000, is sold at one time to a group of persons all age 50.

First Year Amounts of Insurance

1. In force beginning of year = $10,000,000.
2. Amount terminating by death during year = $18,000 (from experience value of $q_{[50]}$).
3. Amount terminating by withdrawal during year = $497,000 (from experience rates of policies failing to continue paying premiums).
4. Amount in force at end of year = $9,485,000. (Subtract the preceding items: $1 - 2 - 3$.)

First Year Asset Share Calculations

1. Premium Income = $70,000 (collected on $10,000,000 of insurance at $7.00 per $1,000).
2. Commissions = $35,000 (50% of item 1).
3. Other Expenses = $45,600 (from forecast of first-year expenses).
4. Premium Tax = $1,400 (2% of item 1).
5. Death Claims = $18,000 (amount of insurance terminating by death shown above).
6. Interest earned on the fund this year = −$840 (7% of items 1 − 2 − 3 − 4). Note that death claims are not subtracted from the fund, because they are considered paid at the end of the year, and interest is earned on the fund which is invested at the beginning of the year.
7. Total fund end of year = − $30,840 (1 − 2 − 3 − 4 − 5 + 6).
8. Asset share end of year = − $3.25 (7 ÷ number of thousands of insurance in force at end of first year shown above).

According to this calculation, the company will pay out more money during the first policy year than it takes in during that year. This often happens in the first year of a policy because first-year expenses and commissions are much higher than in subsequent years. The first-year's asset share is a negative $3.25 per $1,000 of insurance still in force.

The asset share calculation for the second policy year might appear as follows:

Second Year Amounts of Insurance

1. In force beginning of year = $9,485,000 (same as item 4 for the first year).
2. Amount terminating by death during year = $25,000 (from experience value of $q_{[50]+1}$).
3. Amount terminating by withdrawal during year = $359,000 (from experience rates of policies failing to continue paying premiums).
4. Amount in force at end of year = $9,101,000 (1 − 2 − 3).

Second Year Asset Share Calculations

1. Premium Income = $66,395 (collected on $9,485,000 of insurance at $7.00 per $1,000).
2. Commissions = $5,312 (8% of 1).
3. Other Expenses = $1,639 (from forecast of second-year expenses).
4. Premium Tax = $1,328 (2% of 1).
5. Death Claims = $25,000 (amount of insurance terminating by death shown above).
6. Interest earned on the fund this year = $1,909 (7% of 7 from previous year + 1 − 2 − 3 − 4).
7. Total fund at end of year = $4,185 (7 previous year + 1 − 2 − 3 − 4 − 5 + 6).

8. Asset share at end of year = $0.46 (7 ÷ number of thousands of insurance in force at end of second year shown above).

Chart 12–3 shows the continued calculations of amounts of insurance in force for the entire five-year period. At the end of the fifth year, the policies all expire, since they are five-year term policies. Hence, column (3) shows all remaining insurance terminating at that time, and column (4) shows no insurance in force at the end of the fifth year.

CHART 12–3

Amounts of Insurance

Year	(1) Amount in Force Beginning of Year	(2) Amount Terminating by Death	(3) Amount Terminating by Withdrawal	(4) Amount in Force End of Year
1	$10,000,000	$18,000	$ 497,000	$9,485,000
2	9,485,000	25,000	359,000	9,101,000
3	9,101,000	31,000	304,000	8,766,000
4	8,766,000	38,000	253,000	8,475,000
5	8,475,000	45,000	8,430,000	0

Chart 12–4 shows the calculations of asset shares for all five years. Chart

CHART 12–4

Asset Share Calculations

Year	(1) Premium Income	(2) Commissions	(3) Other Expenses	(4) Premium Tax	(5) Death Claims	(6) Interest Income	(7) Fund End of Year	(8) Asset Share
1	$70,000	$35,000	$45,600	$1,400	$18,000	−$ 840	−$30,840	−$3.25
2	66,395	5,312	1,639	1,328	25,000	1,909	4,185	0.46
3	63,707	5,097	1,573	1,274	31,000	4,196	33,144	3.78
4	61,362	4,909	1,515	1,227	38,000	6,080	54,935	6.48
5	59,325	4,746	1,464	1,187	45,000	7,480	69,343	——

12–5 compares year by year the predicted asset shares and the statutory terminal reserves per $1,000. The reserves are calculated using the 1958 C.S.O. Table and 3% interest.

CHART 12–5

End of Year	Asset Share	Statutory Terminal Reserve
1	−$3.25	$1.66
2	0.46	2.59
3	3.78	2.70
4	6.48	1.88
5	—	0

The company will realize no profit from this group by the end of two years, since the liabilities (reserves) still exceed the assets (asset share) at that time. However, from the end of the third year, the asset shares exceed the reserves and this group becomes profitable. The time required for a group of policies to become profitable is called the *validation period*. Technically, validation takes place in the first year in which the asset share equals or exceeds the reserve.

At the end of the five-year period, based on the set of assumptions used, the total fund is predicted to be $69,343 (Chart 12–4, column (7)). Since the company owes nothing further at that point, this represents a predicted profit of $6.93 for each $1,000 of insurance originally issued (that is, $69,343 ÷ 10,000). The actuary may or may not feel that this represents an adequate profit on the money the company would be investing, considering the risk it would be taking. Alternative asset shares, based on lower or higher gross premium assumptions, can be calculated to determine potential profit levels. In practice, the gross premium finally selected is one which balances the considerations of producing an adequate profit with that of being competitive in the market.

Similarly, the same kinds of calculations can be made using different assumptions as to mortality rates, expenses, etc., to show, for example, what would happen to the profits if experience in some of these areas turned out to be unexpectedly adverse.

MORE REFINED CALCULATIONS. While the asset share calculations shown above are quite simple, many refinements are often added in practice. For example, the calculations generally include the nonforfeiture values paid to policyowners who terminate their insurance by withdrawing from the group. In addition, dividends which the company expects to pay to the policy owners each year are generally included. Other refinements could include taking into account the following things:

1. Premiums will be received in different frequencies (semiannual, monthly, etc.), so that those withdrawing in any policy year may not have paid the premium for the entire year.
2. Death benefits are actually paid at the time of death, rather than at the end of the year of death; since these payments are actually spread out over the year, calculation of the interest earned on the fund should allow for the fact that the fund constantly decreases throughout the year as death payments are made.
3. The company may refund a portion of the premium at the death of the insured person in addition to paying the amount of insurance—a very common practice; for example, if the policyowner paid an annual premium and then died after a fourth of that policy year had elpased, the company may refund three fourths of that annual premium in addition to paying the amount of insurance.
4. The company will have to pay United States or Canadian income taxes on

the interest income and the mortality profits on this particular group of policies; such calculations can become very complex.

5. The average size of the policies in the group can have a considerable effect on the asset shares, particularly if the gross premium includes a policy fee (that is, a certain amount for each policy).

6. The proportion of the group which is male and which is female is important; thus, the mortality results expected will be considerably different if the group is expected to contain a higher than normal proportion of females.

EXERCISES, SET 29

1. What is the principal reason for a company to use modified reserves instead of net level reserves?

2. Which modified reserve method produces modified net annual premiums that have a present value at the time a policy is issued not equal to the present value of the benefits?

3. A $1,000 endowment-at-age-65 policy issued at age 35 has its reserved calculated by the Full Preliminary Term Method. The modified net premiums are equal to $3.24 the first year and $28.10 for each of the subsequent years. Calculate (a) the mean reserve for the first year, (b) the initial reserve for the second year, and (c) the terminal reserve for the 30th year.

4. What are the two principal differences between the calculation of GAAP reserves and regular (statutory) reserves?

5. Given the following figures from a company's own experience, calculate the valuation premium which would be used in a company's GAAP reserve calculations for an ordinary life policy.

> Present value at date of issue of:
> Benefits $314.14
> Maintenance expenses 21.01
> Whole life annuity of 1 per year 19.77

6. The following figures have been calculated using a company's own experience for a $1,000 20-year endowment policy

> Present value at date of issue:
> Benefits $610.10
> Acquisition expenses 42.08
> Maintenance expenses 15.55
> 20-year life annuity of 1 per year 14.221

The company decides to charge a gross annual premium of $49.20 per $1,000. How much profit does the company anticipate showing each year on its GAAP statement for each $1,000 of this policy which is still in force?

7. If an asset share calculation assumes a group of policies is issued totaling $1,000,000 of insurance, and it further assumes that the mortality rate for the first year is $q_{[x]} = .00168$, how much insurance will be shown is in force at the end of the first year if none are assumed to withdraw?

8. The following is a portion of an asset share calculation table:

Year	Insurance in Force Beginning of Year	Fund End of Year
1	$1,000,000	−$ 64,200
2	960,000	31,400
3	900,000	216,300
4	820,000	488,400
5	720,000	714,700

Calculate the asset shares per $1,000 of insurance at the end of years 1 through 4.

9. Using the answers to Exercise 8, at what policy year will this group of policies first show an overall profit since date of issue, if the terminal reserves per $1,000 are as follows:

Year	Terminal Reserve
1	$160
2	325
3	497
4	675
5	866

10. The following is a portion of an asset share calculation table:

Year	Insurance in Force Beginning of Year	Fund End of Year
12	$687,000	$317,900
13	635,000	592,800
14	574,000	785,600

According to this table, the asset share per $1,000 of insurance at the end of the 13th year is

(1) $500.63   (3) $1,032.75
(2) $933.54   (4) $1,368.64

CHAPTER SUMMARY

- A policy's *initial reserve* (at the beginning of a policy year) equals the previous year's terminal reserve plus the current year's net annual premium.

- A policy's *mean reserve* (that is, at the middle of a policy year) equals

$$\frac{\text{Initial Reserve} + \text{Terminal Reserve}}{2}$$

- Mean reserves are often used to represent the company's liability in its December 31 financial statement. This is done because all policies issued in the year just ended can be assumed to be half a year old, those issued the previous year can be assumed to be one and a half years old, etc.

- A policy's *net amount at risk* equals the amount of insurance minus the terminal reserve.

- The net amount at risk is generally used to represent the amount of insurance for each policy when studies are made of mortality experience.

- The progress of a policy's reserve for a year can be described as follows: The initial reserve accumulates at interest, the tabular cost of insurance is then deducted, and the result is the terminal reserve.

- The *tabular cost of insurance* can be calculated as follows:

$$\left(\begin{array}{c} \text{Initial} \\ \text{Reserve} \end{array} \right)(1 + i) - \left(\begin{array}{c} \text{Terminal} \\ \text{Reserve} \end{array} \right)$$

- The tabular cost of insurance can be calculated by a second method by multiplying the net amount at risk by the mortality rate for that year. The answer will be the same by either method.

- The tabular cost of insurance is sometimes called the *expected mortality*. The results of studies of actual mortality experience are often expressed as a ratio of actual mortality to expected mortality (that is, the net amount at risk on those policies were the insured died divided by the total expected mortality on all policies being studied).

- State laws have special requirements for calculating reserves on policies with very low gross premiums (that is, where the gross annual premium is less than the net annual premium calculated using *minimum standards*).

- Reserves on such policies must be at least as large as

$$\left(\begin{array}{c} \text{Present Value of} \\ \text{Future Benefits} \end{array} \right) - \left(\begin{array}{c} \text{Present Value of} \\ \text{Future Gross Premiums} \end{array} \right)$$

calculated using minimum standards. These reserves are sometimes called *premium deficiency reserves*, using a name which once applied to special reserves formerly required under old laws.

- The modified net premiums described in Chapter 10 are used to calculate modified reserves. This can be done in the same way as calculating net level reserves (by the retrospective or prospective method).

- Under the Full Preliminary Term Method, the first year's terminal reserve is always zero. Terminal reserves for all subsequent years are equal to those for one year less on a policy issued at one age higher and having a one year shorter premium-paying period.

- Under the Commissioners Method, higher-premium policies have reserves which are larger than Full Preliminary Term reserves but smaller than net level reserves.

- Under the Canadian Method, the early years may have *negative terminal reserves*. Generally, the reserves are the lowest of any method presented in this book.

- At the time a policy is issued (at duration zero), its terminal reserve is equal to zero under all methods presented except for the Canadian Method. Under the Canadian Method, such a terminal reserve is negative.

- At the end of a policy's final year, all methods produce a terminal reserve equal to the amount then owed to the policyowner (that is, it equals zero for a term policy or equals the amount of the pure endowment under an endowment policy).

- In the United States, the National Association of Insurance Commissioners has prepared the Standard Valuation Law, which prescribes a mortality table, interest rate, and modified reserve method for calculating minimum reserves. A company is free to use larger reserves than these. The Standard Valuation Law has been amended several times. Generally, the law and its amendments are enacted in all states with little variation.

- Reserves calculated in accordance with generally accepted accounting principles are referred to as *GAAP reserves*. They are completely different from the reserves discussed so far, which are called statutory reserves because they are required by statute to appear in a company's financial statement submitted to state regulatory authorities.

- In calculating GAAP reserves, a net annual premium (called a *GAAP valuation premium*) is first calculated. It is calculated on a net level basis and is sufficient to provide for all anticipated benefits and yearly maintenance expenses. The mortality, interest, and expense assumptions are those which are expected to occur.

- The policy's *acquisition expenses* are shown as an asset in a GAAP financial statement. Each year this asset is reduced over the life of the policy.

- GAAP reserves can be figured similar to that described in Chapter 11 for regular reserves, that is, a fund can be accumulated involving all persons shown in a mortality table. Each year valuation premiums and interest are added to the fund, and death claims and maintenance expenses are deducted. All such calculations are based on assumptions which are expected to occur.

- As with the regular reserves, the GAAP reserve at the end of the final year will equal the amount then owed to the policyowner. The reason for this is that the GAAP valuation premium is calculated to provide for exactly the same benefits and maintenance expenses which are used in the GAAP reserve calculations.

- The profit from a policy which is expected to appear in a GAAP statement each year is equal to the excess of the gross premium over the valuation premium minus the year's decrease in the acquisition expense asset.

- An *asset share* is the amount of assets a policy is forecast to accumulate at a given point in the future. The calculation is made using presumed actual mortality, interest, expenses, voluntary terminations, nonforfeiture values, and dividends. Many more refinements are often added besides these.

- Asset shares are generally less than the reserves in a policy's early years. By comparing asset shares with reserves, the actuary can forecast the particular point in time when a group of policies can be expected to become profitable. By using different assumptions, the actuary can determine the optimum premiums to charge, as well as the effects of possible future changes in the company's experience.

LEARNING OBJECTIVES

After reading this chapter, the student should know

- The definition of initial reserve.
- How to calculate initial reserves.

- The definition of mean reserve.
- How to calculate mean reserves.
- How mean reserves are used in December 31 annual statements.
- The definition of net amount at risk.
- How to calculate the net amount at risk.
- The definition of the tabular cost of insurance.
- How to calculate the tabular cost of insurance using two different approaches.
- The definition of premium deficiency reserves.
- How to calculate premium deficiency reserves.
- That the Full Preliminary Term Method produces a first year terminal reserve of zero.
- How reserves compare between various methods:

  Net Level
  Full Preliminary Term
  Commissioners
  Canadian

- What amount of terminal reserve is produced by the various methods at duration zero and at the end of the final year.
- When GAAP reserves are used.
- What principles and assumptions are used in calculating GAAP reserves.
- How to calculate the profit anticipated from a policy in a GAAP financial statement.
- The meaning of asset shares.
- How asset shares are calculated.
- How asset shares are useful.

13

Nonforfeiture Values

In previous chapters, we have made some references to the values (called *nonforfeiture values*) which a life insurance company pays to a policyowner when that policyowner decides to stop paying premiums, that is, withdraw or voluntarily terminate the policy. In this chapter, nonforfeiture values will be explained in more detail, along with the methods used to calculate them.

Nonforfeiture values are required by law and explanations will be given of how these laws set forth the calculation of the minimum amounts which must be given.

This chapter will also describe the various options that are generally made available to the policyowner at the time premium payments are stopped. For example, we will see that insurance coverage may remain in force (possibly on a different basis) even though no more premiums are paid.

13.1 INTRODUCTION

In the United States, most life insurance policies are required by law to contain a provision which guarantees that nonforfeiture values will be available if the policyowner decides to stop paying the premiums. The amounts guaranteed for the various policy years are stated in a policy when it is issued, and these values cannot be changed thereafter.

Another required policy provision gives the policyowner the right to borrow money from the insurance company at an interest rate stated in the policy, pledging the policy's guaranteed value as collateral. Generally, such a *policy loan* can be made at any time, but it can never be for more than the guaranteed value which the policyowner is entitled to receive if he or she stops paying premiums. If premium payments are stopped after a loan has been made and before it is repaid, the amount of the loan still unpaid is generally deducted from the guaranteed nonforfeiture value stipulated in the policy.

At the time premium payments are stopped, the policyowner may also be entitled to certain additional values if the policy has been credited with policy *dividends* from the company. The subject of policy dividends will be presented in Chapter 14. It will be sufficient here to state that the *total value* available when premium payments are stopped is generally:

Guaranteed Nonforfeiture Value
+ Value of Dividend Credits (if any)
− Loan (if any)

This total value can generally be taken by the policyowner in any one of the following ways:

1. Received in a lump sum
2. Used to provide a periodic income as provided in the Tables of Settlement Options (Section 8.4)
3. Used to continue the policy in force as *reduced paid-up insurance*
4. Used to continue the policy in force as *extended term insurance*

13.2 CASH VALUE

The *guaranteed nonforfeiture value* is often referred to as the *cash value*. Section 13.2 presents three methods of calculating this cash value: (1) the Surrender Charge Method, (2) the method specified in the Standard Nonforfeiture Law, and (3) the method based on Nonforfeiture Factors. Sections 13.3 and 13.4 describe how to calculate the amount of reduced paid-up and extended term insurance which can be provided from the total value.

RELATIONSHIP TO RESERVES. The statutory reserve is the amount a company is legally required to have on hand for a policy. The cash value is the amount a company guarantees is payable (in a lump sum) if the policy is terminated. State laws specify minimums for both, although companies are permitted to maintain reserves and pay cash values which are higher than the minimums. The minimum cash value specified for any policy at any time is less than the minimum statutory reserve. In actual practice, guaranteed cash values are generally less than the statutory reserve actually held during the early years of a policy. After the early years, however, the cash value is often equal to the statutory reserve. It cannot legally exceed this reserve since the company cannot, in effect, promise that a policyowner could receive more money than the company has set up as its liability for that policy.

SURRENDER CHARGE METHOD. Prior to 1948, state laws in the United States generally required that, beginning at the end of the third year, a policy must provide a guaranteed cash value at least equal to the terminal reserve minus $25 per $1,000 of insurance. This deduction was known as a *surrender charge*. It was customary in practice, however, for the surrender charge to be progressively reduced by policy duration and eliminated after a period of time, such as ten years. Thus, the cash value actually guaranteed at the expiration of such a period was equal to the full terminal reserve.

The surrender charge method is still used by a number of companies in their currently issued policies, although the state laws were changed to specify a different method for policies issued beginning in 1948. This method is described below (see Standard Nonforfeiture Law). A company using the surrender charge method for policies being issued today must check to make certain that all cash values are equal to or greater than the minimums specified in today's laws.

STANDARD NONFORFEITURE LAW. The Standard Nonforfeiture Law, originally drafted by the National Association of Insurance Commissioners, has been enacted into law, with few modifications, in all states. According to this law, the *minimum cash value* at any time is defined to be the present value of future benefits minus the present value of future special premiums, called *adjusted premiums*. These adjusted premiums are precisely defined in the law. In general, the present value of the adjusted premiums (at time of issue) is meant to represent the present value of the policy's benefits, plus the excess of the first-year expenses over the annual expenses for subsequent years. In equation form, the minimum cash value is:

$$\begin{pmatrix} \text{Minimum} \\ \text{Cash} \\ \text{Value} \end{pmatrix} = \begin{pmatrix} \text{Present Value} \\ \text{of Future} \\ \text{Benefits} \end{pmatrix} - \begin{pmatrix} \text{Present Value} \\ \text{of Future} \\ \text{Adjusted Premiums} \end{pmatrix}$$

The adjusted premiums are greater than the net level premiums, and therefore, their present value is greater than the present value of the policy's net level premiums, if the same mortality table and interest rate are used. This, in turn, produces minimum cash values which are less than the net level terminal reserve during the entire premium-paying period of a policy. The reason for this can be seen by examining the two equations:

$$\begin{pmatrix} \text{Terminal} \\ \text{Reserve} \end{pmatrix} = \begin{pmatrix} \text{Present Value of} \\ \text{Future Benefits} \end{pmatrix} - \begin{pmatrix} \text{Present Value of} \\ \text{Future Net Premiums} \end{pmatrix}$$

$$\begin{pmatrix} \text{Minimum} \\ \text{Cash Value} \end{pmatrix} = \begin{pmatrix} \text{Present Value of} \\ \text{Future Benefits} \end{pmatrix} - \begin{pmatrix} \text{Present Value of} \\ \text{Future Adjusted Premiums} \end{pmatrix}$$

The item subtracted on the right-hand side of the Minimum Cash Value equation is larger than the item so subtracted in the Terminal Reserve equation. Therefore, the value of the minimum cash value is less than the value of the net level terminal reserve.

The Standard Nonforfeiture Law generally became effective in 1948. It has subsequently been amended several times. This law specifies the particular mortality table, interest rate, and amount of excess first-year expenses which are to be used to calculate the adjusted premiums. Different bases are specified for policies issued in different time periods. The basis in effect in any particular state for a policy issued at a particular time may be ascertained by making inquiry to that state's department or division of insurance.

In 1980, the Standard Nonforfeiture Law was amended in a similar way to the amendment for the Standard Valuation Law (as described in Chapter 12). According to the amendment, the interest rate for calculating minimum cash values will be determined automatically each year, for policies to be issued the following year, without further legal enactment. The amendment provides that the interest rate for calculating *minimum cash values* will always be higher than the interest rate for calculating *minimum reserves*. Therefore, the minimum cash values themselves will always be smaller than the minimum reserves for any policy. The mortality table specified by the amendment is the 1980 C.S.O. Table, but the states' insurance commissioners may approve new tables without the need for legal enactment by the states. The amendment will become effective on January 1, 1989, but companies can adopt the minimum reserves and cash values earlier if they wish.

The cash value of each individual policy must be at least as large *at every policy year* as the minimum prescribed for that policy year. A company is free to use any basis for calculating its cash values, provided that each and every value equals or exceeds the minimum for that policy year.

To Illustrate—Calculate the minimum cash value at the end of ten years for a $1,000 30-payment life policy issued at age 25. The following information is given, calculated on the bases applicable to this policy under the law:

Net single premium at age 35 for $1,000 whole life insurance $358.66
Present value at age 35 of 20-year life annuity due of 1 . . . . 14.80519
Adjusted premium for this policy . . . . $ 15.83

Solution—The *adjusted premiums* run for 30 years under this policy (to age 55). At any time, their present value is calculated as a temporary life annuity due to age 55. The attained age at the end of ten years is $25 + 10 = 35$; the temporary life annuity then runs for 20 more years:

Basic equation:

$$\begin{pmatrix} \text{Minimum} \\ \text{Cash} \\ \text{Value} \end{pmatrix} = \begin{pmatrix} \text{Present Value} \\ \text{of Future} \\ \text{Benefits} \end{pmatrix} - \begin{pmatrix} \text{Present Value} \\ \text{of Future} \\ \text{Adjusted Premiums} \end{pmatrix}$$

Express this equation in equivalent form:

$$= \begin{pmatrix} \text{Net Single Premium} \\ \text{at Age 35} \end{pmatrix} - \begin{pmatrix} \text{Adjusted} \\ \text{Premium} \end{pmatrix}\begin{pmatrix} \text{20-year Annuity} \\ \text{Factor at Age 35} \end{pmatrix}$$

Substitute values given above:

$$= \$358.66 - \$15.83(14.80519)$$
$$= \$358.66 - \$234.37$$
$$= \$124.29$$

In actual practice, many companies would guarantee a cash value for the above policy equal to the full terminal reserve at the end of ten years. If the net level method were used, this terminal reserve would be $146.68. However, the student can see that the law does allow a cash value in this case which is less than this terminal reserve by as much as

$$\text{Terminal Reserve} - \text{Minimum Cash Value} = \$146.68 - \$124.29$$
$$= \$22.39$$

In a sense, this $22.39 may be thought of as a surrender charge available at that time. Similarly, if the Commissioners modified reserve method were used, the terminal reserve would be $136.71. In that event, the law allows a cash value which is less than this modified terminal reserve by as much as

$$\text{Terminal Reserve} - \text{Minimum Cash Value} = \$136.71 - \$124.29$$

$$= \$12.42$$

NONFORFEITURE FACTORS. Many companies calculate their policies' actual cash values in a manner similar to that set forth in the law for calculating the legal minimums. The cash values are calculated to be the present value of future benefits minus the present value of future *special premiums*. These *special premiums* are not greater than the legally prescribed adjusted premiums and are usually called *nonforfeiture factors*. In equation form, this method of calculating cash values is as follows:

$$\left(\begin{array}{c}\text{Cash}\\\text{Value}\end{array}\right) = \left(\begin{array}{c}\text{Present Value}\\\text{of Future}\\\text{Benefits}\end{array}\right) - \left(\begin{array}{c}\text{Present Value}\\\text{of Future}\\\text{Nonforfeiture Factors}\end{array}\right)$$

Each company using this method calculates its own nonforfeiture factors. Since the nonforfeiture factors are not greater than the adjusted premiums, their present value is not greater than the present value of the adjusted premiums. This, in turn, produces actual cash values which are at least as great as the legal minimums (as they must be).

One widely used method is to specify a certain nonforfeiture factor applicable to the first several years the policy will be in effect and a second factor applicable to the remaining years.

To Illustrate—Calculate the cash value which a certain company would specify at the end of ten years for a $1,000 ordinary life policy issued at age 35. This company specifies that its nonforfeiture factor on this policy is $17.50 for the first 30 years and $16.29 thereafter. The following information is given:

Present value at age 45 of 20-year life annuity due of 1 . . . .   14.14529
Present value at age 45 of whole life annuity due of 1, deferred for
  20 years 4.43261
Net single premium at age 45 for $1,000 whole life insurance $458.89

Solution—The cash value at any time is calculated as the present value of future benefits minus the present value of future nonforfeiture factors. At the end of ten years, the attained age is 35 + 10 = 45. The remaining nonforfeiture factors at that time are shown in the following line diagram.

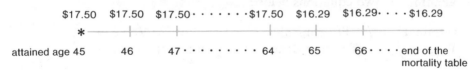

$17.50 $17.50 $17.50· · · · · · ·$17.50 $16.29 $16.29· · · ·$16.29

attained age 45   46   47 · · · · · · · · · 64   65   66 · · · · end of the
                                                                              mortality table

At age 45, there are 20 remaining factors of $17.50 each (due at ages 45 to 64, inclusive), plus $16.29 thereafter each year for the remainder of life (beginning at age 65). The present value of all of them can be looked on as the present value of a temporary life annuity due ($17.50 per year for 20 years) plus the present value of a deferred whole life annuity due ($16.29 per year deferred 20 years):

Basic equation:

$$\begin{pmatrix} \text{Cash} \\ \text{Value} \end{pmatrix} = \begin{pmatrix} \text{Present Value} \\ \text{of Future} \\ \text{Benefits} \end{pmatrix} - \begin{pmatrix} \text{Present Value} \\ \text{of Future} \\ \text{Nonforfeiture Factors} \end{pmatrix}$$

Express this equation in equivalent form:

$$= \begin{pmatrix} \text{Net Single} \\ \text{Premium} \\ \text{at Age 45} \end{pmatrix} - \left[\begin{pmatrix} \text{First} \\ \text{Nonforfeiture} \\ \text{Factor} \end{pmatrix} \begin{pmatrix} \text{20-Year Life} \\ \text{Annuity Factor} \\ \text{at Age 45} \end{pmatrix} \right.$$

$$\left. + \begin{pmatrix} \text{Second} \\ \text{Nonforfeiture} \\ \text{Factor} \end{pmatrix} \begin{pmatrix} \text{Whole Life Annuity} \\ \text{Factor Deferred} \\ \text{20 Years at Age 45} \end{pmatrix} \right]$$

Substitute values given above:

$$= \$458.89 - [(\$17.50)(14.14529) + (\$16.29)(4.43261)]$$
$$= \$458.89 - [\$247.54 + \$72.21]$$
$$= \$458.89 - \$319.75$$
$$= \$139.14$$

It is interesting to note that the policy in this illustration has a net level annual premium equal to $16.29 and that its *adjusted premium* under the Standard Nonforfeiture Law (using the same mortality and interest bases) is $17.72. Therefore, the particular nonforfeiture factors used ($17.50 and $16.29) are not less than the policy's net premium. This is imperative, since otherwise, cash values would be produced which exceed the policy's terminal reserve (an illegal situation). Furthermore, the particular nonforfeiture factors used are not greater than the policy's adjusted premium under the Standard Nonforfeiture Law. This is also imperative, since otherwise, cash values would be produced which would be less than the policy's legal minimum cash value.

It is also interesting to note that the second nonforfeiture factor ($16.29) used in the above illustration is exactly equal to the policy's net level annual premium. The effect of specifying such a nonforfeiture factor is that, after the period (30 years in this illustration), all of the cash values will then be equal to the full terminal reserve. The reason this is so can be demonstrated by examining the two equations below:

$$\begin{pmatrix} \text{Terminal} \\ \text{Reserve} \end{pmatrix} = \begin{pmatrix} \text{Present Value} \\ \text{of Future Benefits} \end{pmatrix} - \begin{pmatrix} \text{Present Value of} \\ \text{Future Net Premiums} \end{pmatrix}$$

$$\binom{\text{Cash}}{\text{Value}} = \binom{\text{Present Value}}{\text{of Future Benefits}} - \binom{\text{Present Value of}}{\text{Future Nonforfeiture Factors}}$$

If the net premium is equal to the nonforfeiture factor, then the right-hand sides of both equations are the same.

13.3 REDUCED PAID-UP INSURANCE

It was pointed out in Section 13.1 that the policyowner can stop paying premiums at any time and use the policy's total value in one of four ways, one of which is to continue the policy in force as *reduced paid-up insurance*. In such a case, the insurance continues in effect, and the nature of the benefit will be the same (whole life, endowment, etc.), but, since no more premiums will be payable, the insurance will be for a smaller amount. The basis for the calculation rests on the principle that the policy's total value is used as if it were a net single premium at the attained age for the paid-up benefits.

For example, an ordinary life policy issued at age 20 might have the following values at the end of 12 years:

Cash value	$227.04
Value of dividend credits	41.80
Total	$268.84
Less loan	−97.60
Total value	$171.24

At the end of 12 years, the attained age is 20 + 12 = 32. Hence, $171.24 will be used as the net single premium at age 32 for a certain amount of whole life insurance. If the 1958 C.S.O. Table and 3% interest are used, the amount of the reduced paid-up insurance will be $515, since the net single premium for $515 of whole life insurance at age 32 equals the $171.24 which is available.

THE CALCULATION. If the amount of the total value is known, and it is desired to calculate the amount of the reduced paid-up insurance which this total value will purchase, the equation is

$$\binom{\text{Amount of Reduced}}{\text{Paid-Up Insurance}} = \frac{(\text{Total Value})}{\binom{\text{Net Single Premium}}{\text{at Attained Age}}{\text{for \$1 of Insurance}}}$$

The net single premium for $1,000 whole life insurance at age 32 is $332.50. The net single premium for $1 of such insurance would be $\frac{1}{1000}$ of $332.50 or $.33250 (by moving the decimal point three places to the left). Applying the equation to the above example, the amount of reduced paid-up insurance would be calculated as follows:

$$\left(\begin{array}{c}\text{Amount of Reduced} \\ \text{Paid-Up Insurance}\end{array}\right) = \frac{(\text{Total Value})}{\left(\begin{array}{c}\text{Net Single Premium} \\ \text{at Attained Age} \\ \text{for \$1 of Insurance}\end{array}\right)}$$

$$= \frac{\$171.24}{.33250}$$

$$= \$515$$

This kind of calculation is simple in actual practice since published tables of net single premiums at each attained age are usually available.

Amounts of life insurance are usually established in whole dollars without any cents. Therefore, when the amount of reduced paid-up insurance is calculated, the answer is usually expressed in the form of whole dollars only. In this instance, however, the usual rules for rounding off the answer are not followed. It is customary instead to drop off any cents from the answer and to add 1 to the number of dollars. For example, if the amount of reduced paid-up insurance were calculated to be $2,017.12, the company would usually establish $2,018 of such insurance. This is called *rounding up to the next higher dollar* and is an example of maintaining goodwill by not giving less than the policyowner is entitled to.

To Illustrate—Calculate the amount of reduced paid-up insurance which is available at the end of 15 years for a $1,000 20-year endowment policy issued at age 25. Assume the cash value is $676.29 and there are no other credits and no loan. The net single premium at age 40 for $1,000 of five-year endowment insurance is $863.63.

Solution—At the end of 15 years, there are five years still remaining of the original 20-year period. The attained age is $25 + 15 = 40$. Hence, the net single premium needed will be for $1 of five-year endowment insurance at age 40. This will be $\frac{1}{1000}$ of the net single premium for $1,000 of such insurance, as given above. By moving the decimal point three places to the left, the net single premium for $1 of such insurance is obtained:

$$\frac{1}{1000} \text{ of } \$863.63 = \$.86363$$

As stated above, the amount of reduced paid-up insurance is found by dividing the policy's available value by the net single premium for $1 of insurance:

Basic equation:

$$\left(\begin{array}{c}\text{Amount of Reduced}\\ \text{Paid-Up Insurance}\end{array}\right) = \dfrac{(\text{Total Value})}{\left(\begin{array}{c}\text{Net Single Premium}\\ \text{at Attained Age}\\ \text{for \$1 of Insurance}\end{array}\right)}$$

$$= \dfrac{\$676.29}{.86363}$$

$$= \$783.08$$

Round to next higher dollar:

$$= \$784$$

This endowment policy will now provide a death benefit of $784 if death occurs between ages 40 and 45, or a pure endowment of $784 will be payable if the insured is alive at age 45. There are no more premiums due, because the policyowner has elected to stop paying premiums and use the policy's nonforfeiture value to provide reduced paid-up insurance.

In calculating reduced paid-up insurance, it should always be remembered that the form of the benefit will be determined only by the policy's original benefit and that the premium-paying period will not affect the net single premium to be used. For example, this net single premium will be a whole life net single premium whether the policy is a 20-payment life policy, a whole life policy with premiums to age 65, or an ordinary life policy.

After the end of the regular premium-paying period of any policy (such as after 20 years on a 20-payment life policy), a calculation of reduced paid-up insurance would, in effect, be meaningless. Such a policy is already paid-up for its full amount of insurance. Therefore, no reduced paid-up insurance is available in such an instance. However, the policyowner may still terminate the policy voluntarily and be entitled to receive its cash value.

13.4 EXTENDED TERM INSURANCE

The fourth nonforfeiture option is *extended term insurance*. Under this option, the insurance continues in effect with no more premiums payable, but for a shorter period of time. For most extended term insurance cases, it is necessary to calculate the amount of such insurance and the period of time for which such insurance will continue.

AMOUNT OF EXTENDED TERM INSURANCE. The principle underlying the determination of the amount of such insurance is that the death benefit will be the same as the death benefit available at the time the policyowner elects to stop paying premiums. This amount is generally calculated as

Regular death benefit of the policy
+ Additional insurance purchased previously by dividends (if any)
− Loan (if any)

The additional insurance purchased by dividends will be discussed in Chapter 14. It will be sufficient here to state that the amount of any such additional insurance, like the policy's regular death benefit, is payable at the time of death. At such time, of course, any outstanding policy loan plus interest is deducted from the policy's regular death benefit. This accounts for its deduction in calculating the amount of extended term insurance.

To Illustrate—Calculate the total value available to provide extended term insurance and the amount of extended term insurance which may be provided ten years after the date of issue of a $10,000 ordinary life policy issued at age 20, given the following information:

Cash value, end of ten years	$674.40
Dividend additions (face value of the additional insurance purchased previously by dividends)	47.00
Value of dividend credits (cash value of the dividend additions)	14.86
Policy loan	100.00

Solution—The total value which is available to provide extended term insurance is

Cash value	$674.40
Value of dividend credits	14.86
Total	$689.26
Less loan	−100.00
Total value	$589.26

The amount of extended term insurance is

Regular death benefit	$10,000
Additional insurance purchased previously by dividends	47
Total	$10,047
Less loan	−100
Total amount of extended term insurance	9,947

PERIOD OF TIME OF EXTENDED TERM INSURANCE. Determining the period of time for which the insurance will continue is again based on the principle that the policy's total value is used as if it were a net single premium for such insurance. The insurance will be term insurance (with no further premiums payable) and will continue for a limited period of time to be determined.

Only by coincidence will the total value result in providing this extended term insurance for an exact number of years. It is customary, therefore, to calculate the number of years and days that it will continue. Any fractional part of a day in the answer is used as if it added an entire extra day. For example, if the answer were five years and 21.247 days, the insurance would actually be granted for a term of five years and 22 days.

To arrive at the above answer of five years and 21.247 days, it would first be observed that the total value available is greater than the net single premium for five years of term insurance but less than the net single premium for six years of term insurance. A calculation is then made to determine what proportionate part of a year is represented by the value available in excess of the net single premium for five years.

EXTENDED TERM INSURANCE ON ENDOWMENT POLICIES. If the extended term insurance nonforfeiture option is selected for an endowment policy, the total value available may be more than sufficient to carry the policy as term insurance for the number of years remaining in the original endowment period. Under these circumstances, any portion of the total value not needed to pay for the term insurance is used as a net single premium, at the attained age, to provide a pure endowment payable at the end of the original endowment period. It is customary to round the amount of this pure endowment up to the next higher dollar.

For example, at the end of the 15th year, the cash value of a $5,000 20-year endowment policy, which was issued at age 40, might be $3,422.75. Assuming there is no loan or dividend credits, the amount of extended term insurance available at that time would be $5,000. At the end of the 15th year, there are five years remaining in the original 20-year endowment period. The attained age is 40 + 15 = 55. Assuming the net single premium necessary at age 55 to provide the $5,000 of term insurance for the remaining five years is $346.25, the policy's cash value of $3,422.75 is sufficient to pay this amount, and there would be an amount left over of

$$\$3,422.75 - \$346.25 = \$3,076.50$$

This $3,076.50 left over might pay for a pure endowment (due in five years) of $3,859.57. Therefore, the entire benefit under the extended term insurance option, would consist of five-year term insurance for $5,000 plus a pure endowment due in five years of $3,860.

After the end of the regular premium-paying period of any policy, a calculation of extended term insurance is, in effect, meaningless. Such a policy is already in force for its full amount of benefits, and for its full period of time, with no more premiums payable. Therefore, no extended term insurance is available in such an instance. However, the policyowner may still terminate the policy voluntarily and receive its cash value.

MORTALITY TABLE FOR EXTENDED TERM INSURANCE. The Standard Nonforfeiture Law specifies that the mortality rates used to calculate the period of time that extended term insurance will continue may not be more than those shown in a certain designated mortality table which is based on the mortality observed for persons selecting that option. The law has been amended several times, and different tables have been specified at various times. The table applicable to any particular policy is that designated by the law in effect at the time the policy is issued. All of these special *extended term mortality tables* have exhibited mortality rates generally higher than those contained in the table which must be used to calculate minimum cash values. This reflects the generally higher mortality observed for those persons who have elected this particular nonforfeiture option.

This higher than normal mortality observed for policies in force as extended term insurance might be expected, because such an arrangement is attractive to persons who may have cause to anticipate an early death. Their full death benefit remains in force (temporarily) without the necessity of further premium payments.

13.5 INSURANCE PAID-UP OR MATURED BY DIVIDENDS

Generally, life insurance policies contain a provision which states that the company will declare the policy to be fully paid-up (the full benefits will continue in effect, but no more premiums need be paid), if the policyowner so desires, whenever the cash value plus the value of dividend credit equals or exceeds the net single premium at the attained age for the future benefits. In doing this, the company would use the necessary amount of dividend credits, and the paid-up policy would then have only the remaining amount of dividend credits still available. If a loan had been made before the policy was made paid-up, this generally would not affect the paid-up transaction. The policy would still have the same loan against it after becoming paid-up.

For example, assume a $1,000 endowment-at-age-65 policy issued at age 30 has a cash value of $775.47 at the end of 30 years. It also has dividend credits valued at $131.18. The total of these values is

$$\$775.47 + \$131.18 = \$906.65$$

In order for this policy to be declared fully paid-up, this total value must equal or exceed the net single premium at the attained age. The attained age is $30 + 30 = 60$. Using the 1958 C.S.O. Table and 3% interest, the net single premium at age 60 for the future benefits (endowment-at-age-65) is $868.42. Hence, the cash value plus dividend credits ($906.65) exceeds the net single premium ($868.42). If the policyowner so desires, the company will declare this policy fully paid-up. In this instance, there is more value than is needed, amounting to

$$\$906.65 - \$868.42 = \$38.23$$

Generally, this extra $38.23 will either be paid to the policyowner at the time the policy is declared to be paid-up or else it will remain in the form of a dividend credit for the policy (the rest of the dividend credits having been used to make the policy paid-up).

Often, a life insurance policy also contains a specific provision which states that the company will mature the policy as an endowment (will pay out the amount of insurance), if the policyowner so desires, whenever the cash value plus the value of dividend credits equals or exceeds the amount of insurance. Any loan against the policy is deducted from the amount so payable, and any excess dividend credits are added.

It should be recognized, however, that the policyowner would have this right even if there were no such special provision, because there is always the right to terminate the policy and receive the cash value plus the value of dividend credits less any loan.

EXERCISES, SET 30

1. What is generally meant by a *surrender charge*?

2. The present value of a policy's adjusted premiums is equal to the present value of the policy's future benefits plus an additional amount. What is this additional amount intended to represent?

3. Suppose that the policyowner stops paying premiums and elects the extended term insurance option after a 20-year endowment policy has been in force for ten years and the policy's total value is then more than sufficient to provide for ten years of paid-up term insurance. Describe the benefits that the company will actually grant.

4. Calculate the amount of money the policyowner will be entitled to receive in a lump sum if the policy is terminated at a time when it has a $250 loan and the following values:

   Cash value $4,817.12
   Value of dividend credits 304.04

5. Given the following information, calculate the tenth-year minimum cash value for a $1,000 endowment-at-age-65 policy issued at age 30.

   Net single premium at age 40 for $1,000 25-year endowment $515.63
   Present value at age 40 of 25-year life annuity due of 1 . . . .   16.6299
   Adjusted premium for this policy . . . .$ 20.58

6. Given the following information, calculate the fourth-year minimum cash value for a $1,000 ordinary life policy issued at age 25. The adjusted premium is $12.41.

Age	Net Single Premium for $1,000 Whole Life Insurance	Present Value of Whole Life Annuity Due of 1
25	$279.14	24.7497
26	286.13	24.5095
27	293.33	24.2623
28	300.74	24.0080
29	308.36	23.7464
30	316.19	23.4776
31	324.23	23.2014
32	332.50	22.9176
33	340.99	22.6260
34	349.71	22.3266
35	358.66	22.0193

7. Using the table given in Exercise 6, calculate the minimum cash value at attained age 30 for a $1,000 20-payment life policy issued at age five. The adjusted premium is $13.10.

8. A company calculates its cash values as being equal to the present value of future benefits minus the present value of future nonforfeiture factors. Using the

following figures, calculate that company's tenth-year cash value for a $1,000 ordinary life policy issued at age 22.

> Nonforfeiture factor for this policy ....$ 10.40
> Net single premium at age 32 for $1,000 whole life insurance 332.50
> Present value at age 32 of whole life annuity due of 1 .... 22.9176

9. Calculate the fifth-year cash value for a $1,000 20-payment life policy issued at age 30. Assume the company specifies a nonforfeiture factor of $23.00 for the first ten years and $21.15 for the remainder of the premium-payment period. The following information is given:

> Net single premium at age 35 for $1,000 whole life insurance $358.66
> Present value at age 35 of five-year life annuity due of 1 .... 4.69286
> Present value at age 35 of ten-year life annuity due of 1,
>   deferred five years 7.33180

10. Calculate the amount of reduced paid-up insurance which is available at the end of 20 years for a 30-year endowment policy issued at age 18. The following information is given:

> Net single premium at age 38 for $1 ten-year endowment insurance ..$ 0.74817
> Cash value at end of 20 years for this policy 553.80
> There is no loan and no dividend credit.

11. Using the table in Exercise 6, calculate the amount of reduced paid-up insurance which is available at the end of 15 years for an ordinary life policy issued at age 20. Assume the policy's total value is $12,853.50.

12. Calculate the amount of the death benefit if extended term insurance is elected 12 years after the date of issue for a 20-payment life policy issued at age 40. The following information is given:

> Regular death benefit of the policy $5,000.00
> Additional insurance purchased previously by dividends 845.00
> Loan 200.00

13. May the following policy be declared fully paid-up at the present time?

> Net single premium, at attained age, for future benefits $5,412.70
> Value of dividend credits 418.99
> Cash value 4,988.18

14. Assume the following figures apply to a $1,000 whole-life policy:

> 20th-year cash value $495
> Dividend additions 55
> Value of dividend credits 30
> Policy loan 125

If the owner of this policy discontinues premium payments at the end of the 20th policy year, the amount of extended term insurance available would be

   (1) $400   (3) $930
   (2) $425   (4) $1,055

CHAPTER SUMMARY

- If a policyowner decides to stop paying premiums, the policy guarantees that certain values, called *nonforfeiture values*, will be available.

- At any time a policyowner can borrow from the company any amount of money up to the amount of the policy's nonforfeiture value at that time. This is called a *policy loan*.

- The total value available when premium payments are stopped is: guaranteed nonforfeiture value + value of dividend credits (if any) − policy loan (if any).

- One of the policyowner's options is to receive this total value in a lump sum. The *guaranteed* value which can be received in a lump sum is usually called the *cash value*.

- In the United States, state laws specify minimum cash values, as well as minimum reserves. The legal minimum cash values are less than the legal minimum reserves. In practice, companies often choose to guarantee cash values which are equal to the policy's reserves after a number of years after issue, such as ten years. No cash value can legally exceed the policy's reserve.

- One method of calculating cash values is called the *surrender charge method*. Under that method cash values are equal to the reserve minus a surrender charge. The surrender charge generally decreases year-by-year, down to zero after a number of years. After that the cash value equals the full reserve.

- The National Association of Insurance Commissioners drafted the Standard Nonforfeiture Law, which was adopted by all states. It sets forth legal minimum cash values as being

$$\begin{pmatrix} \text{Minimum} \\ \text{Cash Value} \end{pmatrix} = \begin{pmatrix} \text{Present Value of} \\ \text{Future Benefits} \end{pmatrix} - \begin{pmatrix} \text{Present Value of} \\ \text{Future Adjusted Premiums} \end{pmatrix}$$

- The adjusted premiums to be used in the above equation are defined in the law. Their present value at the time the policy is issued equals the present value of future benefits plus an amount intended to represent the excess of first-year expenses over annual expenses for subsequent years. The bases to be used in making the calculations have been changed several times by amending the law, but the bases applicable to any particular policy are those that are in effect at the time the policy is issued.

- Many companies calculate their actual cash values as follows:

$$\begin{pmatrix} \text{Cash} \\ \text{Value} \end{pmatrix} = \begin{pmatrix} \text{Present Value} \\ \text{of Future} \\ \text{Benefits} \end{pmatrix} - \begin{pmatrix} \text{Present Value} \\ \text{of Future} \\ \text{Nonforfeiture Factors} \end{pmatrix}$$

The nonforfeiture factors to be used in the above equation are calculated by each company to suit its own purposes, but they cannot be greater than a policy's adjusted premiums nor less than its net annual premiums, so that the cash values will not be less than the legal minimums nor more than the policy's reserves.

- Upon terminating premium payments, there are other options besides receiving the total value in a lump sum. One such option is called *reduced paid-up insurance*. Under this option the insurance continues in effect but for a smaller amount. The amount of such insurance is calculated as follows:

$$\begin{pmatrix} \text{Amount of Reduced} \\ \text{Paid-Up Insurance} \end{pmatrix} = \frac{(\text{Total Value})}{\begin{pmatrix} \text{Net Single Premium} \\ \text{at Attained Age} \\ \text{for \$1 of Insurance} \end{pmatrix}}$$

The answer is then generally used as the next higher number of whole dollars.

- Another option upon terminating premium payments is called *extended term insurance*. Under that option the insurance continues in effect but for a shorter period of time. The amount of extended term insurance is generally calculated as: regular death benefit + additional insurance previously purchased by dividends (if any) − loan (if any)

The period of time for which the extended term insurance will continue is calculated so the present value of those benefits equals the policy's total value at the time premium payments are stopped.

For an endowment policy, if the period of the extended insurance extends to the date of the pure endowment then any portion of the total value not needed to pay for the term insurance to that date is used as a net single premium to provide a pure endowment (of whatever amount it will provide) payable on that original endowment date.

- Mortality rates are observed to be quite high for policyowners who have selected the extended term insurance option. The Standard Nonforfeiture Law allows special tables with higher mortality rates to be used to calculate the period of extended term insurance.

- The policyowner is often given the option of having the policy declared fully paid-up (that is, full benefits will continue, but no more premiums need be paid) whenever the cash value plus value of dividend credits equals or exceeds the net single premium for the future benefits at the attained age.

- Another option often given is having a policy mature as an endowment whenever the cash value plus the value of dividend credits equals or exceeds the amount of insurance.

LEARNING OBJECTIVES

After reading this chapter, the student should know

- The meaning of nonforfeiture values.
- The meaning of cash value.
- What a loan on a policy is.
- How to calculate a policy's total value.
- The meaning of nonforfeiture options.
- What the four nonforfeiture options are.
- How cash values compare with reserves.
- How to calculate cash values using the surrender charge method.
- How minimum cash values are calculated under the Standard Nonforfeiture Law.
- The meaning of adjusted premiums.

- How to calculate cash values using the nonforfeiture factor method.
- How to calculate the amount of reduced paid-up insurance.
- How to calculate the amount of extended term insurance.
- How extended term insurance is calculated for an endowment policy.
- How the provisions work which allow a policy to be paid-up or matured by use of dividends.

14

Dividends and Cost Comparisons

In previous chapters, we have referred to *dividends* which are paid by a life insurance company to its policyowners. For example, in Chapter 13, a policy's total value at any time was defined as including the value of *dividend credits*. Dividends were also mentioned in Chapter 12 as being accounted for in the calculation of GAAP reserves and asset shares. In Chapter 10, we discussed the calculation of gross premiums for participating policies, in which savings from operations are returned to the policyowner in the form of dividends.

Chapter 14 will explain more about the nature of these dividends and describe the most important methods used by life companies to compute the dividends. In addition, as each dividend is paid, the policyowner can choose from among various options for using the amount payable. These options will be explained and illustrated. For example, instead of receiving the dividend in cash, the policyowner may elect to have the dividend applied to purchase additional insurance.

In the final section of this chapter, we will describe some of the methods used to analyze the dividends, premiums, and cash values of various policies and determine which policy represents the best buy. Such methods are generally called *cost comparison methods*. The advantages and disadvantages of the various methods are a topic of lively debate among life insurance persons, and many attempts have been made to encourage the enactment of laws which would require the use of one or another method of cost comparison and prohibit the use of others.

14.1 INTRODUCTION

In calculating gross premiums for participating life insurance policies, the actuary makes conservative assumptions about interest, mortality, and expenses. These conservative assumptions result in gross premiums which are generally more than adequate to cover operating conditions as they currently exist or are anticipated. Therefore, unless the company experiences unfavorable interest rates, mortality rates, or expenses, there are savings from operations each year. These savings can be returned to the policyowners in the form of dividends. Such policy dividends are generally paid annually on the anniversary date of each policy. They are meant to reflect savings which have been realized in the policy year just past. They are payable at the end of each policy year and are considered a return of part of the premium which was paid at the beginning of that same year.

The dividends paid to policyowners on participating policies should not be confused with dividends paid to shareholders of corporations. Policy dividends are, in effect, refunds of part of the gross premiums. Dividends to stock owners represent a share of the corporation's income paid to those who have invested funds in the company.

In calculating the dividend to be paid at the end of the policy's current policy year, the actuaries make use of the company's actual current experience, that is, interest, mortality, and expenses. In connection with marketing new policies, dividends must also be calculated that would be paid in future years. These dividend figures are used in dividend illustrations and cost comparisons. The normal practice is to use the same current experience in calculating such illustrative future dividends as is used in calculating currently-paid dividends. However, they are always published with a warning that they are based on present-day experience, are not guaranteed, and would be equal to the amount shown only if present-day experience remains unchanged in the future.

14.2 THREE-FACTOR CONTRIBUTION METHOD

A number of different methods are used for calculating annual policy dividends. In this chapter, two of the methods will be described: the three-factor contribution method and the experience premium method. The one most commonly used is the three-factor contribution method. Under this method, a contribution is made toward the dividend each year from the areas of interest, mortality, and expenses. The contribution which each factor makes may fluctuate from year to year and may even be negative under unfavorable circumstances.

CONTRIBUTION FROM INTEREST. The contribution for any policy year from interest to the dividend is usually based on the year's initial reserve. This reserve at the beginning of the policy year is used because it represents an amount which is invested during the policy year. In general, the contribution from interest to the dividend for a specific policy year is shown by the equation:

$$\binom{\text{Contribution}}{\text{from Interest}} = \binom{\text{Initial}}{\text{Reserve}} \left[\binom{\text{Dividend}}{\text{Interest}}_{\text{Rate}} - \binom{\text{Tabular}}{\text{Interest}}_{\text{Rate}} \right]$$

The *dividend interest rate* is that interest rate which the company chooses to use for dividend purposes. It approximates the rate actually being earned on the company's present investments, although some actuaries use the rate actually being earned on the investments accumulated by that particular policy or by all the policies issued the same year as that policy. The *tabular interest rate* is the rate used in calculating the policy's reserves. In instances where *dual interest rates* are used to calculate reserves, the tabular interest rate is the rate used for the particular policy year for which the dividend is being calculated. To find the contribution from interest, the initial reserve is multiplied by the difference between these two rates.

To Illustrate—Calculate the contribution from interest to the dividend at the end of the sixth year on a $1,000 30-year endowment policy issued at age 30. Use the following information:

5th terminal reserve	$113.62
Net annual premium	22.82
Dividend interest rate	$4\frac{1}{2}\%$
Tabular interest rate	3%

Solution—The initial reserve for the sixth year is the fifth-year terminal reserve plus the net annual premium.

6th Initial Reserve = 5th Terminal Reserve + Net Annual Premium

= $113.62 + $22.82

= $136.44

The sixth year's contribution from interest may thus be calculated by using the equation given above:

$$\begin{pmatrix} \text{Contribution} \\ \text{from Interest} \end{pmatrix} = \begin{pmatrix} \text{Initial} \\ \text{Reserve} \end{pmatrix} \left[\begin{pmatrix} \text{Dividend} \\ \text{Interest} \\ \text{Rate} \end{pmatrix} - \begin{pmatrix} \text{Tabular} \\ \text{Interest} \\ \text{Rate} \end{pmatrix} \right]$$

= $136.44 (.045 − .03)

= $136.44 (.015)

= $2.05

The contribution from interest may be positive, zero, or negative, depending on whether the dividend interest rate is greater than, equal to, or less than the tabular interest rate. Note that the contribution varies directly with the amount of the initial reserve.

CONTRIBUTION FROM MORTALITY. For each policy, the contribution from mortality to the dividend is usually based on the year's net amount at risk. In general, this contribution is shown by the equation

$$\begin{pmatrix} \text{Contribution} \\ \text{from Mortality} \end{pmatrix} = \begin{pmatrix} \text{Net Amount} \\ \text{at Risk} \end{pmatrix} \left[\begin{pmatrix} \text{Tabular} \\ \text{Rate of} \\ \text{Mortality} \end{pmatrix} - \begin{pmatrix} \text{Dividend} \\ \text{Rate of} \\ \text{Mortality} \end{pmatrix} \right]$$

The *tabular rate of mortality* is the value of q_x as shown in the mortality table which is used in calculating the policy's reserves. The *dividend rate of mortality* for each age is that mortality rate which the company chooses to use for dividend purposes. It approximates the mortality rate currently being experienced on the company's own insurance. The age at which these rates apply is the insured's age at the beginning of the particular policy year. To find the contribution from mortality, the net amount at risk is multiplied by the difference between these two years.

To Illustrate—Calculate the contribution from mortality to the dividend at the end of the sixth year on a $1,000 30-year endowment policy issued at age 30 (the same as the policy used for the interest calculation). Use the following information:

6th terminal reserve	$138.38
Tabular rate of mortality, age 35	.00251
Dividend rate of mortality, age 35	.00124

Solution—For the sixth policy year, the age used is the age at the beginning of the year, which is the same as at the end of five years (30 + 5 = 35). Hence, the rates of mortality are used for age 35. The net amount at risk for the sixth year is the amount of insurance minus the terminal reserve at the end of the year (the sixth terminal reserve).

6th-Year Net Amount at Risk = Amount of Insurance − 6th Terminal Reserve

$$= \$1,000 - \$138.38$$

$$= \$861.62$$

The sixth year's contribution from mortality may be calculated by using the equation given above:

$$\left(\begin{array}{c}\text{Contribution}\\\text{from Mortality}\end{array}\right) = \left(\begin{array}{c}\text{Net Amount}\\\text{at Risk}\end{array}\right)\left[\left(\begin{array}{c}\text{Tabular}\\\text{Rate of}\\\text{Mortality}\end{array}\right) - \left(\begin{array}{c}\text{Dividend}\\\text{Rate of}\\\text{Mortality}\end{array}\right)\right]$$

$$= \$861.62 \, (.00251 - .00124)$$

$$= \$861.62 \, (.00127)$$

$$= \$1.09$$

If the dividend rate of mortality is lower than the tabular rate of mortality, there will be a gain from mortality. Conversely, if the dividend rate of mortality is greater than the tabular rate of mortality, there will be a loss from mortality, and the dividend contribution from this source will be negative.

It should be observed that, for policies with reserves which increase with the age of the policy, the net amount at risk progressively decreases. The contribution from mortality would therefore be expected to decrease with increasing age. However, an increase in the difference between the tabular and dividend mortality rates may more than offset the rate of decrease of the net amount at risk. On the other hand, since the contribution from interest varies directly with the initial reserve, the contribution from interest usually increases for policies with increasing reserves. When opposing factors are combined, it may be that the decreases offset the increases or the increases offset the decreases.

CONTRIBUTION FROM EXPENSES. The excess of the gross premium over the net annual premium, called loading, is the principal source to which the company looks for funds to pay its expenses from the policy. If the policy reserves are being calculated by the net level premium method, this loading will be the same for each year during the premium-paying period. If the policy reserves are being calculated by one of the modified reserve methods described in earlier chapters, the loading in the first year will be greater than in subsequent years. If the policy is past its premium-paying period, the loading each year will be zero, indicating that expenses must be paid for from other sources. These other sources might include a portion of the year's contribution from interest and mortality.

In general, the contribution from expenses to the policy dividend for a specific policy year is shown by the equation

$$\left(\begin{array}{c}\text{Contribution}\\\text{from Expenses}\end{array}\right) = \left[(\text{Loading}) - \left(\begin{array}{c}\text{Dividend}\\\text{Expenses}\end{array}\right)\right]\left(1 + \frac{\text{Dividend}}{\text{Interest Rate}}\right)$$

The *dividend expenses* are those expenses which the actuary chooses to use for dividend purposes. They are determined by careful studies of actual expenses with consideration given to allocation of expenses to the appropriate policies by kind, age, duration, and size of policy. Consideration may also be given to the general trend of expenses. The contribution to the dividend from expenses is the difference between the loading and the dividend expenses, this difference then being accumulated at interest for one year. This accumulation reflects the fact that the loading is received and the expenses are mostly incurred at the beginning of the policy year, while the dividend is paid at the end.

To Illustrate—Calculate the contribution from expenses to the dividend at the end of the sixth year on a $1,000 30-year endowment policy issued at age 30. Use the following data:

Gross annual premium	$28.40
Net annual premium	22.82
6th year dividend expenses	4.99
Dividend interest rate	$4\frac{1}{2}\%$

Solution—The loading is the gross annual premium minus the net annual premium:

Loading = Gross Annual Premium − Net Annual Premium

= $28.40 − $22.82

= $5.58

The sixth year's contribution from expenses may be calculated by using the equation given above:

$$\left(\begin{array}{c}\text{Contribution}\\ \text{from Expenses}\end{array}\right) = \left[\text{(Loading)} - \left(\begin{array}{c}\text{Dividend}\\ \text{Expenses}\end{array}\right)\right]\left(1 + \begin{array}{c}\text{Dividend}\\ \text{Interest Rate}\end{array}\right)$$

$$= (\$5.58 - \$4.99)(1.045)$$

$$= (\$.59)(1.045)$$

$$= \$.62$$

SUMMARY OF THE THREE-FACTOR CONTRIBUTION METHOD. Under the three-factor contribution method, the policy dividend is equal to the total of the contributions from the three sources. For example, the dividend for the sixth policy year for the 30-year endowment policy in the above illustrations would be

Contribution from interest	$2.05
Contribution from mortality	1.09
Contribution from expenses	.62
Total dividend	$3.76

This amount would be payable to the policyowner at the end of the sixth policy year.

To Illustrate—Given the following data pertaining to a particular $1,000 policy, calculate the dividend for the eighth policy year for a company using the three-factor contribution method for distributing dividends:

Basis for calculating reserves	1958 C.S.O. Table, 3%
Issue age	65
Gross annual premium	$ 74.10
Net annual premium	64.75
7th terminal reserve	237.69
8th terminal reserve	268.61
Dividend interest rate	6%
Dividend rate of mortality	80% of tabular rate
Dividend expenses	110% of loading

Solution—The contribution from interest depends on the initial reserve, dividend interest rate, and tabular interest rate. The initial reserve for the eighth year is the seventh-year terminal reserve plus the net annual premium:

8th Initial Reserve = 7th Terminal Reserve + Net Annual Premium

$$= \$237.69 + \$64.75$$

$$= \$302.44$$

The dividend interest rate is given as 6%. The tabular interest rate is 3%, as given above.

$$\left(\begin{array}{c}\text{Contribution}\\\text{from Interest}\end{array}\right) = \left(\begin{array}{c}\text{Initial}\\\text{Reserve}\end{array}\right)\left[\left(\begin{array}{c}\text{Dividend}\\\text{Interest}\\\text{Rate}\end{array}\right) - \left(\begin{array}{c}\text{Tabular}\\\text{Interest}\\\text{Rate}\end{array}\right)\right]$$

$$= \$302.44(.06 - .03)$$

$$= \$302.44(.03)$$

$$= \$9.07$$

The contribution from mortality depends on the net amount at risk, tabular rate of mortality, and dividend rate of mortality. The net amount at risk for the eighth year is the amount of insurance minus the eighth terminal reserve:

8th-Year Net Amount at Risk = Amount of Insurance − 8th Terminal Reserve

$$= \$1,000 - \$268.61$$

$$= \$731.39$$

For the eighth policy year, the age at the beginning of the year is $65 + 7 = 72$. Hence, the rates of mortality are used for age 72. Using Table III, this tabular rate is found to be .05865. It is given that the dividend rate of mortality is 80% of this tabular rate (80% of .05865 = .04692).

$$\left(\begin{array}{c}\text{Contribution}\\\text{from Mortality}\end{array}\right) = \left(\begin{array}{c}\text{Net Amount}\\\text{at Risk}\end{array}\right)\left[\left(\begin{array}{c}\text{Tabular}\\\text{Rate of}\\\text{Mortality}\end{array}\right) - \left(\begin{array}{c}\text{Dividend}\\\text{Rate of}\\\text{Mortality}\end{array}\right)\right]$$

$$= \$731.39(.05865 - .04692)$$

$$= \$731.39(.01173)$$

$$= \$8.58$$

The contribution from expenses depends on the loading, the dividend expenses, and the dividend interest rate. The loading is the gross annual premium minus the net annual premium:

Loading = Gross Annual Premium − Net Annual Premium

$$= \$74.10 - \$64.75$$

$$= \$9.35$$

It is given that the dividend expenses are 110% of the loading (110% of $\$9.35 = \$10.29$).

$$\left(\begin{array}{c}\text{Contribution}\\\text{from Expenses}\end{array}\right) = \left[(\text{Loading}) - \left(\begin{array}{c}\text{Dividend}\\\text{Expenses}\end{array}\right)\right]\left(1 + \begin{array}{c}\text{Dividend}\\\text{Interest Rate}\end{array}\right)$$

$$= (\$9.35 - \$10.29)(1.06)$$

$$= (-\$.94)(1.06)$$

$$= -\$1.00$$

The answer indicates a negative contribution from expenses, because the dividend expenses are higher than the loading.

The policy dividend is equal to the total of the contributions from the three sources, taking into account the fact that in this instance, one number is negative:

Contribution from interest	$ 9.07
Contribution from mortality	8.58
Contribution from expenses	−1.00
Total dividend	$16.65

(The total $16.65 is found by adding $9.07 and $8.58 and subtracting the $1.00 which is negative.)

It should be noted that in current practice it is rare for the contributions from interest or mortality to be negative, but a negative contribution from expenses would not be unusual.

14.3 EXPERIENCE-PREMIUM METHOD

The use of the three-factor contribution method often results in dividends which fluctuate and do not increase smoothly from year to year for a particular policy. One reason for this is that some of the expenses, such as the agent's commission, may change considerably for a particular policy from one year to the next. A second approach, the *experience-premium method*, is intended to achieve dividends which increase fairly evenly each year.

THE FIRST STEP. The experience-premium method involves a two-step calculation. The first step starts with calculating level *experience premiums* for all policies. The actuary calculates these experience premiums by using dividend rates for mortality and expenses but the tabular rate of interest. Generally, the dividend rates of mortality and expenses are chosen as if the three-factor method were being used, that is, they represent a close approximation to the mortality and expenses currently experienced. In that way, the resulting dividends reflect current conditions and will be recalculated in the future if there are significant changes in experience. The actual calculation of the level experience premium is done by first calculating the present value of all the policy's future benefits and expenses (using dividend rates of mortality and expenses and the tabular rate of interest). This present value is then divided by an *annuity factor* (which is based on dividend rates of mortality and the tabular rate of interest). This step is similar to one method of calculating net level annual premiums explained in Section 10.5, that is, the net single premium divided by an annuity factor.

Experience premiums are lower than the actual gross premiums received. The first part of the dividend which can be paid each year is equal to the difference between the two accumulated at interest for one year (using the dividend rate of interest):

$$\begin{pmatrix} \text{First Part} \\ \text{of Dividend} \end{pmatrix} = \left[\begin{pmatrix} \text{Gross} \\ \text{Premium} \end{pmatrix} - \begin{pmatrix} \text{Experience} \\ \text{Premium} \end{pmatrix}\right]\begin{pmatrix} 1 + \dfrac{\text{Dividend}}{\text{Interest Rate}} \end{pmatrix}$$

This part of the dividend remains the same each year. For example, if a policy's gross premium is $112.82, the experience premium is $94.99, and the dividend interest rate is 5%, then the first part of each year's dividend is

$$(\$112.82 - \$94.99)(1.05) = \$18.72$$

Note that although the actuary uses the tabular rate of interest to calculate the experience premium, the dividend rate of interest (approximating the rate the company is actually earning) is used to accumulate the difference between the gross premium and the experience premium.

THE SECOND STEP. The second step in calculating the dividend consists of adding the contribution from interest (calculated exactly as described in Section 14.2):

$$\begin{pmatrix} \text{Contribution} \\ \text{from Interest} \end{pmatrix} = \begin{pmatrix} \text{Initial} \\ \text{Reserve} \end{pmatrix}\left[\begin{pmatrix} \text{Dividend} \\ \text{Interest} \\ \text{Rate} \end{pmatrix} - \begin{pmatrix} \text{Tabular} \\ \text{Interest} \\ \text{Rate} \end{pmatrix}\right]$$

As in the three-factor method, the dividend interest rate generally approximates the rate currently being earned on the company's investments, even though certain of the dividends being calculated might be payable several years in the future and are being calculated currently only for illustrative purposes. If the interest rate actually earned is different in the future when those dividends become payable, they would be recalculated at that time using the *then* current dividend interest rate. This contribution from interest is then added to the first part of the dividend to determine the policy's dividend for the particular year.

To Illustrate—Using the experience-premium method, calculate all of the dividends which it is anticipated would be paid in the future, if current conditions do not change, for a $1,000 10-year endowment policy issued at age 20. Use the following data which include current experience:

Reserve basis	1958 C.S.O. 3%
Gross annual premium	$ 94.85
Experience premium (calculated using 3%)	91.17
Dividend interest rate	6%
Initial reserve	
1st year	$ 85.60
2nd year	172.13
3rd year	261.39
4th year	353.46
5th year	448.46
6th year	546.49
7th year	647.63
8th year	752.01
9th year	859.72
10th year	970.88

Solution—The difference between the gross annual premium and the experience premium, accumulated at interest for one year, represents the first part of the dividend which can be paid each year:

$$\left[\left(\begin{matrix}\text{Gross}\\\text{Premium}\end{matrix}\right) - \left(\begin{matrix}\text{Experience}\\\text{Premium}\end{matrix}\right)\right]\left(1 + \begin{matrix}\text{Dividend}\\\text{Interest Rate}\end{matrix}\right) = (\$94.85 - \$91.17)(1.06)$$

$$= (\$3.68)(1.06)$$

$$= \$3.90$$

The second part of the dividend is the contribution from interest. The basic equation, as given above, is

$$\left(\begin{matrix}\text{Contribution}\\\text{from Interest}\end{matrix}\right) = \left(\begin{matrix}\text{Initial}\\\text{Reserve}\end{matrix}\right)\left[\left(\begin{matrix}\text{Dividend}\\\text{Interest}\\\text{Rate}\end{matrix}\right) - \left(\begin{matrix}\text{Tabular}\\\text{Interest}\\\text{Rate}\end{matrix}\right)\right]$$

In this illustration, the dividend interest rate is given as 6%. The tabular interest rate is given as 3%. Hence, the contribution from interest is

$$\left(\begin{matrix}\text{Contribution}\\\text{from Interest}\end{matrix}\right) = \left(\begin{matrix}\text{Initial}\\\text{Reserve}\end{matrix}\right)(.06 - .03)$$

$$= \left(\begin{matrix}\text{Initial}\\\text{Reserve}\end{matrix}\right)(.03)$$

Each year's total dividend is therefore calculated as $3.90 (the first part of the dividend) plus the initial reserve multiplied by .03 (the contribution from interest):

$$\text{First Dividend} = \$3.90 + \left(\begin{matrix}\text{First}\\\text{Initial}\\\text{Reserve}\end{matrix}\right)(.03)$$

$$= \$3.90 + (\$85.60)(.03)$$

$$= \$3.90 + \$2.57$$

$$= \$6.47$$

$$\text{Second Dividend} = \$3.90 + \left(\begin{array}{c} \text{Second} \\ \text{Initial} \\ \text{Reserve} \end{array} \right)(.03)$$

$$= \$3.90 + (\$172.13)(.03)$$

$$= \$3.90 + \$5.16$$

$$= \$9.06$$

The remaining dividends, calculated in the same manner, are as follows:

Third Dividend = $11.74

Fourth Dividend =   14.50

Fifth Dividend =   17.35

Sixth Dividend =   20.29

Seventh Dividend =   23.33

Eighth Dividend =   26.46

Ninth Dividend =   29.69

Tenth Dividend =   33.03

It should be observed that these anticipated dividends increase each year and exhibit a fairly smooth progression.

There are, of course, other methods besides those mentioned above which actuaries use to calculate dividends. For example, asset share calculations (described in Section 12.7) are used to determine dividends. This usually means setting up goals for the asset shares to reach at the end of certain policy years. For example, a company may want the asset share which is predicted for a certain newly-issued policy (using actual present experience for mortality, expenses, etc.) to be equal to 110% of the policy's statutory reserve at the end of the 20th policy year. So each year's dividend (per $1,000 of insurance) is set at a level to assure that the asset share calculation will meet this desired goal (after the other assumptions have been set for mortality rates, expenses, interest rates, etc.).

In a life company's dividend calculations, it is important that strict *equity* (fairness) be maintained. Careful consideration must be given to the sources of gain, so that policies which make greater contributions to the gain receive proportionately greater dividends. To achieve this end, extensive studies are regularly made in the areas of actual mortality, expenses, and interest. Most actuaries make individual studies of their own company's experience, as well as studies based on the *pooled* or combined experience of several companies.

14.4 DIVIDEND OPTIONS

A dividend apportioned to a particular policy may generally be used by the policyowner in any one of the following ways, called *dividend options*:

1. Withdrawn in cash

2. Applied toward any premium payment then due
3. Left as a deposit with the company to accumulate at interest but withdrawable at any time
4. Used to purchase paid-up insurance, called *paid-up additions*

The first three options require no further explanation, but the fourth will be discussed.

CALCULATING PAID-UP ADDITIONS. The fourth option above is called *paid-up additions.* Paid-up additions represent additional insurance payable in the same manner as the basic policy itself. The amount of such additional insurance is calculated by using the dividend as if it were a net single premium for the paid-up benefits. This is comparable to the calculation of reduced paid-up insurance described in Section 13.3. There it was stated that the amount of paid-up insurance purchased by the cash value was found by dividing the cash value by the net single premium at the attained age for $1 of insurance. Similarly, the amount of paid-up additions is found by dividing the dividend by the net single premium at the attained age for $1 of insurance. In equation form, this is

$$\left(\begin{array}{c}\text{Amount of Paid-Up}\\\text{Additions}\end{array}\right) = \frac{\text{Dividend}}{\left(\begin{array}{c}\text{Net Single Premium}\\\text{at Attained Age}\\\text{for \$1 of Insurance}\end{array}\right)}$$

The answer is usually rounded to the nearest dollar, not necessarily up to the next higher dollar as is customary for reduced paid-up insurance. (However, some companies do round to the next higher dollar as good public relations, and some companies figure this amount of paid-up insurance to the nearest cent.)

To Illustrate—The dividend at the end of the tenth year on an ordinary life policy, issued at age 30, is $45. Calculate the amount of paid-up additions which this dividend will purchase. It is given that the net single premium at age 40 for $1,000 of whole life insurance is $406.58. Assume the amount of paid-up additions will be rounded to the nearest dollar.

Solution—At the end of the tenth year, the attained age is 30 + 10 = 40. Hence, the net single premium needed will be for $1 of whole life insurance at age 40. This can easily be obtained; it will be $\frac{1}{1000}$ of the net single premium given above (the value above being for $1,000 of such insurance). By moving the decimal point three places to the left, the net single premium for $1 of such insurance is obtained:

$$\frac{1}{1000} \text{ of } \$406.58 = \$.40658$$

As stated above, the amount of paid-up additions is found by dividing the dividend by the net single premium at the attained age for $1 of insurance:

Basic equation:

$$\left(\begin{array}{c}\text{Amount of Paid-Up}\\ \text{Additions}\end{array}\right) = \cfrac{\text{Dividend}}{\left(\begin{array}{c}\text{Net Single Premium}\\ \text{at Attained Age}\\ \text{for \$1 of Insurance}\end{array}\right)}$$

Substitute the given amount for the dividend and the calculated amount for the net single premium:

$$= \frac{\$45.00}{.40658}$$

$$= \$110.68$$

Round to the nearest dollar:

$$= \$111$$

CASH VALUE OF PAID-UP ADDITIONS. The paid-up additions purchased by dividends are, in many ways, like a separate paid-up policy. They have reserves and cash values which are equal to the present value of the future benefits, that is, the reserve (and cash value) is equal to the net single premium at the attained age for $1 of insurance multiplied by the amount of paid-up additions. The paid-up additions may also provide gains to the company in the form of savings in mortality and interest, and those gains are often returned to the policyowner in the form of a dividend in addition to the regular dividend on the basic policy.

If the policyowner should later elect to surrender the basic policy and receive its cash value, then the paid-up additions must be similarly terminated in exchange for their cash value. On the other hand, the paid-up additions may be terminated by the policyowner without terminating the basic policy.

14.5 ONE-YEAR TERM DIVIDEND OPTION

Some policies contain a provision stipulating that the dividend apportioned each year (or a part thereof) may be used to purchase one-year term insurance. This is often referred to as the *fifth dividend option*. In a sense, this is not a true option comparable to the four basic options listed in Section 14.4, because generally only a portion of each dividend is so applied. The remainder of the dividend is then used for one of the basic options.

The usual purpose of the fifth dividend option or *one-year term dividend option* is to provide one-year term insurance with a death benefit equal to the next cash value. This would allow the policyowner to borrow the full next cash value without impairing the total amount of money which would be paid on death.

In practice, gross single premiums per $1,000 are computed for each attained age. The interest and mortality rates are chosen to reflect experienced conditions, and a loading is added for expenses. The company is then free to change these gross rates at any time. This is in contrast to the practice used to calculate paid-up additions and reduced paid-up insurance (under the nonforfeiture options). In the latter instances, net single premiums, based on the same interest and mortality rates assumed in the calculation of the basic policy's reserves, are almost always used.

To Illustrate—The dividend at the end of the tenth policy year on a policy issued at age 35 is $24.07. The cash value of the policy at the end of 11 years is $865. Calculate the amount of the current dividend which will be used to buy one-year term insurance, if the policyowner is using the one-year term dividend option and the gross premium rate at age 45 for this option is currently $5.03 per $1,000.

Solution—The attained age on this policy is $35 + 10 = 45$. The amount of one-year term insurance to be purchased is equal to the next cash value, $865. Since $1,000 of one-year term insurance costs $5.03 at this age, $865 of one-year insurance will cost

$$\$5.03\left(\frac{865}{1000}\right) = \$4.35$$

The remainder of the $24.07 dividend is

$$\$24.07 - \$4.35 = \$19.72$$

This remainder may be used for any one of the basic dividend options which the policyowner elects.

It sometimes happens that the amount of the year's dividend is not enough to buy one-year term insurance equal to the full cash value. In that case, the extra amount needed to purchase such insurance may be withdrawn from any dividend credits the policy may have from previous dividend distributions. If the total available from both these sources is insufficient, the amount of one-year term insurance will be that amount (smaller than the cash value) which can be purchased.

OTHER OPTIONS. Some companies offer other ways of using dividends, most of which are variations of the one-year term dividend option. For example, part of the dividend may be used to buy one-year term insurance equal to the total premiums paid for the policy up to that time. As an example of that option, at the beginning of the eighth policy year, one-year term insurance would be purchased with a death benefit equal to eight times the policy's annual premium (using the necessary portion of the dividend payable at the end of the seventh year to buy that one-year term insurance).

Another option sometimes offered is to use the entire dividend to purchase one-year term insurance each year. Generally, however, there is a maximum amount stipulated for such one-year term insurance. For example, it may be limited to an amount equal to the basic policy's death benefit. When the dividend is large enough to buy insurance of that amount, then the total death benefit (basic policy plus one-year term) equals two times the benefit of the basic policy. Furthermore, when such a stipulated maximum is purchased, then any remaining part of the year's dividend (in excess of the amount needed to buy the one-year term insurance) is applied under any of the four regular options. When the dividend is not large enough to buy one-year term insurance for the stipulated maximum amount, then the amount of such insurance purchased in any year is found by dividing the dividend by the gross premium for $1 of one-year term insurance:

$$\begin{pmatrix} \text{Amount of} \\ \text{One-Year} \\ \text{Term Insurance} \end{pmatrix} = \begin{pmatrix} \dfrac{\text{Dividend}}{\text{One-Year Term}} \\ \text{Gross Premium} \\ \text{at Attained Age} \\ \text{Per \$1} \end{pmatrix}$$

One type of policy is designed to use the dividends (under a special option) so that the policy's total death benefit will remain level, that is, the same every year:

$$\text{Total Death Benefit} = \text{Basic Policy Death Benefit}$$

$$+ \text{Amount of Paid-Up Additions}$$

$$+ \text{Amount of One-Year Term Insurance}$$

The basic policy's death benefit may be, for example, $1,000 during the first year and $800 thereafter. Each dividend (beginning at the end of the first year) is used to buy part paid-up additions and part one-year term insurance. The calculation is made each year so that the total amount of paid-up additions (including that purchased by the current year's dividend) plus the current year's one-year term insurance will equal $200 exactly. This benefit, when added to the $800 death benefit of the basic policy, will equal $1,000 exactly each year. The mathematics for making the calculation, while not difficult, is beyond the scope of this textbook. Policies where this is done are usually called *enhancement type policies* (because the dividend is used to enhance the basic death benefit).

EXERCISES, SET 31

1. What is meant by dividend rates of interest, mortality, and expenses?

2. Compared to other methods, what is the principal advantage of using the experience-premium method for calculating dividends?

3. For what reason might a policyowner wish to have the fifth dividend option (one-year term dividend option) wherein a death benefit equal to the cash value is purchased with dividend credits?

4. Given the following data for a $1,000 life insurance policy, calculate the dividend

for the tenth policy year according to the three-factor contribution method:

Gross annual premium	$ 42.68
Net annual premium	33.90
9th-year terminal reserve	228.98
10th-year terminal reserve	254.18
Tabular rate of interest	3%
Dividend rate of interest	$5\frac{3}{4}$%
Tabular mortality rate	.02224
Dividend mortality rate	.01793
Dividend expenses incurred	$ 5.12

5. Using Table III (3%) and the three-factor contribution method, calculate the dividend to be paid at the end of the year on a $1,000 paid-up life policy if the insured is age 60 at the beginning of that year and the dividend interest and mortality rates and expenses are as given in Exercise 4. Whole life net single premiums per $1,000 are

Age 60	$632.00
Age 61	643.71

6. Using Table III (3%) and the three-factor contribution method, calculate the dividend to be paid at the end of the year on a $1,000 one-year term insurance policy issued at age 62 for a premium of $30, ignoring the small contribution from interest. Dividend interest, expenses, and mortality are as given in Exercise 4.

7. Using the experience-premium method, calculate the tenth-year dividend on a $1,000 ordinary life policy issued at age 30. Use the following data:

Basis for calculating reserves	1958 C.S.O. 3%
Experience premium (using 3%)	$ 14.07
Gross premium	15.10
Dividend rate of interest	7%
10th-year initial reserve	$131.09

8. Calculate the amount of paid-up whole life additions which a dividend of $15.12 will purchase at attained age 22. It is given that the net single premium at age 22 for $1,000 of whole life insurance is $259.33.

9. The net single premium for a $1,000 eight-year endowment policy, issued at age 62, is $808.83. The dividend for the 12th policy year on a $5,000 20-year endowment policy, issued at age 50, is $42.30. Calculate the amount of paid-up endowment additions which the dividend will purchase.

10. Given the following information, how much of the dividend which is due at the end of the tenth policy year on a $5,000 insurance policy issued at age 35 will be used to buy one-year term insurance under the one-year term dividend option?

11th-year cash value per $1,000	$351.95
Premium for 1-year term insurance at age 45, per $1,000	5.08

11. If the actual dividend paid on the policy in Exercise 10 were only $8 and the entire dividend were used to buy one-year term insurance under the one-year term dividend option, how much such insurance would it purchase?

12. A life insurance company uses the three-factor contribution method of calculating policy dividends. For one of its policies, the net annual premium is $27.83, the sixth-year terminal reserve is $159.42, the tabular interest rate is 3%, and the dividend interest rate is 7%. The seventh-year dividend for this policy would include a contribution from interest of

      (1) $5.62   (3) $7.49
      (2) $6.38   (4) $13.11

14.6 COST COMPARISON METHODS

The amount of the dividends a company pays participating policyowners is obviously an important factor in determining the total cost to a policyowner of a life policy. Similarly, the levels of cash values guaranteed for a policy (as described in Chapter 13) represent another important consideration in arriving at the total cost.

In this section, we will describe some of the methods commonly used to determine total cost figures which can be used to compare policies. Such calculations are valuable both to consumers facing a choice among various offerings and to the life insurance companies who must sell their policies in a competitive market.

While a great many cost comparison methods have been developed or proposed—each with certain advantages and disadvantages—we will deal in this section with only four of the most widely-used approaches:

      The traditional method
      The interest-adjusted method
      The rate of return (*Linton yield*) method
      The company retention method

TRADITIONAL METHOD. For many years, it was customary to calculate the average yearly payment and the average yearly cost for a new policy. Each such average was usually calculated for both a ten-year and a 20-year period (that is, looking forward to the policy's first ten and first 20 years).

The calculations for a ten-year period were made as follows:

$$\begin{pmatrix} \text{Average} \\ \text{Yearly} \\ \text{Payment} \end{pmatrix} = \frac{\begin{array}{c} \text{Total Premiums for 10 Years} \\ - \text{Total Dividends for 10 Years} \end{array}}{10}$$

$$\begin{pmatrix} \text{Average} \\ \text{Yearly} \\ \text{Cost} \end{pmatrix} = \frac{\begin{array}{c} \text{Total Premiums for 10 Years} \\ - \text{Total Dividends for 10 Years} \\ - \text{10th Year Cash Value} \end{array}}{10}$$

In both equations, the dividends were those being then illustrated by the company (calculated using mortality, interest, and expenses then being experienced). In addition, these averages were customarily compared on a *per $1,000* basis. Therefore, if the calculations were performed using the values from a policy for a different amount than $1,000, the desired result was obtained by dividing the average by the number of thousands (for example, dividing by 25 for a $25,000 policy).

If the calculations were made for a 20-year period, then 20 would replace ten in the above equations. In any case, the lower the average figure turned out to be, the better (or cheaper) the policy was said to be.

The reason for having both a payment and a cost average was that buyers who did not expect to stop paying the premiums before their death or count on receiving the policy's cash value argued that the calculation should ignore cash values since these buyers would never receive such values.

The traditional method of calculating average cost or average payment was criticized because the *incidence* or timing of the dividend payments was not accounted for in the calculation. In fact, the earlier a dividend is paid, the greater value it actually has to the policyowner. For this reason, the supervisory authorities in a number of states have forbidden companies to show customers any calculations which are based on the traditional method.

INTEREST-ADJUSTED METHOD. To give proper weight to dividends and cash values according to how far in the future the various amounts are payable, the interest-adjusted method was devised. The National Association of Insurance Commissioners has drafted and a number of states have adopted a model regulation which requires that the interest-adjusted method be used to calculate costs of new policies and that such figures be made available to all new policyowners.

Under this method, one figure is calculated which uses only premiums and dividends and is commonly called the *interest-adjusted payment*. The model regulation calls it the *net payment cost index*.

A second figure which includes a consideration of cash values (in addition to premiums and dividends) is commonly called the *interest-adjusted cost*. The model regulation calls it the *surrender cost index*.

The calculations are made as follows:

$$\left(\begin{array}{c}\text{Interest-Adjusted}\\\text{Payment}\end{array}\right) = \frac{\begin{array}{c}\text{Accumulated Premiums}\\ -\text{ Accumulated Dividends}\end{array}}{\ddot{s}_{\overline{n}|i}}$$

$$\left(\begin{array}{c}\text{Interest-Adjusted}\\\text{Cost}\end{array}\right) = \frac{\begin{array}{c}\text{Accumulated Premiums}\\ -\text{ Accumulated Dividends}\\ -\text{ Cash Value}\end{array}}{\ddot{s}_{\overline{n}|i}}$$

The model regulation specifies that 5% interest be used in the calculation, that is, the premiums and dividends are to be accumulated, each at 5% from its respective due date to the end of the period (ten or 20 years after issue). In the denominator, the value of n is either ten or 20, depending on the number of years being calculated, and i is 5%.

The calculations are made for the policy's first ten and first 20 years. This follows the custom used previously for the traditional method. In addition, the results are shown on the basis of *per $1,000 of insurance*, and a lower payment or cost figure represents a better buy. This is similar to the traditional method.

The interest-adjusted cost is, in effect, a level annual amount that is equivalent to (has the same accumulated value as) the annual premiums less the annual illustrated dividends and less a level annual contribution to a sinking fund that builds up to equal the cash value. The interest-adjusted cost is often seen as representing a level annual payment for insurance protection for the particular period.

The model regulation also requires yet another amount to be calculated and made available to buyers; it is called the *equivalent level annual dividend*. This amount (for both ten and 20 years) is calculated as follows:

$$\left(\begin{array}{c}\text{Equivalent Level} \\ \text{Annual Dividend}\end{array}\right) = \frac{\text{Accumulated Dividends}}{\ddot{s}_{\overline{n}|i}}$$

The equivalent level annual dividend is meant to represent the part of the interest-adjusted payment and cost which is, in effect, not guaranteed by the insurance company, because dividends will change in the future as the company's experience changes. The interest-adjusted payment and cost are based on dividends being illustrated at the time the policy is issued, and the equivalent level annual dividend gives the buyer an indication of the extent to which these nonguaranteed amounts affect the interest-adjusted payment and cost figures.

RATE OF RETURN METHOD. By still another method of seeking cost comparisons, the key figure calculated is a *rate of interest* or *yield*. This is in contrast to the interest-adjusted method where the rate was assumed in advance (5% in the model regulation). This method is called the *rate of return method* or the *Linton yield method* named after the late M. Albert Linton, a famous actuary.

The mathematics for performing the calculation is fairly simple when the yield sought is for a one-year period. The method sets up an equation to be solved. One side of the equation accumulates (for one year) the total of the cash value at the end of the previous year plus the current year's gross annual premium. This accumulation is at an unknown rate of interest—the yield figure to be determined. The other side of the equation adds together the year-end cash value, the year-end dividend, and an amount representing the cost of insurance for the year. The rate of interest being the unknown, the equation can be solved for this rate. The policy with the higher rate would be considered the better buy.

In instances where the rate of return method is to be applied over a ten- or 20-year period (instead of a one-year period), the method is extended to solving for *a level annual rate of interest* at which the various amounts paid in and taken out over this period will be accumulated. The accumulated value of all these "ins and outs" must equal the policy's cash value at the end of that period. In this calculation, the amounts paid in are made up of the policy's annual premiums. The amounts coming out include annual dividends and the premiums the policyowner would expect to pay for one-year term insurance each year. Generally, a computer is employed to calculate such a rate of interest over a ten- or 20-year period.

The figures produced by the rate of return method are usually considered to be quite understandable to the typical purchaser of life insurance. However, this method has been criticized because the rate of return figure is so drastically influenced by the particular figures used in the calculation to represent the cost of insurance for each year. Authorities do not agree on the appropriate costs of insurance to be used, and use of inappropriate assumptions may result in rate of return figures being calculated which do not at all represent the interest rates actually being credited by the insurance company on the policyowner's funds.

COMPANY RETENTION METHOD. The final method we will explain, the *company retention method*, attempts to arrive at an amount which represents the policyowner's cost by calculating the present value (per person) of all the amounts to be paid in by a large group of policyowners less the present value of amounts to be paid out to this group. The calculation is generally made to cover a period such as 20 years and uses prescribed rates of interest, mortality, and withdrawal. The present values of all the payments (in and out) are calculated by multiplying each such future payment by the appropriate interest-discount factor v^n and also by the probability that such a payment will actually be made. The resulting figure is called the *company retention*, and this is the figure which is used to make comparisons between two policies, the one with the lower figure being considered the better buy.

One advantage claimed for this method is that every year's cash value (during the period) enters the calculation, instead of just the cash value at the end of the period. Hence, extra *weight* or *value* is given to the policy which offers higher cash values in the earlier years. Another advantage is that, by including the probabilities each year that the policyowner will terminate the policy, the dividends and cash values in the earlier years are given relatively greater weight than is the case where the discounting or accumulating involves only the interest factor. This is seen as being more realistic, since each item is *weighted* by the probability that it will actually be paid.

The disadvantages of this method include the fact that a complex computer arrangement is necessary to perform the calculations, plus the fact that the resulting *company retention* figures can be misleading, because a large part of this *retention* is not retained but is actually paid out in expenses and taxes. Furthermore, there may be such large differences between the assumptions that might be prescribed (interest, mortality, and withdrawal rates to be used uniformly by all companies) and the actual experience of any particular company, that the picture presented by the company retention calculation may bear little resemblance to what the company is actually retaining for expenses, taxes, and profits.

EXERCISES, SET 32

1. Which two cost comparison methods derive a level annual amount which is meant to represent the gross premium less the portions used to provide cash value and dividends over a period of time?

2. Which cost comparison method derives the present value of the premiums less the present value of the insurance coverage, dividends, and the cash value payments over a period of time?

3. Which one of the cost comparison methods produces a figure for comparison which represents the best buy if this figure is as large as possible?

4. Use the traditional method to calculate the average yearly payment and the average yearly cost of a $1,000 policy for ten and 20 years. The following facts are given:

Gross annual premium	$ 29.10
10th-year cash value	158.06
20th-year cash value	508.42
Total 10 years' dividends	31.11
Total 20 years' dividends	111.83

5. A $1,000 nonparticipating policy has an annual premium of $19.47. The tenth-year cash value is $127.50. Using the traditional method, calculate the ten-year average yearly payment and average yearly cost.

6. Using 5% interest, calculate the 20-year interest-adjusted payment and interest-adjusted cost of a $1,000 policy. The following facts are given:

Gross annual premium	$ 34.07
20th-year cash value	659.80
20 dividends accumulated at 5% to end of 20 years	89.45

7. How much is the equivalent level dividend over 20 years in Exercise 6?

8. Using the interest-adjusted method of cost comparison and 5% interest, the ten-year interest-adjusted cost (surrender cost index) for a $1,000 nonparticipating life insurance policy with a gross annual premium of $24.70 and a tenth-year cash value of $128.57 is

    (1) $8.97   (3) $14.96
    (2) $11.84   (4) $24.70

CHAPTER SUMMARY

• Participating policies have gross premiums which are calculated using conservative assumptions, and the savings from operations are returned at the end of each policy year to the policyowner in the form of a *dividend* (actually a return of part of the gross premium).

• Perhaps the most common method of calculating dividends is the three-factor contribution method. Under this method, each dividend is calculated as the total of the year's contribution from interest, mortality, and expenses:

$$\begin{pmatrix} \text{Contribution} \\ \text{from Interest} \end{pmatrix} = \begin{pmatrix} \text{Initial} \\ \text{Reserve} \end{pmatrix} \left[\begin{pmatrix} \text{Dividend} \\ \text{Interest} \\ \text{Rate} \end{pmatrix} - \begin{pmatrix} \text{Tabular} \\ \text{Interest} \\ \text{Rate} \end{pmatrix} \right]$$

$$\begin{pmatrix} \text{Contribution} \\ \text{from Mortality} \end{pmatrix} = \begin{pmatrix} \text{Net Amount} \\ \text{at Risk} \end{pmatrix} \left[\begin{pmatrix} \text{Tabular} \\ \text{Rate of} \\ \text{Mortality} \end{pmatrix} - \begin{pmatrix} \text{Dividend} \\ \text{Rate of} \\ \text{Mortality} \end{pmatrix} \right]$$

$$\begin{pmatrix} \text{Contribution} \\ \text{from Expenses} \end{pmatrix} = \left[(\text{Loading}) - \begin{pmatrix} \text{Dividend} \\ \text{Expenses} \end{pmatrix} \right] \begin{pmatrix} \text{Dividend} \\ 1 + \text{Interest} \\ \text{Rate} \end{pmatrix}$$

The *tabular rates* referred to in the equations are those according to the mortality table and interest rate used to calculate the policy's statutory reserves. The *dividend rates* are those which the company chooses to use in calculating its dividends. They usually approximate its current experience.

• Another method, called the experience-premium method, is sometimes used to produce dividends which increase each year and which exhibit a smooth sequence from year to year. (The three-factor contribution method may not always achieve these two features.) There are two steps to the experience-premium method. The amount calculated by the first step remains the same each year for a policy. The amount calculated by the second step generally increases each policy year. The two parts are added together each year to produce the total dividend:

$$\begin{pmatrix} \text{First Part} \\ \text{of Dividend} \end{pmatrix} = \left[\begin{pmatrix} \text{Gross} \\ \text{Premium} \end{pmatrix} - \begin{pmatrix} \text{Experience} \\ \text{Premium} \end{pmatrix} \right] \begin{pmatrix} 1 + \dfrac{\text{Dividend}}{\text{Interest Rate}} \end{pmatrix}$$

$$\begin{pmatrix} \text{Contribution} \\ \text{from Interest} \end{pmatrix} = \begin{pmatrix} \text{Initial} \\ \text{Reserve} \end{pmatrix} \left[\begin{pmatrix} \text{Dividend} \\ \text{Interest} \\ \text{Rate} \end{pmatrix} - \begin{pmatrix} \text{Tabular} \\ \text{Interest} \\ \text{Rate} \end{pmatrix} \right]$$

• Dividends are sometimes arrived at by making asset share calculations, the desired asset share amounts being set in advance and the dividend amounts then being determined so that the desired asset shares are produced.

• A prime consideration in calculating dividends is *equity*, that is, policies which make greater contributions to the gain should receive proportionately greater dividends.

• Normally, there are four options for using each dividend. The dividend may be

a) withdrawn in cash,
b) applied toward payment of any premium then due,
c) left with the company to accumulate at interest, or
d) used to buy paid-up additional insurance.

• Paid-up additional insurance purchased by dividends is referred to as *paid-up additions*. The form of such additional insurance is generally the same as the basic policy (whole life or endowment). The amount of paid-up additional insurance purchased by any dividend is found as follows:

$$\begin{pmatrix} \text{Amount of Paid-Up} \\ \text{Additions} \end{pmatrix} = \frac{\text{Dividend}}{\begin{pmatrix} \text{Net Single Premium} \\ \text{at Attained Age} \\ \text{for \$1 of Insurance} \end{pmatrix}}$$

- Some policies provide that part of each dividend will be applied to buy one-year term insurance. This is called the *one-year term dividend option* or the *fifth dividend option*. The amount of such insurance generally equals the next cash value. The part of the dividend needed to buy this insurance is calculated by charging a gross one-year term premium, based on the mortality, interest, and expenses experienced by the company. If the dividend is not large enough to buy the stipulated amount of such insurance, some of the policy's dividend credits from previous years may be used for this purpose.

- Some variations of the one-year term dividend option include (a) buying one-year term insurance with part of each dividend, with the death benefit of such insurance being equal to the total premiums paid to date for the policy, or (b) buying one-year term insurance with the entire dividend, provided such insurance does not exceed a stipulated maximum amount.

- *Enhancement type* policies use a part of each dividend to buy paid-up additions and a part to buy one-year term insurance. The intent is to produce a level total death benefit from the basic policy, the paid-up additions, and the one-year term insurance. As the amount of paid-up additions in force increases year by year, the amount of one-year term insurance purchased is correspondingly less each year.

- In order for a buyer to determine which of two life insurance policies is the better buy, it is necessary to consider the policies' premiums, cash values, and dividends over a period of time. Several methods have been devised to make the comparison easier. They are generally called *cost comparison methods*. When a new policy is being purchased, such methods generally make use of the dividends which a company illustrates for future years, even though those dividends would actually be different in the future if conditions change from current experience.

- For many years the *traditional method* was used for cost comparison. For a ten-year period, the equations would be

$$\begin{pmatrix} \text{Average} \\ \text{Yearly} \\ \text{Payment} \end{pmatrix} = \frac{\begin{array}{l} \text{Total Premiums for 10 Years} \\ - \text{ Total Dividends for 10 Years} \end{array}}{10}$$

$$\begin{pmatrix} \text{Average} \\ \text{Yearly} \\ \text{Cost} \end{pmatrix} = \frac{\begin{array}{l} \text{Total Premiums for 10 Years} \\ - \text{ Total Dividends for 10 Years} \\ - \text{ 10th Year Cash Value} \end{array}}{10}$$

If a 20-year period is used, then 20 would replace 10 in the above equations. A policy with a lower figure represents a better buy.

This method came into disrepute because the timing of the dividend payments was not taken into account. Therefore, many states have adopted regulations prohibiting use of the traditional method.

- Under the *interest-adjusted method* dividends are accumulated at interest in the calculation, thus giving different *weights* to each dividend, depending on the year in which it is payable. If a ten-year period is used, the equations are

$$\binom{\text{Interest-Adjusted}}{\text{Payment}} = \frac{\text{Accumulated Premiums} - \text{Accumulated Dividends}}{\ddot{s}_{\overline{10}|i}}$$

$$\binom{\text{Interest-Adjusted}}{\text{Cost}} = \frac{\text{Accumulated Premiums} - \text{Accumulated Dividends} - \text{Cash Value}}{\ddot{s}_{\overline{10}|i}}$$

If a 20-year period is used, then 20 would replace 10 in the above equations. A policy with a lower figure represents a better buy. Many states require that such interest-adjusted figures be made available to the purchasers of new policies.

- When the interest-adjusted method is used, a figure called *equivalent level annual dividend* is sometimes also shown. It is intended to represent the part of the payment or cost calculation which involves nonguaranteed amounts:

$$\binom{\text{Equivalent Level}}{\text{Annual Dividend}} = \frac{\text{Accumulated Dividends}}{\ddot{s}_{\overline{n}|i}}$$

- The *rate of return method*, sometimes called the *Linton yield* method, attempts to determine what interest rate the buyer would have to earn, by investing the premium, to achieve comparable results. The method assumes that the gross premiums plus interest allowed each year less amounts taken out each year to provide dividends and the cost of the insurance coverage, accumulate forward to provide the exact amount of the cash value each year.

If only one year is being covered, the calculation is quite simple. Normally, however, a period of ten or 20 years is covered, and then the calculation usually must be done by a computer. A policy with a higher *rate of return* represents a better buy. The result is drastically affected by the annual *cost of insurance* assumption used in the calculation.

- The *company retention method* attempts to compare policies by measuring the present value of premiums less present value of cash values, dividends, and the cost of insurance coverage. Each present value is calculated taking into account mortality, interest, and the probability that the policy will still be in force at that time (that is, withdrawal rates are included). A policy with a lower figure represents a better buy. However, if the assumptions used are unrealistic or inappropriate for the company, the results may be misleading.

LEARNING OBJECTIVES

After reading this chapter, the student should know

- What is meant by participating policies.
- What is meant by
  a) conservative interest rates,
  b) conservative mortality rates, and
  c) conservative expense assumptions.

- What is meant by dividends.
- What is meant by the three-factor contribution method.
- How to calculate the contribution from interest.
- What is meant by dividend interest rate.
- What is meant by tabular interest rate.
- How to calculate the contribution from mortality.
- What is meant by tabular rate of mortality.
- What is meant by dividend rate of mortality.
- How to calculate the contribution from expenses.
- What is meant by dividend expenses.
- How the experience premium method attempts to improve on the three-factor contribution method.
- How the experience premium is calculated.
- How to calculate dividends using the experience premium method.
- What the four dividend options are.
- What is meant by paid-up additions.
- How to calculate the amount of paid-up additions which a dividend will buy.
- How to calculate the cash value of paid-up additions.
- What is meant by the one-year term or fifth dividend option.
- What amount of one-year term insurance is purchased under the fifth dividend option.
- How to calculate the cost of one-year term insurance under the fifth dividend option.
- The principles underlying the calculation of the average yearly payment and average yearly cost, using the traditional method of cost comparison.
- The reasons for criticizing the traditional method.
- The principles underlying the calculation of the interest-adjusted payment and interest-adjusted cost, using the interest-adjusted method.
- Why the interest-adjusted method is considered an improvement over the traditional method.
- The principles underlying the calculation of a rate of return to compare policies.
- The principles underlying the calculation of a company retention to compare policies.
- The principal advantages and disadvantages of the company retention method.

15

Group Life Insurance

In Chapters 9 through 14 we have dealt with life insurance policies which are issued to individuals and are therefore called *individual life policies.* In this chapter, we will discuss the actuarial aspects of a second major type of policy, *group life insurance*, under which all or most members of a particular group are insured under one policy.

A group must meet several important requirements, most of them required by law, before a policy can be issued to cover its members. These requirements will be examined first.

Next, descriptions will be given of the principal types of group life insurance and of the various methods used to calculate the premiums charged for each. Methods of calculating group life reserves and dividends will also be explained. Special note will be taken of the substantial differences between the approaches used for group policies and those used for individual policies.

Finally, this chapter will present some of the methods that are used to compare costs between different group policies in order to select the "better buy."

15.1 INTRODUCTION

Group life insurance is granted to most or all members of a specified group under one policy. The most common example is a group life insurance policy issued to an *employer*, under which most or all of the employees are insured. The employer is the policyowner in that case. Generally, each employee is allowed to name the beneficiary who would receive the death benefit upon that employee's death.

Typically, no evidence is required about the good health of any of the members of the group so insured. This is in contrast to individual insurance, where each applicant is either accepted, rejected, or insured at a higher than normal premium based on the medical evidence submitted. Group insurance is issued on the premise that in any group covered there will be some persons who would be rejected for individual insurance or issued insurance at a higher than normal premium. However, if the group is a large one and a substantial portion of the people in the group are included in the coverage, then the actuary can be assured in most cases that there is a good *spread of risk*, that is, the large number of healthy persons in the group will offset the claims of the few unhealthy ones.

It is only necessary to be certain that the group itself affords no reason to believe that a larger-than-normal proportion will be unhealthy. The same caution would hold true with respect to hazardous occupations. For example, a labor union representing race car drivers would probably not have normal group mortality experience.

Since its beginnings early in the 20th century, the amount of group insurance in force has grown tremendously, and many types of group insurance have been developed. While the designs and details of the group insurance coverages in force are many and varied, they generally conform to the basic framework described in this chapter.

REQUIREMENTS FOR A GROUP. To be considered for insurance, a group must meet certain criteria which allow the actuary to predict with reasonable accuracy what its mortality experience will be. Therefore, the insurance company sets certain requirements (many of which are also required by state laws) before any group insurance can be effected. The three most important such requirements are:

1. The group must have been formed for a purpose other than to obtain insurance. As mentioned above, the most commonly insured group is one made up of employees of a common employer.
2. A large percentage of the persons in the group will be included in the insurance plan. This rule ensures that a sufficiently large number of healthy persons are included to offset the unhealthy ones (who would almost certainly want to participate). The laws of many states require that any group insured must have a minimum participation of 75 percent of the members.
3. No individual in the group will be able to select how much insurance he or she personally will have. Many states have laws which set forth the maximum amount of group life insurance which may be issued on one person, as well as restrictions on the relative amounts that may be issued to different persons in the same group. Typically, a group will have a *schedule* which sets down the allowable amounts of insurance within the group (usually pegged to wages or salaries received). For example, for a large company, this schedule might appear as follows:

Employee's Annual Salary	Amount of Life Insurance
Under $10,000	$20,000
$10,000 to $20,000	$40,000
$20,000 to $40,000	$60,000
$40,000 and over	$80,000

Under this schedule, an employee whose salary is $18,000 per year, for example, would have $40,000 of group life insurance.

Schedules may be set up which are based on criteria other than salary. For example, the amount of insurance is sometimes based on a job classification, such as officer, manager, supervisor, clerk.

Conforming to legal requirements, insurance companies usually establish their own rules for setting up the limits for these schedules. For example, the maximum benefit on any one person in the group might be limited to $2\frac{1}{2}$ or 3 times the average amount of insurance on all persons in the group. Or again, the maximum benefit on any one person might be limited to 10% of the total of all the insurance for the group. Within the limits set, an insured group sets up the schedule it desires.

Besides insuring only groups whose mortality experience can be reasonably predicted, a company must be sure that a given group's insurance will remain in force for a reasonable number of years, since substantial expenses are incurred when a new group is insured, just as for individual policies (see Chapter 10).

In Canada, there are fewer legal restrictions on the types of groups for which group insurance may be written and there are no laws setting forth maximum amounts, as in the United States.

PAYING FOR THE COVERAGE. The person (or corporation) to whom the policy is issued normally pays the premiums to the insurance company as they come due. However, the policyowner may actually collect part or all of this money from the insured members of the group before sending it to the insurance company.

Three different arrangements are possible in this regard:

1. *Noncontributory*—where the members of the group pay nothing themselves, and the policyowner (often the employer of the members) pays 100% of the premiums.
2. *Contributory*—where the members of the group share the cost with the policyowner.
3. *Fully Contributory*—where the members of the group pay the entire cost.

Generally, the insurance company prefers that the noncontributory arrangement be in effect for a group, because that will assure full participation in the program and, in turn, improve the spread of risk. At the other end of the scale, the fully contributory arrangement is often discouraged by an insurance company and, in some states, is prohibited by law.

The contributory arrangement is quite commonly found in practice. While an insurance company bases the premium it charges a group on the age and sex of persons in the group, the contribution toward the premium which each person actually makes is normally not dependent on that person's age or sex. As an example, the contributions required from any insured member of a given group might be set as follows:

Monthly Contribution per $1,000 of Insurance
On the first $20,000 ....None
On the remaining amount (in excess of $20,000) ......$.60 per $1,000

If a member has $60,000 of group life insurance, the monthly contribution required from that member would then be calculated as follows:

On the first $20,000 .... None
On the remaining $40,000 (40 × $.60) $24.00
   Total $24.00

This $24 would be collected from the member by the policyowner. However, the premium which the policyowner then pays to the insurance company is based on the monthly premium being charged by the company for the member's age and sex. In most instances this is more than the member's contribution, and the total premium for the entire group will always exceed the total contributions from the members, so that the policyowner and the members are sharing the cost.

THE GROUP ACTUARY'S RESPONSIBILITIES. In life insurance companies which sell large amounts of group insurance, there is generally a separate division of the actuarial department which is devoted entirely to group work. There may even be a separate department, called the *group actuarial department.*

The primary responsibility of the group actuary is the calculation of the premium rates and the dividends or *experience refunds* for group insurance. These calculations will be explained later in this chapter.

In addition, these actuaries regularly conduct studies to determine the actual mortality experienced and the amount of expenses incurred on its group insurance operations.

Group actuaries also play important roles in the development of new group insurance policies, often as part of a team of representatives from various areas of the company. The actuaries on the team are principally responsible for ensuring that the proposed new group policies are mathematically sound and workable.

15.2 TYPES OF GROUP LIFE INSURANCE

Three of the most common types of group life insurance arrangements are

1. One-year renewable term,
2. Group permanent, and
3. Group life with paid-up insurance.

They are described in this section.

ONE-YEAR RENEWABLE TERM. Under this arrangement, each year's premium pays for just that year's coverage. This is by far the most common type of group life insurance. (The student will recognize this arrangement as being similar to the one-year term insurance issued to individuals, as described in Chapter 9). The premium is recalculated each year based on the then attained ages of all members of the group. This premium is usually paid monthly.

The attractiveness of this arrangement to the policyowner is that it provides coverage at the lowest current cost. However, this one-year term premium can become very expensive for older employees. Consequently, most one-year term group life plans provide for reducing the amount of coverage when a member becomes age 65 or 70.

Since the one-year term arrangement accounts for such a large portion of the total group life insurance in force today, the later sections of this chapter will deal almost exclusively with this arrangement.

GROUP PERMANENT.   Some group life insurance is issued on an *other-than-term* arrangement. This includes: ordinary life, 20-payment life, whole life paid-up at age 65, etc. The gross annual premium charged for such coverage is level, just as in the case of an individual policy issued on such a basis. Also, group permanent insurance provides nonforfeiture values on termination, as individual policies do.

Normally, group permanent is offered to members of a group as being available to replace part or all of their regular one-year term group insurance. Thus, any participant can elect to have part of his or her group insurance continue in force as one-year term and part as group permanent. The total death benefit would be the same as before such an election.

The principal reason for purchasing group permanent life insurance is to provide for some type of benefit to continue after the member leaves the group (most commonly at retirement). Such a benefit can be either in the form of insurance coverage or else in the form of income provided by applying the cash value under the settlement options.

GROUP LIFE WITH PAID-UP INSURANCE.   Under this arrangement, the total death benefit is made up of regular one-year term insurance plus paid-up whole life insurance. A part of the premium (as chosen by each insured individual in the group) is used each year to buy the paid-up whole life insurance, the amount of which is calculated in a manner similar to the purchase of paid-up additions each year from the dividend on an individual life policy. The total amount of paid-up insurance in force at any time represents a part of the total death benefit. The remainder (so that the combination equals the amount shown in the schedule) is provided by the regular one-year term group insurance arrangement.

When a member leaves the group, the one-year term portion coverage ceases, but the paid-up insurance remains in force for the member's entire lifetime. The cash value is also available if the member (after leaving the group) should decide to terminate the paid-up insurance.

15.3 PREMIUMS FOR GROUP LIFE INSURANCE

The process of calculating gross premiums for group life insurance is usually called *rate making*. In practice, the calculations can become very complex, and many refinements are often added. In this book, only the fundamental principles will be explained.

When a policy is issued to a group for the first time, the insurance company usually sets a premium rate which is guaranteed for only the first 12 months of the policy. At the end of the first year, a new rate may be established for that group and this new rate, in turn, is generally guaranteed for only a limited period of time. Thus, the actuary can use the actual mortality experience of any particular group, and can also take into account any changes in the company's expenses in calculating the premiums for that group (after the first policy year in most states). This is in contrast to the situation for individual term policies, where the premium rate is guaranteed for the entire premium-paying period of the policy at the time it is issued.

MINIMUM PREMIUMS. Some states have legal requirements which first-year group life insurance must meet. Most important in this respect is New York State, because its laws set forth such requirements as being applicable to group policies issued in any state if the insurance company is licensed to do business in New York.

The purpose of these legal requirements (first adopted in 1926) is to prevent competitive pressures from forcing insurance companies into setting inadequate premiums, since financial losses from such inadequate premiums could harm the insurance company and impair its ability to pay death claims.

Originally, the New York law specified the minimum first-year group premiums for each age which could be charged to any group. In 1974, the law was relaxed so that now it applies only to the first-year premiums of groups that are acquiring insurance for the first time.

Some states also require that first-year group life insurance premium rates must be approved by that state's department or division of insurance before the policy can be issued in that state.

After the first policy year, the insurance company is free to change the rates for subsequent years.

PREMIUM RATING CLASSES. In calculating premiums for any group, the actuary may choose from three possible approaches in determining what expected *mortality* to use. Premiums resulting from each of these approaches are said to fall into one of three *rating classes*:

1. *Manually Rated.* These premium rates are developed independently of the mortality experience of any particular group and are really based on the experience of an average group. Such rates could theoretically be used for every group to be insured. In practice, however, this is undesirable because some groups will have distinctly above-average or below-average mortality.

2. *Experience Rated.* These premium rates are developed by using the actual mortality experience only of the particular group (usually a large one) which will pay the rates. Such premiums will be prepared only if the group's mortality experience is significantly better or worse than average and only if actual experience is likely to be the best basis for predicting the group's mortality in the future.

3. *Blended.* These premium rates are developed by basing mortality figures partly on manual and partly on experience rated data. If the actuary believes the group's actual mortality experience is soundly based and

reliable, then a fairly large proportion of each premium rate will be derived from the experience rated approach and vice versa. The proportion of the blend representing the experience rated approach is called the *credibility percentage* or *credibility factor.*

To Illustrate—The actuary has calculated the following gross annual one-year term group premiums per $1,000 for females age 40:

Manually Rated $2.72
Experience Rated for this particular group 2.05

If the actuary assigns a credibility percentage of 75% to this group, what blended rate will actually be charged for females age 40?

Solution—Seventy-five percent of the premium rate will be determined from the experience rated approach and the remaining 25% from the manually rated approach. Therefore, the blended premium rate is calculated as follows:

Blended Premium Rate = .75 (Experience Rate) + .25 (Manual Rate)

$$= .75\ (\$2.05) + .25\ (\$2.72)$$

$$= \$1.54 + \$.68$$

$$= \$2.22$$

CALCULATION OF PREMIUMS. The starting point in calculating group life insurance premium rates is to produce net premium rates in a manner similar to that shown for individual policies in Chapter 10. These net premium rates are generally for one-year term coverage and are calculated by taking account of only mortality and interest with no allowance for expenses, profit, or unforeseen contingencies.

In calculating *experience rated premiums*, the mortality experience of that one particular group is the basis for that group's net premiums. The actuary must decide on the particular period of time to be studied, such as the most recent 12 months. Frequently, a period of several years is studied, since mortality experience is likely to fluctuate somewhat from year to year. Whatever the period used, the results may also be adjusted for changes expected in the near future.

Sometimes the experience of several small groups may be combined to produce experience rated premiums which will be applicable to each of those particular groups. This allows a small group which has a favorable mortality experience to gain the advantages of paying experience rated premiums. It would obviously be impossible to do this with each small group separately, because not enough deaths occur in any one year to produce meaningful mortality rates. In fact, a group with less than 100 persons may have no death claims at all in any one year.

For *manually rated premiums*, the mortality assumptions used are generally those rates actually experienced by the insurance company on all those groups that would be expected to have normal mortality. Sometimes these mortality rates are adjusted to reflect changes expected in the near future.

Net premium rates are generally calculated separately for each age and sex. Manually rated net premiums may also be calculated separately for different types of industries. For example, groups that consist entirely of police would generally have higher premium rates than groups consisting of clerical workers in an office. In order to add a margin for possible higher than anticipated death claims, it is also customary to increase the mortality rates before they are used to calculate net premiums. The interest rate used in calculating net premiums is not important in one-year term policies. The companies generally use a currently-earned interest rate, although some companies ignore the interest factor in making the calculation.

Loading is added to the net premium rates in order to produce the gross premium rates. The loading provides for the insurance company's expenses, profit, and unforeseen contingencies, as well as the *conversion privilege* included in the group policy, as explained below. A part of the premium is often refunded to the policyowner if it proves to be too large.

The calculation of loading is comparable to the simple approach described in Section 10.7 for participating individual policies. A common approach is to use the equation

Gross = Net + Constant + Percent of Gross

The actual expenses an insurance company incurs for group life insurance are small compared with individual life insurance. This is true because there are no medical examinations and agents' commissions are lower, as are administrative expenses, since only one person is dealt with (the policyowner) in connection with a large amount of insurance. Just as with individual insurance, the first-year expenses are larger than for succeeding years. This requires that a part of the loading in years after the first be used to repay the insurance company for the larger first-year expenses. Since only certain expenses will be constant regardless of the size of the group, it is typical to charge slightly smaller rates per $1,000 for larger groups.

Members who leave the insured group are guaranteed the right to convert their group coverage to regular individual life insurance policies (other than term policies) without any medical examination. This is an extremely valuable privilege since it represents an opportunity for those in poor health to get a bargain. Group premium rates must include a factor to provide this privilege unless the insurance company decides to make such charges at the time of conversion.

To Illustrate—Calculate the gross annual premium rate per $1,000 to be charged for group coverage for males age 55, if the net premium rate per $1,000 has the following loading factors to be added in order to produce the gross rate:

> For expenses, contingencies, and profit .. $.55
> For conversion privilege .... .40
> For commissions and taxes .... 25% of gross
> premium

Assume that the net premium rate per $1,000 is $6.40.

Solution—

Basic equation:

Gross = Net + Constant + Percent of Gross

Substitute $6.40 for Net, $.55 + $.40 for Constant, and .25 for the Percent:

Gross = $6.40 + $.55 + $.40 + (.25)(Gross)

Solve the equation for Gross:

$$Gross - (.25)(Gross) = \$6.40 + \$.55 + \$.40$$

$$Gross\ (1 - .25) = \$7.35$$

$$Gross\ (.75) = \$7.35$$

$$Gross = \$9.80$$

In the above illustration, the $6.40 net premium rate could have been arrived at by a manually rated, experience rated, or blended approach.

CALCULATION OF MONTHLY PAYMENTS. Group life insurance premiums are most often paid monthly. At each yearly anniversary of a particular group policy, a listing is prepared of the total amount of insurance in force for that group for each age and sex. The appropriate gross monthly premium rate is multiplied by the amount in force for each age and sex, and the total monthly premium is found by adding. The total monthly premium thus calculated is divided by the total insurance in force, thus deriving an average monthly premium rate per $1,000. At each monthly premium-paying date throughout the policy year, this average rate is multiplied by the new total of insurance in force to derive that month's payment. The basic premise in applying the average rate is that the composition of the group by age and sex will not change significantly in a year's time.

Consider a simplified example of such a calculation. (In this example, it will be assumed that only a few ages are represented among the members.) The insurance in force by age and sex is shown, as well as the gross monthly premium rates for each such category. At the right-hand side is shown the total monthly premiums for each such category, derived by multiplying the number of thousands of insurance in force by the premium rate.

Anniversary In-Force for XYZ Company Employees

Sex and Age	Insurance in Force	Monthly Premium per $1,000	Total Monthly Premium
Male, 25	$100,000	$ .13	$ 13.00
Female, 25	200,000	.08	16.00
Male, 35	400,000	.20	80.00
Female, 35	300,000	.13	39.00
Male, 45	1,000,000	.55	550.00
Female, 45	1,500,000	.39	585.00
Total	$3,500,000		$1,283.00

To derive the average monthly premium per $1,000, the $1,283 (total monthly premium) is divided by 3,500 (number of thousands of insurance in force):

$$\$1,283 \div 3,500 = \$.37$$

If the total insurance in force the following month were found to be $3,850,000, the next payment would be calculated as follows (using the same average rate):

$$\$.37 \times 3,850 = \$1,424.50$$

15.4 RESERVES FOR GROUP LIFE INSURANCE

UNEARNED PREMIUM RESERVES. When group life insurance is issued on the one-year term basis, the reserve liability which the insurance company must establish each December 31 for the Annual Statement is equal to the portion of the last premium paid which is not yet used up. This is known as an *unearned premium reserve.* In other words, if an annual premium were paid on October 1, then $\frac{3}{12}$ of it would be used up by December 31, and the other $\frac{9}{12}$ of the premium would equal the reserve liability. If premiums are payable monthly on the first day of the month, then the December 31 reserve would be zero (the December 1 monthly premium having been entirely used up by December 31).

Just as with individual insurance, it is the net premium which is considered in calculating reserves. The net premium must be calculated from mortality tables which are prescribed or approved by the state authorities. However, it should be noted that some companies choose to follow the more conservative approach of using gross premiums instead of net premiums when calculating reserves on the one-year renewable term type of policy.

GROUP PERMANENT RESERVES. In the case of group permanent or group ordinary insurance, the method of calculating reserves is identical with that for individual insurance, as described in Chapters 11 and 12.

CONVERSION PRIVILEGE RESERVES. An additional reserve is usually calculated for the individual policies which are issued from exercise of the conversion privilege in group insurance (over and above the regular required reserve on the individual policy). This is done because death rates on such policies are generally very high, and the *present value of future benefits* in the reserve calculation is quite inadequate when a standard mortality table is used. In practice, a company may apply a simple approximation, such as figuring an additional reserve to be $70 per $1,000 of insurance the first year, decreasing by $7 per year for ten years.

CONTINGENCY RESERVES. In selling group insurance, a company is faced with the possibility of catastrophic death claims, a contingency not generally found in the case of individual insurance. This results from the fact that many of the members of an insured group may be closely concentrated, especially employees who work in one building. Therefore, such possible disasters as earthquakes, fires, floods, explosions, or epidemics could cause death claims far in excess of those predicted in the premium calculation.

To afford protection against the effects of such possible disasters, it is customary for insurance companies to set aside money into a *contingency reserve.* Such a reserve is voluntary and not legally required.

A typical approach is to allocate each year 2% of the excess group premiums received over dividends paid out in order to build up this reserve. At the suggestion of the New York Insurance Department, the maximum size of this reserve is usually set as 50% of this annual excess.

The contingency reserve then represents money which is available to the insurance company to help pay catastrophic death claims, should they occur.

15.5 DIVIDENDS FOR GROUP LIFE INSURANCE

Participating group life insurance policies receive policy dividends just as in the case of individual insurance. In the case of nonparticipating group life policies, companies accomplish the same thing as dividends by refunding part of the premiums. These refunds for nonparticipating policies are called *experience refunds* or *retroactive rate reductions.* The same process is used to calculate either dividends or experience refunds.

CALCULATION OF DIVIDENDS. To determine how much can be refunded to a particular group at the end of each policy year, the actuary calculates the *accumulated financial position* of that group's insurance as of that date. This means that the amount available at any date equals the total of the premiums collected to date plus interest and minus the following: actual death claims, expenses, charges for the conversion privilege, contribution to surplus (that is, profit to the insurance company), and all previous years' refunds or dividends. The balance is generally available to pay out as that year's dividend.

Before demonstrating a simplified example of this procedure, we should consider briefly how the most important elements in the calculation are determined.

DEATH CLAIMS. Because the death claims of any particular group are likely to fluctuate from year to year, it is customary to use a part of the actual death claims and a part of the expected death claims each year in calculating a group's dividend. The proportion representing the actual death claims is usually called the *credibility percentage,* the same term used for the blending of experience rated and manually rated premiums. The credibility percentage used in the dividend calculation can range from zero to 100%. Small groups and new groups would normally be assigned a very small percentage, while large groups (for example, over 5,000 persons) might be assigned 100%.

To Illustrate—A particular group has experienced $250,000 in death claims during the last policy year. The actuary has calculated the group's expected death claims for that year to be $400,000 and has assigned a credibility percentage of 30% to the group's actual claims. What amount is used for death claims in the year's dividend calculation?

Solution—Thirty percent of the death claim amount will be determined from the actual claims and the remaining 70% from the expected claims. The amount to be used, then, is calculated as follows:

$$\text{Death Claims to be Used} = .30(\text{Actual Claims}) + .70(\text{Expected Claims})$$
$$= .30(\$250,000) + .70(\$400,000)$$
$$= \$75,000 + \$280,000$$
$$= \$355,000$$

A second technique, often used to minimize the effects of fluctuations in the death claims, is to place a limit on the amount of the claims that will be used in any one year's calculations. This amount is called a *loss limit*, and it is set (by a method of higher mathematics) so that it should be exceeded only a predetermined number of times or a predetermined portion of the times.

EXPENSES. For any particular insured group, the year's expenses to be charged in the dividend calculation include actual costs incurred by that group plus that group's allocated share of general expenses. A group can be charged directly for its own commissions and certain taxes. Examples of expenses allocated among all groups include the company's group claim expenses and its general administration expenses.

CHARGE FOR CONVERSION PRIVILEGE. A deduction is also made to allow for the higher than normal mortality which is expected of a person who leaves the group and exercises the privilege to obtain an individual policy without presenting evidence of good health. This represents money taken out of group operations and transferred to individual operations, which is then used to establish the additional individual reserve described in Section 15.4.

Such charges in a group's dividend calculation typically are about $60 to $75 per $1,000. This rate is multiplied by the amount of insurance actually converted during the year. For example, if $150,000 of group insurance is converted to individual insurance in the year, then the group may be charged $70 × 150 = $10,500 in the year's dividend calculation.

NEGATIVE FINANCIAL POSITION. It sometimes happens that a particular group's accumulated financial position at a certain point in time may be negative (that is, more has been paid out than has been collected in premiums). This could happen, for example, because of unexpectedly large death claims in one year or because the high first-year expenses have not yet been recouped. In such a case, no dividend is paid. Moreover, positive gains in future years have to be applied against a negative position before any dividend would be paid in the future.

EXAMPLE OF DIVIDEND CALCULATION. Below is a simplified example of how group dividends are generally calculated (for only the first two policy years):

First Year's Financial Position

1. Premiums Collected = $840,000.
2. Interest Earned = $40,000. (This represents any interest earned during the year on the fund accumulated to date.)
3. Death Claims = $780,000. (This is the amount arrived at after applying the credibility percentage.)
4. Expenses = $115,000. (This includes commissions, taxes, and a share of general administrative expenses.)
5. Conversion Privilege = $3,250 on $50,000 of conversions. (This is calculated, in this example, as $65 for each $1,000 converted during the year.)
6. Contribution to Company's Surplus = $2,000.
7. Amount Available for Dividend = −$20,250 (Items 1 + 2 − 3 − 4 − 5 − 6).

In this case, the financial position (item 7) is negative, so no dividend is paid.

Second Year's Financial Position

1. Premiums Collected = $920,000.
2. Interest Earned = $42,000.
3. Death Claims = $820,000.
4. Expenses = $65,000.
5. Conversion Privilege = $9,750.
6. Contribution to Surplus = $10,000.
7. Negative Position from Preceding Year = $20,250.
8. Amount Available for Dividend = $37,000 (Items 1 + 2 − 3 − 4 − 5 − 6 − 7).

In this case, the insurance company has $37,000 which is available for a dividend or experience refund. Typically, most or all of the $37,000 would actually be paid to the policyowner.

15.6 COST COMPARISON FOR GROUP LIFE INSURANCE

A group seeking life insurance will customarily make a comparison among several insurance companies to find the best buy. To facilitate comparison, each insurance company prepares illustrations of the anticipated *net cost* for that particular group. For this purpose, net cost is equal to the anticipated premium less the anticipated dividend or experience refund. Such figures are generally calculated using present day experience on mortality and expenses and then applied to the particular group. The prospective buyer is cautioned that the net costs shown will be achieved only if all the assumptions are realized. The anticipated figures are typically shown for a period of ten years (that is, the group policy's first ten years).

In the example shown above in Section 15.5, the actual net cost for the first two years of this group is:

Year 1: $840,000 − 0 = $840,000
Year 2: $920,000 − $37,000 = $883,000 (assuming the entire $37,000 is paid as a dividend)

EXERCISES, SET 33

1. How can an actuary satisfactorily predict the mortality rates for group life insurance given the fact that all persons in the group are insured with no evidence of good health?

2. What is the purpose of providing a schedule which shows exactly how much insurance coverage each person in the group will have?

3. Why do insurance companies generally prefer to sell noncontributory instead of contributory group life insurance?

4. Why is one-year renewable term the most popular form of group life insurance?

5. Given the following information, calculate the blended annual premium rate per $1,000 to be charged for females age 25 in a certain group.

> *Annual Premium Rate per $1,000 for Females Age 25*
> Manually Rated $1.02
> Experience Rated for this group 92
> The credibility factor for this group has been set at 60%.

6. Calculate the gross annual premium rate per $1,000 (manually rated) to be charged for group coverage for males age 30, if the net annual premium rate per $1,000 (manually rated) is $1.12 and is to be loaded 40¢ per $1,000 plus 20% of the gross premium.

7. On the policy anniversary, a certain group has $10,000,000 of group insurance in force and the monthly premium is calculated to be $6,000. How much will the monthly premium be a few months later when the amount of insurance is $9,400,000?

8. A monthly group premium of $6,200 was due and paid on December 11. What unearned premium reserve is established on December 31, assuming 31 days in the month?

9. Where a group's actual claims are $800,000 but its expected claims were $2,000,000, calculate the amount of death claims to use in the year's dividend calculation. The credibility percentage for this group's dividend calculation has been set at 10%.

10. What is the year's net cost for a certain group policy, given that the year's premiums were $156,000 and the year's experience refund was $3,000?

11. Assume, that in a given year, a certain group was expected to have $550,000 in claims, but the group's actual claims were $700,000. If the credibility percentage

used for this group's dividend calculation is 65%, then the amount of death claims that will be used in the dividend calculations for this year is

(1) $455,000   (3) $647,500
(2) $602,500   (4) $812,500

CHAPTER SUMMARY

• Under group life insurance, one policy insures all or most members of a group. The most common example is a policy insuring the employees of one employer.

• As a rule, no evidence of good health is required from members of a group. To predict mortality rates accurately, a large enough group is needed, or groups must be combined. A group should be looked at for unusual hazards before being issued a policy.

• To be eligible for insurance, a group must meet certain requirements set by both state laws and the insurance companies. Most commonly, the group must exist for a purpose other than obtaining insurance; a large percentage of the group must be insured (many states require 75%); and no person can say how much insurance he or she will have.

• Each person's amount of insurance is generally determined from a schedule related to salary, job position, etc. State laws often stipulate the maximum insurance amount allowable under the schedule, as well as the maximum in relation to other members' amounts.

• Payment of premiums may be *noncontributory* (members themselves pay nothing), *contributory* (the policyowner, who is often the employer, shares the payment with the members), or *fully contributory* (members pay the entire premium).

• The noncontributory arrangement assures that all members will participate; therefore, more healthy persons will be included.

• If the members contribute, their contributions are generally not related to their age and sex. However, the premiums actually paid to the insurance company are so related.

• Actuaries in the group area calculate premiums and dividends for group insurance, as well as conduct studies of their company's mortality and expense experience on group policies.

• The most common types of group life insurance are one-year term (the lowest cost and by far the most popular), group ordinary (with level premiums and cash values, used to replace part of a member's one-year term insurance), and group life with paid-up insurance (part of each premium buys paid-up whole life insurance similar to paid-up additions, used to replace part of a member's one-year term insurance).

• A group's premium rates (for each age and sex) are guaranteed only for the first year of the insurance. Thereafter, the insurance company can change them periodically, based on each group's own experience.

• Some states (most notably New York) specify minimum group life premium rates for a group's first year. Thereafter, the rates can be changed without restrictions.

- Premiums can be calculated using any one of three different approaches for mortality assumptions:

    Manually Rated—in which mortality is based on the average experience of many groups.

    Experience Rated—in which mortality is based on the experience of the particular group which will pay the rates.

    Blended—in which mortality is based party on the manually rated approach and partly on the experience rated approach. (The proportion representing the experience rated approach is called the *credibility percentage* or *factor*.)

- Gross premiums for group life insurance are calculated for each age and sex in a manner similar to that shown in Chapter 10 for participating individual life insurance, that is, net premiums (based on mortality and interest only) plus loading (to provide for expenses, profit, and unforeseen contingencies) equals the gross premiums. A common approach would be

    Gross = Net + Constant + Percent of Gross

- Group life insurance expenses are small compared with individual life insurance. However, first-year expenses are larger than for succeeding years, and therefore, the use of a *level loading* means that part of each year's loading (after the first year) is used to repay the excess first-year expenses.

- Members who leave the group can convert their group life coverage to individual policies at regular premiums without presenting evidence of good health. (In some insurance companies, a part of the loading collected each year on premiums is used to pay for the higher than normal mortality expected on these individual policies.)

- Group premiums are usually paid monthly. On each policy's anniversary, an *average* monthly premium per $1,000 is calculated, taking into account the amounts then in force at each age and sex. This same average premium is then multiplied by the actual total amount in force for each of the next 11 months, as they come due, to determine those months' total premium.

- When group insurance is issued on the one-year term basis, the December 31 reserve liability is equal to the portion of the last premium which is not yet used up. This is called an *unearned premium reserve*.

- When an individual policy is issued as a conversion from group insurance, an extra reserve is generally calculated for that policy. This extra reserve represents the present value of the future extra mortality expected. It is usually calculated by a simple approximation and decreased to zero after a period such as ten years.

- Insurance companies often establish a voluntary *contingency reserve* to have available in event of catastrophic group death claims. A typical approach is to add 2% of each year's excess of group premiums over dividends, with a maximum reserve of 50% of this annual excess.

- Dividends are almost always paid on group life insurance. For nonparticipating policies, they are called *experience refunds*.

- The amount available for a dividend each year is found by calculating the accumulated financial position of the particular group's insurance to that date. This involves adding the total premiums plus interest and subtracting the total death claims, expenses, charges for conversion privilege, profit, and dividends paid since issue of the policy.

- In arriving at the dividends just described, the amount of death claims is generally calculated as being partly actual claims and partly expected claims. The proportion representing the actual death claims in any year is called the *credibility percentage*.

- To assist buyers of group insurance in finding the best buy, insurance companies furnish illustrations of anticipated *net cost* (that is, anticipated premiums less anticipated dividends). The figures are based on present-day experience, and the buyer is cautioned that the net cost results will only be achieved if all the assumptions are actually realized.

LEARNING OBJECTIVES

After reading this chapter, the student should know

- Why the mortality on group policies is reasonably predictable.
- What the usual requirements are for a group to be insurable.
- How each person's amount of insurance is determined.
- What the possible arrangements are for the members themselves to contribute to the premiums.
- What the actuary's responsibilities are in group life insurance.
- What the most common types of group life insurance are.
- What the possible approaches are for arriving at the mortality experience to use in a group's premium calculation.
- What is meant by the credibility percentage.
- How to calculate group life insurance premiums.
- How the group conversion privilege works.
- How monthly group insurance premiums are calculated.
- How unearned premium reserves are calculated.
- What the nature and purpose of a group contingency reserve are.
- What is meant by experience refunds.
- How group dividends are calculated.
- How group insurance net cost is calculated.

16

Health Insurance

Although the principal focus of this book has been on *life* insurance, it is appropriate to explain some of the mathematical bases underlying *health* insurance. Very often, both kinds of insurance are sold by the same insurance company and by the same agents. In fact, the great preponderance of health insurance in the United States is actually sold today by life insurance companies. Actuaries use many of the same principles in calculating premiums, reserves, and dividends for both life and health insurance.

Health insurance, like life insurance, is marketed through individual and group policies, and in this chapter, both types of policies will be discussed.

Because of the variety of benefits available and the great complexity of those benefits, health insurance is a vast subject. Therefore, in this chapter, we will explain briefly only the most popular health insurance benefits, as well as the fundamental principles for calculating their premiums, reserves, and dividends. This should give students useful insights into health insurance and prepare them to explore the subject more thoroughly at another time.

16.1 INTRODUCTION

When a person experiences an injury or sickness, there is often a financial loss (from disruption of income or the expenses of treatment). Health insurance is designed to provide benefits to pay for a portion of these financial losses.

Health insurance first came into being over 100 years ago, but in recent years has undergone a remarkable growth. Today, more than 80% of the population of the United States is protected by one or more forms of health insurance. Group health insurance exceeds individual health insurance in force by a wide margin. In fact, the total yearly premium for group health insurance even exceeds that for group life insurance.

COMPARING LIFE AND HEALTH INSURANCE. There are several important differences between life insurance and health insurance, most of which have had an effect on the way actuarial calculations are performed.

- Life insurance deals with mortality; health insurance deals with morbidity (the general term used to mean sickness, disability, or failure of health).

For purposes of insurance, morbidity is more difficult to define than mortality, because morbidity is more subjective in nature. For example, many physical conditions, such as hernias and back problems, present no particular hazard as far as life insurance is concerned, even though they may lead to health insurance claims. Further, while persons who are insured naturally desire to avoid both death and sickness, they may show less desire to recover quickly from a sickness as long as they are collecting insurance benefits.

- The amount payable for a life insurance claim is definitely defined by the policy. However, the amount payable in event of a valid health insurance claim is often less definite, as will be described later in the chapter.

- The amount paid out in health insurance claims is dramatically affected by swings in the economy, by inflation, and by changes in medical practice, none of which have such a direct effect on death claims.

- There is voluminous data and actual experience available for studying mortality experience, but there is a distinct scarcity of usable morbidity data. This is due mainly to the many types of health insurance coverages in existence, so that each type has a smaller amount in force to study.

- Because of the variation in medical costs in different areas, certain health insurance premiums must be calculated separately for different *geographic areas*. By contrast, life insurance premium rates at given ages generally do not vary by geographical location (within North America).

- The occupation of an insured person is important in calculating a life insurance premium only if it is a hazardous one. On the other hand, many occupations which are generally not considered hazardous may give rise to a higher-than-normal number of health claims. For example, persons in unsteady or seasonal industries show worse claim experience for insurance which covers *inability to work due to injury or sickness*.

- Typical health insurance policies cover losses resulting from sickness *commencing after the policy is issued*. Thus, pre-existing conditions are generally not allowed in the coverage. This is in contrast to life insurance, where a claim is normally paid regardless of the cause of death (unless information was withheld at time of issue, and even then a claim will be paid if the policy had been in force more than two years).

- In health insurance, any one insured person may collect claim payments again and again from the same policy. In life insurance, of course, the claim only occurs once.

- It is common practice to limit the amount of certain health insurance coverages issued to any particular person. For example, payments made to compensate for lost wages while a person is sick and unable to work should not exceed (or even approach) the amount of actual wages being lost. In life insurance, it is rare that the insurance company needs to be concerned about issuing too much insurance for any particular person.

THE ACTUARY'S RESPONSIBILITIES. In companies which sell large amounts of health insurance, it is customary for certain actuaries to specialize in the health insurance area. The responsibilities may be further divided into *group health* and *individual health* if both kinds of policies are sold.

Whether in group or individual health, the primary responsibility of *health actuaries* is to calculate the premium rates, reserves, and dividends for the company's health insurance policies. In addition, these actuaries must continually study and evaluate the actual claims and expenses which the company experiences under each of its different types of health insurance coverages.

As with life insurance (both individual and group), health actuaries also take an active role in the process of developing new types of coverages for sale.

16.2 HEALTH INSURANCE COVERAGES

The particular types of health coverages offered for sale are continually changing as new concepts are developed. However, it may be generalized that health insurance provides reimbursement to cover the two principal areas of monetary loss when health is impaired:

1. Loss of income (through inability to work) and
2. Expenses of medical treatment.

Insurance covering loss of income is normally sold to the breadwinners of a family. Insurance covering expenses of medical treatment, however, is normally sold to insure all of the members of a family (since all, obviously, may need medical treatment).

The expenses of medical treatment are generally divided into four major categories, each usually being covered under a separate section in a health insurance policy:

> Hospital expense
> Surgical expense
> Medical (doctor's) expense
> Major medical expense

Each of these categories, as well as insurance covering loss of income, will be explained below. Generally, these benefits are approximately the same whether they are provided through group health insurance policies or individual health insurance policies. There are, of course, other categories of expenses sometimes covered by health insurance (such as expenses of diagnostic tests and dental expenses), but these are less common, and we will not discuss them in this book.

In Canada, all of the provinces cover their residents for most of the expenses that are included in the categories of hospital expense, surgical expense, and medical (doctor's) expense. However, major medical expense coverage is sold in Canada by insurance companies for certain items of expense not covered by the government insurance. Insurance covering loss of income is also sold.

DISABILITY INCOME INSURANCE. This is the name generally given to the insurance covering loss of income through inability to work. Such inability to work, called *disability*, must be caused by injury or sickness. Occasionally the details of the coverage are different for injury than for sickness, but we will not go into those differences here.

The benefit payable under disability income insurance is in the form of an annuity, that is, monthly payments are made, each contingent on the insured person being alive and still disabled. Such an annuity is called a *disabled-life annuity*. Since the insured person may recover and later qualify for benefits again, the policy is considered to be still in force during any benefit-paying period. However, all regular premiums due during that time are waived.

Disability income insurance differs in two major ways from life insurance:

1. It is often difficult to determine (it is subjective) whether or not disability, as defined in the policy, actually exists.
2. The claim amount itself is always payable in the form of an annuity, rather than a single sum.

Premium rates for disability income insurance are generally calculated and published for units of $10 or $100 of monthly benefit. For example, the annual premium rate for a certain person might be $1.82 for each $10 of monthly disability income benefit. If that person wanted $850 per month of benefit, the annual premium would be $1.82 × 85 = $154.70.

Individual and group premium rates for disability income insurance are generally calculated and published on the basis of the following breakdowns:

1. *Age*: With advancing age, the frequency of becoming disabled increases significantly, as does the length of time a person then stays disabled.
2. *Sex*: Experience shows that, at most ages, females become disabled more frequently than males, although the opposite is true at the highest ages.
3. *Occupation*: Common practice is to assign all occupations to *occupation classes*.

In group health insurance, there are often further breakdowns by type of industry involved.

Disability income benefits begin only after the insured person has been actually disabled for a specified period of time known as the *waiting period* or *elimination period*. This waiting period saves the insurance company considerable claim outlay because a very large portion of persons becoming disabled actually recover and go back to work in a short time. The most common waiting periods provided are one or two weeks, or one, two, three, or six months.

Normally, disability income benefit payments stop after a specified number of monthly payments have been made, even if the person continues to be disabled at that time. This period of time is called the *maximum benefit period.* Since most disabilities actually last for a relatively short period of time, most buyers of the insurance are unwilling to pay the higher premiums that would be required to provide a very long maximum benefit period. *Short-term disability income* policies specify a maximum benefit period of six months or so, while *long-term disability income* policies specify a period of one, two, or five years, or one ending when the insured person reaches age 65. In rare instances, policies specify that payments will be made for the person's lifetime (if he or she continues to be disabled that long).

Typically, an insurance company's rate manual offers an array of different waiting periods and maximum benefit periods. To find the premium rate (per $10 of monthly income benefit) in the rate manual for a particular person's policy, one must refer to the age, sex, occupation class, waiting period, and maximum benefit period which are applicable.

As mentioned in Section 16.1, there is an upper limit to the amount of disability income insurance which may be issued to any particular person. A typical rule is that the total monthly income benefit from all of a person's policies, including disability income insurance under government plans like social security, shall not exceed two thirds of that person's current monthly salary. If such limits were not imposed and the benefit could exceed the insured person's salary, then there would be much less incentive to return to work.

Some disability income policies provide encouragement for a disabled person to become *rehabilitated* by continuing to pay benefits while the person is participating in a rehabilitation program, even though he or she may be receiving some wages during that time.

HOSPITAL EXPENSE INSURANCE. This first category of medical treatment coverage pays both a daily benefit toward the cost of a hospital room and all other hospital charges up to specified limits.

The administration of claims under hospital expense insurance is much simpler than that for disability income insurance because the hospital bill proves that insured loss has taken place and also specifies the exact amount of the loss. This is also true for the other three medical treatment categories to be described below—surgical expense, doctor's expense, and major medical expense.

Premiums for hospital expense insurance are generaly calculated separately for each age and sex. Older persons experience considerably higher hospital claim frequencies than younger persons. Females require hospitalization more frequently than males, except at high ages. Higher premiums are often charged to persons in occupations or industries which are hazardous or involve exposure to poisons, dust, etc. Finally, because of the large differences in hospital charges among regions, hospital insurance premiums must be calculated separately for different geographical areas.

SURGICAL EXPENSE INSURANCE. This coverage pays an amount toward the surgeon's fee for performing operations. Different amounts of benefits are paid for different types of operations. As with hospital expense insurance, the surgeon's bill provides proof that the loss has actually happened and provides information on the exact amount. Again, premiums for surgical expense insurance are calculated separately for each age, sex, and geographical area, and higher premiums may be charged for hazardous occupations or industries.

For this benefit, the insured person does not specify the amount of insurance being applied for (as with life insurance or disability income insurance or, perhaps, hospital expense insurance). Instead, there are generally two or three options on *schedules* to choose from. For example, there might be two available schedules set forth as follows:

Maximum Payment for Surgical Procedures

Procedure	Schedule A	Schedule B
Abdomen:		
Removal of Appendix	$300	$450
Removal of Gall Bladder	450	675
Removal of Spleen	450	675
Etc.		

Higher premium rates will be charged for coverage under Schedule B than under Schedule A

MEDICAL (DOCTOR'S) EXPENSE INSURANCE. This coverage pays benefits toward doctors' bills other than surgical. It is usually limited to hospital visits by the doctor. Sometimes it is called simply *medical expense insurance*, but this name is not very descriptive of the benefit. An example of the benefit might be:

Doctor's Hospital Visits

First day of hospitalization $10
Each day thereafter, up to 30 days . . . .$20 per day

The amounts shown are the maximums which the insurance would pay each day.

Once more, premiums for this coverage are calculated separately for each age, sex, and geographical area.

MAJOR MEDICAL INSURANCE. This coverage is issued on one of the following bases:

1. *Supplemental Major Medical*—which provides a benefit toward almost all expenses of medical treatment over and above the amounts paid by the person's hospital, surgical, and doctor's expense insurance described above. (Since all three of these categories specify the maximum amounts which the insurance will pay, very large medical bills are often inadequately covered by the three categories.)
2. *Comprehensive Major Medical*—which provides a benefit toward almost

all expenses of medical treatment without any regular hospital, surgical, and doctor's expense insurance.

In either case, the premium for major medical insurance is kept reasonable by requiring that the insured person pay the first portion of the expenses each year. This is called the *deductible* and is generally at least $100 to $200. Then, to stimulate interest by the insured person in the amount of expenses being charged, the insurance pays less than 100% of each dollar charged. This is called the *coinsurance feature*. The insurance company generally pays 75% to 85% of the expenses, and the insured must pay the remaining 15% to 25%. Finally, there is a maximum total amount, such as $250,000 or $1,000,000, which will be paid to any one person.

Thus, typical major medical benefit provisions might look like this:

Supplemental Major Medical

Pays 80% of all eligible medical bills over and above that paid by the basic insurance, after first deducting $150 per year (which the insured person must pay), up to a maximum total payment of $500,000.

Comprehensive Major Medical

Pays 80% of all eligible medical bills, after first deducting $150 per year (which the insured person must pay), up to a maximum total payment of $500,000.

In these examples, $150 is the deductible, 80% represents the coinsurance feature, and $500,000 is the maximum benefit.

16.3 INDIVIDUAL HEALTH INSURANCE CALCULATIONS

Like individual life insurance, individual health insurance policies require the person applying to submit evidence of good health, and the gross premiums are generally calculated on a level premium basis.

However, unlike individual life insurance policies, the insurance company often has the right to change the premium rate for health insurance to a different level premium after the policy has been issued. Various approaches are used, but usually an individual health insurance policy specifies one of the following arrangements:

1. *Cancellable or Renewable at the Company's Option*—in which the company can terminate the policy.
2. *Guaranteed Renewable*—in which the company cannot terminate the policy but may change the premium rates for broad classes of policies.
3. *Noncancellable and Guaranteed Renewable*—in which the company cannot terminate the policy and cannot change the premium.

If the evidence of good health submitted to the company shows that a problem exists which could lead to a health insurance claim later on, such as the existence of a stomach ulcer or the participation of the applicant in a hazardous sport, then the policy is usually issued with a special provision stating that no benefits will be payable if disability or medical treatment arises from that specified problem. This is in contrast to life insurance policies, where the claim is generally payable regardless of the cause, though life policies sometimes do not cover deaths if the person insured is killed flying an airplane or engaging in certain hazardous activities. Another approach is to issue a health insurance policy with a higher premium if a problem exists (a procedure like that followed on individual life insurance policies).

PREMIUMS FOR INDIVIDUAL HEALTH POLICIES. Morbidity experience is used to calculate net annual premiums for health insurance, just as mortality experience is used to calculate life insurance net premiums. As mentioned earlier, there is often a scarcity of morbidity data available, because the amount of *published* experience data is limited and quickly goes out of date. If available, the best source is a company's own experience on the same type of policy being calculated. The next best source is from group health insurance which can be used for individual policies. The last resort is health statistics which are available from a wide range of government studies.

In individual health insurance, as in life insurance, net annual premiums may be calculated either on a net level basis or a modified basis. From these net annual premiums, reserves are calculated for each policy year.

For disability income policies, net annual premiums are usually calculated in a manner quite similar to that shown in Chapter 10 for life insurance policies. In that chapter, the net single premium for $1,000 of life insurance covering one year was shown to be

$$\$1,000\left(\frac{d_x v}{l_x}\right)$$

In calculating disability premiums, the same approach is used, except for these differences:

1. d_x in the numerator represents the number becoming disabled instead of the number dying.
2. The benefit takes the form of a disabled-life annuity instead of a single payment, and its value is represented by the present value of such an annuity.

Therefore, $\dfrac{d_x v}{l_x}$ is multiplied by the present value of the disabled life annuity. This value, of course, is a different amount for each age at which disability could occur.

The present value of all years' benefits, then, would appear as follows (assuming the present value of the disabled-life annuity is $5,612 if disability occurs at age x, \$5,920 if it occurs at age $x + 1$, \$6,418 if it occurs at age $x + 2$, etc.):

$$\binom{\text{Present Value of}}{\text{Benefits}} = \frac{\$5,612\,d_x v + \$5,920\,d_{x+1} v^2 + \$6,418\,d_{x+2} v^3 + \cdots \text{ etc.}}{l_x}$$

As explained above, the d's represent the number becoming disabled.

The present value of the net annual premiums is expressed the same as that shown in Chapter 10 for life insurance:

$$\binom{\text{Present Value of}}{\text{Net Annual Premiums}} = \binom{\text{Net Annual}}{\text{Premium}} \left(\frac{l_x + l_{x+1} v + l_{x+2} v^2 + \cdots \text{ etc.}}{l_x} \right)$$

In practice, special commutation functions are often calculated to simplify the work.

Another approach, often used for hospital, surgical, and major medical coverages, will be shown in an example below. Typically, no nonforfeiture values are available for an individual health insurance policy. The premium calculation shown below takes account of this fact, and the premiums, therefore, are kept lower. In such a calculation, those dying and those terminating are combined since no benefit is paid in either instance.

The basic morbidity figures, which are derived from experience and used in calculating net annual premiums, are called *annual claim costs*. These are equal to the expected frequency of claims in a year's time multiplied by the average amount payable in the event of each claim. In a sense, this is comparable to $\$1,000\,q_x$ which would be used in a life insurance calculation. Such annual claim costs are derived as separate figures for each type of coverage and for each age and sex. If appropriate, they are derived by occupation class or geographic area. For example, the annual claim cost for a certain surgical expense coverage for a male age 55 living in the Midwest might be \$29.50, and this might have been derived by multiplying .05 (frequency of claims in a year) by \$590 (average amount payable for each claim) which equals \$29.50.

The following simplified example demonstrates this approach in the net annual premium calculation. It is based on the familiar principle that, at the time a policy is issued, the present value of the net annual premiums is equal to the present value of the future benefits. The calculation is based on assumptions about the number of persons that will still be paying premiums at the beginning of each year and the annual claim costs. Interest is assumed to be 6%, and it is assumed that the policy covers a period of five years.

Chart 16–1 shows the calculation of the present value of \$1 per year in premium payments for a group of 1,000 males age 55 who buy a hospital expense insurance policy.

CHART 16–1

Present Value of $1 Per Year in Premiums, Male Age 55

(1) Year n	(2) Number Beginning of Year	(3) Number Withdraw and Die	(4) v^{n-1} at 6%	(5) Present Value of $1 Premium (Col. 2 × Col. 4)
1	1,000	310	1.000000	$1,000.00
2	690	105	.943396	650.94
3	585	51	.889996	520.65
4	534	32	.839619	448.36
5	502	—	.792094	397.63
	Total Present Value			$3,017.58

Chart 16–2 shows the calculation of the present value of the annual claim costs for a certain surgical expense coverage issued to males age 55 living in the Midwest. This example assumes that claim costs are incurred at the end of each year, and the frequency of claim assumed in the annual claim costs is based on the number of persons at the beginning of each year.

CHART 16–2

Present Value of Annual Claim Costs, Male Age 55, Midwest

(1) Year n	(2) Number Beginning of Year	(3) Annual Claim Cost	(4) v^n at 6%	(5) Present Value of Annual Claim Costs (Col. 2 × Col. 3 × Col. 4)
1	1,000	$29.50	.943396	$27,830.18
2	690	31.75	.889996	19,497.59
3	585	34.25	.839619	16,822.82
4	534	37.00	.792094	15,650.19
5	502	40.30	.747258	15,117.48
	Total Present Value			$94,918.26

Note that no use is made in Chart 16–2 of the number dying or terminating, because no benefit is payable on either occurrence. Instead, the annual claim costs are associated with the number of persons still in the group who are exposed to the risk being insured against. Annual claim costs are equal to the frequency of the expected claim multiplied by the amount of the average claim, and therefore, the total amount of claims expected each year in Chart 16–2 is found by multiplying column (2) by column (3). In the first year, the total amount of claims expected from this hypothetical group is $1000 \times \$29.50 = \$29,500$. From another point of view, this amount may be seen as the number of persons insured, multiplied by the frequency of claim, multiplied by the average amount of claim. If we assume the frequency to be .05 and the average amount to be $590, this becomes:

$$1,000 \times .05 \times \$590 = \$29,500$$

From this point of view, 50 persons may each be expected to incur $590 in claims, for a total of 50 × $590 = $29,500.

To calculate the net level annual premium per person, the following equation is solved:

$$\left(\begin{array}{c}\text{Net Level} \\ \text{Annual Premium}\end{array}\right)\left(\begin{array}{c}\text{Present Value of} \\ \text{\$1 Premium Per Year}\end{array}\right) = \left(\begin{array}{c}\text{Present Value of} \\ \text{Annual Claim Costs}\end{array}\right)$$

$$\left(\begin{array}{c}\text{Net Level} \\ \text{Annual Premium}\end{array}\right)(\$3,017.58) = \$94,918.26$$

$$\left(\begin{array}{c}\text{Net Level} \\ \text{Annual Premium}\end{array}\right) = \$31.46$$

In practice, special commutation functions are sometimes calculated from annual claim costs and used to calculate net annual premiums and reserves.

In calculating net annual premiums for hospital, surgical, and major medical coverages, it is common to assume that, because of the recent history of inflating medical care costs, annual claim costs will increase in the future over their current levels. Such assumptions, however, generally project only moderate increases, because premiums must be kept in line with competitors' premiums.

A loading is added to the net annual premiums to produce the gross annual premiums. The methods and considerations for loading are virtually the same as those explained in Chapter 10 for individual life insurance gross premiums. The loading must be sufficient to cover commissions, expenses, taxes, and an amount for unforeseen contingencies. Since the risk is more uncertain for health insurance than for life insurance, a greater amount for unforeseen contingencies is generally included.

Actuaries generally consider *asset share tests* to be very important for health insurance policies to ensure, among other things, that there will not be a loss if more persons than expected terminate their policies. The profit or loss picture in health insurance is keenly affected by the number of such terminations.

A number of states require that the gross premiums for health insurance policies must be "reasonable." As a measure of "reasonableness," a calculation is generally required of the *anticipated loss ratio* for a group of similar policies. The anticipated loss ratio is generally calculated (as of the time of issue) as follows:

$$\text{Anticipated Loss Ratio} = \frac{\text{Present Value of Future Benefits}}{\text{Present Value of Future Gross Premiums}}$$

The actuary calculates the anticipated loss ratio at the time gross premiums are calculated. Some states require that an anticipated loss ratio of at least 50% be the dividing line between reasonable and unreasonable.

RESERVES FOR INDIVIDUAL HEALTH POLICIES. Since individual health policies involve level premiums along with claim costs which increase each year, reserves must be set up for the policies. The terminal reserves can be calculated in a manner similar to that for life insurance. If the prospective method is used, this would involve the usual equation:

$$\begin{pmatrix} \text{Terminal} \\ \text{Reserve} \end{pmatrix} = \begin{pmatrix} \text{Present Value} \\ \text{of Future Benefits} \end{pmatrix} - \begin{pmatrix} \text{Present Value of} \\ \text{Future Net Premiums} \end{pmatrix}$$

Alternatively, the calculation may show the accumulation of a fund for a large number of persons, and thereby calculate reserves in a manner similar to that shown in Section 11.1 for life insurance.

The net premiums and the resulting reserves for individual health insurance may be on a net level basis, or the first year (or each of the first two years) may be considered one-year term insurance and the remaining years calculated as net level. This latter approach is the same as the Full Preliminary Term Method for life insurance. The legal requirements for health insurance reserves are not as explicit as for life insurance. However, a two-year preliminary term approach is generally allowed. Legal reserve requirements apply only to those policies which the company cannot terminate.

Instead of using mean reserves for the December 31 financial statement, as in life insurance, the December 31 health insurance reserves are usually shown in two parts. One such part is called a *midterminal reserve* and is calculated as follows:

$$\begin{pmatrix} \text{Midterminal} \\ \text{Reserve} \end{pmatrix} = \frac{\text{(Previous Terminal Reserve)} + \text{(Terminal Reserve)}}{2}$$

The student should recognize this as being the same as the mean reserve except that the net annual premium is not included in the numerator. The second part is called an *unearned premium reserve* and is calculated the same as the unearned premium reserves described in Section 15.4 for group insurance, that is, the part of the last premium paid which is not yet used up.

For instance, the surgical expense coverage in the example above was shown to have a net level annual premium of $31.46 when issued to males age 55 living in the Midwest. The terminal reserves for this same policy are as follows:

End of Year 1 = $5.57

End of Year 2 = 8.84

End of Year 3 = 9.27

End of Year 4 = 6.56

End of Year 5 =   0

The December 31 reserve which occurs during the policy's second year (that is, approximately one and a half years after the date of issue) would be a midterminal reserve calculated as follows:

$$\left(\begin{array}{c}\text{Midterminal}\\\text{Reserve}\end{array}\right) = \frac{(\text{1st Terminal Reserve}) + (\text{2nd Terminal Reserve})}{2}$$

$$= \frac{\$5.57 + \$8.84}{2}$$

$$= \frac{\$14.41}{2}$$

$$= \$7.21$$

The second part (usually shown separately in the financial statement) is the December 31 unearned premium. Let us assume that one particular policy's premium is paid annually on April 1. In that case, as of December 31, $\frac{3}{12}$ of the annual premium is still unearned (the portion covering the period from January 1 to April 1). Therefore, if the unearned premium is to be based on the net premium, it would be $\frac{3}{12} \times \$31.46 = \$7.87$. On the other hand, the more conservative approach may be used of basing this amount on the gross premium. If we assume this policy's gross annual premium is $47.00, then the unearned premium to be shown is $\frac{3}{12} \times \$47.00 = \$11.75$.

In addition to the policy reserves described above, a *claim reserve* must be established when a claim is incurred and reported to the company. Such a claim reserve is calculated as the present value of future claim payments which, it is anticipated, will result from that particular claim. For disability income insurance, the claim reserve is the present value of the monthly payments remaining to be made in the future to those persons who are actually disabled and receiving benefits on the date of the company's financial statement. This present value is calculated using disabled-life annuities, such as those referred to in Section 16.2 above. Several tables of disabled-life annuities, based on the combined experience of several companies, are published and widely used.

An *actual loss ratio* is calculated yearly in the company's financial statement. The actual loss ratio is generally calculated (for a period of time such as a year) as follows:

$$\text{Actual Loss Ratio} = \frac{\begin{array}{c}(\text{Claim Payments Made})\\ + (\text{Increase in Claim Reserves})\end{array}}{\begin{array}{c}(\text{Premiums Collected})\\ - (\text{Increase in Policy Reserves})\end{array}}$$

Here again, as in the anticipated loss ratio described earlier, a ratio of at least 50% is often taken to mean that gross premiums are reasonable.

To Illustrate—A company's individual major medical policy shows the following amounts for the year 1985:

Premiums collected $1,500,000
Claim payments made 440,000
Claim reserves, beginning of year 300,000
Claim reserves, end of year 500,000
Policy reserves, beginning of year 800,000
Policy reserves, end of year 1,200,000

Does the year's actual loss ratio indicate that the gross premiums are reasonable for this policy?

Solution—The increase in claim reserves for the year is equal to $500,000 − $300,000 = $200,000. The increase in policy reserves is equal to $1,200,000 − $800,000 = $400,000. The actual loss ratio is calculated as follows:

Basic Equation:

$$\text{Actual Loss Ratio} = \frac{\text{(Claim Payments Made)} + \text{(Increase in Claim Reserves)}}{\text{(Premiums Collected)} - \text{(Increase in Policy Reserves)}}$$

Substitute $440,000 for Claim Payments, $200,000 for Increase in Claim Reserves, $1,500,000 for Premiums, and $400,000 for Increase in Policy Reserves:

$$= \frac{\$440,000 + \$200,000}{\$1,500,000 - \$400,000}$$

$$= \frac{\$640,000}{\$1,100,000}$$

$$= .58, \text{ or } 58\%$$

Since the actual loss ratio exceeds 50%, most states would probably deem the gross premiums to be reasonable for this policy.

It should be noted that a new group of policies will generally show very low actual loss ratios in the first year or two after the company starts issuing them, because all the persons insured have very recently submitted evidence of good health. This is a temporary situation and not taken to mean that the gross premiums are unreasonable.

Because of the sensitivity of health insurance to economic conditions, health insurance is not as predictable as life insurance. Therefore, it is common for companies to establish (voluntarily) a *contingency reserve* for their health insurance business. Such a reserve is built up over a number of years, ultimately reaching an amount which is typically 50% of one year's premium income from the company's health insurance business.

DIVIDENDS FOR INDIVIDUAL HEALTH POLICIES. A large portion of the individual health insurance sold today is nonparticipating. For those policies which are participating, the dividends are typically paid only after the policy has been in force for a period of time such as three or five years.

The purpose of this delay is to allow the company to recover more of its expenses from selling and issuing the policy.

Dividends paid on individual health insurance policies are very often quoted as a percent of the premium. For example, a dividend might be quoted as being equal to 10% of the premium, payable beginning at the end of the policy's fifth year. If the annual premium is $256.00, then the annual dividend is .10 × $256.00 = $25.60, with the first four years excluded. Such dividends, of course, stay at the same amount each year and do not increase.

One method actuaries use to determine such dividends is to calculate the actual gross premium by making conservative assumptions (for morbidity, interest, expenses, etc.) and then calculate what the gross premium would be, using actually expected assumptions. The difference between the two amounts is available to pay each year as a dividend. The student will recognize this as being similar to the first part of the life insurance dividend calculation using the experience-premium method shown in Section 14.3.

For example, assume the gross annual premium for a certain health insurance policy is calculated as follows:

Using conservative assumptions $314.85
Using actually expected assumptions 288.98

The difference, which may be paid each year as a dividend, is $314.85 − $288.98 = $25.87. If the dividend were to be quoted as a percent of the gross premium, then the percentage would be found by dividing the dividend by the gross premium to be charged:

$25.87 ÷ $314.85 = .082, or 8.2%

In this case the dividend would probably be quoted as being 8% of the premium. In addition, a dividend might not be paid for the first few years. An attempt would usually be made to use the same percent as the dividend figure for all ages buying this particular policy, by calculating the percentage (as shown above) for several ages and using an average of the results.

16.4 GROUP HEALTH INSURANCE CALCULATIONS

Group health insurance for disability and medical treatment is issued to all or most of the members of a group under one policy. Generally, no evidence is required as to the good health of any of the members of the group. The arrangements and calculations generally follow the same principles explained in Chapter 15 for group life insurance.

The requirements for a group to be insured are the same as those outlined in Section 15.1 for group life insurance, and the arrangements possible for collecting the premium money are the same as for group life insurance—noncontributory, contributory, or fully contributory.

Group health insurance is issued on the one-year renewable term basis, whereby each year's premium pays for just that year's coverage. A new premium is charged each year based on the sex and attained ages of the members of the group. The considerations of geographic location, occupations, and type of industry, referred to in section 16.2, are also taken into account. The premium is usually paid monthly.

PREMIUMS FOR GROUP HEALTH INSURANCE. When a health policy is issued to a group for the first time, the insurance company usually guarantees the premium rates for only the first 12 months of the policy. At the end of the first year, new rates may be established by the insurance company for that group. In turn, these new rates are generally guaranteed for only a limited period of time. Thus, the actuary can use the actual morbidity experience and expenses of any particular group to calculate the premiums for that group (after the first policy year).

Some states require that all first-year group health insurance premium rates be approved by that state's department or division of insurance before the policy can be issued in that state. The purpose is to prevent the setting of inadequate rates, as explained in Chapter 15 in connection with group life insurance. The New York law specifies that an insurance company operating in New York cannot use group health rates in the first year in any state which are lower than those approved by New York.

The net annual premiums (on the one-year term basis) are the same as the annual claim costs described in Section 16.3. They are equal to the expected claim frequency in a year's time multiplied by the average amount payable in event of each claim.

As in group life insurance, there are three possible rating classes: *manually rated, experience rated,* and *blended.* In calculating manually rated premiums, the annual claim costs used are generally derived from the morbidity actually experienced by the insurance company on all those groups expected to have normal morbidity. In calculating experience rated premiums, the morbidity experience of the one particular group is the basis for that group's net premiums. Sometimes the experience of several small groups is combined to produce experience rated premiums to be applicable to those particular groups, as was explained in Chapter 15 in connection with group life insurance. And like individual health insurance, it is common to assume that the average amount of each claim (and hence, the annual claim costs) will increase in the future over the current levels.

A loading is added to the net one-year premiums to produce the gross premiums. The methods and considerations are virtually the same as those explained in Chapter 15 for group life insurance gross premiums. A common approach would be to use the equation:

$$\text{Gross} = \text{Net} + \text{Constant} + \text{Percent of Gross}$$

This loading must be sufficient to cover the commissions, expenses, taxes, unforeseen contingencies, and the conversion privilege (that is, the extra morbidity that is expected when a person leaves the group and converts his or her group health coverage to an individual health policy). The insurance company's expenses are smaller for group health than for individual health insurance, because there are no medical examinations, the agents' commissions are not as large, and only one person is dealt with (the policyowner) in connection with a large amount of insurance. However, expenses for the first year are still larger than for succeeding years. This requires that a part of the loading in years after the first year be used to repay the insurance company for the larger first-year expenses.

To Illustrate—Calculate the gross one-year premium rate to be charged for group comprehensive major medical coverage for females age 25 living in the Los Angeles area. Use the following information:

Frequency of claim in one year .... .09
Average amount of claim $2,060.00
Annual loading needed per person for expenses,
    contingencies, conversion privilege, and profit $13.15
Annual loading needed for commissions and taxes .... 20% of gross premium

Solution—The annual claim cost (that is, the net one-year term premium) equals the frequency of claim times the average-size claim:

Annual Claim Cost = .09 × $2,060.00 = $185.40

Using $185.40 as the net premium for that year, the gross premium can be calculated using the common equation given above:

Basic equation:

Gross = Net + Constant + Percent of Gross

Substitute $185.40 for Net, $13.15 for Constant, and .20 for Percent:

Gross = $185.40 + $13.15 + (.20)(Gross)

Solve the equation for Gross:

Gross − (.20)(Gross) = $185.40 + $13.15

Gross(1 − .20) = $198.55

Gross(.80) = $198.55

Gross = $248.19

Note that, in the above calculation, no present values are calculated using a rate of interest. It is common to ignore the interest factor for group coverages where only a one-year term arrangement is used.

Loss ratios for group health insurance are calculated in the same manner as shown in Section 16.3 for individual health insurance. However, since group insurance normally is on a one-year term basis, the reference to policy reserves is eliminated, and the equation for actual loss ratio used is:

$$\text{Actual Loss Ratio} = \frac{\text{(Claim Payments Made)} + \text{(Increase in Claim Reserves)}}{\text{(Premiums Collected)}}$$

RESERVES FOR GROUP HEALTH INSURANCE. The terminal reserves for group health insurance are zero, because it is issued on a one-year term basis. The December 31 reserves used for the company's financial statement are unearned premium reserves, calculated in the same manner as shown in Chapter 15 for group life insurance.

In addition to the unearned premium reserve, group health insurance requires that a reserve be established equal to the present value of the payments to be made in the future to those persons who are actually disabled or receiving benefits. Such a reserve is calculated in the same manner as explained in Section 16.3 for individual health insurance.

A *voluntary contingency reserve* is also common for group health insurance, just as it is for individual health insurance. A typical amount for such a reserve is 50% of a year's premium income from the company's group health business.

DIVIDENDS FOR GROUP HEALTH INSURANCE. The principles and methods used in calculating dividends for group health insurance are virtually identical to those explained in Section 15.5 for group life insurance. They will be outlined briefly here, and the student should note the similarities to group life insurance dividend calculations.

Participating policies pay dividends on group health insurance, while nonparticipating policies pay *experience refunds* which are calculated in the same manner as dividends. The dividend payable to any particular group is determined by looking at that group's *accumulated financial position*. This is equal to the premiums collected and interest to date minus the actual claims, expenses, conversion privilege charges, contributions to surplus, and dividends paid to date. The balance is generally available to pay as that year's dividend.

The amounts representing claims used in such calculations are generally part of the actual claims and part of the expected claims each year. The portion representing the actual claims is usually called the *credibility percentage*. Small groups and new groups are assigned a very small credibility percentage. In addition, a limit is often placed on the amount of any single claim which is used in the calculation. This amount is called a *loss limit*, and is set at so large an amount that only rarely is it actually exceeded.

It sometimes happens that a group's accumulated financial position may be negative. This could happen because of unexpectedly large claims or because the high first-year expenses have not yet been recouped. In that case, no dividend would be paid, and gains in future years would be used to make up the negative position before any dividend would be paid.

A large group seeking group health insurance often asks several insurance companies to prepare *net cost illustrations*. Net cost in such a case is defined to be the anticipated premiums less the anticipated dividends. Such calculations are generally based on each company's present-day claim experience and expenses.

EXERCISES, SET 34

1. What are the two major areas of financial loss often suffered when a person experiences an injury or sickness?

2. What is meant by the word morbidity?

3. Why is it more difficult to predict morbidity than mortality?

4. What particular characteristics must be known about the applicant and the insurance coverage in order to determine the premium when an individual disability income policy is being applied for?

5. What is the difference between supplemental major medical coverage and comprehensive major medical coverage?

6. Calculate the annual claim cost expected for a particular health coverage. Use the following actual experience for this coverage as the basis of the calculation.

Last year's number of persons insured 1,000
Last year's number of claims incurred 40
Last year's amount of claims incurred $80,000

7. Given the following information, calculate the gross annual premium to be charged for a particular individual health insurance policy.

Present value of annual claim costs $540,000
Present value of $1 per year premium 13,500
Loading needed .... 25% of net premium

8. Given the following information, calculate the actual loss ratio experienced in a year for a particular group of individual health policies.

Premiums collected $350,000
Claim payments made 150,000
Claim reserves, beginning of year 100,000
Claim reserves, end of year 200,000
Policy reserves, beginning of year 40,000
Policy reserves, end of year 30,000

9. Given the following information, calculate the midterminal reserve that would be included in the company's December 31, 1986 financial statement for a certain individual health insurance policy.

Date of issue .... June 1, 1984
Net annual premium .... $306.12 (after first year)
1st terminal reserve 0
2nd terminal reserve 31.60
3rd terminal reserve 66.48

10. If a company wished to express the dividend for an individual health insurance policy as a percent of the premium, what percent would be used for a policy having a gross premium of $612.00, assuming the same premium would be $581.40 if it were calculated using actually expected assumptions?

11. Calculate the net one-year term premium for an experience rated group's health insurance coverage for males age 40. Use the following data from the experience of that particular group:

Frequency of claim in one year for males age 40 .... .072
Average amount of claim for males age 40 .... $2,860

12. Calculate the loss ratio which the actuary would predict on the policies referred

to in Exercise 11. Assume that the gross one-year term premium for a male age 40 is $298.44.

13. Calculate the company's December 31 liability for the policy in Exercise 12. Assume that one-twelfth of the gross premium is paid on the 15th day of each month, and assume 30 days in each month.

14. Where a group's actual health insurance claims were $1,200,000 and the groups expected claims were $900,000, calculate the amount of claims to use in the year's dividend calculation. The credibility percentage for this group's dividend calculation has been set at 70%.

15. A person has individual comprehensive major medical insurance coverage which provides for a deductible of $100 and a coinsurance feature of 75%. If this person incurs covered medical expenses of $5,473, the insurance company will pay

(1) $1,368.25   (3) $4,029.75
(2) $1,443.25   (4) $4,104.75

CHAPTER SUMMARY

- Health insurance pays a portion of the financial losses (loss of income and expenses of medical treatment) caused by injury or sickness.

- There is more subjectivity in determining morbidity than mortality, and the amount payable for a claim on morbidity is not always as easy to determine as a claim on mortality. Furthermore, the claim experience for morbidity is greatly affected by swings in the economy and inflation.

- Limits are placed on the amount of health insurance sold to one person, so that the benefit will not exceed the loss suffered.

- Health insurance benefits are generally the same whether they are on an individual or a group.

- Insurance that pays benefits when an injury or sickness prevents a person from working is called *disability income insurance*. The benefit is paid in the form of a disabled-life annuity (monthly), wherein each payment is contingent upon the person being alive and still disabled. Such payments begin after the *waiting period* and continue for no longer than the *maximum benefit period*. Premium rates are published for each age, sex, and *occupation class*.

- The four most common categories of medical expenses that are covered in a health insurance policy are: hospital expense, surgical expense, medical (doctor's) expense, and major medical expense (either *supplemental* or *comprehensive*).

- In either type of major medical insurance, the insured person must pay an amount of expenses (called the *deductible*) before the insurance will begin to pay. Furthermore, this insurance pays only a certain percent of the remaining expenses (the *coinsurance feature*). There is also a maximum total amount which this insurance will pay.

- Individual health insurance policies are issued on a level premium basis. Generally, one of the following arrangements is specified:

  1. *Cancellable* (the company can terminate the policy)
  2. *Guaranteed Renewable* (the company cannot terminate the policy but can change the premiums for broad classes)

3. *Noncancellable and Guaranteed Renewable* (the company cannot terminate the policy and cannot change the premium)

- If the person applying has a specific problem that may cause a claim, an individual health policy can be issued with a stipulation that claims resulting from that problem will not be paid.

- Net annual premiums for individual health policies may be net level or modified. The calculation takes into account the fact that there are no nonforfeiture values, resulting in lower premiums than would otherwise be the case.

- *Annual claim costs* are defined as the expected frequency of claim in a year's time multiplied by the average amount of each claim. These are derived from actual experience and form the basis of the net premium calculations.

- Net annual premiums are calculated using the principle that, at the time the policy is issued, the present value of the net premiums is equal to the present value of the benefits.

- Loading is added to the net premium to cover commissions, expenses, taxes, and a generous amount for unforeseen contingencies.

- Many states require that health insurance premiums be reasonable. When policies are first issued, reasonableness is determined by the *anticipated loss ratio* of a group of similar policies, where

$$\text{Anticipated Loss Ratio} = \frac{\text{Present Value of Future Benefits}}{\text{Present Value of Future Gross Premiums}}$$

A common requirement is that the anticipated loss ratio must exceed 50%.

- Reserve factors for individual health policies may be calculated by special commutation functions or by accumulating a fund of a large number of identical hypothetical policies. States generally allow these reserves to be calculated as if the first two years were both one-year term insurance.

- December 31 reserves for individual health policies are generally calculated as being *midterminal reserves* and *unearned premium reserves* (the two parts being shown separately), where:

$$\left(\begin{array}{c}\text{Midterminal}\\\text{Reserve}\end{array}\right) = \frac{(\text{Previous Terminal Reserve}) + (\text{Terminal Reserve})}{2}$$

- In addition, claim reserves must be established (when a claim is reported) which are equal to the present value of anticipated future payments for that claim. For disability income insurance, this is a disabled-life annuity for the monthly payments still to be made for persons who are disabled on the date of the financial statement.

- The *actual loss ratio* for a group of policies for the year is calculated as follows:

$$\text{Actual Loss Ratio} = \frac{\begin{array}{c}(\text{Claim Payments Made})\\+ (\text{Increase in Claim Reserves})\end{array}}{\begin{array}{c}(\text{Premiums Collected})\\- (\text{Increase in Policy Reserves})\end{array}}$$

- It is common to establish a voluntary contingency reserve for health insurance, because the claims are not as easily predictable as for life insurance. A common amount is a reserve of 50% of a year's premium income.

- Dividends on individual health policies are usually quoted as being a percent of the premium, beginning after the policy has been in force for a few years. The annual dividend thereafter would be level. The amount available for a dividend is the difference between the gross premium (calculated using conservative assumptions) and what the premium would have been if calculated using actually expected assumptions.

- The arrangements and calculations for group health insurance generally follow the same principles as explained in Chapter 15 for group life insurance.

- Some states require that first-year group health premiums must be approved by the state. A company operating in New York cannot use first-year premiums in any state lower than those approved by New York.

- Net annual premiums (one-year term) for group health insurance are the same as the annual claim costs defined above. The premiums can be *manually rated*, *experience rated*, or *blended*, as defined in Chapter 15. In addition, it is common to assume that annual claim costs will increase in the future.

- Loading, added to produce gross one-year term premiums, must include the cost of the extra morbidity expected when a person leaves the group and converts to an individual health policy.

- Actual loss ratios for group health insurance are calculated the same as for individual health, except that there is no reference to policy reserves:

$$\text{Actual Loss Ratio} = \frac{\begin{array}{c}\text{(Claim Payments Made)} \\ + \text{ (Increase in Claim Reserves)}\end{array}}{\text{(Premiums Collected)}}$$

- December 31 reserves for group health insurance are generally unearned premium reserves plus a reserve for those who are actually receiving disability income or medical benefits plus a voluntary contingency reserve (often 50% of a year's premium income).

- As with group life insurance, the amount available in group health insurance for a dividend each year is found by calculating the accumulated financial position of the particular group to date, and the amount of claims to be used is calculated using the *credibility percentage*.

LEARNING OBJECTIVES

After reading this chapter, the student should know

- How morbidity differs from mortality.
- The principal differences between life insurance and health insurance.
- The principal types of health insurance coverage.
- What requirements must be met in order to receive disability income benefits.
- What is meant by the *waiting period* and the *maximum benefit period*.
- What breakdowns are generally used to quote premium rates for different types of health insurance.
- What is meant by *supplemental*, *comprehensive*, *deductible*, and *coinsurance* in connection with major medical insurance.

- What is meant by individual health policies being *cancellable, guaranteed renewable*, or *noncancellable and guaranteed renewable*.

- How individual health policies may be issued to persons with problems that may lead to a claim.

- How premiums are calculated for individual health insurance policies.

- What is meant by *annual claim costs*.

- How loss ratios are calculated for health insurance.

- How reserves are calculated for the December 31 financial statement for individual health insurance policies.

- How dividends are calculated for individual health policies.

- How premiums are calculated for group health insurance.

- How reserves are calculated for group health insurance.

- How dividends are calculated for group health insurance.

Glossary

These words and phrases are described in the way they are used in this text. *Many of them have other meanings in other contexts.*

Accidental Death Benefit—Insurance which promises to pay money when death occurs because of an accident (as defined by the policy).

Accumulated Cost of Insurance—The amount which would have to be paid at the end of the term of coverage (by the survivors) to provide the death benefits for those who had died during the term.

Accumulated Value—The total of the amount of money originally invested plus the interest.

Accumulation Factor—The number to be multiplied by the amount of money paid now, to derive the accumulated value of that money. (May be calculated with interest only or with benefit of survivorship.)

Acquisition Expenses—Additional expenses incurred in a policy's first year, related to selling and issuing the policy.

Actuary—A person who deals with contingent events, that is, finds probabilities and uses probabilities to make calculations and forecasts.

Adjusted Premiums—Special premiums (greater than net premiums) which are defined in the Standard Nonforfeiture Law and are used in calculating the legal minimum cash values.

Agent—A person who represents a life insurance company for the purpose of selling the company's contracts.

Amortize—To repay a debt by means of regular periodic payments.

Amortization Payments—Regular periodic payments made for the purpose of repaying a debt.

Annual Claim Costs—Frequency of a health claim in a year multiplied by the average amount of each claim; same as net one-year term premium.

Annuity—A series of payments made or received at regular intervals of time.

Annuity Certain—A series of payments involving a fixed number of such payments.

Annuity Due—A series of payments in which the payments are made at the beginning of each interval of time.

Annuity Factor—The present value at age x of a temporary life annuity of 1.

Annuity Immediate—A series of payments in which the payments are made at the end of each interval of time.

Annuity Mortality Table—A tabulation of probabilities of dying at each age for use with contracts where benefits are paid only if a designated person is alive.

Assets—Things of value owned.

Asset Share—The actual amount which it is forecast will have accumulated at any given time from a policy.

Assumptions—The particular mortality and interest bases used to calculate premiums and reserves.

Attained Age—The current age at the time of calculation, that is, the age at the time the policy was issued plus the number of years elapsed since the policy was issued.

Average Yearly Cost—A cost comparison figure representing the average yearly cost of a policy, calculated with the traditional method (involves premiums, dividends, and cash values).

Average Yearly Payment—A cost comparison figure representing the average yearly payment for a policy, calculated with the traditional method (involves premiums and dividends).

Band Grading—Treating policies as groups according to face amounts for the purpose of calculating loading.

Base—A number which has an exponent appearing at the upper right. (See also *exponent.*)

Beneficiary—The person who is named to receive the benefits of a policy upon the death of the person who is insured.

Benefit of Survivorship—Describes the fact that payments made to surviving persons include a portion of the shares which are forfeited by those in the original group who did not survive.

Blended—Describes group premiums calculated partly on the manually rated approach and partly on the experience rated approach.

Bond—A certificate of indebtedness agreeing to reimburse the purchaser and pay periodic interest.

Canadian Method—A method prescribed in Canada for calculating modified net premiums and reserves.

Cancellable—Describes individual health policies which can be terminated by the company.

Cash Refund Option—A settlement method in which the insurance company makes a series of equal payments for as long as the recipient lives; if the recipient dies before the total payments equal the proceeds of the policy, the balance is paid at once.

Cash Values—The amounts, as printed in a policy, which the insurance company guarantees to pay in cash if a person voluntarily terminates the policy.

Certain Payment—A payment which will definitely be made under any circumstances, its payment not being contingent upon any predesignated condition.

Coinsurance Feature—Refers to the situation where health insurance pays a certain percent of expenses.

Commissioners Method—A method prescribed in the United States for calculating modified net premiums and reserves.

Commissions—The amounts of money paid to the agents for selling insurance policies (almost always calculated as a percentage of the premium).

Common Multiplier—A number which is being multiplied by each of several other numbers.

Commutation Functions—Symbols representing a combination of mortality-table figures and interest-table figures, used to simplify calculations of annuities, premiums, and reserves.

Company Retention Method—A cost comparison method wherein the present value of premiums, cash values, and dividends is calculated by weighting each item each year by the probability that it will be paid.

Complementary Probabilities—Two probabilities whose total equals 1.

Compound—To add interest to the amount invested, so that this interest may earn interest.

Compound Interest—Interest which is earned upon previous interest.

Comprehensive Major Medical—Medical insurance that pays benefits toward most medical expenses not covered by any regular hospital, surgical, or medical insurance.

Conservative Mortality Table—Describes rates of mortality that are higher than expected if used for life insurance calculations or lower than expected if used for annuity calculations.

Contingencies—Events which are possible but may or may not actually happen.

Contingency Reserves—Voluntary reserves (liabilities) established by insurance companies to help pay unexpectedly large claim amounts.

Contingent Payment—A payment which will be made only if some predesignated condition is met, such as the recipient being alive.

Contributory—A kind of arrangement where members of an insured group share the cost of their insurance.

Conversion Privilege—The promise that a person may change the insurance to another type, in certain prescribed situations.

Coupon—A detachable portion of a bond, which may be presented on or after a specified date to receive interest payments.

Coupon Bond—A bond wherein the promised interest is represented in the form of coupons to be detached.

Credibility Percentage—The percentage of a blended group insurance premium which is represented by the experience rated approach; or the percentage of claims used in a group dividend which is represented by actual claims.

Current Settlement Option Rates—Special settlement option rates quoted for new settlement options when payments begin during periods of very high interest rates.

Death Benefit—The amount of the payment to be made when a designated insured person dies.

Death Claims—The amounts of money which are actually paid out by an insurance company because of deaths under its life insurance policies.

Decimal Form—A form of writing numbers in which numbers to the right of the decimal point constitute a fraction with a value of less than 1.

Decimal Places—The number of digits appearing to the right of a decimal point in a number.

Deductible—The first dollars of expenses that must be paid by the insured person before the health insurance will begin to pay for expenses.

Deferred Annuity—A series of payments which has its first payment postponed for one or more periods. It also refers to an annuity contract where premiums are accumulated at interest and then used to provide a life annuity.

Deferred Life Annuity—A series of payments, each of which is made only if a designated person is alive, with the first payment postponed one or more periods.

Disability—Inability to work due to an injury or sickness.

Disability Benefits—Benefits which are payable periodically while the insured continues to be disabled. "Being disabled" is generally defined in terms of inability to work.

Disability Income Insurance—Insurance that pays a monthly benefit if the person insured is unable to work due to an injury or sickness.

Disability Table—A tabulation of the probabilities of becoming disabled at each age, plus certain related figures. A second kind of disability table is a tabulation of the number of persons who are still disabled at each age and the duration of disability, plus certain related figures.

Disabled Life Annuities—A series of payments, each of which is contingent on a person being alive and still disabled.

Discounting (as used in this text)—Finding the present value at a specified rate of interest of an amount due in the future.

Dividend Credits—The values resulting from dividends having been left with the company under a dividend option; the values are available to be used (along with the cash value) under the nonforfeiture options.

Dividend Expenses—The amount which a company chooses to use in calculating dividends, as representing its present year's cost for maintaining a certain policy in force.

Dividend Interest Rate—The interest rate which a company chooses to use in calculating dividends, as repesenting the actual rate being earned on its present investments.

Dividend Options—The various ways in which a policyowner may choose to receive the dividends from the policy.

Dividend Rate of Mortality—The rate of mortality (for a given age) which a company chooses to use in calculating dividends; it represents the mortality rate currently experienced by a company on its own insurance.

Dividends (as used in this text)—That part of the profits, or savings from operations, which is returned to the owner of a participating policy each year.

Dual Interest Rates—The use of two different rates of interest over the time span involved, one rate for part of the period and the second rate for the remainder of the period.

EDP—The letters stand for "electronic data processing" and refer to computers or their use.

Effective Interest Rate—An annual interest rate which produces the same accumulated values as the nominal rate compounded more frequently than annually.

Elimination Period—The period of time after an insured person becomes disabled before disability income payments begin.

Endowment Insurance—Insurance which provides a benefit (1) if death occurs during a specified number of years or (2) if, at the end of the specified number of years, the person is then alive.

Enhancement Type Policies—Policies in which part of each dividend provides paid-up additions and part provides one-year term insurance to produce a predetermined total death benefit.

Equation—A statement that two expressions are equal to each other.

Equity—Fairness, in the sense that each person gets benefits in proportion to his or her contribution.

Equivalent Level Annual Dividend—A level annual amount, a series of which has the same accumulated value as a policy's dividends.

Equivalent Rates—Two interest rates which produce the same accumulated value in the same period of time.

Equivalent Single Payment—One payment which can replace several other payments, because it equals the value of the other payments.

Evaluation Date—The date as of which the accumulated value or present value is being calculated.

Excess Interest—Amounts of interest above the guaranteed amounts that companies pay on settlement options when interest rates are high.

Expected Mortality—Means the same as *tabular cost of insurance.*

Experience Premiums—Special annual premiums which are calculated using dividend rates of mortality and expenses but the tabular rate of interest.

Experience-Premium Method—A method for calculating dividends, wherein a basic amount is calculated (difference between gross premium and experience premium), to which the year's contribution from interest is added.

Experience Rated—Describes group premiums calculated using the claim experience of the particular group which pays those premiums.

Experience Refunds—Amounts paid by nonparticipating insurance companies on group insurance, calculated in the same way as a dividend.

Exponent—A number appearing at the upper right of another number, indicating how many times this other number (known as the *base*) is multiplied by itself. The exponent is also called the *power* to which the base is raised.

Extended Term Insurance—A nonforfeiture option in which the full amount of insurance continues in effect but for a shorter period of time, and no more premiums are payable.

Face Amount—The amount of the death benefit in a life insurance policy.

Factoring—Removing a common multiplier from several numbers, that is, writing the expression as the common multiplier times a quantity.

Factors—Those numbers which, when multiplied together, equal a certain specified number.

Fifth Dividend Option—The use of the policy dividend (or part thereof) to purchase one-year term insurance.

Fixed Payment Option—A settlement option in which the company pays out a series of equal payments of a certain amount, such as $100 per year.

Fixed Period Option—A settlement option in which the company pays out a series of equal payments for a certain period of time only, such as for ten years.

Formula—An equation that expresses the method used to calculate a certain desired value.

Fractional Premiums—Premiums which are paid in installments over each year, such as semiannually, quarterly, or monthly.

Full Preliminary Term Method—A method for calculating modified net premiums and reserves, wherein the first year of insurance is considered to be one year term insurance.

Fully Contributory—A kind of arrangement where members of a group pay the entire cost of their insurance.

GAAP Reserves—Reserves which are calculated in accordance with "generally accepted accounting principles" as defined by the American Institute of Certified Public Accountants.

Graduation—A mathematical process to smooth out an observed series of numbers so that the series more nearly represents the average expected results.

Gross Premium—The actual amount to be paid by the policyowner for life insurance, calculated to include the net premium plus loading.

Group Insurance—Insurance which is granted to members of a group under a master policy.

Group Permanent—Group life insurance which is issued on an other-than-term arrangement, such as on ordinary life.

Guaranteed Renewable—Describes individual health policies which an insurance company cannot terminate, but upon which the company can change the premium rates for broad classes.

Hospital Expense Insurance—Insurance which pays a benefit toward daily hospital room and other hospital charges.

Individual Insurance—Insurance which is issued to an individual person, as contrasted with group insurance.

Initial Reserve—The reserve on a policy at the beginning of any given policy year, which includes the net annual premium then due.

Installment Refund Option—A settlement option in which the insurance company guarantees a series of equal payments until such time as the total paid out equals the proceeds of the policy; thereafter, the payments will continue only as long as the original recipient lives.

Insurance Mortality Table—A tabulation (for use with insurance contracts) of the probabilities of dying at each age.

Insured—The person whose death (or disability) is the subject of the insurance.

Interest—Money which is paid for the use of money.

Interest-Adjusted Cost—A figure representing the average yearly cost of a policy, calculated using the interest-adjusted method (involves premiums, dividends, and cash values).

Interest-Adjusted Method—A cost or payment comparison method wherein dividends are accumulated at interest to give greater weight to earlier dividends.

Interest-Adjusted Payment—A figure representing the average yearly payment for a policy, calculated using the interest-adjusted method (involves premiums and dividends).

Interest Conversion Period—The period of time between interest compoundings.

Interest Option—A settlement option under which the insurance company holds the proceeds of a policy and periodically pays out the interest thereon.

Interest Rate—The percentage by which an amount of money is multiplied to derive the amount paid for the use of that money.

Invest—To lay out money in the expectation of receiving interest or other gain therefrom.

Investment—The property or rights which are acquired in the expectation of receiving interest or other gain therefrom; or the money laid out to acquire such property or rights; or the act of so laying out money.

Lapse—Termination of an insurance policy because premiums were not paid.

Liabilities—Amounts owed or to be paid in the future.

Life Annuity—A series of payments at regular intervals, each of which is made only if a designated person is then alive.

Life Income Option—A settlement option in which the insurance company pays out a series of equal payments for as long as the recipient lives.

Life Income Option with Period Certain—A settlement option in which the insurance company guarantees a series of equal payments for a designated period of time, such as ten years; thereafter, the payments will continue only as long as the original recipient lives.

Life Income Option with Refund—A settlement option in which the insurance company pays out a series of equal payments until such time as the total paid out equals the proceeds of the policy; thereafter, the payments will continue only as long as the original recipient lives.

Linton Yield Method—A cost comparison method wherein the key figure calculated is an annual interest rate, representing a rate of return. (The method is also called the *Rate of Return Method*.)

Loading—An amount which is added to net premiums to provide for expenses and adverse contingencies.

Loss Limit—The maximum amount for any one claim which is allowed to enter the calculation of group dividends.

Loss of Time Insurance—The same as disability income insurance.

Loss Ratio—A ratio calculated for health insurance business which is intended, in general, to represent the ratio of claims to premiums. Such ratio may be either anticipated (calculated at time of issue) or actual (calculated using actual experience).

Major Medical Insurance—Insurance which pays a stipulated percentage (such as 80%) of hospital, surgical, and medical bills, after first deducting certain amounts, with an upper limit on benefits.

Manually Rated—Describes group premiums calculated using the claim experience of a number of average groups.

Mature (as an Endowment)—Describes the situation where the endowment amount becomes due and payable at the end of the contract period or earlier by the use of dividends.

Maximum Benefit Period—The maximum length of time for which disability income payments continue to be made.

Mean Reserve—The average of the initial and terminal reserves of a policy in any given policy year.

Medical Expense Insurance—Insurance which pays benefits toward doctors' bills.

Midterminal Reserve—The average of a policy's terminal reserve at the beginning of the policy year and the end of the policy year.

Modified Net Premiums—Net premiums which are other than level, generally being lower for the first year than for subsequent years.

Modified Reserves—Reserves calculated using modified net premiums.

Morbidity—Sickness, disability, or failure of health.

Mortality Rate—The probability of dying within one year after attaining a specified age.

Mortality Table—A tabulation of the probabilities of dying at each age, plus certain related figures.

National Association of Insurance Commissioners (NAIC)—An organization composed of the insurance supervisory authorities (commissioners) of each of the states.

Net Amount at Risk—That portion of a policy's death benefit which exceeds its terminal reserve.

Net Cost—For individual insurance, net cost is any one of several different figures used to indicate the cost of an insurance policy; for group insurance, net cost is the premiums less the dividends.

Net Level Annual Premium—A net premium which stays the same each year during the premium-payment period.

Net Level Premium Reserve—The amount of liability which an insurance company establishes for a policy, calculated using net level annual premiums.

Net Payment Cost Index—A figure representing the average yearly payment for a policy, calculated using the interest-adjusted method (involves premiums and dividends).

Net Premium—An amount necessary to provide insurance benefits, calculated by using the assumed rate of interest and the tabular mortality rate.

Net Single Premium—A net premium of an amount equal to the present value of death and endowment benefits.

Nominal Interest Rate—An annual interest rate which is quoted with the understanding that interest is compounded more than once a year.

Noncancellable and Guaranteed Renewable—Describes individual health policies which the company cannot terminate and on which the premiums cannot be changed.

Noncontributory—The arrangement where members of an insured group pay nothing themselves for their insurance.

Nonforfeiture Factors—Special values, similar to annual premiums, which some companies calculate and use for deriving cash values.

Nonforfeiture Values—The benefits, as printed in the policy, which the insurance company guarantees if a policyowner stops paying premiums. These amounts may be used in a variety of options.

Nonparticipating—A type of insurance or annuity in which the policyowner does not receive any policy dividends.

Occupation Class—A group of occupations that use the same premium rates for health insurance.

Operations Research—Using mathematical techniques to explore the effect that certain events or courses of action would have on the company's operations.

Option—A choice which a policyower can make about settlements, dividends, or nonforfeiture values.

Ordinary Life Policy—An insurance policy on which premiums are payable for the person's entire life, and which provides a benefit whenever death occurs.

Paid-Up—Describes an insurance policy that provides benefits in the future but requires no further premium payments.

Paid-Up Additions—Additional insurance purchased from policy dividends, with no premiums payable on this insurance.

Participating—A type of insurance or annuity on which policy dividends are paid.

Payment Certain—A payment which is not contingent on any predesignated condition.

Percent—Hundredths—for example, 3 percent means $\frac{3}{100}$ or .03.

Policy Charge—An amount which a company may include in the gross premium each year. This amount is the same regardless of the size of the policy. (A *policy charge* is sometimes called a *policy fee*.)

Policy Loan—Borrowing from the insurance company (by the policyowner) for an amount that does not exceed the policy's cash value.

Policyowner—The person who actually controls the policy and has all of its rights and privileges as long as it is in force (not necessarily the same person whose life is insured).

Policy Reserve—Amount which an insurance company is required by law to establish as a liability for each policy at any given time.

Policy Year—The period of time between a policy's anniversaries.

Pre-existing Condition—A sickness or injury which began or happened before health insurance was issued.

Premium Deficiency Reserve—Refers to the special requirements for calculating reserves when the gross premium is less than the net premium.

Present Value—The amount of money which must be invested on the evaluation date in order to accumulate to a specified amount at a later date.

Present Value Factor—The number by which the amount of money to be paid later is multiplied in order to derive the present value of that money on the evaluation date. (May be calculated with interest only or with benefit of survivorship.)

Probability—The likelihood of some event occurring.

Proceeds—The amount of money which the insurance company is obligated to pay for the settlement of a policy (death benefit, endowment benefit, or cash value).

Prospective Method—A method of calculating reserves by looking to the future: The terminal reserve equals the present value of future benefits minus the present value of future net premiums.

Pure Endowment—An amount which is paid at the end of the endowment period only if a designated person is then alive.

Quantity—That which is included inside a pair of parentheses or brackets.

Rate Making—Calculating gross premiums for group life or health insurance.

Rate of Return Method—A cost comparison method wherein the key figure calculated is an annual interest rate, representing a rate of return. (This method is also called the *Linton Yield Method*.)

Rating Classes—The three different approaches to mortality assumptions in group premium calculation (manually rated, experience rated, and blended).

Reduced Paid-Up Insurance—A nonforfeiture option in which the insurance continues in effect for a smaller amount with no more premiums payable.

Reducing Fractions—Dividing the numerator and denominator by the same number without changing the value of the fraction.

Retirement Annuity—A contract where amounts paid to the company (minus amounts needed for expenses) are accumulated at interest until such time as the accumulation is used to provide a life annuity.

Retroactive Rate Reduction—Also called an *experience refund*, it is a refund of part of the premium paid for group insurance, similar to a policy dividend.

Retrospective Method—A method for calculating reserves by using past occurrences: The terminal reserve equals the accumulated value of net premiums received minus the accumulated cost of insurance.

Rider—An agreement providing separate benefits and premiums which is attached to a basic insurance policy.

Scatter Diagram—Graphs of observed data before being smoothed or graduated.

Select and Ultimate Mortality Table—A tabulation of basic mortality information during the *select period* and the period beyond it.

Select Mortality Table—A mortality table for the *select period.*

Select Period—The period of years during which there is a significant difference in mortality rates between persons whose good health was proved at the beginning of the period and other persons of the same age.

Setback—The number of years subtracted from the true age in insurance calculations.

Settlement Option Payments—Periodic payments made by an insurance company in lieu of an immediate lump-sum settlement of a policy.

Settlement Option Table—A tabulation of the various amounts which the insurance company is willing to pay as periodic payments in the settlement of a policy.

Sinking Fund—A fund which is being accumulated by periodic payments for the purpose of attaining a certain amount by a certain date.

Sinking Fund Payment—A regular periodic payment into a sinking fund.

Spread of Risk—Having a large enough number of healthy persons insured to offset the few unhealthy ones.

Standard Nonforfeiture Law—A law, which is virtually uniform in all states, specifying minimum cash values.

Standard Risk—An average risk not subject to higher premiums or restrictions because of poor health.

Standard Valuation Law—A law, which is virtually uniform in all states, specifying minimum standards for calculating insurance reserves.

Statutory Reserves—Reserves which are reported to government authorities, as required by statutes.

Subscript—A part of a symbol appearing at the lower right of the main part of the symbol.

Substandard Risk—A risk with insurable qualifications below the standard of risks on which the premium for the coverage was based.

Supplemental Major Medical—Major medical insurance providing benefits over and above those benefits paid by basic hospital, surgical, and medical coverage.

Surgical Expense Insurance—Insurance which pays a benefit toward a surgeon's fee for performing operations.

Surrender Charge—An amount which is deducted from a policy's reserve to arrive at its cash value.

Surrender Cost Index—A figure used in cost comparisons representing the average yearly cost of a policy. It is calculated using the interest-adjusted method (involves premiums, dividends, and cash values).

Tabular Cost of Insurance—The contribution which must be made by each of those insured in order to make up the full amount of the death claims payable in any year, according to the particular mortality table which is being used to calculate reserves.

Tabular Cost of Insurance Based on the Net Amount at Risk—Refers to a method of calculating the tabular cost of insurance by multiplying the net amount at risk by the mortality rate. (It means the same thing as *tabular cost of insurance*.)

Tabular Interest Rate—The interest rate which is used in calculating the policy's reserves.

Tabular Rate of Mortality—The rate of mortality (for a given age) shown in the mortality table which is used in calculating the policy's reserves.

Temporary Life Annuity—A series of payments, each of which is made only if a designated person is then alive, with the number of such payments limited to a specified number. Each such payment is made at the *end* of an interval of time.

Temporary Life Annuity Due—A series of payments, each of which is made only if a designated person is then alive, with the number of such payments limited to a specified number. Each such payment is made at the *beginning* of an interval of time.

Term Insurance—Insurance which provides a benefit only if death occurs during a specified period.

Terminal Reserve—The reserve on a policy at the end of any given policy year.

Three-Factor Contribution Method—A method for calculating policy dividends, considering separately the contributions arising from interest, mortality, and expenses.

Traditional Method—A cost comparison method wherein total dividends are used in the calculation without any reference to the timing of the dividend payments.

Ultimate Mortality Table—A mortality table covering years beyond the *select period*.

Unearned Premium Reserve—A liability equal to the portion of the premium which is not yet " used up" as of the date of the financial statement.

Validation Period—The period of time required for a block of policies to become profitable after they are issued, as shown by an asset share calculation.

Valuation Premium—The net annual premium used to calculate reserves (most often used to describe the GAAP net premium).

Waiting Period—Generally, this means the same as *elimination period*.

Whole Life Annuity—A series of payments, each of which is made only if a designated person is then alive, with the payments continuing for that person's entire lifetime. Each such payment is made at the *end* of an interval of time.

Whole Life Annuity Due—A series of payments, each of which is made only if a designated person is then alive, with the payments continuing for that person's entire lifetime. Each such payment is made at the *beginning* of an interval of time.

Whole Life Insurance—Insurance which provides a benefit whenever death occurs.

With Benefit of Survivorship—Describes the fact that payments made to surviving persons include a portion of the shares which are forfeited by those of the original group who did not survive.

Withdrawal—Voluntarily terminating the insurance contract.

Yield Rate—The interest rate which the purchaser of a bond will actually realize on the investment.

List of Equations

The number in parentheses refers to the section where the equation is first presented.

(3.1) Expression for the accumulated value of money invested:

$$S = A + I$$

(3.1) Expression for the amount of interest earned in 1 period:

$$I = Ai$$

(3.1) Expression for the accumulated value at the end of 1 period:

$$S = A(1 + i)$$

(3.2) Expression for the accumulated value at the end of n periods:

$$S = A(1 + i)^n$$

(3.5) Equation for calculating the effective rate of interest corresponding to a given nominal rate (in a decimal form):

$$\text{Effective Rate (decimal)} = (1 + i)^n - 1$$

(3.5) Equation for calculating the effective rate of interest corresponding to a given nominal rate (in percentage form):

$$\text{Effective Rate (\%)} = [(1 + i)^n - 1]100$$

(4.2) Expression for the symbol, $s_{\overline{n}|i}$:

$$s_{\overline{n}|i} = (1 + i)^{n-1} + (1 + i)^{n-2} + \cdots + (1 + i)^2 + (1 + i)^1 + 1$$

(4.3) Equation for calculating values of $s_{\overline{n}|i}$ when n is larger than shown in the table (25 in this case):

$$s_{\overline{n}|i} = s_{\overline{25}|i} + s_{\overline{n-25}|i}(1 + i)^{25}$$

(4.4) Expression for the symbol, $\ddot{s}_{\overline{n}|i}$:

$$\ddot{s}_{\overline{n}|i} = (1 + i)^n + (1 + i)^{n-1} + \cdots + (1 + i)^2 + (1 + i)^1$$

(4.4) Relationship between accumulated values of an annuity due and an annuity immediate:

$$\ddot{s}_{\overline{n}|i} = (1 + i)s_{\overline{n}|i}$$

(4.4) Another expression for the relationship between the accumulated values of an annuity due and an annuity immediate:

$$\ddot{s}_{\overline{n}|i} = s_{\overline{n+1}|i} - 1$$

(4.5) Equation for calculating a sinking fund payment (made at the end of each period):

$$\left(\begin{array}{c}\text{Sinking Fund}\\\text{Payment}\end{array}\right) = \frac{\text{Accumulated Value}}{s_{\overline{n}|i}}$$

(4.5) Equation for calculating a sinking fund payment (made at the beginning of each period):

$$\left(\begin{array}{c}\text{Sinking Fund}\\\text{Payment}\end{array}\right) = \frac{\text{Accumulated Value}}{\ddot{s}_{\overline{n}|i}}$$

(5.2) Expression for the present value n periods earlier:

$$\frac{S}{(1 + i)^n} = A$$

(5.2) Another expression for the present value n periods earlier:

$$A = Sv^n$$

(5.3) Equation for calculating values of v^n at i when n is larger than shown in the table (25 in this case):

$$v^n \text{ at } i = v^{25} \text{ at } i \times v^{n-25} \text{ at } i$$

(5.4) Expression for the symbol, $a_{\overline{n}|i}$:

$$a_{\overline{n}|i} = v + v^2 + \cdots + v^{n-1} + v^n$$

(5.5) Relationship between successive values of $a_{\overline{n}|i}$:

$$a_{\overline{n+1}|i} = a_{\overline{n}|i} + v^{n+1}$$

(5.5) Equation for calculating values of $a_{\overline{n}|i}$ when n is larger than shown in the table (25 in this case):

$$a_{\overline{n}|i} = a_{\overline{25}|i} + a_{\overline{n-25}|i}v^{25}$$

(5.6) Expression for the symbol, $\ddot{a}_{\overline{n}|i}$:

$$\ddot{a}_{\overline{n}|i} = 1 + v + v^2 + \cdots + v^{n-2} + v^{n-1}$$

(5.6) Relationship between the present value of an annuity due and an annuity immediate:

$$\ddot{a}_{\overline{n}|i} = (1 + i)a_{\overline{n}|i}$$

(5.6) Another expression for the relationship between the present value of an annuity due and an annuity immediate:

$$\ddot{a}_{\overline{n}|i} = a_{\overline{n-1}|i} + 1$$

(6.2) Equation for calculating amortization payment (made at the end of each period):

$$\left(\begin{array}{c}\text{Amortization}\\\text{Payment}\end{array}\right) = \frac{\text{Present Value}}{a_{\overline{n}|i}}$$

(6.2) **Equation** for calculating amortization payment (made at the beginning of each period):

$$\left(\begin{array}{c}\text{Amortization}\\\text{Payment}\end{array}\right) = \frac{\text{Present Value}}{\ddot{a}_{\overline{n}|i}}$$

(6.6) Relationship between the present value and the accumulated value of an annuity:

$$s_{\overline{n}|i} = a_{\overline{n}|i}(1 + i)^n$$

(6.6) Another expression for the relationship between the present value and the accumulated value of an annuity:

$$a_{\overline{n}|i} = s_{\overline{n}|i}v^n$$

(7.4) Relationship between successive values of l_x:

$$l_{x+1} = l_x - d_x$$

(7.4) Equation for calculating values of d_x:

$$d_x = l_x q_x$$

(7.4) Equation for calculating values of q_x:

$$\frac{d_x}{l_x} = q_x$$

(7.6) Equation for calculating values of p_x:

$$p_x = \frac{l_{x+1}}{l_x}$$

(7.6) Relationship between p_x and q_x:

$$p_x + q_x = 1$$

(7.6) Equation for calculating values of $_np_x$:

$$_np_x = \frac{l_{x+n}}{l_x}$$

(7.6) Equation for calculating values of $_nq_x$:

$$_nq_x = \frac{l_x - l_{x+n}}{l_x}$$

(7.6) Relationship between $_np_x$ and $_nq_x$:

$$_np_x + _nq_x = 1$$

(8.1) Expression for the present value n years earlier, with benefit of survivorship:

$$\begin{pmatrix} \text{Present Value of \$1} \\ \text{Due in } n \text{ Years to a} \\ \text{Life Now Age } x, \text{ with} \\ \text{Benefit of Survivorship} \end{pmatrix} = \$1 \left(\frac{l_{x+n} v^n}{l_x} \right)$$

(8.2) Relationship between the present value of a whole life annuity due and a whole life annuity immediate:

$$\begin{pmatrix} \text{Present Value at Age } x \\ \text{of Whole Life Annuity Due} \end{pmatrix} = \begin{pmatrix} \text{Present Value at Age } x \\ \text{of Whole Life Annuity} \end{pmatrix} + 1$$

(8.2) Relationship between the present value of a temporary life annuity due and a temporary life annuity immediate:

$$\begin{pmatrix} \text{Present Value at Age } x \\ \text{of } n\text{-Year Life Annuity Due} \end{pmatrix} = \begin{pmatrix} \text{Present Value at Age } x \\ \text{of } (n-1)\text{-Year Life Annuity} \end{pmatrix} + 1$$

(8.2) Relationship between temporary, deferred, and whole life annuities:

$$\begin{pmatrix} \text{Present Value at Age } x \\ \text{of } n\text{-Year Temporary} \\ \text{Life Annuity} \end{pmatrix} + \begin{pmatrix} \text{Present Value at Age } x \\ \text{of Life Annuity} \\ \text{Deferred } n \text{ Years} \end{pmatrix} = \begin{pmatrix} \text{Present Value at Age } x \\ \text{of Whole Life} \\ \text{Annuity} \end{pmatrix}$$

(8.3) Expression for the accumulated value at the end of n years, with benefit of survivorship:

$$\begin{pmatrix} \text{Accumulated Value of \$1} \\ \text{at End of } n \text{ Years to a} \\ \text{Life Age } x \text{ at the Beginning,} \\ \text{with Benefit of Survivorship} \end{pmatrix} = \$1 \left[\frac{l_x(1+i)^n}{l_{x+n}} \right]$$

(8.5) Definition of the commutation symbol, D_x:

$$D_x = l_x v^x$$

(8.5) Expression for the present value, n years earlier, with benefit of survivorship (using commutation functions):

$$\begin{pmatrix} \text{Present Value of \$1} \\ \text{Due in } n \text{ Years to a} \\ \text{Life Now Age } x, \text{ with} \\ \text{Benefit of Survivorship} \end{pmatrix} = \$1 \left(\frac{D_{x+n}}{D_x} \right)$$

(8.5) Expression for the accumulated value at the end of n years, with benefit of survivorship (using commutation functions):

$$\begin{pmatrix} \text{Accumulated Value of \$1} \\ \text{at End of } n \text{ Years to a} \\ \text{Life Age } x \text{ at the Beginning,} \\ \text{with Benefit of Survivorship} \end{pmatrix} = \$1 \left(\frac{D_x}{D_{x+n}} \right)$$

(8.5) Definition of the commutation symbol, N_x:

$$N_x = (D_x + D_{x+1} + D_{x+2} + \cdots \text{ to end of the mortality table})$$

(9.1) Expression for the net single premium for one-year term insurance:

$$\begin{pmatrix} \text{Net Single Premium for} \\ \text{\$1,000 Death Benefit} \\ \text{to a Life Age } x, \text{ for} \\ \text{One Year of Insurance} \end{pmatrix} = \$1,000 \left(\frac{d_x v}{l_x} \right)$$

(9.4) Expression for the net single premium for a pure endowment:

$$\begin{pmatrix} \text{Net Single Premium for} \\ \text{\$1,000 Pure Endowment to} \\ \text{a Life Age } x, \text{ Due at the} \\ \text{End of } n \text{ Years} \end{pmatrix} = \$1,000 \left(\frac{l_{x+n} v^n}{l_x} \right)$$

(9.7) Definition of the commutation symbol, C_x:

$$C_x = d_x v^{x+1}$$

(9.7) Expression for the net single premium for one-year term insurance (using commutation functions):

$$\begin{pmatrix} \text{Net Single Premium for} \\ \text{\$1,000 Death Benefit} \\ \text{to a Life Age } x, \text{ if} \\ \text{Death Occurs in One Year} \end{pmatrix} = \$1,000 \left(\frac{C_x}{D_x} \right)$$

(9.7) Definition of the commutation symbol, M_x:

$$M_x = (C_x + C_{x+1} + C_{x+2} + \cdots \text{ to the end of the mortality table})$$

(10.5) Relationship between net premiums and life annuities:

$$\begin{pmatrix} \text{Net Annual} \\ \text{Premium} \end{pmatrix} \begin{pmatrix} \text{Annuity} \\ \text{Factor} \end{pmatrix} = \begin{pmatrix} \text{Net Single} \\ \text{Premium} \end{pmatrix}$$

(10.5) Another expression for the relationship between net premiums and life annuities:

$$\begin{pmatrix} \text{Net Annual} \\ \text{Premium} \end{pmatrix} = \frac{\begin{pmatrix} \text{Net Single} \\ \text{Premium} \end{pmatrix}}{\begin{pmatrix} \text{Annuity} \\ \text{Factor} \end{pmatrix}}$$

(10.7) Relationship between net and gross premiums and loading:

Gross Premium − Net Premium = Loading

(10.7) Another expression for the relationship between net and gross premiums and loading:

Net Premium + Loading = Gross Premium

(10.7) A simple equation that might be used to calculate gross annual premiums:

Gross = Net + Percent of Gross

(10.7) Another equation that might be used to calculate gross **annual premiums:**

Gross = Net + Constant + Percent of Gross

(11.2) Expression for the retrospective method of calculating **terminal reserves:**

$$\begin{pmatrix}\text{Terminal}\\\text{Reserve}\end{pmatrix} = \begin{pmatrix}\text{Accumulated Value}\\\text{of Net Premiums}\\\text{Received}\end{pmatrix} - \begin{pmatrix}\text{Accumulated}\\\text{Cost of}\\\text{Insurance}\end{pmatrix}$$

(11.3) Expression for the prospective method of calculating terminal **reserves:**

$$\begin{pmatrix}\text{Terminal}\\\text{Reserve}\end{pmatrix} = \begin{pmatrix}\text{Present Value}\\\text{of Future Benefits}\end{pmatrix} - \begin{pmatrix}\text{Present Value of}\\\text{Future Net Premiums}\end{pmatrix}$$

(12.1) Expression for the mean reserve:

$$\text{Mean Reserve} = \frac{\text{Initial Reserve} + \text{Terminal Reserve}}{2}$$

(12.1) Another expression for the mean reserve:

$$\text{Mean Reserve} = \frac{\begin{array}{c}\text{Net Premium} + \text{Previous Terminal Reserve}\\ + \text{Terminal Reserve}\end{array}}{2}$$

(12.2) Definition of the net amount at risk:

$$\begin{pmatrix}\text{Net Amount}\\\text{at Risk}\end{pmatrix} = \begin{pmatrix}\text{Amount of}\\\text{Insurance}\end{pmatrix} - \begin{pmatrix}\text{Terminal}\\\text{Reserve}\end{pmatrix}$$

(12.3) An equation for calculating the tabular cost of insurance:

$$\begin{pmatrix}\text{Tabular Cost}\\\text{of Insurance}\end{pmatrix} = \begin{pmatrix}\text{Initial}\\\text{Reserve}\end{pmatrix}(1 + i) - \begin{pmatrix}\text{Terminal}\\\text{Reserve}\end{pmatrix}$$

(12.3) A second equation for calculating the tabular cost of insurance:

$$\begin{pmatrix}\text{Tabular Cost}\\\text{of Insurance}\end{pmatrix} = \left[\begin{pmatrix}\text{Net}\\\text{Premium}\end{pmatrix} + \begin{pmatrix}\text{Previous}\\\text{Terminal Reserve}\end{pmatrix}\right](1 + i) - \begin{pmatrix}\text{Terminal}\\\text{Reserve}\end{pmatrix}$$

(12.3) A third equation for calculating the tabular cost of insurance:

$$\begin{pmatrix}\text{Tabular Cost}\\\text{of Insurance}\end{pmatrix} = \begin{pmatrix}\text{Net Amount}\\\text{at Risk}\end{pmatrix}q_x$$

(12.3) A fourth equation for calculating the tabular cost of insurance:

$$\begin{pmatrix}\text{Tabular Cost}\\\text{of Insurance}\end{pmatrix} = \left[\begin{pmatrix}\text{Amount of}\\\text{Insurance}\end{pmatrix} - \begin{pmatrix}\text{Terminal}\\\text{Reserve}\end{pmatrix}\right]q_x$$

(13.2) Equation for calculating a policy's minimum cash value, as set forth in the Standard Nonforfeiture Law:

$$\begin{pmatrix}\text{Minimum}\\\text{Cash Value}\end{pmatrix} = \begin{pmatrix}\text{Present Value}\\\text{of Future Benefits}\end{pmatrix} - \begin{pmatrix}\text{Present Value of}\\\text{Future Adjusted Premiums}\end{pmatrix}$$

(13.2) Equation for calculating a policy's cash value when nonforfeiture factors are used:

$$\begin{pmatrix} \text{Cash} \\ \text{Value} \end{pmatrix} = \begin{pmatrix} \text{Present Value} \\ \text{of Future Benefits} \end{pmatrix} - \begin{pmatrix} \text{Present Value of} \\ \text{Future Nonforfeiture Factors} \end{pmatrix}$$

(13.3) Equation for calculating the amount of reduced paid-up insurance which is available:

$$\begin{pmatrix} \text{Amount of Reduced} \\ \text{Paid-Up Insurance} \end{pmatrix} = \frac{\text{Total Value}}{\begin{pmatrix} \text{Net Single Premium} \\ \text{at Attained Age} \\ \text{for \$1 of Insurance} \end{pmatrix}}$$

(14.2) In the three-factor contribution method, the contribution toward the dividend from the area of interest:

$$\begin{pmatrix} \text{Contribution} \\ \text{from Interest} \end{pmatrix} = \begin{pmatrix} \text{Initial} \\ \text{Reserve} \end{pmatrix} \left[\begin{pmatrix} \text{Dividend} \\ \text{Interest} \\ \text{Rate} \end{pmatrix} - \begin{pmatrix} \text{Tabular} \\ \text{Interest} \\ \text{Rate} \end{pmatrix} \right]$$

(14.2) In the three-factor contribution method, the contribution toward the dividend from the area of mortality:

$$\begin{pmatrix} \text{Contribution} \\ \text{from Mortality} \end{pmatrix} = \begin{pmatrix} \text{Net Amount} \\ \text{at Risk} \end{pmatrix} \left[\begin{pmatrix} \text{Tabular} \\ \text{Rate of} \\ \text{Mortality} \end{pmatrix} - \begin{pmatrix} \text{Dividend} \\ \text{Rate of} \\ \text{Mortality} \end{pmatrix} \right]$$

(14.2) In the three-factor contribution method, the contribution toward the dividend from the area of expenses:

$$\begin{pmatrix} \text{Contribution} \\ \text{from Expenses} \end{pmatrix} = \left[(\text{Loading}) - \begin{pmatrix} \text{Dividend} \\ \text{Expenses} \end{pmatrix} \right] \begin{pmatrix} 1 + \dfrac{\text{Dividend}}{\text{Interest Rate}} \end{pmatrix}$$

(14.3) In the experience-premium method, the first part of the dividend:

$$\begin{pmatrix} \text{First Part} \\ \text{of Dividend} \end{pmatrix} = \left[\begin{pmatrix} \text{Gross} \\ \text{Premium} \end{pmatrix} - \begin{pmatrix} \text{Experience} \\ \text{Premium} \end{pmatrix} \right] \begin{pmatrix} 1 + \dfrac{\text{Dividend}}{\text{Interest Rate}} \end{pmatrix}$$

(14.3) In the experience-premium method, the second part of the dividend (that is, the contribution from interest):

$$\begin{pmatrix} \text{Contribution} \\ \text{from Interest} \end{pmatrix} = \begin{pmatrix} \text{Initial} \\ \text{Reserve} \end{pmatrix} \left[\begin{pmatrix} \text{Dividend} \\ \text{Interest} \\ \text{Rate} \end{pmatrix} - \begin{pmatrix} \text{Tabular} \\ \text{Interest} \\ \text{Rate} \end{pmatrix} \right]$$

(14.4) Equation for calculating the amount of paid-up additions which a dividend will purchase:

$$\begin{pmatrix} \text{Amount of Paid-Up} \\ \text{Additions} \end{pmatrix} = \frac{\text{Dividend}}{\begin{pmatrix} \text{Net Single Premium} \\ \text{at Attained Age} \\ \text{for \$1 of Insurance} \end{pmatrix}}$$

(14.6) Equation for calculating average yearly payment (traditional method):

$$\begin{pmatrix} \text{Average Yearly} \\ \text{Payment} \end{pmatrix} = \frac{\begin{array}{c} \text{Total Premiums for 10 Years} \\ - \text{Total Dividends for 10 Years} \end{array}}{10}$$

(14.6) Equation for calculating average yearly cost (traditional method):

$$\begin{pmatrix} \text{Average} \\ \text{Yearly} \\ \text{Cost} \end{pmatrix} = \frac{\begin{array}{c} \text{Total Premiums for 10 years} \\ - \text{Total Dividends for 10 years} \\ - \text{10th Year Cash Value} \end{array}}{10}$$

(14.6) Equation for calculating interest-adjusted payment:

$$\begin{pmatrix} \text{Interest-Adjusted} \\ \text{Payment} \end{pmatrix} = \frac{\begin{array}{c} \text{Accumulated Premiums} \\ - \text{Accumulated Dividends} \end{array}}{\ddot{s}_{\overline{n}|i}}$$

(14.6) Equation for calculating interest-adjusted cost:

$$\begin{pmatrix} \text{Interest-Adjusted} \\ \text{Cost} \end{pmatrix} = \frac{\begin{array}{c} \text{Accumulated Premiums} \\ - \text{Accumulated Dividends} \\ - \text{Cash Value} \end{array}}{\ddot{s}_{\overline{n}|i}}$$

(14.6) Equation for calculating equivalent level annual dividend:

$$\begin{pmatrix} \text{Equivalent Level} \\ \text{Annual Dividend} \end{pmatrix} = \frac{\text{Accumulated Dividends}}{\ddot{s}_{\overline{n}|i}}$$

(16.3) Equation for calculating anticipated loss ratio for health insurance:

$$\text{Anticipated Loss Ratio} = \frac{\text{Present Value of Future Benefits}}{\text{Present Value of Future Gross Premiums}}$$

(16.3) Equation for calculating midterminal reserve for individual health policies:

$$\begin{pmatrix} \text{Midterminal} \\ \text{Reserve} \end{pmatrix} = \frac{(\text{Previous Terminal Reserve}) + (\text{Terminal Reserve})}{2}$$

(16.3) Equation for calculating actual loss ratio for health insurance:

$$\text{Actual Loss Ratio} = \frac{(\text{Claim Payments Made}) + (\text{Increase in Claim Reserves})}{(\text{Premiums Collected}) - (\text{Increase in Policy Reserves})}$$

Tables

TABLE I

2%

n	(1) *Accumulated* *Value of 1* $(1 + i)^n$	(2) *Present* *Value of 1* $v^n \text{ or } \dfrac{1}{(1 + i)^n}$	(3) *Accumulated* *Value of 1* *per Period* $s_{\overline{n}|i}$	(4) *Present* *Value of 1* *per Period* $a_{\overline{n}|i}$
1	1.020000	.980392	1.000000	0.980392
2	1.040400	.961169	2.020000	1.941561
3	1.061208	.942322	3.060400	2.883883
4	1.082432	.923845	4.121608	3.807729
5	1.104081	.905731	5.204040	4.713460
6	1.126162	.887971	6.308121	5.601431
7	1.148686	.870560	7.434283	6.471901
8	1.171659	.853490	8.582969	7.325481
9	1.195093	.836755	9.754628	8.162237
10	1.218994	.820348	10.949721	8.982585
11	1.243374	.804263	12.168715	9.786848
12	1.268242	.788493	13.412090	10.575341
13	1.293607	.773033	14.680332	11.348374
14	1.319479	.757875	15.973938	12.106249
15	1.345868	.743015	17.293417	12.849264
16	1.372786	.728446	18.639285	13.577709
17	1.400241	.714163	20.012071	14.291872
18	1.428246	.700159	21.412312	14.992031
19	1.456811	.686431	22.840559	15.678462
20	1.485947	.672971	24.297370	16.351433
21	1.515666	.659776	25.783317	17.011209
22	1.545980	.646839	27.298984	17.658048
23	1.576899	.634156	28.844963	18.292204
24	1.608437	.621721	30.421862	18.913926
25	1.640606	.609531	32.030300	19.523456

TABLE I—(Continued)

$2\frac{1}{2}$%

n	(1) Accumulated Value of 1 $(1 + i)^n$	(2) Present Value of 1 v^n or $\dfrac{1}{(1 + i)^n}$	(3) Accumulated Value of 1 per Period $s_{\overline{n}|i}$	(4) Present Value of 1 per Period $a_{\overline{n}|i}$
1	1.025000	.975610	1.000000	0.975610
2	1.050625	.951814	2.025000	1.927424
3	1.076891	.928599	3.075625	2.856024
4	1.103813	.905951	4.152516	3.761974
5	1.131408	.883854	5.256329	4.645828
6	1.159693	.862297	6.387737	5.508125
7	1.188686	.841265	7.547430	6.349391
8	1.218403	.820747	8.736116	7.170137
9	1.248863	.800728	9.954519	7.970866
10	1.280084	.781198	11.203382	8.752064
11	1.312087	.762145	12.483466	9.514209
12	1.344889	.743556	13.795553	10.257765
13	1.378511	.725420	15.140442	10.983185
14	1.412974	.707727	16.518953	11.690912
15	1.448298	.690466	17.931927	12.381378
16	1.484506	.673625	19.380225	13.055003
17	1.521618	.657195	20.864730	13.712198
18	1.559659	.641166	22.386349	14.353364
19	1.598650	.625528	23.946007	14.978891
20	1.638616	.610271	25.544658	15.589162
21	1.679582	.595386	27.183274	16.184549
22	1.721571	.580865	28.862856	16.765413
23	1.764611	.566697	30.584427	17.332110
24	1.808726	.552875	32.349038	17.884986
25	1.853944	.539391	34.157764	18.424376

TABLE I—(Continued)

3%

n	(1) Accumulated Value of 1 $(1 + i)^n$	(2) Present Value of 1 v^n or $\dfrac{1}{(1 + i)^n}$	(3) Accumulated Value of 1 per Period $s_{\overline{n}|i}$	(4) Present Value of 1 per Period $a_{\overline{n}|i}$
1	1.030000	.970874	1.000000	0.970874
2	1.060900	.942596	2.030000	1.913470
3	1.092727	.915142	3.090900	2.828611
4	1.125509	.888487	4.183627	3.717098
5	1.159274	.862609	5.309136	4.579707
6	1.194052	.837484	6.468410	5.417191
7	1.229874	.813092	7.662462	6.230283
8	1.266770	.789409	8.892336	7.019692
9	1.304773	.766417	10.159106	7.786109
10	1.343916	.744094	11.463879	8.530203
11	1.384234	.722421	12.807796	9.252624
12	1.425761	.701380	14.192030	9.954004
13	1.468534	.680951	15.617790	10.634955
14	1.512590	.661118	17.086324	11.296073
15	1.557967	.641862	18.598914	11.937935
16	1.604706	.623167	20.156881	12.561102
17	1.652848	.605016	21.761588	13.166118
18	1.702433	.587395	23.414435	13.753513
19	1.753506	.570286	25.116868	14.323799
20	1.806111	.553676	26.870374	14.877475
21	1.860295	.537549	28.676486	15.415024
22	1.916103	.521892	30.536780	15.936917
23	1.973587	.506692	32.452884	16.443608
24	2.032794	.491934	34.426470	16.935542
25	2.093778	.477606	36.459264	17.413148

TABLE I—(Continued)

4%

n	(1) Accumulated Value of 1 $(1 + i)^n$	(2) Present Value of 1 v^n or $\dfrac{1}{(1 + i)^n}$	(3) Accumulated Value of 1 per Period $s_{\overline{n}|i}$	(4) Present Value of 1 per Period $a_{\overline{n}|i}$
1	1.040000	.961538	1.000000	0.961538
2	1.081600	.924556	2.040000	1.886095
3	1.124864	.888996	3.121600	2.775091
4	1.169859	.854804	4.246464	3.629895
5	1.216653	.821927	5.416323	4.451822
6	1.265319	.790315	6.632976	5.242137
7	1.315932	.759918	7.898294	6.002055
8	1.368569	.730690	9.214226	6.732745
9	1.423312	.702587	10.582795	7.435332
10	1.480244	.675564	12.006107	8.110896
11	1.539454	.649581	13.486351	8.760477
12	1.601032	.624597	15.025806	9.385074
13	1.665074	.600574	16.626838	9.985648
14	1.731676	.577475	18.291911	10.563123
15	1.800944	.555264	20.023588	11.118387
16	1.872981	.533908	21.824531	11.652296
17	1.947900	.513373	23.697512	12.165669
18	2.025817	.493628	25.645413	12.659297
19	2.106849	.474642	27.671229	13.133939
20	2.191123	.456387	29.778079	13.590326
21	2.278768	.438834	31.969202	14.029160
22	2.369919	.421955	34.247970	14.451115
23	2.464716	.405726	36.617889	14.856842
24	2.563304	.390121	39.082604	15.246963
25	2.665836	.375117	41.645908	15.622080

TABLE I—(Continued)

5%

n	(1) Accumulated Value of 1 $(1 + i)^n$	(2) Present Value of 1 v^n or $\dfrac{1}{(1 + i)^n}$	(3) Accumulated Value of 1 per Period $s_{\overline{n}\mid i}$	(4) Present Value of 1 per Period $a_{\overline{n}\mid i}$
1	1.050000	.952381	1.000000	0.952381
2	1.102500	.907029	2.050000	1.859410
3	1.157625	.863838	3.152500	2.723248
4	1.215506	.822702	4.310125	3.545950
5	1.276282	.783526	5.525631	4.329477
6	1.340096	.746215	6.801913	5.075692
7	1.407100	.710681	8.142008	5.786373
8	1.477455	.676839	9.549109	6.463213
9	1.551328	.644609	11.026564	7.107822
10	1.628895	.613913	12.577892	7.721735
11	1.710339	.584679	14.206787	8.306414
12	1.795856	.556837	15.917126	8.863252
13	1.885649	.530321	17.712983	9.393573
14	1.979932	.505068	19.598632	9.898641
15	2.078928	.481017	21.578564	10.379658
16	2.182875	.458112	23.657492	10.837770
17	2.292018	.436297	25.840366	11.274066
18	2.406619	.415521	28.132385	11.689587
19	2.526950	.395734	30.539004	12.085321
20	2.653298	.376889	33.065954	12.462210
21	2.785963	.358942	35.719252	12.821153
22	2.925261	.341850	38.505214	13.163003
23	3.071524	.325571	41.430475	13.488574
24	3.225100	.310068	44.501999	13.798642
25	3.386355	.295303	47.727099	14.093945

TABLE I—(Continued)

6%

n	(1) Accumulated Value of 1 $(1 + i)^n$	(2) Present Value of 1 $v^n \text{ or } \dfrac{1}{(1 + i)^n}$	(3) Accumulated Value of 1 per Period $s_{\overline{n}|i}$	(4) Present Value of 1 per Period $a_{\overline{n}|i}$
1	1.060000	.943396	1.000000	0.943396
2	1.123600	.889996	2.060000	1.833393
3	1.191016	.839619	3.183600	2.673012
4	1.262477	.792094	4.374616	3.465106
5	1.338226	.747258	5.637093	4.212364
6	1.418519	.704961	6.975319	4.917324
7	1.503630	.665057	8.393838	5.582381
8	1.593848	.627412	9.897468	6.209794
9	1.689479	.591898	11.491316	6.801692
10	1.790848	.558395	13.180795	7.360087
11	1.898299	.526788	14.971643	7.886875
12	2.012196	.496969	16.869941	8.383844
13	2.132928	.468839	18.882138	8.852683
14	2.260904	.442301	21.015066	9.294984
15	2.396558	.417265	23.275970	9.712249
16	2.540352	.393646	25.672528	10.105895
17	2.692773	.371364	28.212880	10.477260
18	2.854339	.350344	30.905653	10.827603
19	3.025600	.330513	33.759992	11.158116
20	3.207135	.311805	36.785591	11.469921
21	3.399564	.294155	39.992727	11.764077
22	3.603537	.277505	43.392290	12.041582
23	3.819750	.261797	46.995828	12.303379
24	4.048935	.246979	50.815577	12.550358
25	4.291871	.232999	54.864512	12.783356

TABLE I—(Concluded)

10%

n	(1) Accumulated Value of 1 $(1 + i)^n$	(2) Present Value of 1 $v^n \text{ or } \dfrac{1}{(1 + i)^n}$	(3) Accumulated Value of 1 per Period $s_{\overline{n}|i}$	(4) Present Value of 1 per Period $a_{\overline{n}|i}$
1	1.100000	.909091	1.000000	0.909091
2	1.210000	.826446	2.100000	1.735537
3	1.331000	.751315	3.310000	2.486852
4	1.464100	.683013	4.641000	3.169865
5	1.610510	.620921	6.105100	3.790787
6	1.771561	.564474	7.715610	4.355261
7	1.948717	.513158	9.487171	4.868419
8	2.143589	.466507	11.435888	5.334926
9	2.357948	.424098	13.579477	5.759024
10	2.593742	.385543	15.937425	6.144567
11	2.853117	.350494	18.531167	6.495061
12	3.138428	.318631	21.384284	6.813692
13	3.452271	.289664	24.522712	7.103356
14	3.797498	.263331	27.974983	7.366687
15	4.177248	.239392	31.772482	7.606080
16	4.594973	.217629	35.949730	7.823709
17	5.054470	.197845	40.544703	8.021553
18	5.559917	.179859	45.599173	8.201412
19	6.115909	.163508	51.159090	8.364920
20	6.727500	.148644	57.274999	8.513564
21	7.400250	.135131	64.002499	8.648694
22	8.140275	.122846	71.402749	8.771540
23	8.954302	.111678	79.543024	8.883218
24	9.849733	.101526	88.497327	8.984744
25	10.834706	.092296	98.347059	9.077040

TABLE II

1971 Individual Annuity Mortality Table (male)—6% Interest

Age x	l_x	d_x	q_x	D_x	N_x
5	10,000,000	4,560	.000456	7,472,582	128,564,758
6	9,995,440	4,238	.000424	7,046,390	121,092,176
7	9,991,202	4,026	.000403	6,644,720	114,045,786
8	9,987,176	3,915	.000392	6,266,078	107,401,066
9	9,983,261	3,884	.000389	5,909,077	101,134,988
10	9,979,377	3,892	.000390	5,572,432	95,225,911
11	9,975,485	3,960	.000397	5,254,961	89,653,479
12	9,971,525	4,039	.000405	4,955,542	84,398,518
13	9,967,486	4,116	.000413	4,673,147	79,442,976
14	9,963,370	4,205	.000422	4,406,808	74,769,829
15	9,959,165	4,312	.000433	4,155,612	70,363,021
16	9,954,853	4,420	.000444	3,918,691	66,207,409
17	9,950,433	4,547	.000457	3,695,236	62,288,718
18	9,945,886	4,685	.000471	3,484,480	58,593,482
19	9,941,201	4,831	.000486	3,285,696	55,109,002
20	9,936,370	4,998	.000503	3,098,207	51,823,306
21	9,931,372	5,184	.000522	2,921,367	48,725,099
22	9,926,188	5,400	.000544	2,754,568	45,803,732
23	9,920,788	5,615	.000566	2,597,235	43,049,164
24	9,915,173	5,860	.000591	2,448,835	40,451,929
25	9,909,313	6,134	.000619	2,308,856	38,003,094
26	9,903,179	6,437	.000650	2,176,818	35,694,238
27	9,896,742	6,770	.000684	2,052,267	33,517,420
28	9,889,972	7,140	.000722	1,934,777	31,465,153
29	9,882,832	7,541	.000763	1,823,943	29,530,376
30	9,875,291	7,989	.000809	1,719,389	27,706,433
31	9,867,302	8,486	.000860	1,620,752	25,987,044
32	9,858,816	9,030	.000916	1,527,696	24,366,292
33	9,849,786	9,634	.000978	1,439,903	22,838,596
34	9,840,152	10,292	.001046	1,357,071	21,398,693
35	9,829,860	11,029	.001122	1,278,916	20,041,622
36	9,818,831	11,822	.001204	1,205,171	18,762,706
37	9,807,009	12,700	.001295	1,135,585	17,557,535
38	9,794,309	13,683	.001397	1,069,919	16,421,950
39	9,780,626	14,759	.001509	1,007,947	15,352,031
40	9,765,867	15,948	.001633	949,459	14,344,084
41	9,749,919	17,442	.001789	894,254	13,394,625
42	9,732,477	19,465	.002000	842,126	12,500,371
43	9,713,012	21,952	.002260	792,869	11,658,245
44	9,691,060	24,896	.002569	746,300	10,865,376
45	9,666,164	28,245	.002922	702,247	10,119,076
46	9,637,919	31,978	.003318	660,562	9,416,829
47	9,605,941	36,061	.003754	621,104	8,756,267
48	9,569,880	40,461	.004228	583,748	8,135,163
49	9,529,419	45,170	.004740	548,376	7,551,415
50	9,484,249	50,124	.005285	514,885	7,003,039
51	9,434,125	55,284	.005860	483,173	6,488,154
52	9,378,841	60,597	.006461	453,152	6,004,981
53	9,318,244	66,047	.007088	424,740	5,551,829
54	9,252,197	71,612	.007740	397,858	5,127,089
55	9,180,585	77,273	.008417	372,433	4,729,231
56	9,103,312	83,014	.009119	348,394	4,356,798
57	9,020,298	88,849	.009850	325,676	4,008,404
58	8,931,449	94,790	.010613	304,216	3,682,728
59	8,836,659	100,835	.011411	283,950	3,378,512

(Continued on next page)

TABLE II—(Continued)

1971 Individual Annuity Mortality Table (male)—6% Interest

Age x	l_x	d_x	q_x	D_x	N_x
60	8,735,824	107,005	.012249	264,821	3,094,562
61	8,628,819	113,322	.013133	246,771	2,829,741
62	8,515,497	119,839	.014073	229,745	2,582,970
63	8,395,658	126,632	.015083	213,690	2,353,225
64	8,269,026	133,834	.016185	198,555	2,139,535
65	8,135,192	141,593	.017405	184,283	1,940,980
66	7,993,599	150,016	.018767	170,827	1,756,697
67	7,843,583	159,146	.020290	158,132	1,585,870
68	7,684,437	168,996	.021992	146,155	1,427,738
69	7,515,441	179,544	.023890	134,850	1,281,583
70	7,335,897	190,733	.026000	124,177	1,146,733
71	7,145,164	202,502	.028341	114,103	1,022,556
72	6,942,662	214,757	.030933	104,593	908,453
73	6,727,905	227,410	.033801	95,621	803,860
74	6,500,495	240,362	.036976	87,159	708,239
75	6,260,133	253,498	.040494	79,185	621,080
76	6,006,635	266,652	.044393	71,678	541,895
77	5,739,983	279,624	.048715	64,619	470,217
78	5,460,359	292,129	.053500	57,991	405,598
79	5,168,230	303,825	.058787	51,782	347,607
80	4,864,405	314,235	.064599	45,979	295,825
81	4,550,170	322,616	.070902	40,575	249,846
82	4,227,554	328,346	.077668	35,563	209,271
83	3,899,208	331,203	.084941	30,945	173,708
84	3,568,005	331,374	.092874	26,714	142,763
85	3,236,631	329,130	.101689	22,861	116,049
86	2,907,501	324,628	.111652	19,374	93,188
87	2,582,873	317,818	.123048	16,236	73,814
88	2,265,055	308,326	.136123	13,433	57,578
89	1,956,729	295,603	.151070	10,947	44,145
90	1,661,126	279,136	.168040	8,768	33,198
91	1,381,990	258,635	.187147	6,881	24,430
92	1,123,355	234,171	.208457	5,277	17,549
93	889,184	206,189	.231885	3,940	12,272
94	682,995	175,629	.257146	2,856	8,332
95	507,366	144,011	.283841	2,001	5,476
96	363,355	113,209	.311565	1,352	3,475
97	250,146	85,103	.340214	878	2,123
98	165,043	61,028	.369769	546	1,245
99	104,015	41,626	.400194	325	699
100	62,389	26,915	.431413	184	374
101	35,474	16,436	.463312	99	190
102	19,038	9,438	.495756	50	91
103	9,600	5,075	.528599	24	41
104	4,525	2,541	.561692	10	17
105	1,984	1,180	.594884	4	7
106	804	505	.628022	2	3
107	299	198	.660949	1	1
108	101	70	.693503	0	0
109	31	22	.725521	0	0
110	9	7	.756852	0	0
111	2	2	.787390	0	0
112	0	0	.817125	0	0
113	0	0	.846198	0	0
114	0	0	.874915	0	0
115	0	0	1.000000	0	0

(Continued on next page)

TABLE II—(Continued)

1971 Individual Annuity Mortality Table (female)—6% Interest

Age x	l_x	d_x	q_x	D_x	N_x
5	10,000,000	2,340	.000234	7,472,582	129,715,937
6	9,997,660	1,929	.000193	7,047,956	122,243,355
7	9,995,731	1,620	.000162	6,647,732	115,195,399
8	9,994,111	1,429	.000143	6,270,429	108,547,667
9	9,992,682	1,339	.000134	5,914,653	102,277,238
10	9,991,343	1,319	.000132	5,579,114	96,362,585
11	9,990,024	1,428	.000143	5,262,620	90,783,471
12	9,988,596	1,549	.000155	4,964,026	85,520,851
13	9,987,047	1,667	.000167	4,682,318	80,556,825
14	9,985,380	1,798	.000180	4,416,543	75,874,507
15	9,983,582	1,927	.000193	4,165,800	71,457,964
16	9,981,655	2,046	.000205	3,929,241	67,292,164
17	9,979,609	2,175	.000218	3,706,072	63,362,923
18	9,977,434	2,305	.000231	3,495,532	59,656,851
19	9,975,129	2,444	.000245	3,296,910	56,161,319
20	9,972,685	2,593	.000260	3,109,530	52,864,409
21	9,970,092	2,742	.000275	2,932,757	49,754,879
22	9,967,350	2,910	.000292	2,765,990	46,822,122
23	9,964,440	3,079	.000309	2,608,663	44,056,132
24	9,961,361	3,258	.000327	2,460,243	41,447,469
25	9,958,103	3,455	.000347	2,320,224	38,987,226
26	9,954,648	3,663	.000368	2,188,132	36,667,002
27	9,950,985	3,881	.000390	2,063,515	34,478,870
28	9,947,104	4,118	.000414	1,945,954	32,415,355
29	9,942,986	4,375	.000440	1,835,045	30,469,401
30	9,938,611	4,662	.000469	1,730,412	28,634,356
31	9,933,949	4,957	.000499	1,631,700	26,903,944
32	9,928,992	5,292	.000533	1,538,571	25,272,244
33	9,923,700	5,646	.000569	1,450,708	23,733,673
34	9,918,054	6,031	.000608	1,367,814	22,282,965
35	9,912,023	6,452	.000651	1,289,606	20,915,151
36	9,905,571	6,914	.000698	1,215,817	19,625,545
37	9,898,657	7,424	.000750	1,146,197	18,409,728
38	9,891,233	7,983	.000807	1,080,507	17,263,531
39	9,883,250	8,588	.000869	1,018,524	16,183,024
40	9,874,662	9,263	.000938	960,036	15,164,500
41	9,865,399	9,993	.001013	904,845	14,204,464
42	9,855,406	10,782	.001094	852,763	13,299,619
43	9,844,624	11,676	.001186	803,613	12,446,856
44	9,832,948	12,645	.001286	757,226	11,643,243
45	9,820,303	13,719	.001397	713,446	10,886,017
46	9,806,584	14,896	.001519	672,122	10,172,571
47	9,791,688	16,196	.001654	633,114	9,500,449
48	9,775,492	17,615	.001802	596,289	8,867,335
49	9,757,877	19,194	.001967	561,524	8,271,046
50	9,738,683	20,948	.002151	528,697	7,709,522
51	9,717,735	23,040	.002371	497,698	7,180,825
52	9,694,695	25,604	.002641	468,413	6,683,127
53	9,669,091	28,679	.002966	440,733	6,214,714
54	9,640,412	32,305	.003351	414,551	5,773,981
55	9,608,107	36,424	.003791	389,777	5,359,430
56	9,571,683	41,005	.004284	366,319	4,969,653
57	9,530,678	45,995	.004826	344,104	4,603,334
58	9,484,683	51,303	.005409	323,059	4,259,230
59	9,433,380	56,760	.006017	303,125	3,936,171

(Continued on next page)

TABLE II—(Concluded)

1971 Individual Annuity Mortality Table (female)—6% Interest

Age x	l_x	d_x	q_x	D_x	N_x
60	9,376,620	62,149	.006628	284,246	3,633,046
61	9,314,471	67,241	.007219	266,379	3,348,800
62	9,247,230	71,878	.007773	249,487	3,082,421
63	9,175,352	76,018	.008285	233,536	2,832,934
64	9,099,334	79,847	.008775	218,491	2,599,398
65	9,019,487	83,791	.009290	204,315	2,380,907
66	8,935,696	88,356	.009888	190,960	2,176,592
67	8,847,340	93,977	.010622	178,369	1,985,632
68	8,753,363	100,978	.011536	166,486	1,807,263
69	8,652,385	109,574	.012664	155,249	1,640,777
70	8,542,811	119,847	.014029	144,608	1,485,528
71	8,422,964	131,828	.015651	134,508	1,340,920
72	8,291,136	145,493	.017548	124,908	1,206,412
73	8,145,643	160,811	.019742	115,770	1,081,504
74	7,984,832	177,711	.022256	107,062	965,734
75	7,807,121	196,115	.025120	98,753	858,672
76	7,611,006	215,916	.028369	90,823	759,919
77	7,395,090	237,013	.032050	83,251	669,096
78	7,158,077	259,301	.036225	76,022	585,845
79	6,898,776	282,677	.040975	69,121	509,823
80	6,616,099	306,895	.046386	62,536	440,702
81	6,309,204	331,315	.052513	56,260	378,166
82	5,977,889	355,140	.059409	50,289	321,906
83	5,622,749	377,624	.067160	44,623	271,617
84	5,245,125	398,100	.075899	39,270	226,994
85	4,847,025	415,729	.085770	34,236	187,724
86	4,431,296	429,384	.096898	29,527	153,488
87	4,001,912	437,561	.109338	25,157	123,961
88	3,564,351	438,337	.122978	21,138	98,804
89	3,126,014	429,852	.137508	17,489	77,666
90	2,696,162	411,089	.152472	14,231	60,177
91	2,285,073	382,453	.167370	11,378	45,946
92	1,902,620	345,850	.181776	8,937	34,568
93	1,556,770	304,171	.195386	6,899	25,631
94	1,252,599	260,630	.208071	5,237	18,732
95	991,969	218,130	.219896	3,912	13,495
96	773,839	178,832	.231097	2,879	9,583
97	595,007	144,117	.242211	2,089	6,704
98	450,890	114,446	.253823	1,493	4,615
99	336,444	89,646	.266452	1,051	3,122
100	246,798	69,236	.280535	728	2,071
101	177,562	52,638	.296449	493	1,343
102	124,924	39,293	.314535	328	850
103	85,631	28,697	.335121	212	522
104	56,934	20,413	.358537	133	310
105	36,521	14,065	.385122	80	177
106	22,456	9,325	.415238	47	97
107	13,131	5,899	.449274	26	50
108	7,232	3,527	.487649	13	24
109	3,705	1,966	.530787	6	11
110	1,739	1,007	.579040	3	5
111	732	463	.632529	1	2
112	269	186	.690903	1	1
113	83	62	.753081	0	0
114	21	17	.817218	0	0
115	4	4	1.000000	0	0

Note: l_x, d_x, D_x, and N_x values adjusted by author to display only whole numbers.

TABLE III

1958 C.S.O. Table (male)

Age x	l_x	d_x	q_x	Age x	l_x	d_x	q_x
0	10,000,000	70,800	.00708	50	8,762,306	72,902	.00832
1	9,929,200	17,475	.00176	51	8,689,404	79,160	.00911
2	9,911,725	15,066	.00152	52	8,610,244	85,758	.00996
3	9,896,659	14,449	.00146	53	8,524,486	92,832	.01089
4	9,882,210	13,835	.00140	54	8,431,654	100,337	.01190
5	9,868,375	13,322	.00135	55	8,331,317	108,307	.01300
6	9,855,053	12,812	.00130	56	8,223,010	116,849	.01421
7	9,842,241	12,401	.00126	57	8,106,161	125,970	.01554
8	9,829,840	12,091	.00123	58	7,980,191	135,663	.01700
9	9,817,749	11,879	.00121	59	7,844,528	145,830	.01859
10	9,805,870	11,865	.00121	60	7,698,698	156,592	.02034
11	9,794,005	12,047	.00123	61	7,542,106	167,736	.02224
12	9,781,958	12,325	.00126	62	7,374,370	179,271	.02431
13	9,769,633	12,896	.00132	63	7,195,099	191,174	.02657
14	9,756,737	13,562	.00139	64	7,003,925	203,394	.02904
15	9,743,175	14,225	.00146	65	6,800,531	215,917	.03175
16	9,728,950	14,983	.00154	66	6,584,614	228,749	.03474
17	9,713,967	15,737	.00162	67	6,355,865	241,777	.03804
18	9,698,230	16,390	.00169	68	6,114,088	254,835	.04168
19	9,681,840	16,846	.00174	69	5,859,253	267,241	.04561
20	9,664,994	17,300	.00179	70	5,592,012	278,426	.04979
21	9,647,694	17,655	.00183	71	5,313,586	287,731	.05415
22	9,630,039	17,912	.00186	72	5,025,855	294,766	.05865
23	9,612,127	18,167	.00189	73	4,731,089	299,289	.06326
24	9,593,960	18,324	.00191	74	4,431,800	301,894	.06812
25	9,575,636	18,481	.00193	75	4,129,906	303,011	.07337
26	9,557,155	18,732	.00196	76	3,826,895	303,014	.07918
27	9,538,423	18,981	.00199	77	3,523,881	301,997	.08570
28	9,519,442	19,324	.00203	78	3,221,884	299,829	.09306
29	9,500,118	19,760	.00208	79	2,922,055	295,683	.10119
30	9,480,358	20,193	.00213	80	2,626,372	288,848	.10998
31	9,460,165	20,718	.00219	81	2,337,524	278,983	.11935
32	9,439,447	21,239	.00225	82	2,058,541	265,902	.12917
33	9,418,208	21,850	.00232	83	1,792,639	249,858	.13938
34	9,396,358	22,551	.00240	84	1,542,781	231,433	.15001
35	9,373,807	23,528	.00251	85	1,311,348	211,311	.16114
36	9,350,279	24,685	.00264	86	1,100,037	190,108	.17282
37	9,325,594	26,112	.00280	87	909,929	168,455	.18513
38	9,299,482	27,991	.00301	88	741,474	146,997	.19825
39	9,271,491	30,132	.00325	89	594,477	126,303	.21246
40	9,241,359	32,622	.00353	90	468,174	106,809	.22814
41	9,208,737	35,362	.00384	91	361,365	88,813	.24577
42	9,173,375	38,253	.00417	92	272,552	72,480	.26593
43	9,135,122	41,382	.00453	93	200,072	57,881	.28930
44	9,093,740	44,741	.00492	94	142,191	45,026	.31666
45	9,048,999	48,412	.00535	95	97,165	34,128	.35124
46	9,000,587	52,473	.00583	96	63,037	25,250	.40056
47	8,948,114	56,910	.00636	97	37,787	18,456	.48842
48	8,891,204	61,794	.00695	98	19,331	12,916	.66815
49	8,829,410	67,104	.00760	99	6,415	6,415	1.00000

TABLE IV

1958 C.S.O. Table (male)—3% Interest

Age x	D_x	N_x	C_x	M_x
0	10,000,000	288,963,016	68,738	1,583,602
1	9,640,000	278,963,016	16,472	1,514,864
2	9,342,751	269,323,016	13,788	1,498,392
3	9,056,845	259,980,265	12,838	1,484,604
4	8,780,216	250,923,420	11,934	1,471,766
5	8,512,547	242,143,204	11,157	1,459,832
6	8,253,452	233,630,657	10,417	1,448,675
7	8,002,643	225,377,205	9,789	1,438,258
8	7,759,766	217,374,562	9,267	1,428,469
9	7,524,487	209,614,796	8,839	1,419,202
10	7,296,488	202,090,309	8,572	1,410,363
11	7,075,398	194,793,821	8,450	1,401,791
12	6,860,869	187,718,423	8,393	1,393,341
13	6,652,645	180,857,554	8,526	1,384,948
14	6,450,353	174,204,909	8,705	1,376,422
15	6,253,773	167,754,556	8,865	1,367,717
16	6,062,760	161,500,783	9,065	1,358,852
17	5,877,110	155,438,023	9,244	1,349,787
18	5,696,688	149,560,913	9,347	1,340,543
19	5,521,418	143,864,225	9,327	1,331,196
20	5,351,273	138,342,807	9,300	1,321,869
21	5,186,111	132,991,534	9,214	1,312,569
22	5,025,845	127,805,423	9,076	1,303,355
23	4,870,385	122,779,578	8,937	1,294,279
24	4,719,593	117,909,193	8,752	1,285,342
25	4,573,377	113,189,600	8,570	1,276,590
26	4,431,602	108,616,223	8,433	1,268,020
27	4,294,094	104,184,621	8,296	1,259,587
28	4,160,727	99,890,527	8,200	1,251,291
29	4,031,341	95,729,800	8,141	1,243,091
30	3,905,782	91,698,459	8,077	1,234,950
31	3,783,944	87,792,677	8,046	1,226,873
32	3,665,687	84,008,733	8,008	1,218,827
33	3,550,912	80,343,046	7,998	1,210,819
34	3,439,489	76,792,134	8,014	1,202,821
35	3,331,295	73,352,645	8,118	1,194,807
36	3,226,149	70,021,350	8,269	1,186,689
37	3,123,915	66,795,201	8,492	1,178,420
38	3,024,435	63,671,286	8,838	1,169,928
39	2,927,506	60,646,851	9,237	1,161,090
40	2,833,002	57,719,345	9,709	1,151,853
41	2,740,778	54,886,343	10,218	1,142,144
42	2,650,731	52,145,565	10,732	1,131,926
43	2,562,794	49,494,834	11,271	1,121,194
44	2,476,878	46,932,040	11,831	1,109,923
45	2,392,905	44,455,162	12,429	1,098,092
46	2,310,779	42,062,257	13,079	1,085,663
47	2,230,396	39,751,478	13,772	1,072,584
48	2,151,661	37,521,082	14,519	1,058,812
49	2,074,472	35,369,421	15,307	1,044,293

(Continued on next page)

TABLE IV—(Concluded)

1958 C.S.O. Table (male)—3% Interest

Age x	D_x	N_x	C_x	M_x
50	1,998,744	33,294,949	16,145	1,028,986
51	1,924,383	31,296,205	17,020	1,012,841
52	1,851,313	29,371,822	17,902	995,821
53	1,779,489	27,520,509	18,814	977,919
54	1,708,845	25,741,020	19,743	959,105
55	1,639,330	24,032,175	20,691	939,362
56	1,570,892	22,392,845	21,672	918,671
57	1,503,465	20,821,953	22,683	896,999
58	1,436,992	19,318,488	23,717	874,316
59	1,371,420	17,881,496	24,752	850,599
60	1,306,724	16,510,076	25,805	825,847
61	1,242,859	15,203,352	26,836	800,042
62	1,179,823	13,960,493	27,846	773,206
63	1,117,613	12,780,670	28,830	745,360
64	1,056,231	11,663,057	29,780	716,530
65	995,688	10,606,826	30,692	686,750
66	935,995	9,611,138	31,569	656,058
67	877,164	8,675,143	32,395	624,489
68	819,220	7,797,979	33,151	592,094
69	762,208	6,978,759	33,752	558,943
70	706,256	6,216,551	34,140	525,191
71	651,546	5,510,295	34,254	491,051
72	598,315	4,858,749	34,069	456,797
73	546,819	4,260,434	33,584	422,728
74	497,308	3,713,615	32,890	389,144
75	449,933	3,216,307	32,050	356,254
76	404,779	2,766,374	31,117	324,204
77	361,872	2,361,595	30,109	293,087
78	321,223	1,999,723	29,022	262,978
79	282,844	1,678,500	27,787	233,956
80	246,819	1,395,656	26,354	206,169
81	213,275	1,148,837	24,713	179,815
82	182,351	935,562	22,868	155,102
83	154,171	753,211	20,863	132,234
84	128,818	599,040	18,761	111,371
85	106,305	470,222	16,631	92,610
86	86,578	363,917	14,527	75,979
87	69,529	277,339	12,497	61,452
88	55,007	207,810	10,588	48,955
89	42,818	152,803	8,832	38,367
90	32,738	109,985	7,251	29,535
91	24,533	77,247	5,854	22,284
92	17,965	52,714	4,638	16,430
93	12,803	34,749	3,596	11,792
94	8,834	21,946	2,716	8,196
95	5,861	13,112	1,999	5,480
96	3,692	7,251	1,436	3,481
97	2,148	3,559	1,019	2,045
98	1,067	1,411	692	1,026
99	344	344	334	334

Note: Values adjusted by author to display only whole numbers.

Answers to Exercises

Answers	Explanations

SET 1

1. X multiplied by Y, or X times Y.

2. 20 — Perform division first: $20 - 6 + 6$.

3. $9 + 3A - 3B$ — Multiply each item inside the parentheses by 3.

4. $\dfrac{14B}{9}$ — A fraction indicates numerator is divided by denominator.

5. They must all be expressed with a common denominator.

6. 12 — Multiply the two denominators. In this case, this is the smallest common denominator that can be found.

7. $\frac{13}{10}$ — $\frac{1}{2} \times \frac{5}{5} + \frac{4}{5} \times \frac{2}{2} = \frac{5}{10} + \frac{8}{10} = \frac{5+8}{10}$

8. $\frac{1}{12}$ — $\frac{5}{6} \times \frac{2}{2} - \frac{3}{4} \times \frac{3}{3} = \frac{10}{12} - \frac{9}{12} = \frac{10-9}{12}$. The same answer would result from using $6 \times 4 = 24$ as the common denominator and then reducing the answer.

9. $\frac{17}{8}$ — Use 8 as the common denominator. Multiply second fraction by $\frac{4}{4}$, third fraction by $\frac{2}{2}$.

10. $\dfrac{3A}{4(B + 6)}$ — Multiply two numerators; multiply two denominators.

11. $\frac{4}{3}$ — Invert $\frac{1}{4}$ and multiply: $\frac{1}{3} \times \frac{4}{1}$.

12. $\frac{2}{7}$ — Invert $\frac{11}{1}$ and multiply: $\frac{22}{7} \times \frac{1}{11} = \frac{22}{77}$. Reduce by dividing numerator and denominator by 11.

13. $\frac{3}{8}$ — This problem is easier to work if the student looks for factors common to both numerator and denominator and

Answers	Explanations

divides by them before actually multiplying: $\frac{2 \times 15}{5 \times 16}$ may have numerator and denominator both divided by 2 and by 5 before actually multiplying. Try using the cancellation method.

14. 37 — Perform multiplication first: $27 + 12 - 2$.

SET 2

1. .00002 — Five decimal places because there are five zeros in 100,000.

2. 31.507 —
12.000
4.620
.007
14.880
31.507

3. Six — Three places in 18.773 plus three places in .005.

4. 1.880004 — The total decimal places in the two numbers is six; hence, there are six decimal places in the answer.

5. .4286 — $3.00000 \div 7 = .42857$, then round off to four decimal places.

6. a) 334.3 — Move decimal point one place to the right.

   b) 6.74 — Move decimal point two places to the right.

   c) 1,070 — Move decimal point two places to the right.

   d) 74.6 — Move decimal point one place to the left.

   e) .138147 — Move decimal point two places to the left.

   f) .04277 — Move decimal point three places to the left.

7. 13.175, 13.17 — Three places: Drop all digits after three places; add 1 in last place because first digit dropped is 5.

   Two places: Drop all digits after two places; do not add 1, because first digit dropped is 4.

8. a) 300 — Factor out 12, multiply by the total of $14 + 8 + 3$.

Answers	**Explanations**

b) $2,100 — $1.05 \times \$2,000.$

c) $370.37 — $\$400 \times \frac{1}{1.08}$, or $\$400 \div 1.08.$

9. a) $A(4 + x)$ — Common multiplier is A.

b) $5(B - 3BC + 4C)$ — Common multiplier is 5.

10. 4,310 — Move decimal point three places to the right.

SET 3

1. 782.86 — Approximately $250 \times 3 = 750$

2. 22.1073 — Approximately $40 \times .5 = 20$

3. 2.8434 — Approximately multiplying by 1

4. 437.69 — Approximately multiplying by .01; move decimal point two places to the left.

5. 20.644 — Approximately dividing by 100; move decimal point two places to the left.

6. .000313 — Approximately dividing by 100; move decimal point two places to the left.

SET 4

1. 13 — Add 3 to both sides.

2. 3 — Subtract D from both sides.

3. 4 — $4A = 16$; divide both sides by 4.

4. 4 — Add C to both sides, subtract 1 from both sides, divide both sides by 4.

5. 15 — Multiply both sides by 5; the fraction disappears.

6. $\frac{2}{5}$ — Multiply both sides by 2: $6B - 2 = B.$

7. $\frac{7}{2}$ — $2L - 4 = 3$

8. 9 — $3E + 3 = 2E + 12$

9. 2 — $6R - 3 = 9$

10. $\frac{1}{8}$ — Multiply both sides by R: $2 + R = 17R.$

11. $\frac{4}{5}$ — Multiply both sides by 3: $L - 2 = 6L - 6.$

12. $\frac{7}{13}$ — Multiply both sides by 14: $2K = 28K - 14.$

13. $\dfrac{9R}{13}$ — Multiply both sides by 3: $3R + N = 12R - 12N$; then $13N = 9R.$

14. 10^7 — Add exponents: $3 + 4 = 7.$

15. 10^{11}

16. 10^{16}

Answers	Explanations
Answers	**Explanations**

17. 10^3 — Subtract exponents: $8 - 5 = 3$.

18. 10^1 — or simply 10

19. B^{18} — Add exponents: $7 + 8 + 3 = 18$.

20. $(1.08)^{12}$

21. v^8 — Subtract exponents: $18 - 10 = 8$.

22. $\left(\dfrac{1}{1+i}\right)^{11}$ — Add exponents: $8 + 2 + 1 = 11$; where no exponent is shown, the exponent is understood to be 1.

23. $\left(\dfrac{a}{4}\right)^2$ — Subtract exponents: $3 - 1 = 2$.

24. $A(A + 1)$ — A is the common multiplier: $A \times A = A^2$, $A \times 1 = A$.

25. $5(1.075)[1 + 3\,(1.075) + 5(1.075)^2]$

26. $\dfrac{50}{1.06}\left[1 + \dfrac{3}{(1.06)} + \dfrac{1}{(1.06)^2} + \dfrac{4}{(1.06)^3}\right]$

27. $(b + c)^{12}$ — First add the exponents in the numerator: $\dfrac{(b+c)^{16}}{(b+c)^4}$; then subtract the exponents: $16 - 4$.

SET 5

3. $38,906.13 — $15,000 \times 1.10^{10}$, that is, $15,000 \times 2.593742$.

4. $607.75 — 500×1.05^4, that is, 500×1.215506.

5. 4.549383 — 4.291871×1.06.

6. 3.946088 — $(1.04)^{25}(1.04)^{10} = (2.665836)(1.480244)$

7. $(1.08)^{20} \div (1.08)$ — Dividing $(1.08)^{20}$ by (1.08) gives the preceding accumulated interest rate, $(1.08)^{19}$

SET 6

1. $3.00 — Interest for a whole year $= .06 \times 100 or $6.00.
180 days is half of 360 days.

2. $1,058.00 — $80.00 \times \dfrac{261}{360} + $1,000$.

3. $121.84 — 100×1.025^8.

4. $1,796.98 — $1,000 \times 1.06^7$ on March 15, 1990; $1,000 \times 1.06^7 \times 1.02^9$ on June 15, 1992.

5. The lender — The more frequent the compounding, the larger the resulting effective annual rate will be.

Answers	Explanations

6. 10.25%

$(1.05^2 - 1) \times 100.$

7. 4.0604%

Calculate 1.01^4 by performing the actual multiplications.

8. 4%

$\dfrac{\$2,191.12}{\$1,000.00} = (1 + i)^{20}$, that is, $2.19112 = (1 + i)^{20}$ at what interest rate?

9. Between 5% and 6%

$\dfrac{\$2,600}{\$2,000} = (1 + i)^{10}$, that is, $1.3 = (1 + i)^{10}$; i is between $2\frac{1}{2}\%$ and 3%.

10. $\$1,300\ (1.03)^2(1.015)^6$

$\$1,300 \times 1.03^2$ on October 1, 1980 (after two semiannual compounding periods); $\$1,300 \times 1.03^2 \times 1.015^6$ on April 1, 1982 (after six quarterly compounding periods).

SET 7

1. $s_{\overline{30}|11\%}$

2. 3.1525

$s_{\overline{1}|5\%} = 1$
$s_{\overline{2}|5\%} = 1(1.05) + 1 = 2.05$
$s_{\overline{3}|5\%} = 2.05(1.05) + 1 = 3.1525$

3. 3.1525

$1.05^2 + 1.05^1 + 1$
$= 1.1025 + 1.05 + 1$
$= 3.1525$

4. $8,622.22

$\$625 \times 13.795553$

5. $1,093.65

$\$250 s_{\overline{4}|6\%} = \$250 \times 4.374616$

6. $2,429.74

$\$100 s_{\overline{20}|2\%}$

7. June 1, 1987

The five deposits are made in 1983, 1984, 1985, 1986, and 1987.

8. 112.7969, rounded to four decimal places

$s_{\overline{25}|3\%} + 1.03^{25} s_{\overline{25}|3\%}$

9. $252.70

Borrower will owe $\$500(1.10)^5$; savings account will have $\$100 s_{\overline{5}|5\%}$.

SET 8

1. 14.140442

$(1.025)s_{\overline{12}|2\frac{1}{2}\%}$ or $s_{\overline{13}|2\frac{1}{2}\%} - 1$

2. 3.310125

First method:
$\ddot{s}_{\overline{1}|5\%} = 1.05$
$\ddot{s}_{\overline{2}|5\%} = (1.05 + 1)(1.05) = 2.1525$
$\ddot{s}_{\overline{3}|5\%} = (2.1525 + 1)(1.05) = 3.310125$

Answers	**Explanations**

Second method:
$$1.05^3 + 1.05^2 + 1.05^1$$
$$= 1.157625 + 1.102500 + 1.050000$$
$$= 3.310125$$

3. $1,320.68 $100(s_{\overline{11}|5\%} - 1)$

4. $2,957.54 $400\ddot{s}_{\overline{6}|6\%} = \$400(s_{\overline{7}|6\%} - 1)$

5. $1,963.75 $75\ddot{s}_{\overline{20}|2\frac{1}{2}\%} = \$75(s_{\overline{21}|2\frac{1}{2}\%} - 1)$

6. $170.05   This is the same as the accumulated value of a five-payment annuity due, plus a sixth payment made on the evaluation date. It is also the same as a six-payment annuity immediate.

7. $39.42 $300\ddot{s}_{\overline{5}|2\frac{1}{2}\%} - \$300s_{\overline{5}|2\frac{1}{2}\%}$ or
$300(s_{\overline{6}|2\frac{1}{2}\%} - 1) - \$300s_{\overline{5}|2\frac{1}{2}\%}$

8. $79.05 $\dfrac{\$750}{s_{\overline{7}|10\%}}$

9. $403.50 $\dfrac{\$10,000}{\ddot{s}_{\overline{20}|2\%}} = \dfrac{\$10,000}{s_{\overline{21}|2\%} - 1}$

10. $24.12 $24(1 + i) = \$24(1.005)$

11. $2,983.43 $200\ddot{s}_{\overline{11}|5\%} = \$200(s_{\overline{12}|5\%} - 1)$

12. $(1.07)^3 + (1.07)^2 + (1.07)$

SET 9

1. $800 \div 1.07 = \$747.66$, etc.

2. $1,500.00 \times v^5$ at 3% = $1,500.00 \times .862609$, etc.

3. $100(1 + i)^5$

4. $1,415.09 $1,500.00 \div 1.06$ or $1,500.00(v^1$ at 6%)

5. $837.59 $1,500.00(v^{10}$ at 6%)

6. $610.27 $1,000(v^{20}$ at $2\frac{1}{2}\%$)

7. $7,006.88 $20,000(v^{18}$ at 6%)

8. $6,434.10   Find the present value of each of the four payments separately and add: $1,751.72 + $1,652.57 + $1,559.03 + $1,470.78

9. .411987   Any two values of v^n at 3%, the exponents of which add up to 30, can be multiplied together.

10. $5,000v^{16}$ at 3%

Answers	Explanations

SET 10

1. $(v^1 + v^2 + v^3$ at $5\% = .952381 + .907029 + .863838)$

2. $528.16 50×10.563123

3. $3,399.29 $350a_{\overline{15}|6\%} = \$350 \times 9.712249$

4. $892.65 $60a_{\overline{20}|3\%} = \$60 \times 14.877475$

5. $278.95 $25a_{\overline{19}|6\%}$

6. $2,735.55 $100a_{\overline{40}|2\%}$; that is, $100(a_{\overline{25}|2\%} + a_{\overline{15}|2\%}v^{25})$

7. $1,500a_{\overline{4}|12\%}(v^8$ at $10\%)$ $+ \$1,500a_{\overline{8}|10\%}$

8. 3.993 $a_{\overline{4}|i} + v^5$

SET 11

1. 3.723248 $1 + .952381 + .907029 + .863838$

2. 10.514209 $9.514209 + 1; 1.025 \times 10.257765$

3. $583.11 $40 \times (13.577709 + 1)$

4. $1,170.25 $150\ddot{a}_{\overline{10}|6\%} = \$150(6.801692 + 1)$

5. $482.31 $25\ddot{a}_{\overline{24}|2\%} = \$25(18.292204 + 1)$

6. $1,089.86 and $2,157.86 There are 15 payments; present value of annuity due; accumulated value of annuity immediate since the evaluation date is the same as the date of the last payment: $100\ddot{a}_{\overline{15}|5\%}$ and $100s_{\overline{15}|5\%}$.

7. $7,472 $1,000\ddot{a}_{\overline{8}|2\%} = \$1,000(6.471901 + 1)$

SET 12

1. $62.25 $10(a_{\overline{10}|4\%} - a_{\overline{2}|4\%})$ or $10a_{\overline{8}|4\%}v^2$

2. $64.74 $10(\ddot{a}_{\overline{10}|4\%} - \ddot{a}_{\overline{2}|4\%})$ or $10\ddot{a}_{\overline{8}|4\%}v^2$; derive each annuity value using $\ddot{a}_{\overline{n}|i} = a_{\overline{n-1}|i} + 1$. It is also possible to view this annuity as an eight-payment annuity immediate deferred for one year.

3. $641.28 $200(a_{\overline{9}|3\%} - a_{\overline{5}|3\%})$ or $200a_{\overline{4}|3\%}v^5$

4. Amortization payment

5. $25.38 $\dfrac{\$164.26}{a_{\overline{7}|2\%}}$

| **Answers** | **Explanations** |

6. $24.88

$$\frac{\$164.26}{\ddot{a}_{\overline{7}|2\%}} = \frac{\$164.26}{a_{\overline{6}|2\%} + 1} = \frac{\$164.26}{6.601431};$$

or $25.38 from Exercise 2 ÷ 1.02

7. $2,441.18

$$\frac{\$15,000}{a_{\overline{10}|10\%}}$$

8. $263.97

$$\frac{\$1,200}{\ddot{a}_{\overline{5}|5\%}} = \frac{\$1,200}{a_{\overline{4}|5\%} + 1}$$

9. $266.74

$$\frac{\$1,000(1.06)^2}{a_{\overline{5}|6\%}} \text{ or } \frac{\$1,000}{a_{\overline{7}|6\%} - a_{\overline{2}|6\%}}$$

10. $1,850.07

$$\frac{\$15,000}{\ddot{a}_{\overline{10}|5\%}} = \frac{\$15,000}{a_{\overline{9}|5\%} + 1}$$

11. $4,233.76

Each payment $= \dfrac{\$5,000}{a_{\overline{20}|6\%}} = \$435.92;$ at the end of five years there are 15 payments remaining, so the balance is $435.92a_{\overline{15}|6\%}$.

12. $1,043.30

$60a_{\overline{5}|5\%} + \$1,000v^5$ at 5%

13. $4,729.14

$100a_{\overline{6}|3\%} + \$5,000v^6$ at 3%

14. $229

$$\frac{\$1,200}{a_{\overline{6}|4\%}}$$

SET 13

(Review Exercises for Chapters 3 through 6)

1. $640.04

$500(1.025)^{10} = \$500(1.280084)$

2. $390.60

$500(v^{10}$ at $2\frac{1}{2}\%) = \$500(.781198)$

3. $494.87

$50s_{\overline{8}|6\%} = \$50(9.897468)$

4. $1,371.89

$75s_{\overline{14}|4\%} = \$75(18.291911)$

5. $792.23

$75a_{\overline{14}|4\%} = \$75(10.563123)$

6. $2,098.26

$200\ddot{s}_{\overline{8}|6\%} = \$200(s_{\overline{9}|6\%} - 1)$

7. $1,316.48

$200\ddot{a}_{\overline{8}|6\%} = \$200(a_{\overline{7}|6\%} + 1)$

8. $140.02

$$\frac{\$1,000}{\ddot{s}_{\overline{6}|5\%}} = \frac{\$1,000}{s_{\overline{7}|5\%} - 1} = \frac{\$1,000}{7.142008}$$

9. $4,463.24

$300a_{\overline{20}|3\%}$

10. $2,327.27

$75\ddot{s}_{\overline{24}|2\%} = \$75(s_{\overline{25}|2\%} - 1)$

11. $215.47

$$\frac{\$1,000}{s_{\overline{4}|10\%}}$$

Answers	**Explanations**
13. 12.6162%	$100[(1.02)^6 - 1]\% = 100[1.126162 - 1]\%$
14. $190.27	$20(a_{\overline{20}|2\frac{1}{2}\%})v^{20}$
15. $1,950.28	$\dfrac{\$4,000(1.06)^{10}}{\ddot{a}_{\overline{4}|6\%}} = \dfrac{\$4,000(1.06)^{10}}{a_{\overline{3}|6\%} + 1}$
16. $2,228.73	$1,000v + \$750v^2 + \$500v^3 + \$250v^4,$ all at 6%
17. $377.88	$84.63\ddot{a}_{\overline{5}|6\%} = \$84.63(a_{\overline{4}|6\%} + 1)$
18. $700.21	$\dfrac{\$1,000s_{\overline{4}|5\%}(1.05)^2}{\ddot{a}_{\overline{8}|5\%}}$
19. $2,252.75	$180a_{\overline{5}|6\%} + \$2,000v^5$ at 6%
20. $455.34	$1,208.15v^{20}$ at 5%
21. $600.31	$405.55(1.04)^{10}$

SET 14

1. The number of times an event can be expected to occur compared to (or divided by) the number of opportunities for it to occur.

2. Complementary probabilities

3. The law of large numbers

4. $\frac{1}{6}$ — Only one of the six faces has a 3; all faces are equally likely.

5. $\frac{1}{36}$ — Two independent events: $\dfrac{1}{6} \times \dfrac{1}{6}$

6. .0134 — Only one can occur; the probability that one of the events will actually occur is the total.

7. .00079952 — The probability that both will happen $= .9994 \times .0008$.

8. .4961 — The two are complementary, that is, add up to 1.

9. Accidental fluctuations occur in the acutal experience.

10. $\frac{2}{1,000}$ or .002 — The probability of occurrence = the number of occurrences divided by the number of opportunities.

11. $\frac{998}{1,000}$ or .998 — The probability of living = the number living divided by the number of opportunities.

Answers	Explanations

12. .18033

There were $100 + 22 = 122$ a year ago at age 88; $22 \div 122 = .18033$

13. $\frac{4}{52} + \frac{13}{52} - \frac{1}{52}$

A standard deck of playing cards contains four aces and thirteen clubs. However, one of the aces is a club. Therefore, the number of chances of drawing either an ace or a club is 16.

SET 15

1. Buyers of the contracts are often aware that their own probabilities of dying are better or worse than average.

2. Lower

3. .012249

The value of q_{60} from male table

4. $\frac{2,034}{100,000}$

The value of $q_{60} = .02034$, which is written $\frac{2,034}{100,000}$ in fractional form.

5. 797

$.00742 \times 107,412$

6. .89881

It is a certainty that he will either live or die; $1 - q_{79}$.

7. Use of an age set-back for females or construction of separate tables for males and females

8. .00189

Consider that a female is subject to the rate of mortality for a male six years younger.

9. 993,737

$l_{19} = l_{18} - d_{18}$

10. 33,869

$d_{42} = l_{42} - l_{43}$

11. 2,092

$d_{36} = l_{36} \times q_{36}$

12. 948,911

$l_{37} = l_{36} - d_{36}$

13. .07317 rounded to five decimal places

$q_{75} = \dfrac{d_{75}}{l_{75}}$

14. *Age*

$d_{20} = 92,637 - 91,914;$

$q_{20} = \dfrac{d_{20}}{l_{20}}$; etc.

x	d_x	q_x
20	723	.00780
21	722	.00786
22	721	.00791

15. $\dfrac{l_x - l_{x+1}}{l_x}$

$\dfrac{l_x - l_{x+1}}{l_x} = \dfrac{d_x}{l_x}$

Answers	**Explanations**

SET 16

1. The probability that a person age 42 will still be alive eight years later (at age 50).

2. $_{10}q_{65}$

3. .9982 $\qquad$ $\dfrac{l_{21}}{l_{20}}$

4. .9363 $\qquad$ $\dfrac{l_{45}}{l_{20}}$

5. .9243 $\qquad$ $\dfrac{l_{50}}{l_{30}}$

6. .9443 $\qquad$ $\dfrac{l_{42}}{l_{17}}$

7. 7,255 $\qquad$ $\dfrac{l_{65}}{l_{35}} \times 10{,}000$

8. .2827 $\qquad$ $\dfrac{l_{30} - l_{65}}{l_{30}}$

9. 1,944 $\qquad$ $\dfrac{l_{21} - l_{31}}{l_{21}} \times 100{,}000$

10. .9243 $\qquad$ $\dfrac{l_{40}}{l_{30}} \times \dfrac{l_{50}}{l_{40}}$

11. .0013 $\qquad$ $\dfrac{l_{30} - l_{40}}{l_{30}} \times \dfrac{l_{40} - l_{50}}{l_{40}}$

12. .0587 $\qquad$ $\dfrac{d_{70}}{l_{20}} + \dfrac{d_{80}}{l_{20}}$

13. The number is the age at which good health was proved.

14. .0556 $\qquad$ $q_{[79]+1}$

15. .9393 $\qquad$ $1 - q_{[75]+3}$

16. .0013626 $\qquad$ $(q_{[72]})(q_{77})$

17. 98,250 $\qquad$ $(100{,}000)(1 - q_{[70]})$

18. $\dfrac{l_{[25]+1} - l_{[25]+4}}{l_{[25]+1}}$

19. $\dfrac{l_{35} + d_{34}}{l_{32}}$ $\qquad$ $\dfrac{l_{34}}{l_{32}} = \dfrac{l_{35} + d_{34}}{l_{32}}$

Answers	Explanations

SET 17

1. The payment certain.

2. $250 $\left(\dfrac{l_{35}\,v^{25}}{l_{10}}\right)$

3. $50 $\left(\dfrac{l_{65} + l_{66}\,v + l_{67}\,v^2 + l_{68}\,v^3}{l_{65}}\right)$

4. $750 $\left(\dfrac{l_{42}\,v^{22} + l_{43}\,v^{23} + l_{44}\,v^{24}}{l_{20}}\right)$

5. $1,000 $\left(\dfrac{l_{97}\,v + l_{98}\,v^2 + l_{99}\,v^3}{l_{96}}\right)$

6. $14.81 $40 $\left(\dfrac{l_{80}\,v^{10}}{l_{70}}\right)$

7. $17.67 $10 $\left(\dfrac{l_{30}\,v^8 + l_{31}\,v^9 + l_{32}\,v^{10}}{l_{22}}\right)$

8. $3.15 $1,000 $\left(\dfrac{l_{113}\,v^7 + l_{114}\,v^8 + l_{115}\,v^9}{l_{106}}\right)$

9. $165.67 $100 $\left(\dfrac{l_{97} + l_{98}\,v + l_{99}\,v^2}{l_{97}}\right)$

10. $153.06 $15\,(18.713 - 8.509)$

11. $481.12   Add the amount of one payment.

12. $100 $\left(\dfrac{l_{26}\,v + l_{27}\,v^2 + l_{28}\,v^3}{l_{25}}\right)$

SET 18

1. $1000 $\left[\dfrac{l_{20}(1 + i)^{45}}{l_{65}}\right]$

2. $25 $\left[\dfrac{l_{21}(1 + i)^4 + l_{22}(1 + i)^3 + l_{23}(1 + i)^2 + l_{24}(1 + i)}{l_{25}}\right]$

3. $148.40 $100 $\left[\dfrac{l_{65}(1.06)^5}{l_{70}}\right]$; use male table.

4. $2,665.16 $565\,\ddot{a}_{\overline{5}|3\%}$

5. $616.45 $\dfrac{\$5,000}{a_{\overline{10}|4\%}}$

6. $38.81 per $1,000 of proceeds $\dfrac{\$1,000}{24.764575 + 1}$

7. Excess interest payments and current option figures.

Answers	**Explanations**

8. 200 payments

$1,000 \div \$5 = 200$

9. Because the proceeds must provide for payments over a much longer period of time.

10. $\$1,000 \left[\dfrac{l_{31}(1 + i)^2 + l_{32}(1 + i) + l_{33}}{l_{33}} \right]$

SET 19

1. $\$1,000 \left(\dfrac{D_{62}}{D_{24}} \right) = \$93.82$

2. $\$500 \left(\dfrac{D_{21}}{D_{63}} \right) = \$6,835.53$

3.

With Benefit of Survivorship	*Interest Only*
.553918	.558395
.411225	.417265
.304154	.311805
.223004	.232999

$\dfrac{1,278,916}{2,308,856}, \dfrac{949,459}{2,308,856},$ etc.

4. $328.78

Use $\dfrac{D_{25}}{D_{45}}$ from the male table.

5. $\$1 \left(\dfrac{N_{23}}{D_{23}} \right) = \$16.57$

$\$1 \left(\dfrac{N_{24}}{D_{23}} \right) = \$15.57$

$\$1 \left(\dfrac{N_{55}}{D_{23}} \right) = \$1.82$

6. $\$100 \left(\dfrac{N_{46} - N_{56}}{D_{36}} \right) = \$419.86$

7. $23,506.18

$\$1,500 \left(\dfrac{N_{35}}{D_{35}} \right)$

8. $7,675.14

$\$1,000 \left(\dfrac{N_{45} - N_{55}}{D_{45}} \right)$

9. $258.49

$\$100 \left(\dfrac{N_{65} - N_{68}}{D_{64}} \right)$

10.

Fund Beginning of Year	*Interest Added*	*Payments End of Year*	*Fund End of Year*
2,137,460,531	128,247,632	813,519,200	1,452,188,963
1,452,188,963	87,131,338	799,359,900	739,960,401
739,960,401	44,397,624	784,358,300	(−275)

Answers	**Explanations**

11. $297.76

$$\$18.09 \left(\frac{N_{25}}{D_{25}}\right)$$

12. The present value at age 20 of a deferred whole life annuity of $100 per year, first payment at age 69.

The present value at age 20 of a deferred temporary life annuity of $100 per year, first payment at age 69, last payment at age 78.

13. Nine-year life annuity of $100 per year, issued at age 25.

SET 20

1. a) net single premium
   b) accumulated cost of insurance

2. Generally at the end of the year in which death occurs (unless specified differently), even though in actual practice it is usually paid very soon after death.

3. Payment of a benefit upon death within a specified number of years or payment of a benefit at the end of that time if still living.

4. The death benefit for those who die in the final year of the coverage and the pure endowment paid to those alive at the end of the period.

5. $\$4,000 \left(\dfrac{d_{25}\,v}{l_{25}}\right) = \$7.50$

6. $\$1,000 \left(\dfrac{d_{45}\,v + d_{46}\,v^2 + d_{47}\,v^3}{l_{45}}\right) = \$16.42$

7. $\$10,000 \left(\dfrac{d_{97}\,v + d_{98}\,v^2 + d_{99}\,v^3}{l_{97}}\right) = \$9,517.47$

8. $\$1,000 \left(\dfrac{l_{65}\,v^{15}}{l_{50}}\right) = \$498.16$

9. $\$5,000 \left(\dfrac{d_{20}\,v + d_{21}\,v^2 + d_{22}\,v^3 + l_{23}\,v^3}{l_{20}}\right) = \$4,576.46$

10. $25.78 and $4,550.68

Pure endowment part =

$$\$5,000 \left(\frac{l_{23}\,v^3}{l_{20}}\right)$$

Answers	Explanations

11. $\$1,000 \left[\dfrac{d_{19}(1 + i)^2 + d_{20}(1 + i) + d_{21}}{l_{22}} \right] = \$5.54$

12. $\$1,000 \left[\dfrac{d_{49}(1 + i) + d_{50}}{l_{51}} \right]$

SET 21

1. $\$10,000 \left(\dfrac{C_{10}}{D_{10}} \right) = \$11.75$ $\$10,000 \left(\dfrac{8,572}{7,296,488} \right)$

2. $\$10,000 \left(\dfrac{M_{10} - M_{40}}{D_{10}} \right) = \$354.29$

3. $\$1,000 \left(\dfrac{M_{65}}{D_{65}} \right) = \$689.72$

4. $\$2,000 \left(\dfrac{D_{30}}{D_5} \right) = \$917.65$

5. $\$5,000 \left(\dfrac{M_{40} - M_{70} + D_{70}}{D_{40}} \right) = \$2,352.48$

6. $\$10,000 \left(\dfrac{M_{18} - M_{30}}{D_{30}} \right) = \$270.35$

7. a) Net single premium at age 43 for $1,000 one-year term insurance
   b) Net single premium at age 43 for $1,000 four-year term insurance
   c) Net single premium at age 43 for $1,000 four-year term insurance
   d) Net single premium at age 62 for $5,000 whole life insurance
   e) Net single premium at age 25 for $15,000 25-year endowment insurance (or endowment-at-age-50 insurance)
   f) Net single premium at age 25 for $1,500 40-year pure endowment (or pure endowment due at age 65)

8. $\$4,000 \left(\dfrac{M_{32} - M_{35} + D_{35}}{D_{32}} \right)$

SET 22

1. A net annual premium is calculated using only a mortality table and interest.

   A gross annual premium, the premium actually paid by the policy-owner, includes amounts for expenses and profits.

2. Temporary (ten-year) life annuity due.

3. Lower.

Answers	**Explanations**

4. a) $\left(\begin{array}{c}\text{Net Annual}\\\text{Premium}\end{array}\right)(l_{75}) = \$1{,}000(d_{75}\,v);\ \$71.23$

b) $\left(\begin{array}{c}\text{Net Annual}\\\text{Premium}\end{array}\right)(l_{69} + l_{70}\,v + l_{71}\,v^2) = \$1{,}000(d_{69}\,v + d_{70}\,v^2 + d_{71}\,v^3);\ \$48.18$

c) $\left(\begin{array}{c}\text{Net Annual}\\\text{Premium}\end{array}\right)(l_{97} + l_{98}\,v + l_{99}\,v^2) = \$1{,}000(d_{97}\,v + d_{98}\,v^2 + d_{99}\,v^3);\ \$574.49$

d) $\left(\begin{array}{c}\text{Net Annual}\\\text{Premium}\end{array}\right)(l_{97} + l_{98}\,v) = \$1{,}000(d_{97}\,v + d_{98}\,v^2 + d_{99}\,v^3);\ \$635.91$

e) $\left(\begin{array}{c}\text{Net Annual}\\\text{Premium}\end{array}\right)(l_{10} + l_{11}\,v + l_{12}\,v^2)$

$$= \$1{,}000(d_{10}\,v + d_{11}\,v^2 + d_{12}\,v^3 + l_{13}\,v^3);\ \$314.52$$

f) $\left(\begin{array}{c}\text{Net Annual}\\\text{Premium}\end{array}\right)(l_{25} + l_{26}\,v)$

$$= \$1{,}000(d_{25}\,v + d_{26}\,v^2 + d_{27}\,v^3 + d_{28}\,v^4 + l_{29}\,v^4);\ \$451.40$$

5. a) $19.96   \$406.58 \div 20.374

b) $27.95   \$406.58 \div 14.546

c) $86.87 $\dfrac{\$43.37 + \$705.52}{8.621}$

d) $32.35 $\dfrac{\$221.20 + \$249.30}{14.546}$

6. 7.914 $\left(\begin{array}{c}\text{Annuity}\\\text{Factor}\end{array}\right) = \dfrac{\left(\begin{array}{c}\text{Net Single}\\\text{Premium}\end{array}\right)}{\left(\begin{array}{c}\text{Net Annual}\\\text{Premium}\end{array}\right)}$

7. $412.37 $\left(\begin{array}{c}\text{Net Single}\\\text{Premium}\end{array}\right)$

$$= \left(\begin{array}{c}\text{Net Annual}\\\text{Premium}\end{array}\right)\left(\begin{array}{c}\text{Annuity}\\\text{Factor}\end{array}\right)$$

8. $\$Z(l_{22} + l_{23}\,v)$

SET 23

1. a) $\$1{,}000\left(\dfrac{M_{25} - M_{45}}{N_{25} - N_{45}}\right) = \$2.60$

b) $\$1{,}000\left(\dfrac{M_{65} - M_{66}}{N_{65} - N_{66}}\right)$, or $\$1{,}000\left(\dfrac{C_{65}}{D_{65}}\right) = \$30.82$

Answers	**Explanations**

c) $\$1,000\left(\dfrac{M_{40} - M_{65}}{N_{40} - N_{65}}\right) = \$9.87$

d) $\$1,000\left(\dfrac{M_0}{N_0}\right) = \$5.48$

e) $\$1,000\left(\dfrac{M_{21}}{N_{21} - N_{51}}\right) = \$12.91$

f) $\$1,000\left(\dfrac{M_{30}}{N_{30} - N_{70}}\right) = \$14.45$

g) $\$1,000\left(\dfrac{M_{28} - M_{53} + D_{53}}{N_{28} - N_{53}}\right) = \$28.37$

h) $\$1,000\left(\dfrac{M_{15} - M_{45} + D_{45}}{N_{15} - N_{35}}\right) = \$28.20$

i) $\$1,000\left(\dfrac{M_{22} - M_{70} + D_{70}}{N_{22} - N_{52}}\right) = \$15.08$

2. $148.45 $\qquad\qquad \$20,000\left(\dfrac{M_{12}}{N_{12}}\right)$

3. a) Net annual premium for a $1,000 20-payment 30-year endowment insurance policy issued at age five
   b) Net annual premium for a $1,000 20-payment life policy issued at age 60
   c) Net annual premium for a $1,000 five-payment ten-year term insurance policy issued at age 14

4. $\$7,000\left(\dfrac{M_{35}}{N_{35} - N_{55}}\right)$

SET 24

1. The amount by which the gross premium exceeds the net premium, that is, the difference between the two. It is generally thought of as the amount available to cover expenses and profit.

2. Because any savings in the future, that is, any amount of the premium

Answers	Explanations

that proves to be excessive, can be returned to policyowners in the form of dividends.

3. Derive a level annual amount which has the same present value as the present value of all the expected future expenses.

4. Establishing several "size-of-policy" categories and setting different premium rates (per $1,000 of coverage) for each category. The actual premium rate for any particular policy is then determined by which of the size categories the policy falls into.

5. $15.06

$$Gross = Net + .20\ Gross$$
$$.80\ Gross = Net$$
$$Gross = \frac{Net}{.80}$$

6. $158.60

$15.06 × 10, add $8

7. $26.17

$$Gross = Net + \$2.50 + .10\ Gross$$
$$.90\ Gross = Net + \$2.50$$
$$Gross = \frac{Net + \$2.50}{.90}$$

8. $404.55

$26.17 × 15, add $12

9. $657.60

Per $1,000:

$$Gross = Net + \$5 + .15\ Gross$$
$$.85\ Gross = Net + \$5$$
$$Gross = \frac{Net + \$5}{.85}$$

For the policy:

$$Gross × 10 + \$20$$

10. $800.50

25 × $32.02

11. $27.56

$$\$314.95 × 1.05 × \frac{1}{12}$$

12. $75.92

Annual Premium = 10 × $14.10, add $5; Semiannual Premium = Annual Premium × 1.04 × $\frac{1}{2}$

Answers	Explanations

Answers

Explanations

13. $228.24

Per $1,000:

$$\text{Gross} = \text{Net} + \$6 + .12 \text{ Gross}$$

$$.88 \text{ Gross} = \text{Net} + \$6$$

$$\text{Gross} = \frac{\text{Net} + \$6}{.88}$$

For the policy:

$$\text{Gross} \times 5$$

SET 25

1. Full Preliminary Term Method

2. Canadian Method

3. Because it is always the one-year term net premium, regardless of the kind of policy.

4. $17.14

$$\$5,000\left(\frac{d_{40}\,v}{l_{40}}\right)$$

5. $22.57

Same as two-year term policy issued at age 61:

$$\$1,000\left(\frac{M_{61} - M_{63}}{N_{61} - N_{63}}\right)$$

6. $50.61

Net Level Loading = Gross − $84.36, Commissioners Loading = Gross − $33.75

7. $11.16

Gross annual premium
  − Net annual premium = Loading

$$\$30.60 - \$21.25 = \$9.35$$

First year expenses:

Issue and administration expenses	$ 7.35
First-year commission expense	12.24
Premium taxes	.92
	$20.51

First-year expenses − Loading

$$\$20.51 - \$9.35 = \$11.16$$

Answers	Explanations

SET 26

1. Terminal reserve

2. a) Zero
   b) $1,000
   c) Zero

3. a) Prospective
   b) Retrospective
   c) Prospective
   d) Prospective

4. $403.27 $816.04 − $412.77 or $584.60 − $181.33

5. $144.22 $491.82 − ($19.92)(17.45)

6. $450.97

$$\text{Net annual premium} = \frac{\$351.30}{33.083} =$$

$10.62; Reserve = $643.86 − ($10.62) (18.163)

7. $$\begin{pmatrix} \text{Accumulated Value} \\ \text{of Net Premiums} \\ \text{Received} \end{pmatrix} - \begin{pmatrix} \text{Accumulated} \\ \text{Cost of} \\ \text{Insurance} \end{pmatrix}$$

SET 27

1. a) Retrospective:

$$\$6.308 \left(\frac{N_{40} - N_{50}}{D_{50}} \right) - \$1,000 \left(\frac{M_{40} - M_{50}}{D_{50}} \right)$$

Prospective:

$$\$1,000 \left(\frac{M_{50} - M_{55}}{D_{50}} \right) - \$6.308 \left(\frac{N_{50} - N_{55}}{D_{50}} \right)$$

Value = $15.61

b) Retrospective:

$$\$11.278 \left(\frac{N_{25} - N_{65}}{D_{65}} \right) - \$1,000 \left(\frac{M_{25} - M_{65}}{D_{65}} \right)$$

Prospective:

$$\$1,000 \left(\frac{M_{65}}{D_{65}} \right) - \$11.278 \left(\frac{N_{65}}{D_{65}} \right)$$

Value = $569.58

c) Retrospective:

$$\$21.145 \left(\frac{N_{30} - N_{35}}{D_{35}} \right) - \$1,000 \left(\frac{M_{30} - M_{35}}{D_{35}} \right)$$

Answers	Explanations

Prospective:

$$\$1,000 \left(\frac{M_{35}}{D_{35}}\right) - \$21.145 \left(\frac{N_{35} - N_{50}}{D_{35}}\right)$$

Value = $104.40

d) Retrospective:

$$\$37.266 \left(\frac{N_0 - N_8}{D_8}\right) - \$1,000 \left(\frac{M_0 - M_8}{D_8}\right)$$

Prospective:

$$\$1,000 \left(\frac{M_8 - M_{20} + D_{20}}{D_8}\right) - \$37.266 \left(\frac{N_8 - N_{20}}{D_8}\right)$$

Value = $323.81

2. $57.37

Net annual premium

$$= \$1,000 \left(\frac{M_{35} - M_{65}}{N_{35} - N_{65}}\right)$$

$$= \$8.097$$

$$\text{Reserve} = \$1,000 \left(\frac{M_{45} - M_{65}}{D_{45}}\right)$$

$$- \$8.097 \left(\frac{N_{45} - N_{65}}{D_{45}}\right)$$

3. $236.31

$$\$1,000 \left(\frac{M_{40}}{D_{40}}\right) - \$14.32 \left(\frac{N_{40} - N_{55}}{D_{40}}\right)$$

4. $133.53; $400.59

Net annual premium

$$= \$1,000 \left(\frac{M_{30} - M_{65} + D_{65}}{N_{30} - N_{50}}\right)$$

$$= \$26.435$$

$$\text{Reserve} = \$26.435 \left(\frac{N_{30} - N_{35}}{D_{35}}\right)$$

$$- \$1,000 \left(\frac{M_{30} - M_{35}}{D_{35}}\right)$$

5. $10,000 $\left(\dfrac{M_{47} - M_{50}}{D_{47}}\right)$

SET 28

1. Mean reserves
2. Net amount at risk
3. Net amount at risk

Answers	Explanations

4. Tabular cost of insurance

5. The particular mortality table and interest rate specified in the law for calculating
   a) a special net premium to compare with the gross premium and
   b) the minimum reserve required if the gross premium is less than such a special net premium.

6. $1,107.65

Same as net annual premium, since the previous terminal reserve is zero.

7. $3,197.35

Fifth terminal reserve plus net annual premium.

8. $773.53

First initial reserve + first
$$\frac{\text{terminal reserve}}{2}$$

9. $8,708.70

Amount of insurance, minus third terminal reserve.

10. $398.17

$8,502.00 \times 1.035 - $8,401.40

11. $9.33

$5,100 \times q_{21} = $5,100 \times .00183

12. $23.43

($10,000 - $1,124.00)(q_{36})

13. Third-year mean reserve

SET 29

1. Because the lower first-year net premium releases more loading to help cover the high first-year expenses.

2. Canadian Method

3. a) $1.62

a) Initial reserve = $3.24
   Terminal reserve = 0

   b) $28.10

b) Previous terminal reserve = 0
   Net annual premium = $28.10

   c) $1,000

c) 30th year is final year

4. The inclusion of maintenance expenses and the use of true assumptions.

5. $16.95

$$\frac{$314.14 + $21.01}{19.77}$$

Answers	Explanations

6. $2.25

Valuation premium

$$= \frac{\$610.10 + \$15.55}{14.221}$$

$$= \$43.99$$

(Gross Premium)   (Valuation Premium)

$$= \$49.20 - \$43.99$$

$$= \$5.21 \text{ profit}$$

This is reduced by the yearly amount needed to repay acquisition expense:

$$\frac{\$42.08}{14.221} = \$2.96$$

Final yearly profit = $5.21 − $2.96

7. $998,320

Amount terminating by death
= .00168 × $1,000,000
= $1,680
Amount still in force
= $1,000,000 − $1,680

8. −$66.88, $34.89, $263.78, $678.33

Fund ÷ Number of thousands in force at the beginning of the following year.
− $64,200 ÷ 960, etc.

9. Year 4

Asset share first exceeds terminal reserve, that is, $678.33 exceeds $675.

10. $1,032.75

$592,800 ÷ 574

SET 30

1. The amount which would be deducted from a policy's reserve in order to produce its cash value.

2. The excess of its first-year expenses over the annual expenses for the subsequent years.

3. Paid-up term insurance for ten years plus a pure endowment (less than the amount of insurance) payable at the end of that time.

4. $4,871.16

$4,817.12 + $304.04 − $250.00

5. $173.39

$515.63 − $20.58(16.6299)

6. $13.67

$308.36 − $12.41(23.7464)

Answers	Explanations
7. $316.19	At that age, this policy has no more premiums payable; minimum value is simply present value of future benefits.
8. $94.16	$332.50 − $10.40(22.9176)
9. $95.66	$358.66 − $23.00(4.69286) − $21.15(7.33180)
10. $741	$553.80 ÷ .74817, round to next higher dollar.
11. $35,838	$12,853.50 ÷ .35866
12. $5,645	$5,000 + $845 − $200
13. No	$4,988.18 + $418.99 does not equal or exceed $5,412.70.
14. $930	$1,000 + $55 − $125

SET 31

1. The rates the company chooses to use in calculating dividends. They generally approximate the rates currently experienced by the company.

2. Each policy's dividends will increase fairly smoothly from year to year.

3. So that if a policy loan is made for an amount equal to the cash value, then the total death benefit will not be reduced, because the one-year term dividend option will provide a death benefit equal to the loan which is deducted from the death benefit.

4. $14.31

$$\text{Interest} = (\$228.98 + \$33.90)(.0575 - .03)$$
$$= \$7.23$$

$$\text{Mortality} = (\$1,000 - \$254.18)(.02224 - .01793)$$
$$= \$3.21$$

$$\text{Expenses} = (\$42.68 - \$33.90 - \$5.12)(1.0575)$$
$$= \$3.87$$

Answers	Explanations
	Since the policy is paid-up, the net annual premium is zero, and the terminal reserves are equal to the whole life net single premiums at the attained ages.

5. $12.83

$$\text{Interest} = (\$632.00)(.0575 - .03)$$

$$= \$17.38$$

$$\text{Mortality} = (\$1,000 - \$643.71)$$
$$(.02034 - .01793)$$

$$= \$.86$$

$$\text{Expenses} = (-\$5.12)(1.0575)$$

$$= -\$5.41$$

6. $7.73

The net premium is $1000 $\left(\dfrac{d_{62}\,v}{l_{62}}\right)$ = $23.60.

$$\text{Mortality} = (\$1,000 - 0)$$
$$(.02431 - .01793)$$

$$= \$6.38$$

$$\text{Expenses} = (\$30 - \$23.60 - \$5.12)$$
$$(1.0575)$$

$$= \$1.35$$

7. $6.34

$$(\$15.10 - \$14.07)(1.07)$$
$$+ (\$131.09)(.07 - .03)$$

8. $58

$$\frac{\$15.12}{.25933}$$

9. $52

$$\frac{\$42.30}{.80883}$$

10. $8.94

$$\$5.08 \times \frac{5 \times \$351.95}{1,000}$$

11. $1,574.80

$$\frac{\$8.00}{.00508}$$

12. $7.49

$$(\$159.42 + \$27.83)(.07 - .03)$$

SET 32

1. Traditional method and interest-adjusted method.

2. Company retention method.

Answers	**Explanations**

3. Rate of return method.

4. *Average Yearly Payment*
   10 Years = $25.99
   20 Years = $23.51

$$\frac{\$29.10 \times 10 - \$31.11}{10}$$

$$\frac{\$29.10 \times 20 - \$111.83}{20}$$

Average Yearly Cost
10 Years = $10.18
20 Years = −$1.91

$$\frac{\$29.10 \times 10 - \$31.11 - \$158.06}{10}$$

$$\frac{\$29.10 \times 20 - \$111.83 - \$508.42}{20}$$

5. Payment = $19.47
   Cost = $6.72

If there are no dividends, the average yearly payment is the same as the premium.

$$\text{Cost} = \frac{\$19.47 \times 10 - \$127.50}{10}$$

6. Payment = $31.49
   Cost = $12.49

$$\text{Payment} = \frac{\$34.07\ddot{s}_{\overline{20}|5\%} - \$89.45}{\ddot{s}_{\overline{20}|5\%}}$$

$$= \frac{\$34.07(34.719252)}{34.719252}$$
$$- \frac{\$89.45}{34.719252}$$

$$\text{Cost} = \frac{\$34.07\ddot{s}_{\overline{20}|5\%} - \$659.80 - \$89.4}{\ddot{s}_{\overline{20}|5\%}}$$

$$= \frac{\$34.07(34.719252)}{34.719252}$$

$$- \frac{\$659.80}{34.719252} - \frac{\$89.45}{34.719252}$$

7. $2.58

$$\frac{\$89.45}{34.719252}$$

8. $14.96

$$\frac{\$24.70\ddot{s}_{\overline{10}|5\%} - \$128.57}{\ddot{s}_{\overline{10}|5\%}}$$

$$\frac{\$24.70(13.206787)}{13.206787} - \frac{\$128.57}{13.206787}$$

Answers	Explanations

SET 33

1. Each group is generally large enough and has a large enough percentage of its members insured, so that many healthy persons offset the claims expected to occur because of the few unhealthy ones.

2. So that persons in poor health cannot decide that they will have a very large amount of insurance themselves.

3. Because 100% of the members are usually covered if the insurance is noncontributory, resulting in proportionately more healthy persons being included.

4. Because the premium outlay is lower than for any other type.

5. $.96   .60($.92) + .40($1.02)

6. $1.90   Gross = $1.12 + $.40 + .20(Gross)
.80(Gross) = $1.52

7. $5,640   Average monthly premium per $1,000 is $6,000 ÷ 10,000 = $.60, then $.60 × 9,400 = $5,640.

8. $2,000   10 days of coverage remain; $\frac{10}{31} \times \$6,200$.

9. $1,880,000   .10($800,000) + .90($2,000,000)

10. $153,000   ($156,000 − $3,000)

11. $647,500   .65($700,000) + .35($550,000)

SET 34

1. Disruption of income and expenses of medical treatment.

2. Sickness, disability, or failure of health.

3. Because there is a scarcity of experience data, and the experience is dramatically affected by swings in the economy, inflation, and changes in medical practice.

Answers	Explanations

4. The amount being applied for, the waiting period and maximum benefit period being applied for, and the person's age, sex, and occupation class.

5. Supplemental major medical assumes that hospital, surgical, and medical insurance are in force, and covers the excess expenses over and above coverage in force. Comprehensive major medical covers all such expenses.

6. $80

Frequency $= 40 \div 1,000 = .04$; average claim $= \$80,000 \div 40 = \$2,000$

7. $50

Net $= \$540,000 \div 13,500 = \$40$; gross $= \$40 \times 1.25 = \$50$

8. 69%

$$\frac{\$150,000 + \$100,000}{350,000 - (-10,000)} = \frac{250,000}{360,000};$$

note that the increase in the reserve is negative.

9. $49.04

$$\frac{\$31.60 + \$66.48}{2}$$

10. 5%

$$\frac{\$612.00 - \$581.40}{\$612.00}$$

11. $205.92

$.072 \times \$2,860$

12. 69%

Claim cost $\div$ premium; $\$205.92 \div \$298.44$

13. $12.44

Monthly premium $= \$298.44 \div 12 = \$24.87$; half the monthly premium is unearned.

14. $1,110,000

$.70 \times \$1,200,000 + .30 \times \$900,000$

15. $4,029.75

After the person pays the deductible of $100, $5,373 of covered medical expenses remain to be paid $.75(\$5,373) = \$4,029.75$

Index